PARLIAMENTS AND LEGISLATURES SERIES

SAMUEL C. PATTERSON, *General Advisory Editor*

SENATES

BICAMERALISM IN THE CONTEMPORARY WORLD

EDITED BY

Samuel C. Patterson

and Anthony Mughan

Ohio State University Press • Columbus

Credits for photographs: The United States Senate courtesy of U.S. Senate Photographic Studio; German Bundesrat courtesy of German Information Center, photograph no. 114597/22a; the Australian Senate courtesy of Australian Foreign Affairs and Trade Department; official photograph of the Senate of Canada for the first session of the 36th Parliament courtesy of Micheal Bedford Photography; French Sénat courtesy of Sénat Service de la Communication, photograph no. C97/451/6; Spanish Senado courtesy of Foto-Video Industrial.

Library of congress Catatloging-in-Publication Data

Senates : bicameralism in the contemporary world / edited by
    Samuel C. Patterson and Anthony Mughan.
        p.   cm. — (Parliaments and legislatures series)
    Includes bibliographical references and index.
        ISBN 0-8142-0810-x (cl : alk. paper). — ISBN 0-8142-5010-6
    (pb : alk. paper)
        1. Legislative bodies—Upper chambers.   2. Comparative
    government.   I. Patterson, Samuel Charles, 1931–   .
    II. Mughan, Anthony.   III. Series.
    JF541.S43   1999   98-45047
                                                           CIP

Text design by Carrie Nelson House.
Type set in Adobe Minon by G & S Typesetters.
Printed by Maple-Vail.

9 8 7 6 5 4 3 2 1

TO CHARLES O. JONES

Longtime friend, scholar extraordinaire

CONTENTS

The Parliaments and Legislatures Series is the publishing home for studies of parliaments or legislatures, the institutional heartbeat of democratic governments. We refer to parliaments and legislatures in the same breath to denote their kinsmanship. Representative assemblies are best known to Europeans as parliaments and best known to Americans as legislatures. The names may be used interchangeably, although there are those who insist on a distinction—that parliaments' members are expected only to talk, whereas members of legislatures really make laws. Of course, the plain truth is that both parliaments and legislatures, as they may be known, are variously enmeshed in lawmaking and they exercise a variety of distinctive powers.

By the same token, the authors in *Senates: Bicameralism in the Contemporary World* have given the generic term *senates* to the upper houses of the world's parliaments, and indeed most upper houses are given that name. Senates, putatively bodies of the wise and notable of the realm, arose in ancient Greek and Roman times. The Roman Senate held sway during the second century B.C. Although rooted in the parliamentary developments of antiquity, modern parliaments date their origins to medieval times, when bicameral institutions first emerged. The development of European parliaments that included "second chambers" or "upper houses" indicated the preeminence and survival of aristocracy. But senates have long outlived their original purposes and justification. They have, in one way or another, been transformed into modern, viable parliamentary institutions.

The contemporary design of these institutions—how their members are chosen, how they are organized, what powers they exercise, how their processes work, and what impact they have on legislation—provides an important realm of inquiry about parliamentary government. These fundamentals of institutional design, when they are well understood, supply the basis for more extensive comparative analysis. In this book, the authors dissect the upper houses in their own political systems, capturing their development over time and characterizing their relations with the lower house, the government of the day, extraparliamentary political parties, and so forth. From these foundations, future comparative study can press ahead with inquiry into complex questions about parliamentary representation, institutionalization, bicameral linkages, parliamentary responsibility and accountability, and relations between legislature and executive.

These authors take note of the fact that there is very little in the English-language literature about parliaments that focuses on upper houses. Even the U.S. Senate, putatively the most powerful of these bodies, was largely neglected by political scientists until the 1970s. The post–World War II British House of Lords attracted little scholarly attention until the 1990s. Other upper houses have been virtually unknown to the scholarly world. In this sense, this pioneering book brings knowledgeable, penetrating accounts of senate institutions to the forefront, providing baseline analyses of these bodies that will help build a compelling foundation for future research.

SAMUEL C. PATTERSON

Democratic government in political units of any size requires a parliament where citizens may be represented and where public policies may be debated and determined. The institutional design for such a parliament varies in many particulars. A fundamental design issue is the number of houses that the parliament, or legislature, should have: one, two, three, more? In today's world, legislative bodies generally are composed of either one house or two; they are unicameral or bicameral. The U.S. Congress is bicameral, consisting of a House of Representatives and a Senate. The Ohio legislature is similarly designed, as are the legislatures in all the other American states except Nebraska, which has a unicameral legislature. About a third of the world's national parliaments are also bicameral.

Bicameral parliaments consist of a lower house and an upper house. These upper houses, which carry different names in different places, but which we have dubbed "senates," are important political institutions, but they have been neglected. Although Americans give their Senate plenty of attention, most of the world's consideration of parliamentary life is accorded to the lower houses—frequently the popularly elected and more powerful assembly. We have long been curious about the senates of the world and interested in learning more about how they are established, how they are organized, and how they work. Fortunately, we were able to find scholars in nine countries who were willing to analyze and write about their country's upper house and thus compose this book. We owe a tremendous debt of gratitude to these nine scholars, our authors, for their involvement in this project.

We would like to acknowledge the inspiration, guidance, and encouragement we have received over the years from our mentors: Ralph K. Huitt, Leon D. Epstein, John C. Wahlke, and Gerhard Loewenberg. We dedicate this book to Charles O. Jones, intrepid scholar of parliamentary government and close personal friend. From him, much has been learned about the U.S. Congress and about the institutional matrix in which that steadfast parliamentary institution is embedded. More immediately, we have appreciated the opportunity to work on this book with Charlotte Dihoff, Ohio State University Press, who provided us help and encouragement in making this book a reality. Finally, we thank Suzanne and Karen, who nurtured and tolerated us while this project was under way.

1

Senates and the Theory of Bicameralism

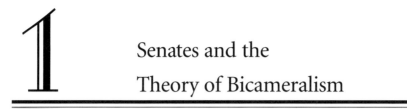

SAMUEL C. PATTERSON AND ANTHONY MUGHAN

Bicameralism is an institutional design for a two-house representative assembly. Unquestioningly accepted in the United States, where the House of Representatives and Senate remain enshrined in the Constitution, bicameralism is neither universally accepted nor practiced. John Stuart Mill, the philosophical architect of representative government, observed in the mid-nineteenth century that "what is known as the question of the Two Chambers" was energetically debated (Mill 1861, 247). Although a powerful inertia in practices of governance constrains serious advocacy of institutional reform, the institutional design feature of "two chambers," or what Henry Jones Ford dubbed "divided representation," remains a cogent focus for inquiry (Ford 1924, 273–94). The contributors to this book dissect senates in nine interesting bicameral systems in order to explore their representational performance and legislative effectiveness in modern polities.

The name *senate* is the common appellation for this house of the legislature (just as *house of representatives* is a common name for the other house). Two-thirds of the bicameral assemblies denote one house a senate—the Australian, Canadian, or United States Senate, the Belgian or French Sénat, the Senado of Argentina, Brazil, Chile, Colombia, Venezuela, or Spain, the Italian Senato. In the parlance of parliamentary studies, these bodies are often referred to as "second chambers" or "upper houses," designating the other houses of the legislatures, the popularly elected assemblies chosen on the basis of population, the first chambers or lower houses. Only in the Netherlands is this convention reversed; that country's national parliament includes a popularly elected house called the Tweede Kamer, or Second Chamber, and an indirectly elected body called the Eerste Kamer, or First Chamber (see van Schendelen et al. 1981). The same was true of the Swedish Riksdag until unicameralism was adopted in 1970 (Metcalf 1987, 189–95). Although we adopt the appellation *senate* to refer generically to these parliamentary houses, in a number of major democratic countries these chambers bear different names— Bundesrat in Austria and Germany, Rajya Sabha in India, Soviet Federatsii in Russia, House of Lords in the United Kingdom.

The multichambered parliament, which most often took bicameral form, is rooted historically in the highly stratified societies of the Middle Ages, and it reflected "the communal spirit of the medieval world" (Marongiu 1968, 54). In those days, the upper and lower nobility, the clergy, and the townspeople and peasants composed distinct classes, or "estates," each of which came to meet independently, mainly to contribute revenues to the coffers of the king. Although it had important English origins in the thirteenth century, it was something of a historical accident that these conclaves emerged as two-house parliaments, a pattern that had largely congealed by the later eighteenth century. Whether embracing bicameralism or unicameralism, all of the emergent polities of that era, and later, were influenced by the historical experience of the British House of Lords.

In 1295, Edward I summoned the barons, the clergy, and the commoners to assemble as a parliament (see Ilbert 1911, 7–25; Luce 1930, 72–81;

Sayles 1974, 70–93). They came to meet in two houses rather than three, apparently because of "a series of fortunate accidents" (Marriott 1910, 6). The lower clergy withdrew; the bishops and abbots united with the barons to form the House of Lords; and the knights of the shire joined the burgesses of the towns to shape the incipient House of Commons (see Pollard 1920). Although "the mistiness of long ago obscures the origin of the bicameral organization in the English Parliament," the House of Lords emerged as a hereditary body whose members, until the enactment of the Life Peerages Act in 1958 permitted nonhereditary membership, were entitled to sit in the House by right of their birth into the nobility (Johnson 1938, 4; Shell 1992). In contrast, the House of Commons evolved as an elected assembly, eventually eclipsing the upper house in legislation and in the formation of governments. British parliamentary practice cast a long shadow over subsequent institutional developments, first on continental Europe and then across an empire.

Parliaments' Upper Chambers

Most of the world's parliaments are unicameral, consisting of a single legislative chamber. When the Inter-Parliamentary Union most recently took inventory of parliaments, it found that 122, more than two-thirds, were one-house legislatures. They are located mainly in small polities, notably in New Zealand and the Nordic countries—Denmark, Norway, Sweden, Finland, Iceland (see Arter 1984, 16–22; Damgaard 1992). In addition, unicameral legislatures are commonplace at the subnational level—in the Canadian provinces, in the American state of Nebraska, in the German *länder* except for Bavaria, and in many municipalities around the globe (see, for example, Levy and White 1989; Breckenridge 1957). Upper chambers were abolished in Denmark in 1953 and in Sweden in 1970. In a modified form of unicameralism, the Norwegian Storting, elected as a unicameral body, divides after elections into two separate entities to deal with legislation.

The larger countries of the world tend to have bicameral parliaments, composed of senates and houses of representatives. A notable exception is Peru, where a unicameral Congress of 120 members replaced the traditional bicameral institution in 1993 following a convention that produced a new constitution. Moreover, China has a very large unicameral assembly, the National People's Congress; its 2,978 members are elected for five-year terms (see O'Brien 1990). When the Czech Republic and Slovakia separated in 1993, the former's constitution prescribed a bicameral parliament, while the latter's provided for unicameralism (see Reschova and Syllova 1996; Malova and Sivakova 1996).

In table 1.1 we array the sixty-one countries whose representative assembly is bicameral, showing the name of the upper house, the size of this body, term of office, and a brief indication of the means of member selection. Two-house parliaments are to be found in all parts of the world. Most of the national representative bodies of countries in the western hemisphere are bicameral, including Canada and the United States. The exceptions are the parliaments of Ecuador and Peru, the assemblies of the small countries of Guyana and Surinam, and the Central American assemblies, except for Belize. Several small island countries of the West Indies have two-house legislatures (e.g., the Dominican Republic and Jamaica). The senates in the United States and Canada are well known, but little is known about Latin American senates outside their own countries (but see Agor 1971; Close 1995; Kelley 1971).

Most of the Western European countries have bicameral parliaments—the United Kingdom, Ireland, France, Belgium, Germany, the Netherlands, Italy, Spain, Austria, Switzerland (see Mastias and Grangé 1987). The national parliament of the Russian Federation is constitutionally bicameral, consisting of a Duma and a Council of the Federation (see Hahn 1996; Remington and Smith 1996, 180–82). In Eastern Europe, bicameralism occurs in Poland, the Czech Republic, Croatia, Romania, and Yugoslavia. Elsewhere in the world, bicameralism is spread more thinly. In the Western Pacific region, two-house parliaments are prominent in Australia, the Philippines, Malaysia, and Japan (and in Fiji and Palau); in Asia the main exemplars of bicameralism are India, Pakistan, and Thailand; in the Middle East, Jordan; and in a scattering of small African countries (Burkina Faso, Congo, Ethiopia, Lesotho, Mauritania, Namibia, Swaziland) and South Africa.

Not only are senates ubiquitous but they vary greatly in size. The British House of Lords is by far the largest, its membership gauged by the number of peers. Although in 1996 this meant that about 1,200 persons were members, fewer than half of these are active participants. Omitting the House of Lords because of its indeterminate active size, the average senate consists of eighty-three members. Nearly half are small bodies, with no more than fifty members. The senates of small countries and island republics are the smallest. Nine senates range in size from one hundred to two hundred members—in Burkina Faso, Canada, Colombia, Ethiopia, Mexico, Poland, Romania, the Russian Federation, and the United States. The U.S. Senate, with its one hundred members, is a bit larger than the average upper house. A few senates are quite large, with more than two hundred members: France, India, Italy, Japan, Spain, and Thailand.

In the United Kingdom and Canada, members of the upper chamber can serve for life, and in both Germany and the Russian Federation, the terms of members are indefinite, though not guaranteed for life. Elsewhere, senators serve for a fixed term, which varies from three years in Burkina Faso and Malaysia to nine years in France. Six-year terms, like that for U.S. senators, are not uncommon, but two-thirds of all members of upper houses serve terms of five years or less. In some cases the terms of members are stratified so that only a third or half of the senate membership is chosen in any one election.

As table 1.2 indicates, senators are elected, directly or indirectly, in 34 of the 61 senates, but in only 19 senates are all members directly elected. Members of the U.S. Senate were elected indirectly—by the state legislatures—until the Constitution was amended in 1913 to require direct popular election of members (Haynes 1906; Abramowitz and Segal 1992, 12–26). In Italy and Spain most senators are directly elected, but some are elected indirectly or appointed. Members of the French Sénat are selected by departmental electoral colleges, composed of members of the National Assembly, and by regional and local council members. In yet another seventeen upper chambers, all of the senators are appointed. Membership in the British upper house is, of course, made up of hereditary peers and persons appointed to peerages for life. Canadian senators are appointed for life, and appointments are a patronage plum for the prime minister. Members of the German Bundesrat are appointed by the state governments in numbers allocated to them roughly in proportion to the state's population. In other senates, members are appointed by the government, by the head of state, or by the king.

Members of senates are appointed on the basis of varying criteria and premises, and they take on different responsibilities and constitutional obligations. Indeed, these bodies are, at least outwardly, unique aggregations, each with its own history, its special traditions and customs,

Table 1.1. Senates of the World

Country	Upper House	No. of Members	Term (Years)	Comments
Antigua & Barbuda	Senate	17	5	All appointed
Argentina	Senado	72	6	$\frac{1}{3}$ indirectly elected every 2 years
Australia	Senate	76	6	$\frac{1}{2}$, plus 4 territorial senators, elected every 3 years
Austria	Bundesrat	64	5–6	Indirectly elected; term varies by province
Bahamas	Senate	16	5	Appointed by the governor-general
Barbados	Senate	21	5	Appointed by the governor-general
Belarus	Soviet Republiki	64	4	56 indirectly elected; 8 appointed by the head of state
Belgium	Sénat	71	4	40 directly elected; 31 elected indirectly or co-opted
Belize	Senate	8	5	Appointed by the governor-general
Bolivia	Cámara de Senadores	27	4	Directly elected
Bosnia-Herzegovina	Dom Naroda	15	2	10 appointed from Bosnia, 5 from Republika Srpska
Brazil	Senado Federal	81	8	$\frac{1}{3}$, then $\frac{2}{3}$, elected every 4 years
Burkina Faso	Chambre des Représentants	178	3	Appointed or indirectly elected
Canada	Senate	104	Life	Appointed by the governor-general
Chile	Senado	46	8	38 elected, $\frac{1}{2}$ every 4 years; others appointed
Colombia	Senado	102	4	Directly elected
Congo	Sénat	60	6	$\frac{1}{3}$ indirectly elected every 2 years
Croatia	Zupanijski Dom	68	4	63 directly elected; 5 appointed by the head of state
Czech Republic	Senat	81	6	$\frac{1}{3}$ directly elected every 2 years
Dominican Republic	Senado	30	4	Directly elected
Ethiopia	Yefedereshn Mekir Bet	120	5	Directly or indirectly elected
Fiji	Senate	34	4	Appointed by the head of state

Country	Chamber	Term	Members	Selection
France	Sénat	9	321	$\frac{1}{3}$ indirectly elected every 3 years
Gabon	Sénat	6	91	Indirectly elected
Germany	Bundesrat	Varies	69	Appointed by the länder
Grenada	Senate	5	13	Appointed by the governor-general
Haiti	Sénat	6	27	$\frac{1}{3}$ elected every 2 years
India	Rajya Sabha	6	245	233 elected by legislatures, $\frac{1}{3}$ every 2 years
Ireland	Seanad Eireann	5	60	49 elected, 11 appointed by the prime minister
Italy	Senato	5	326	315 directly elected; 11 are senators for life
Jamaica	Senate	5	21	Appointed by the governor-general
Japan	Sangiin	6	252	$\frac{1}{2}$ elected every 3 years
Jordan	Majlis al-Aayan	4	40	Appointed by the king
Kazakstan	Senate	4	47	40 indirectly elected every 2 years; 7 appointed
Kyrghyzstan	Myizam Chygaru Palatasy	5	35	Directly elected
Lesotho	Senate	5	33	22 principal chiefs, 11 others appointed by the king
Malaysia	Dewan Negara	3	69	26 indirectly elected; 43 appointed by the head of state
Mauritania	Majlis al-Chouyoukh	6	56	$\frac{1}{3}$ indirectly elected every 2 years
Mexico	Cámara de Senadores	6	128	$\frac{1}{2}$ elected every 3 years
Namibia	National Council	6	26	Indirectly elected
Nepal	Rastriya Sabha	6	60	50 elected, $\frac{1}{3}$ every 2 years; 10 named by the king
Netherlands	Eerste Kamer	4	75	Indirectly elected
Pakistan	Senate	6	87	$\frac{1}{2}$ indirectly elected every 3 years
Palau	Senate	4	14	Directly elected
Paraguay	Cámara de Senadores	5	45	Directly elected
Philippines	Senado	6	24	$\frac{1}{2}$ directly elected every 3 years
Poland	Senat	4	100	Directly elected
Romania	Senatul	4	143	Directly elected
Russian Federation	Soviet Federatsii	Varies	178	Regional authorities; terms vary by republic

(continued)

Table 1.1. (*Continued*)

Country	Upper House	No. of Members	Term (Years)	Comments
Saint Lucia	Senate	11	5	Appointed by the governor-general
South Africa	National Council	90	5	Elected by provincial legislatures
Spain	Senado	257	4	208 elected directly; 49 indirectly elected
Swaziland	Senate	30	5	10 elected; 20 appointed by the head of state
Switzerland	Ständerat	46	4	Directly elected
Thailand	Wuthisapha	260	4	Appointed by the head of state
Trinidad & Tobago	Senate	31	5	Appointed by the head of state
United Kingdom	House of Lords	1,067	Life	633 hereditary peers; 408 life peers; 26 clergy
United States	Senate	100	6	$\frac{1}{3}$ elected every 2 years
Uruguay	Cámara de Senadores	31	5	30 directly elected, plus vice president of Republic
Venezuela	Senado	52	5	50 directly elected, 2 appointed for life
Yugoslavia	Veçe Republika	40	4	Indirectly elected

Sources: Inter-Parliamentary Union, *World Directory of Parliaments* (Geneva: Inter-Parliamentary Union, 1997) and *Chronicle of Parliamentary Elections and Development*, vols. 26–30 (Geneva: Inter-Parliamentary Union, 1982–97). As of 1997, 180 national parliaments existed in the world; 61 (34%) are bicameral.

Table 1.2. Selection of Senators

Method of Selection	Number of Senates	%
Directly elected	19	31.1
Indirectly elected	12	19.7
Some elected directly, some indirectly	3	4.9
Some elected, some appointed	10	16.4
All appointed	17	27.9
Total	61	100.0

Source: calculated from table 1.1.

its time-honored norms and practices, its constitutional status, and its impact on the laws of the land. Yet, for all their wonder and variety, the world's senates share much in common in their underlying justification, purpose, and rationale. In short, senates allow for differentiation in political representation, and they provide the redundancy in policy making that may prevent error, delay action until alternatives have been vetted satisfactorily, or postpone decisions until the disputants achieve consensus. Accordingly, the theory of bicameralism underscores both representation and redundancy.

The Theory of Bicameralism

Why do so many countries, large and small, maintain bicameral parliamentary institutions? What is the theory lying behind the long-standing practice of bicameralism? Articulating a theory of bicameralism has preoccupied both scholars and practitioners for many years (Loewenberg and Patterson 1979, 120–25; see also Lees-Smith 1923; Marriott 1910; Money and Tsebelis 1992; Roberts 1926; and Temperley 1910). It is a tribute to the hidden power of tradition and inertia in the governing affairs of human beings that fundamentals of institutional design are rarely laid open to full appraisal. Institutions tend to be accepted at face value. Whether the legislature has one house or two is taken for granted by practitioners, observers, and citizens. "Bicameralism," says Richard F. Fenno Jr., "is a political commonplace in the United States. The division of our national legislature into two separate bodies was little debated in 1787, and it has been taken for granted ever since" (1982, vii). And yet, especially outside the settled context of the American regime, these insti-tutions can arouse intense debate about their justification, the constitu-tion of their membership, and the rectitude of their leverage, or lack of it, over public policies.

Representation

A powerful justification for a two-house parliament lies in demands for representation. According to the theory, one house is composed of popu-larly elected members representing the citizens directly. The other house, with a different basis of representation, may give voice to the interests of social classes, economic interests, or territorial diversity. The most com-mon basis upon which senates have been constitutionally anointed is to provide territorial representation. In particular, federal systems are highly conducive to bicameralism in which a senate serves as a federal house whose members are selected to represent the states or provinces. The paradigmatic federal house is the U.S. Senate, whose one hundred mem-bers are distributed territorially on the basis of two senators for each of the fifty states regardless of differences in state population size.

Unitary nations tend to establish unicameral parliaments, while federal nations tend to create bicameral assemblies. When the Inter-Parliamentary Union took stock of national parliaments in 1983, it found that only one federal country, Comoros, was managing with a unicameral parliament, the Assemblée Fédérale. In 1992, a new constitution was adopted in Comoros providing for an elected senate, but this body has not yet been formed. The IPU survey found that fifty-four of sixty-six unitary countries had unicameral parliaments; only a dozen were bicameral (Inter-Parliamentary Union 1986, 14). At the same time, most of today's bicameral parliaments are operating in unitary systems. Only eighteen (about a third) of the sixty-one senates shown in table 1.1 are located in federal systems.

This is not to say that territorial considerations are not reflected in the parliamentary structures of unitary states. Certainly, the provision of ter-ritorial representation is not confined to the federal senates. In France, with its unitary constitution, senators are chosen so as to represent the departments and overseas territories and French citizens living outside France (Mastias 1980). The Spanish Senate is based on territorial repre-sentation, although Spain is a unitary state. Each province is accorded four senators, and Senate membership is allocated to islands and other territories. Unitary Bolivia's twenty-seven senators are territorially distributed—three for each of the country's nine departments regardless of their population. By the same token, Chilean senators are elected from the country's thirteen regions, six of which return four senators and seven of which return two senators (Agor 1971; Nef and Galleguillos 1995).

When the founders of the American republic convened in Philadelphia in 1787 to forge a new constitution for the United States, almost all of the delegates to the constitutional convention favored a bicameral national legislature (Baker 1988). Eleven of the states' legislatures were bicameral— all but those in Pennsylvania and Georgia (Main 1967; Moran 1895). It is true that the so-called New Jersey Plan proposed a unicameral Congress, but delegates readily agreed that unicameralism was one of the defects of the Articles of Confederation, which they were bound and determined to replace with a new basic law. The Virginia Plan proposed a bicameral Congress, with the Senate to be elected by members of the House of Representatives. In the Connecticut Compromise, convention delegates agreed on a Congress in which the lower house would be popularly elected (limited to white male suffrage), its membership allocated to the states in accord with their census population, and in which an upper house, the Senate, would be based on equality of state representation, with two senators selected by each state legislature.

This "federal solution" was little discussed by the founders beyond acknowledging their belief that this would resolve worries about the relative advantage of large as opposed to small states in the new constitutional system. At the time of the founding, the Compromise was essential to resolve the fear of the representatives of small states like Delaware or Connecticut that their states would be dominated by large states like New York or Virginia, a fear placated by giving each state two senators regardless of differences in population (see Jillson 1988, 64–100). Conceived as a federal house, the Senate largely ceased to be so after the Civil War of the 1860s, and Lord Bryce noted at the end of the nineteenth century that there never had been "any division of interests or consequent contests between the great States and the small ones" after the implementation of the new federal constitution (Bryce 1893, 1: 99). The Senate simply did not develop as a federal house, a council of states, certainly not in the way in which the German Bundesrat directly represents the länder (see Riker 1955; Swanstrom 1985, 15–18, 154–74).

At the same time, even today the U.S. Senate is thought to reflect the representation of states in the federal governing apparatus, and the equal representation of states in the Senate, however undemocratic as a mode of apportionment, is virtually unchallenged. Moreover, in a number of federal countries—Australia, Canada, Switzerland, Latin American federal systems—states unequal in population are equally represented in the legislature's upper house (see Duchacek 1970, 244–52). The new South African upper chamber, with limited powers, is specifically intended to give voice to the provinces (see O'Brien 1997). Finally, considerations of political representation other than territorial ones may enter into the calculations. Historically, social classes provided an important representational basis for bicameralism. At the time of the founding of the American republic, many advocated a senate that would especially represent the gentry, the rich. Functional representation has been proposed, and most members of the present Senead of Ireland are chosen in functional clusters—in culture and education, agriculture, labor, industry and commerce, public administration, and social services.

Redundancy

A further line of theorizing about bicameralism concerns the value of redundancy. A second chamber, so the theory goes, "provides for a second opinion" (Wheare 1967, 140). There are differences among countries in the gravity of this opinion. In the United States, both for Congress and for the forty-nine bicameral state legislatures, or in Italy, the two houses carry equal powers, and laws must be approved by both. In the American case, a truly "bicameral perspective" is in order, a viewpoint that recognizes the coequality of the two legislative houses such that they provide a checking and balancing of one another (see Fenno 1982). In the Italian case, the Chamber of Deputies and the Senate are coequal constitutionally. Both must enact legislation, and governments must be invested by and enjoy the confidence of both chambers (Furlong 1990). But in most parliaments, the upper house is subordinate to the lower. Like the British House of Lords, upper houses are commonly empowered only to revise, reconsider, or delay, and constitutional provisions govern the circumstances under which the upper house can be overridden by the lower house.

That the strength of bicameralism lay in the capacity of the senate to check the actions of the putatively more popular lower house was firmly defended by John Stuart Mill in the mid-nineteenth century. He argued that "a majority in a single assembly, when it has assumed a permanent character . . . easily becomes despotic and overweening, if released from the necessity of considering whether its acts will be concurred in by another constituted authority" (Mill 1861, 249). Lord Bryce, who wrote profusely about American government and who chaired a commission on the status of the upper chamber in Britain in 1917–18, echoed Mill's view, saying that "the chief advantage of dividing a legislature into two branches is that the one may check the haste and correct the mistakes of the other" (Bryce 1893, 1:183; Lees-Smith 1923, 216–35; Roberts 1926, 37–136).

In the United States, both houses of the 104th Congress were controlled by Republican Party majorities for the first time in four decades. The aggressive House Republican majority passed several bills in 1995 from its partisan "Contract with America" that were not acceptable to Senate Republican leaders. The Senate balked, and compromises were reached. "We are the pause that refreshes," remarked a Senate leadership staff member (*Washington Post National Weekly Edition,* June 5–11, 1995, p. 13). The check of one house upon the actions of another, the institutionalized second opinion provided by bicameralism, is argued in various ways. One line of argument stresses the critical review that one house may accord to the other; the argument usually takes the form of asserting a revisory role for the upper house. The upper house contributes to legislative performance by virtue of its capacity to review and revise.

In so doing, the senate may ferret out and correct errors in lawmaking made by the popular house, permit "second thoughts" about provisions of law, and check the influence of interest groups. Another line of argument stresses the virtues of delay or reconsideration to allow the expression of public sentiments on policy issues of the day or to dampen or mitigate popular passions or hasty judgments (e.g., see Riker 1992). Then a line of argument stresses the importance of a second chamber to prevent the corruption or usurpation of power by the other body, by the executive, or by special interests. But, of course, provision of redundancy may be twisted by institutional design, so that senates may be established or elected to protect a ruling elite, providing, as in Chile in the early 1990s, a "democratic facade" intended to preserve the political influence of authoritarian forces (Nef and Galleguillos 1995, 124–28).

This line of theorizing about bicameralism unfolded most vividly in

the debates over the constitution of the U.S. Senate. The American founders assumed the new Congress would be bicameral in some form. Upper-
most in their thinking was the belief that a second chamber was needed
to provide essential checks on a democratic lower house. James Madison
elaborated the basic theory when he spoke to the Constitutional Convention about the makeup of the Senate (Madison 1893, 241–42):

> In order to judge of the form to be given to this institution, it will
> be proper to take a view of the ends to be served by it. These were,
> first, to protect the people against their rulers, secondly, to protect the
> people against the transient impressions into which they themselves
> might be led. A people deliberating in a temperate moment . . . on the
> plan of government most likely to secure their happiness would first
> be aware that those charged with the public happiness might betray
> their trust. An obvious precaution against this danger would be to di-
> vide the trust between different bodies of men, who might watch and
> check each other.

By the same token, Madison argued that the popular house might be
"liable to err . . . from fickleness and passion" and that a second chamber
would provide "a necessary fence against this danger" (1893, 242). "Great
advantages," said Oliver Ellsworth to the Convention, "will result in having a second branch endowed with the qualifications . . . [of] weight and
wisdom [which] may check the inconsiderate and hasty proceedings of
the first branch" (quoted in Wood 1969, 556).

Madison offered a fulsome and spirited defense of the Senate in *Federalist* no. 62, one of the newspaper articles written in support of ratification
of the proposed new Constitution by the states. There he argued, first,
that bicameralism was essential to prevent "usurpation or perfidy," and,
second, that a senate was needed because of "the propensity of all single
and numerous assemblies to yield to the impulse of sudden and violent
passions, and to be seduced by factious leaders into intemperate and per-
nicious resolutions." This line of theorizing was echoed in the state rati-
fying conventions; for instance, Alexander Hamilton told the New York
Convention that "there ought to be two distinct bodies in our government," including a senate to provide "a certain balance and mutual control" (Elliot 1907, 2:302).

The institutional value of redundancy provided by bicameral parliaments is underscored by a simple story drawn from the dawn of the American republic. Thomas Jefferson, absent from the Constitutional Convention and distant from ratification politics because he was on a diplomatic mission for the United States in France, met George Washington for breakfast upon his return from Paris. He asked Washington why the founders had created a second house of Congress, the Senate. Thereupon Washington asked, "Why did you pour your coffee into your saucer?" Jefferson replied, "To cool it." "Even so," Washington responded, "we pour legislation into the senatorial saucer to cool it" (retold in Sundquist 1992, 27). The metaphor persists. Late in 1995, when the conservative Republican leadership of the House of Representatives and the more moderate Republicans of the Senate were at loggerheads over budgetary legislation, Senate Majority Leader Robert Dole (R-Kans.) said, "We are going to let [the House's] coffee cool" (*National Journal,* November 11, 1995, p. 2800).

In order for the lawmaking process to reach closure in a system of cameral redundancy, processes have to be invented by means of which legislative differences between the two houses may be resolved. Generally speaking, parliaments have developed two essential procedures for intercameral resolution: conference committees and a "shuttle" system. Some senates are primarily involved in one process, some utilize the other, and some senates practice both. When the conference committee procedure is in play, each of the parliamentary houses chooses some of its members to serve on a joint committee, the conference, to iron out differences. When the shuttle system (in some places called the "navette" system) is operating, bills simply pass from lower to upper house until both have adopted the same version of the bill. These interactions between the two bodies of parliament may substantially influence how each component institution operates (see Tsebelis and Money 1997).

The theorizing that leads to parliamentary bicameralism grounded in conceptions of representation and redundancy is, of course, open to challenge. Proponents of unicameralism have attacked the elitism in the selection of members of upper houses, such as the hereditary British House of Lords or the life-appointed Canadian Senate. Elsewhere, national senates are often under fire for their unrepresentativeness, where equal representation is provided to unequal territories, where electoral units are malapportioned, or where electoral processes are undemocratic. In parliamentary regimes, bicameralism may be challenged on the ground that the second house interferes with the normal relationship of political responsibility between the lower house, the putatively democratic body, and the executive.

The existence of a second chamber may be attacked on purely operational grounds. A senate is said to produce obstruction and frustration of the popular will more often than contributing salutary delay, and it may particularly do so when the two houses are in the hands of different political party majorities. Senates introduce inefficiencies in the processing of important legislation, and they may fail to provide a critical review of legislative proposals. Considerations such as these help to account for the fact that most national parliaments have only a single house and the fact that reform and change in the bicameral systems of many countries is, or has been, a zesty aroma in the political air.

Institutional Change

Legislatures, like political institutions generally, are both institutionally tenacious and subject to change. Sometimes landmark legislation epitomizes the profundity of legislative change. The Parliament Act of 1911 effected a fundamental constitutional change in Great Britain, removing the power of the House of Lords to veto legislation passed by the House of Commons and replacing this with merely the power to delay. The Legislative Reorganization Act of 1946, adopted by both houses of the U.S. Congress, streamlined and modernized the operations of Congress, including the Senate, ushering in the "modern" Congress (Davidson 1990).

Garden variety institutional change occurs as senates adapt to major events, changing political realities, and evolving political conventions and norms. The oldest senates have evolved over a very long period. The venerable British House of Lords has survived as an institution because it was possible to make institutional adaptations as conditions changed. Donald Shell has observed (1992, 28):

> Between the House of Lords of today and its predecessor body of 600 years ago there is an unbroken institutional continuity, but along with this continuity there has also been great change. The House of Lords has become more meritocratic and rather less aristocratic. From

being the senior part of Parliament it has become very much a junior part. More recently, from being an ill-attended body sustained by the enthusiasm of a few amateur, part-time or retired politicians, it has become much better attended and a partly professional House. From Parliament to Parliament significant, if subtle, changes are continuously evident. The institution may be the same body as existed centuries ago, yet it is also completely different.

While it may be true that, if there were no House of Lords today, no one would seriously propose establishing one, there is a remarkable inertia that attenuates change in these traditional institutions.

Arguing that the drafters of the U.S. Constitution surreptitiously "intended the Senate first and foremost to resemble in its form the British House of Lords," Elaine K. Swift trenchantly documents the evolution of the Senate over its first half century (1996, 10). She shows that in the early 1800s the Senate was largely reactive legislatively, insulated, and executive-centered, but that by 1841 it had become a body we would largely recognize today, with stronger links to the people and weaker bonds to the state legislatures, more proactive legislatively, and more independent of the executive (Swift 1996, 140). More recently, changes in the Senate as an institution since 1950 have transpired largely because of the rapid growth of policy demands on the body, the enlargement and diversity of groups active in the policy community of the national capital, and dramatic shifts in the policy agenda of the nation (Sinclair 1989). Rarely under any threat of reform from external forces, secure in the constitutional constellation, and under very little pressure for change internally, the Senate has, nevertheless, transmogrified over two centuries so that today it is quite a different institution than it was in the beginning.

Unicameral movements have emerged in some polities with bicameral parliaments, seeking to abolish the senate. The American state of Pennsylvania may have embraced the first bicameral legislature to go unicameral. In the last two decades of the seventeenth century the Pennsylvania legislature was bicameral, but in 1701 proprietor William Penn granted a charter to the colony establishing a one-house legislature, the Assembly (Johnson 1938, 33). Pennsylvania's legislature remained unicameral until a new constitution was approved in 1790. The second switch to unicameralism occurred in the state of Georgia. The colonial legislature was bicameral, but when its leaders framed the first state constitution in 1777, a one-house legislature was established. The state returned to bicameralism when its constitution was revised in 1789 (Moran 1895, 50). After the Vermont legislature went bicameral in 1836, all of the American state legislatures took bicameral form until Nebraska abolished the state senate in 1934 (Breckenridge 1957). Nebraskans call their legislature the "unicameral," its members are referred to as "senators," elections are nonpartisan, and the speaker of the house does not preside (see Comer and Johnson 1978).

There have been three celebrated cases of abolition of upper houses since World War II: in New Zealand (1950), Denmark (1953), and Sweden (1971). All three are small, unitary systems with a parliamentary form of government. All essentially inherited bicameralism from a previous undemocratic regime (see Longley and Olson 1991). In New Zealand a failed upper house, the Legislative Council, was abolished when it became clear that parliament was "functioning smoothly without the effective participation of an upper chamber" (Jackson 1972, 183). At the same time, New Zealanders have not abandoned the concept of bicameralism. On the contrary, "discussion of the values attributed to bicameralism has lingered as an important element permeating New Zealand political life over the past forty years" (Jackson 1991, 43).

In Denmark and Sweden, upper houses were dispatched without regret, and the unicamerals made their adjustments to the new parliamentary realities (see Arter 1991; von Sydow 1991). Over time, the Danish Folketing and the Swedish Riksdag have become weightier, more influential parliaments with firmer party organization and more significant committee systems. The strengthening of parliaments in Denmark and Sweden, as in the Nordic countries generally, owes much to party system changes and particularly to increased party conflict and competition. Cameral change effects have not been trivial, but soon these were eclipsed by adaptation to changed electoral laws, altered intraparliamentary party structure, and a new and stronger hand of parliament in relations with the executive (Damgaard 1992).

Today, the senates of the world are undergoing change. Some, like the Canadian Senate, are under strong pressure to reform. Others, like the U.S. Senate, have become more institutionally open and more electorally sensitive. The British House of Lords has developed greater professionalism as a legislative body and become more effective. The German Bundesrat has been called upon to absorb representation from the states of formerly Communist East Germany. In other settings—Poland, Romania, South Africa, Spain—senates have recently become substantially more democratic. Scholars have yet to fully assay and record institutional development and change in many countries, and the truth is that most senates are little understood and fertile locales for inquiry. The authors of the chapters to follow aim to begin a wider and deeper tradition of research on senates and on parliaments or legislatures more generally.

Senates of the Contemporary World

Comparative analysis of the upper chambers of parliaments should begin with an institutional perspective. Parliaments are political institutions sine qua non—they tend to be firmly rooted in their constituencies, their institutional boundaries are well defined, their internal official and informal organizations tend to be well established, their memberships tend to be highly stable, the rules and norms governing their policy processing are characteristically formalized, and their linkages to other political institutions, particularly the executive and judicial branches of government, are well worn if sometimes controversial. The first steps in the comparative study of institutions like parliaments must entail rich, or "thick," description of their emergence as distinctive bodies, their constitutional status, their powers, their organizational structure and leadership, their modus operandi, and their ties to the other key actors in the political process.

In an ideal scholarly world, we would have available to us detailed descriptions and analyses of every one of the sixty-one upper houses of today's parliaments. This would permit us to understand each of these institutions in their own right, embedded in their own national setting, their distinctive constitutional status, their own institutional history, their own social, political, and economic environment, and their own institutional context. It would give us the basis for constructing and estimating models about how things senatorial actually work, how politicians' and citizens' preferences and interests unfold into public policies through legislative processing.

Moreover, a portfolio of knowledge about the senates of this world would let us make comparisons, constructing informative typologies of senate institutions and taking measurements of aggregate institutional properties for the sake of testing ideas about the institutionalization, representation, or performance of these bodies. Trespassing the micro- and macrolevels of parliamentary life, we could come to better terms with questions about how representative bodies work, what makes them so robust and lasting, why they change and sometimes disappear, and what effects their members and the institutions have upon political legitimacy, public policies, politicians' careers and satisfactions, public well-being and happiness, and the future of human governance. These are heady prospects.

There are nine country chapters in this book. The cases have been chosen because they vary along several interlocking dimensions of potential importance to senates' performance of their representational and redundancy functions in democratic political systems. The executive-controlled senates so prevalent in Third World countries are absent entirely from our purview. The factor most commonly thought to influence the political role of senates is the structure of the state, federal or unitary. Thus we have four federal systems (the United States, Germany, Australia, and Canada) and five unitary ones (France, Britain, Italy, Spain, and Poland). The effects of state structure, however, can be mitigated, even neutralized, by differences that cut across this federal-unitary distinction.

Our selection of cases allows us to take into account the effects of a number of these cross-cutting influences. The first of these is formal powers. Some federal senates (e.g., the United States) enjoy coequal powers with the lower house, but unitary ones can, too (e.g., Italy). Another difference concerns the representation of territories. Federal senates do not always have a territorial representational base—witness Canada. Equally, unitary senates sometimes allow for such representation—witness France and Spain.

Yet another difference taken into account by our selection of cases is the election, direct or indirect, or appointment of senate members. Federal and unitary senates alike are sometimes elected, directly or indirectly, and sometimes appointed. Again, senates vary in their political party makeup and in the parties' linkages out in the countryside. The party composition of the upper house can foster gridlock when partisan differences divide the upper and lower houses or, alternatively, mitigate bicameralism when both houses enjoy the same party structure. Finally, we have age. Some senates, federal and unitary alike, are centuries old and operate within a long-established structure of democratic government (e.g., the U.S. Senate and the British House of Lords), whereas others, like the Polish one, have only recently come into existence and operate within democracies struggling to find their feet. In short, this book provides an in-depth examination of the performance of the representational and redundancy functions in nine upper houses that vary greatly in their constitutional powers and in both the governmental framework and political culture in which they routinely operate.

Although in recent years scholars have given some attention to the U.S. Senate, and there is a bit of new work on the British House of Lords, for the most part these senates are barely known to the scholarly world. There is a small literature in French on the French Sénat. But for some of these parliamentary bodies—the Italian Senato, the Spanish Senado, or the Polish Senat—there is virtually no analytical writing in the language of these countries, not to mention in English. Scholarly inquiry, such as it is, has leaned more in the direction of investigating abolished upper chambers, or relations between bicameral chambers, than dissecting the upper body as an institution in its own right (see Longley and Olson 1991; Tsebelis and Money 1997).

Given the primitive state of knowledge about most parliamentary bodies, we eschewed any attempt to construct a procrustean formula for the chapters. It also seemed to us that comparison and analytical conclusions are better promoted by grouping the chapters in federal and unitary clusters rather than by shared history or geography. Comparing within and across these groupings provides a better understanding of the forces promoting or impeding senates' performance of their representative and redundancy functions. We think of the effort as exploratory, defining the agenda of a larger program of research on parliamentary life as much as, or more than, expanding knowledge about how senates work in a variety of interesting political systems.

Our anthology begins with the senates in federal systems because in these countries bicameralism flowed easily from the rationale that a parliament should include one body representing the people of the nation as a whole and another body representing the component territories of the national federation. Because they were obliged to give strong priority to federal structure in devising their constitutions and institutional arrangements, the Anglo-American countries (the United States, Canada, and Australia) and Germany established a chamber of parliament explicitly to reflect their federal origins and the centrality of subnational units in national territorial expansion. Although the federal character of these upper chambers has, in many cases, diminished in importance, these federal senates experienced elements of common ancestry and purpose.

Bicameralism is readily identifiable with federal systems, where representation and geography entwine. We consider upper houses in five unitary states (France, Britain, Italy, Spain, and Poland) as a cluster to underscore the option of institutional design available to unitary systems. On account of historical inertia, in order to especially represent crucial social classes or interests, or to institutionalize policy processing that would embrace redundancy and protect minorities, unitary systems may establish bicameral parliaments including more or less consequential upper houses. Unitary systems with particularly strong inclinations to create barriers against rash policy decisions, provide extended deliberation before action, or permit checks and balances so that an upper house can correct the errors, technical or political, of a more popular and impulsive lower house, will consider bicameralism. Moreover, formally unitary systems may wish to provide special representation for territorially rooted racial, nationality, or ethnic subgroups, or create institutional recognition of policy devolution to subnational units (states, provinces, or "autonomous communities"). France, Italy, and Spain are systems in which subnational units are, or have sought, some kind of representation in a parliamentary upper house.

In summary, the distinction we are drawing is epitomized by comparing the United States and the United Kingdom, a confederation with a federal senate and a unitary system with an upper house in parliament. As two recent scholars of bicameralism have argued, "Britain and the United States represent two distinct models of institutional development. Other European states experienced some linear combination of these two paths. Confederations tended to adopt a bicameralism in which 'the people' were represented in the lower house, while the constituent states were represented in the upper house. Unitary states tended to reserve the upper house for elite classes to offset the political power of 'the people' in the lower house. In both cases, however, the two houses tended to have equal legislative power." In short, it makes great good sense to begin an inquiry of parliamentary upper chambers by comparing and contrasting federal and unitary senates (Tsebelis and Money 1997, 32).

Table 1.3 presents skeletal information about the four federal senates in our analysis. In these federal systems, significant subnational units exist that possess semisovereign constitutional power. Interestingly, three of these—the American, Australian, and Canadian—grew out of British, or Westminster, parliamentary tradition and practice, despite the fact that the United Kingdom always has been a unitary state. The formation of the post–World War II German parliament was profoundly influenced by the Allies, the United States and Britain, although it took a distinctive federal form. Two of these senates (the American and Australian) are popularly elected; two (the German and Canadian) are appointed. In their own ways, three of these federal senates exercise very substantial legislative power: the U.S. and Australian Senates and the German Bundesrat.

Table 1.3 also provides information about the five bicameral parliaments in unitary systems that are included in our purview. In these unitary systems, although public administration may be delegated by the central government to administrative subdivisions, in constitutional principle all political power that government may exercise lies in the hands of the national government. In Italy, Spain, and Poland, senators are directly elected by the people, but their institutional powers vary considerably. The Italian Senate has lawmaking and cabinet confirming power coequal with the lower house, but the senates in Spain and Poland are effectively subordinate to the lower house. The French senators are elected indirectly by electoral colleges, and peers of the realm are, of course, automatically members of the British House of Lords. The upper houses in France and Britain are relatively weak institutions, but their role in legislation is neither negligible nor trivial.

We sought to open up the institutional life of these major upper chambers by asking scholars expert in their own nation's parliament to analyze its senate. We hoped they would capture the senate's constitutional importance, its legislative roles, its lawmaking functions, its place in the society and political system, the selection of its members, its internal organizational life, and its linkages to its constituencies. We recognized that the level of knowledge and research would vary considerably among the upper chambers we chose to investigate, and much would be left to discover.

We begin with the U.S. Senate. It is the best-known upper chamber, the most stalwart, and the most extensively studied. Barbara Sinclair dissects the origins and development of the U.S. Senate, adumbrating its role in the congressional vortex as a coequal partner with the House of Representatives. Sinclair paints a portrait of the contemporary Senate she calls

Table 1.3. Nine Senates

Upper Chamber	Constitutional System	Size	Term (Years)	Selection	Powers
U.S. Senate	Federal	100	6	Two senators elected in each of the 50 states, by direct popular vote since 1913; before 1913, senators were chosen by state legislatures; one-third are elected every two years.	Lawmaking power, including initiating legislation, coequal with the lower house; confirms presidential appointees; must ratify treaties; may impeach the president for "high crimes and misdemeanors."
German Bundesrat	Federal	69	Varies	Appointed by the 16 länder (state) governments; terms are not fixed, but depend on the office holding of the state governments.	Veto over legislation affecting state powers; if a bill fails by a $\frac{2}{3}$ vote in the Bundesrat, only a $\frac{2}{3}$ vote in the lower house can override the defeat; exercises a voice in the position taken by German ministers in the Council of Ministers of the European Union.
Australian Senate	Federal	76	6	$\frac{1}{2}$ of the members are elected every 3 years except for 4 senators representing the federal territories who serve only 3-year terms; each of the 6 states elects 12 senators by proportional representation.	Role in lawmaking coequal with that of the House of Representatives; may not initiate or amend financial bills, but may return any legislation to the lower house requesting amendments; bicameral deadlock precipitates delay, elections, and joint sessions of the two houses.
Canadian Senate	Federal	104	Life	Appointed by the governor-general on the recommendation of the prime minister.	Primarily revises the details of bills and delays final passage, but has the constitutional power to reject bills passed by the House of Commons; committees may conduct influential investigations.

French Sénat	Unitary	321	9	$\frac{1}{3}$ indirectly elected every 3 years; senators chosen by popularly elected electoral colleges in each department, the number of seats based on department population; election by majority in departments with 4 senators or less, by proportional representation in departments with 5 or more senators.	Generally subordinate to the National Assembly, but with somewhat greater influence regarding "organic laws" and financial bills; Senate may initiate bills or propose amendments, but final decision rests with the lower house; conducts investigations and engages in oversight, but cannot dismiss the government.
British House of Lords	Unitary	1,067	Life	633 hereditary peers; 408 life peers; 26 clergy.	Financial bills must originate in the House of Commons; the Lords cannot alter financial bills once they are approved by the lower house; Lords' amendments to other bills may be rejected by the Commons, and final approval of bills may only be delayed by the House of Lords for one year.
Italian Senato	Unitary	326	5	315 directly elected; 9 appointed by the president of the Republic, 2 ex-officio members (former presidents); majority vote for 75% of the seats, proportional representation for 25%.	The Chamber of Deputies and the Senate are coequal lawmaking bodies; committees may enact legislation (*in sede deliberante*); the prime minister and cabinet must be confirmed by both houses of Parliament.

(*Continued*)

Table 1.3. (*Continued*)

Upper Chamber	Constitutional System	Size	Term (Years)	Selection	Powers
Spanish Senado	Unitary	257	4	208 elected directly from 52 multimember constituencies in the provinces, Ceuta, and Melilla; 49 indirectly elected by the legislative assembly of the 7 autonomous communities.	May propose constitutional reforms; may amend or veto bills adopted by the Congress of Deputies (within 2 months for ordinary bills and 20 days for urgent bills), but the final decision is made by the lower house; may engage in oversight of the executive, but the government is responsible only to the lower house.
Polish Senat	Unitary	100	4	Two senators directly elected from 47 of the 49 provinces; in Warsaw and Katowice, 3 senators are elected; election is by majority vote.	Subordinate to the Sejm; may initiate legislation, propose amendments, or veto bills, but the lower house makes final legislative decisions; Senate must act on ordinary bills within 30 days, and consider budget amendments within 20 days; only the Sejm may vote to override a presidential veto, but only the Senate may approve or block a national referendum.

"individualist," the ego-centered, participant, obstructionist body with its uneasy relations with lower house and president in the White House that, she believes, struggles to maintain a capacity to legislate.

The three other federal senates provide the focus for the next three chapters. First, Werner J. Patzelt analyzes the most federal of upper houses, the German Bundesrat. He characterizes in detail the strong linkages between the governments of the German states and the federal chamber of the German Parliament, and unwraps the unusual, if constrained, lawmaking role of that body. Patzelt's account of the Bundesrat's role underscores the unusual effects of the overlap of federal and state interests, and competition between governing and opposition political parties, within the German parliamentary system. John Uhr recounts the fascinating upsurge of influence exerted by the Australian Senate, where opposition parties have flourished and where parliamentary committees have become stronger. Uhr's analysis depicts the curious Australian version of divided government, where a redundant upper chamber may frustrate the legislative program of the party majority in the lower house. Then, C. E. S. Franks anatomizes the workings of the upper house in a very different Commonwealth parliament—the Canadian Senate. Indeed, Franks describes two Canadian senates, the actual body that meets and acts regularly in Ottawa and the senate of the reform literature, the so-called Triple-E Senate (elected, equal, effective).

The remaining chapters capture senatorial segments of parliamentary life in five unitary systems. Jean Mastias's focus is on the French Sénat, an upper chamber with a rather rocky past and a future that rests on its establishing a permanent identity as an independent parliamentary body. Because senators represent the localities of France in the parliamentary precincts of Paris, the Sénat has achieved a permanence somewhat belied by its limited deliberative and policy-influencing role. Donald Shell has pioneered modern research on the British House of Lords. Here, he locates that chamber within the context of Britain's constitutional development, and explains that this unashamedly undemocratic body has actually come to play new and constructive roles in the British parliamentary context.

Claudio Lodici and Carlos Flores Juberías analyze the senates of Italy and Spain, respectively. As Lodici explains, the Italian Senate is unusual among parliamentary systems in its coequality with the lower house. Indeed, the important role of the Senate in the Italian political structure invites comparison to two other senates considered in this book—the senates in the United States and Australia. These senates are not under the aegis of the lower houses of their parliaments, but participate equally in the exercise of legislative power. In its coequal role in confirming prime ministers and cabinets and in enacting legislation, the Italian Senate overshadows its Mediterranean partner, the Spanish Senate, which has been unable to muster a substantial role in post–Franco Spanish politics. Flores provides an illuminating accounting of the parliamentary role of the senate in Spain, and analyzes the lines along which the Spanish Senate must develop if it is to be a major player in Spanish legislative politics.

Last but not least, David M. Olson considers the most recently constructed senatorial edifice of those presented in this book—the Polish Senate. Poland is something of an outlier, a unitary, parliamentary system which nevertheless opted for a two-house parliament. To be sure, its Senate was intended to be a secondary body, subordinate to the Sejm with only revisory powers. As Olson explains, the Polish Senate continues to seek its proper place in the political system.

References

Abramowitz, Alan I., and Jeffrey A. Segal. 1992. *Senate Elections.* Ann Arbor: University of Michigan Press.

Agor, Weston H. 1971. *The Chilean Senate.* Austin: University of Texas Press.

Arter, David. 1984. *The Nordic Parliaments: A Comparative Analysis.* New York: St. Martin's Press.

———. 1991. "One Ting Too Many: The Shift to Unicameralism in Denmark." In *Two into One: The Politics and Processes of National Legislative Cameral Change,* ed. Lawrence D. Longley and David M. Olson, 77–142. Boulder, Colo.: Westview Press.

Baker, Richard Allan. 1988. *The Senate of the United States: A Bicentennial History.* Malabar, Fla.: Robert E. Krieger.

Breckenridge, Adam C. 1957. *One House for Two: Nebraska's Unicameral Legislature.* Washington, D.C.: Public Affairs Press.

Bryce, James. 1893. *The American Commonwealth.* 2 vols. 3d ed. New York: Macmillan.

Close, David, ed. 1995. *Legislatures and the New Democracies in Latin America.* Boulder, Colo.: Lynne Rienner.

Comer, John C., and James B. Johnson, eds. 1978. *Nonpartisanship in the Legislative Process: Essays on the Nebraska Legislature.* Washington, D.C.: University Press of America.

Damgaard, Erik, ed. 1992. *Parliamentary Change in the Nordic Countries.* Oslo: Scandinavian University Press.

Davidson, Roger H. 1990. "The Advent of the Modern Congress: The Legislative Reorganization Act of 1946." *Legislative Studies Quarterly* 15:357–73.

Duchacek, Ivo D. 1970. *Comparative Federalism: The Territorial Dimension of Politics.* New York: Holt, Rinehart and Winston.

Elliot, Jonathan, ed. 1907. *Debates in the Several State Conventions on the Adoption of the Federal Constitution.* 5 vols. Philadelphia: J. B. Lippincott.

Fenno, Richard F. Jr. 1982. *The United States Senate: A Bicameral Perspective.* Washington, D.C.: American Enterprise Institute for Public Policy Research.

Ford, Henry Jones. 1924. *Representative Government.* New York: Henry Holt.

Furlong, Paul. 1990. "Parliament in Italian Politics." In *Parliaments in Western Europe,* ed. Philip Norton, 52–67. London: Frank Cass.

Hahn, Jeffrey W., ed. 1996. *Democratization in Russia: The Development of Legislative Institutions.* Armonk, N.Y.: M. E. Sharpe.

Haynes, George H. 1906. *The Election of Senators.* New York: Henry Holt.

Ilbert, Courtenay. 1911. *Parliament: Its History, Constitution, and Practice.* New York: Henry Holt.

Inter-Parliamentary Union. 1986. *Parliaments of the World.* Vol. 1. 2d ed. Aldershot, U.K.: Gower.

Jackson, W. Keith. 1972. *The New Zealand Legislative Council: A Study of the Establishment, Failure, and Abolition of an Upper House.* Toronto: University of Toronto Press.

———. 1991. "The Abolition of the New Zealand Upper House of Parliament." In *Two into One: The Politics and Processes of National Legislative Cameral Change,* ed. Lawrence D. Longley and David M. Olson, 43–76. Boulder, Colo.: Westview Press.

Jillson, Calvin C. 1988. *Constitution Making: Conflict and Consensus in the Federal Convention of 1787.* New York: Agathon Press.

Johnson, Alvin W. 1938. *The Unicameral Legislature.* Minneapolis: University of Minnesota Press.

Kelley, R. Lynn. 1971. "The Role of the Venezuelan Senate." In *Latin American Legislatures: Their Role and Influence,* ed. Weston H. Agor, 461–511. New York: Praeger.

Lees-Smith, H. B. 1923. *Second Chambers in Theory and Practice.* London: George Allen and Unwin.

Levy, Gary and Graham White, eds. 1989. *Provincial and Territorial Legislatures in Canada.* Toronto: University of Toronto Press.

Loewenberg, Gerhard, and Samuel C. Patterson. 1979. *Comparing Legislatures.* Boston: Little, Brown.

Longley, Lawrence D., and David M. Olson, eds. 1991. *Two into One: The Politics and Processes of National Legislative Cameral Change.* Boulder, Colo.: Westview Press.

Luce, Robert. 1930. *Legislative Principles.* Boston: Houghton Mifflin.

Madison, James. 1893. *Journal of the Constitutional Convention.* Edited by E. H. Scott. Chicago: Scott, Foresman.

Main, Jackson Turner. 1967. *The Upper House in Revolutionary America, 1763–1788.* Madison: University of Wisconsin Press.

Malova, Darina, and Danica Sivakova. 1996. "The National Council of the Slovak Republic: The Developments of a National Parliament." In *Parliaments and Organised Interests: The Second Steps,* ed. Attila Ágh and Gabriella Ilonszki, 342–64. Budapest: Hungarian Centre for Democracy Studies.

Marongiu, Antonio. 1968. *Medieval Parliaments: A Comparative Study.* London: Eyre and Spottiswoode.

Marriott, J. A. R. 1910. *Second Chambers: An Inductive Study in Political Science.* Oxford: Clarendon Press.

Mastias, Jean. 1980. *Le Sénat de la Ve République: Réforme et renouveau.* Paris: Economica.

Mastias, Jean, and Jean Grange. 1987. *Les secondes chambres du Parlement en Europe occidentale.* Paris: Economica.

Metcalf, Michael F., ed. 1987. *The Riksdag: A History of the Swedish Parliament.* New York: St. Martin's Press.

Mill, John Stuart. 1861. *Considerations on Representative Government.* London: Parker, Son and Bourn.

Money, Jeannette, and George Tsebelis. 1992. "Cicero's Puzzle: Upper House Power in Comparative Perspective." *International Political Science Review* 13 : 25–43.

Moran, Thomas F. 1895. *The Rise and Development of the Bicameral System in America.* Baltimore: Johns Hopkins University Press.

Nef, Jorge, and Nibaldo Galleguillos. 1995. "Legislatures and Democratic Transitions in Latin America: The Chilean Case." In *Legislatures and the New Democracies in Latin America,* ed. David Close, 113–35. Boulder, Colo.: Lynne Rienner.

O'Brien, Gary. 1997. "South Africa's New Upper Chamber." *Canadian Parliamentary Review* 20 : 16–18.

O'Brien, Kevin J. 1990. *Reform without Liberalization: China's National People's Congress and the Politics of Institutional Change.* Cambridge: Cambridge University Press.

Pollard, Albert F. 1920. *The Evolution of Parliament.* New York: Longmans, Green.

Remington, Thomas F., and Steven S. Smith. 1996. "The Early Legislative Process in the Russian Federal Assembly." *Journal of Legislative Studies* 2 : 161–92.

Reschova, Jana, and Jindriska Syllova. 1996. "The Legislature of the Czech Republic." In *Parliaments and Organised Interests: The Second Steps,* ed. Attila Ágh and Gabriella Ilonszki, 322–41. Budapest: Hungarian Centre for Democracy Studies.

Riker, William H. 1955. "The Senate and American Federalism." *American Political Science Review* 49 : 452–69.

———. 1992. "The Justification of Bicameralism." *International Political Science Review* 13 : 101–16.

Roberts, G. B. 1926. *The Functions of an English Second Chamber.* London: George Allen and Unwin.

Sayles, George O. 1974. *The King's Parliament of England.* New York: W. W. Norton.

Shell, Donald. 1992. *The House of Lords.* 2d ed. New York: Harvester Wheatsheaf.

Sinclair, Barbara. 1989. *The Transformation of the U.S. Senate.* Baltimore: Johns Hopkins University Press.

Sundquist, James L. 1992. *Constitutional Reform and Effective Government.* Rev. ed. Washington, D.C.: Brookings Institution.

Swanstrom, Roy. 1985. *The United States Senate, 1787–1801.* Washington, D.C.: Government Printing Office.

Swift, Elaine K. 1996. *The Making of an American Senate: Reconstitutive Change in Congress, 1787–1841.* Ann Arbor: University of Michigan Press.

Temperley, Harold W. V. 1910. *Senates and Upper Chambers.* London: Chapman and Hall.

Tsebelis, George, and Jeannette Money. 1997. *Bicameralism.* New York: Cambridge University Press.

Van Schendelen, M. P. C. M., J. J. A. Thomassen, and H. Daudt. 1981. *Leden van de Staten-General.* The Hague: Vuga-Uitgeverij.

von Sydow, Bjorn. 1991. "Sweden's Road to a Unicameral Parliament." In *Two into One: The Politics and Processes of National Legislative Cameral Change,* ed. Lawrence D. Longley and David M. Olson, 143–201. Boulder, Colo.: Westview Press.

Wheare, K. C. 1967. *Legislatures.* 2d ed. London: Oxford University Press.

Wood, Gordon S. 1969. *The Creation of the American Republic, 1776–1787.* New York: W. W. Norton.

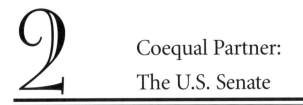

2

Coequal Partner:
The U.S. Senate

BARBARA SINCLAIR

Three characteristics make the U.S. Senate unusual among upper chambers: it shares legislative power equally with the House of Representatives; it operates under a set of rules that vests enormous power in each senator; and when majorities rule in the Senate it is only by leave of minorities. In this chapter, I examine the development and contemporary functioning of the Senate, with special emphasis on these characteristics and on their effects on public policy and governance in the United States.

The Senate of the late twentieth century consists of one hundred senators, two popularly elected from each of the fifty American states for six-year terms. It contrasts with the House of Representatives, in which representation is based on population and terms last two years. Like House members, almost all senators are members of one of the two major American political parties. But, because political parties are relatively weak in the United States, senators do not owe their elections primarily to their party organizations. Party leaders in the states and in Washington, D.C., have only limited influence over the behavior of senators and certainly cannot control them. As one chamber of the legislature in a division-of-powers system, the Senate exercises policy-making power independent of the executive, as does the House of Representatives.

Constitutional Origins and Contours

Political theory and practical politics produced the U.S. Senate. Bicameralism was an essential component of the separation of powers in the Framers' view. As James Madison wrote in *Federalist* no. 51, "In republican government the legislative power necessarily predominates. The remedy for this inconveniency is to divide the legislature into different branches; and to render them, by different modes of election and different principles of action, as little connected with each other as the nature of their common functions and their common dependence on the society will admit" (Hamilton et al. 1961 [1788], 322). The Virginia Plan that formed the basis for the Constitutional Convention's deliberations called for two legislative chambers, and a unicameral legislature was never considered.

If bicameralism was a broadly accepted principle and thus the creation of a second chamber was not controversial, the basis of representation in that second chamber proved to be the most highly contentious issue the Framers faced. Their solution—two senators per state to be chosen by the state's legislature—was a political deal that the small states extracted from the large states by their adamant unwillingness to settle for less. As added insurance, the small states secured a provision making their equal representation in the Senate effectively impossible to change; the provision for amending the Constitution states that "no State, without its Consent, shall be deprived of its equal Suffrage in the Senate" (Article V). In *Federalist* no. 62, Madison does not even try to justify the equal representation in the Senate of states of highly unequal population as anything other than a political deal (Hamilton et al. 1961 [1788], 377).

In the Framers' view, bicameralism would provide a safeguard against "schemes of usurpation and perfidy" by "requiring the concurrence of two distinct bodies" (*Federalist* no. 62, Hamilton et al. 1961 [1788], 379). A well-constructed second chamber would, in addition, provide experience, stability, and a guard against the "propensity of all single and numerous assemblies to yield to the impulse of sudden and violent passions" (Hamilton et al. 1961 [1788], 379). The length of the Senate term and the qualifications for senators were aimed at accomplishing these ends; the special powers vested in the Senate were predicated on the Senate actually displaying these characteristics. Thus, Senate terms were set at six years and were staggered; senators were required to be thirty years old and nine years a citizen.

In a bow to the widespread belief that control over the power to tax was at the heart of popular government, the Framers gave the House of Representatives, the popular chamber, the power to initiate all tax legislation. Despite some discussion of the possibility, they did not limit the Senate's power to amend such legislation. The power of impeaching federal officials was vested in the House; the Senate was charged with trying impeachments. The Senate was also charged with approving treaties and federal appointments.

Constitutional, Institutional, and Electoral Development

The small states expected the Senate to give them a direct voice in the national government. In essence, they expected the Senate to be an assembly of ambassadors from the states. Yet state legislatures never had an effective means of controlling the senators they chose, and so senators were never really just agents of their state legislature. Some state legislatures attempted to direct their senators through the "doctrine of instructions" by which the legislature passed a resolution instructing their senators how to vote. However, since the Constitution unlike the Articles of Confederation that preceded it did not allow recall, state legislatures lacked means of enforcement (Riker 1955, 455–63). Given the lengthy term of senators compared with those of state legislators, even the state legislature's control over the senator's reelection provided little leverage. From the beginning, then, senators had considerable latitude to define their representational role as they chose; they were not required to be mere agents of their states and certainly not of their state legislatures. Consequently, the Senate never served as a mechanism by which the states could control national decisions.

During the first years of the new government, the Senate was the less prestigious chamber (see Swift 1996). Its role was less clear than that of the House: was it to be the protector and voice of the states, the protector of the propertied elite as the discussions of the desired characteristics of senators and of the Senate's insulation from popular opinion suggested, or an advisory council to the president, as some of its special powers seemed to imply? Unlike the House, the Senate met behind closed doors, which made it less visible. In addition, it lagged significantly behind the House in workload, originating legislation much less frequently (Risjord 1994, 99–100).

Like the House, the Senate initially relied on select committees to draft legislation and was slower than the House to develop standing committees. In some cases supposedly select committees did take on much of the character of standing committees as they were repeatedly reestablished, sometimes with the same chairman (Risjord 1994, 100). In 1916, the Senate voted to establish eleven standing committees, and the committee system continued to grow.

The Senate opened its sessions to the public in 1794, and by the 11th Congress (1809) its share of the legislative workload had grown enough to prompt changes in its committee system. The Senate's growing prestige, however, resulted from its role in the great national debates preceding the Civil War. The Senate provided the forum to debate and sometimes to patch together compromises on the salient and divisive issues of slavery and free soil.

New states were admitted to the union, but the Senate remained small: sixty-four members in the 35th Congress (1857–59). As a result, the Senate did not experience the pressure that the much larger House did to curtail debate. Although the House adopted rules restricting debate as early as 1811, the nineteenth-century Senate did not. "Elaborate rules were believed unnecessary, deference and courtesy were expected to prevail" (Bogue 1994, 113; see also Binder 1997). By the time the filibuster became a significant problem in the late nineteenth century, the permissive debate rules had acquired an almost sacred aura; defenders argued that they embodied the will of the Framers of the Constitution. Certainly the usefulness of those rules to individual senators—and the fact that they made changing Senate rules so difficult—acted as a formidable barrier against change (Binder and Smith 1997).

Only when "a small group of willful men" blocked President Woodrow Wilson's proposal to arm American merchant ships in 1917 and Wilson managed to focus intense public attention on the Senate's debate rules did the body agree to a procedure for cutting off debate. Even so, the cloture procedure instituted was cumbersome. Sixteen senators had to file a petition requesting a vote to end debate on the matter at issue; two days after the filing, a vote would be taken, and if two-thirds of those present and voting supported the cloture motion, debate would be limited to one hour per senator.

The rule has been changed several times. Since 1975, three-fifths of the total membership (sixty) is required to cut off debate, although stopping debate on a proposal to change Senate rules still requires a two-thirds vote. Since 1986, all Senate activity following cloture has been limited to thirty hours. Thus, to cut off debate still requires a supermajority.

The Senate's small size and constitutional provisions about Senate leadership contributed to the late and incomplete development of a formal, vigorous party leadership in the chamber. The Constitution makes the vice president of the United States the president of the Senate and specifies that the Senate must also choose a president pro tempore to preside in the vice president's absence. Although it appears that before 1845 the vice president appointed congressional committees, the Senate was loath to vest much power in an outsider. After 1845, the party caucuses assumed the committee assignment function, and the chairman of the Senate Majority Caucus was usually—but not always—the most powerful single figure in the chamber (Bogue 1994, 117; Gamm and Smith 1997). Around the turn of the century, a clique of Republican senators led by Nelson Aldrich of Rhode Island exercised considerable centralized power in the chamber through their control of the Senate Republican Party. It was not until 1911–13 that the parties began electing majority and minority leaders for the entire Congress (Ripley 1969, 26). The formal establishment of these offices did not bring with it any significant new procedural powers; the Senate continued to be stingy in giving central leaders tools for doing their jobs.

The early years of the twentieth century saw a change in Senate elections. The 17th Amendment to the Constitution, passed by Congress and ratified by the states in 1913, provided for popular election of senators.

Actually, in many states senators were popularly elected in fact if not in form in the nineteenth century. The public canvass by which Senate candidates helped elect state legislative candidates pledged to vote for them originated in the 1830s, spread in the 1850s, and became quite common after the Civil War (Riker 1955, 463–69). The famous Lincoln-Douglas debates were part of such a campaign. This practice reduced the influence of state legislatures over their senators even further.

With the rise of the direct primary in the late nineteenth and early twentieth centuries, the parties' candidates for Senate were chosen by the voters in a number of states, and state legislatures ignored the will of the people at their peril. Oregon carried this thrust one step further, providing for a test of popular sentiment between Senate candidates in the November general election and requiring the state legislature to vote for the winner. American political culture had changed since the Constitution was drafted and, in response, practice changed even before formal constitutional change. Senators had never really been agents of their state legislatures; now they were clearly expected to represent the people of their states directly.

Thus, by 1920, the major contours of the modern Senate had emerged. The Senate had long since established itself as an equal legislative partner with the House. It exercised its shared legislative powers fully and on occasion made assertive use of its special powers. In one of the most notorious cases, the Senate refused to ratify the Versailles Treaty containing the League of Nations Covenant that President Wilson had negotiated at the end of World War I. Furthermore, the Senate had outstripped the larger House in visibility and prestige. Moving from the House to the Senate was clearly considered a step up.

To get its legislative work done, the Senate relied on a system of standing committees. Senators obtained their committee assignments through their parties. However, once on a committee, a senator was considered entitled to remain, and committee rank was determined by seniority. Formal party leadership positions had been established, but leaders were not granted much procedural power. The Senate's rules, especially unlimited debate and the loose germaneness rules, vested great power in individual senators should they choose to exploit them.

The formal shift to popular election enhanced senators' legitimacy. It also made them more directly subject to the same currents of public opinion as House members were. However, because of the de facto changes in the mode of election in many states prior to the formal change, this was an incremental rather than a revolutionary change.

The Contemporary Senate

The Senate's position as the more visible and more prestigious chamber was reinforced after World War II. As foreign affairs issues became more salient, the Senate's special powers in that area gave it added prominence. Even more important was the development of television and the increased prominence of the mass media in American politics. Journalists have always been partial to senators (Fenno 1982, 1995). Being fewer in number than House members, senators and the Senate are easier to cover; each senator is seen as more important, and personalities stand out. Furthermore, the six-year term makes the reporter's investment in cultivating senators as news sources more likely to pay off. Of course, as senators become more visible, they are deemed more worthy of coverage. Reporters' need for credible spokespeople, especially in opposition to the president, leads them to senators with their higher visibility and prestige. Senators are more likely to appear on the weekend interview shows and on the evening TV news. Inevitably, given the importance of visibility in a candidate-centered era, the Senate became an important source of presidential candidates, and this, of course, made senators even more interesting to the media.

Senate Elections

The Senate's prestige, long terms, small size, and rules that empower individuals make a Senate seat a valuable prize. Furthermore, most states are now sufficiently competitive that a candidate of either party has a shot at winning statewide. As a result, Senate contests tend to attract quality candidates. Many House members seek to move up to the Senate. Most nonincumbent Senate candidates have either held elective office or have become prominent in some other sphere—as an astronaut or a basketball player, for example. In recent elections, about two-thirds of Senate challengers have had previous experience in elective office (Jacobson 1992, 99).

Within the American weak party system, candidates are frequently "self-recruited." In recent years, the parties' senatorial campaign committees have actively recruited candidates. In 1990, such national Republican efforts were instrumental in persuading three well-regarded women House members to run against presumably vulnerable Democratic incumbents. In 1996, Bob Kerrey, chair of the Democratic Senatorial Campaign Committee, induced Ben Nelson, governor of Nebraska, to run for an open Senate seat. Such recruitment efforts, which have had mixed success, are aimed at persuading strong candidates to run for seats perceived as winnable. What neither the national nor the state party can do, or seldom attempts, is to persuade potential candidates who want to run to step aside for someone perceived to be stronger. Political parties have little ability to prevent well-financed candidates from waging divisive primary battles.

Senate elections are expensive, and access to funding is essential to success. The size of all but the smallest states dictates that Senate candidates rely heavily on electronic media, especially television, to convey their message to the voters. A serious Senate campaign will cost millions; in 1992, the average spent by all general election candidates was $2.9 million; incumbents averaged $3.85 million, and winning challengers averaged a bit over $4 million (Ornstein et al. 1994, 79, 89). Races in the larger states are much more expensive; the 1994 California Senate race saw the challenger spend $28 million, much of it his own money, and the incumbent $11 million. Although the political parties contribute significant amounts to their general election candidates, candidates must be able to raise the bulk of their own money. Campaign finance law and the parties' limited funds prohibit them from being the primary funders of their candidates.

The reliance on the mass media that the size of most states dictates not only increases the cost of Senate campaigns but also accentuates their candidate-centered character. Candidates sell themselves as individuals, not as members of a party; they tout their own experience and character and their own issue agendas, and voters judge them on that basis (Hinckley and Muir 1994).

Senate general election candidates are likely to be able to raise significant amounts of money, if not necessarily as much as they would like and believe they need. A contest between two strong candidates attracts money as it does in House races as well; contributors, whatever their motives, prefer to give to candidates with a good chance of winning. Furthermore, since a senator is 1 of 100 rather than 1 of 435, contributions to Senate races may be seen as more cost-effective.

Senate races, then, are more likely than House races to be competitive. A significant number of House districts are safe for one or the other party; no state falls into that category any longer. The media's interest in senators translates in turn into an interest in Senate candidates, and that translates into the likelihood that Senate challengers will receive some free media coverage. Still, in every election year, often about half of all Senate races are low-key affairs in which one candidate never gets his or her campaign off the ground. Such races are overwhelmingly ones in which a strong incumbent has managed to scare off a significant challenge.

In recent elections, the reelection rate for incumbent senators has varied widely, due in part to the small size of the group up for reelection every two years. In the elections from 1970 to 1994, on average 82 percent of incumbent senators who sought reelection successfully attained it; the low was 55 percent in 1980; the high was 97 percent in 1990 (Ornstein et al. 1994, 59). Senate incumbents who do win reelection usually do so by considerably narrower margins than House incumbents. In the elections from 1980 through 1992, 45 percent of Senate incumbents received less than 60 percent of the vote (Ornstein et al. 1994, 62).

The competitiveness of most states, staggered Senate terms, and the candidate-centered focus of Senate elections leads to states frequently being represented by senators of different parties. During the 103d Congress, twenty of fifty Senate delegations consisted of one Democrat and one Republican; in the 104th and 105th Congresses, nineteen Senate delegations were split between the parties.

The character of Senate elections has also made the body more subject to shifts in partisan control than the House. After a long period of Democratic majorities stretching from 1955 to 1980, Republicans took control and held a majority until the 1986 elections; Democrats remained in the majority until the 1994 elections returned control to the Republicans. The frequency of close races for the Senate combined with the varying size and composition of the states with Senate contests in any given year means that a shift in a relatively few votes can produce a switch in partisan control.

The Senate's Membership

The Framers expected the Senate to be made up of substantial citizens, of the "better elements" of society. In descriptive terms at least, they would not be disappointed. Most senators have been white, male, middle-aged, well educated, and well off. Although the body has become a bit more diverse in recent years, the change is marginal. In the 105th Congress (1997–98), Senate membership included nine women, one African American (who is also female), two Asian Americans, and one Native American. All these figures equal or exceed previous highs.

The average age of senators in the 104th Congress was fifty-eight, a bit higher than the mid-fifties average typical of the last several decades (Freedman 1997, 30). Fifty-three senators identified their prior occupation as law, and thirty-three as business or banking. Law has always been a common profession of senators, and the number of lawyers in the 105th is actually somewhat lower than in the previous several decades (Ornstein et al. 1994, 28–29).

Most senators have held prior elective office. A study of senators who served between 1972 and 1988 found that 32 percent had previously served in the House of Representatives and 14 percent as governor of their state; only 9 percent had held no political office (Hinckley and Muir 1994, 471). Eight of the thirteen freshmen in the 105th Congress were previous members of the House; only two had held no elective office, but as is often the case of winning Senate candidates, both had previous political experience.

Clearly the Senate is not representative of the American people demographically; the Framers never intended it to be. The Senate is also not representative in the now broadly accepted "one person, one vote" sense. In 1990, the 18 percent of the nation's population living in the twenty-six smallest states elected over half the Senate membership; the majority living in the nine largest states elected only 18 percent of the chamber's members (Fenno 1995, 1785). This is, of course, the consequence of the political deal that the Framers were forced to make.

Internal Organization

The Senate confronts an enormous workload that it must process with its small membership. It continues to rely on a well-developed committee system to provide the division of labor that makes doing so possible. The Senate's twenty-one committees vary widely in power and prestige; Appropriations, Finance, Foreign Affairs, and Armed Services have traditionally been considered the Senate's top committees and are so recognized in Senate rules, but the two money committees far outstrip the others in desirability.

Party committees assign members to the Senate's substantive committees. The Democratic Steering Committee, which consists of over half the Democratic membership, makes its decisions through a bargaining and balloting process. The Republican Party bases its decisions strictly on seniority. Party leaders can still influence decisions but only at the margins. For example, at the beginning of the 104th Congress, Majority Leader Bob Dole prevented his rival, Phil Gramm, from assuming a Finance Committee seat by persuading more senior senators to assert their claim. However, when another Finance seat became vacant after Bob Packwood's forced resignation from the Senate, Dole could not induce any senator senior to Gramm to take the seat and Gramm got it.

Traditionally, the member of the majority party with the most seniority on the committee automatically became committee chair; the most senior minority party member became ranking minority member. Seniority seems to have become established as a practice in the Senate by 1840, and during the first half of the twentieth century it was considered inviolate. Both parties now have rules requiring party approval of committee leaders, but in the Senate, unlike the House, seniority has been consistently followed. Few challenges to the most senior member have been mounted, and those that have been mounted have failed. In the past, respect for seniority and the clout that senior members exercised served to maintain the seniority system; now senators' dedication to individualism and independence undergird the seeming deference to seniority. Discretion in the choice of committee leaders is perceived as a possible threat to a senator's independence.

The majority leader and the minority leader, elected by the members of their respective parties, are the only real central leaders in the Senate. Although he is president of the Senate, the vice president's only real power is to break the occasional tie vote. President pro tempore has become an honorary title bestowed automatically on the most senior member of the majority party.

Formal party organization was slow to develop in the Senate but has become relatively elaborate. In addition to their leaders, the party caucuses elect whips and several other leaders—on the Republican side, Conference chairman and secretary and Policy Committee chairman. Both parties have established whip systems and have a number of party committees charged with internal party maintenance and external public relations and outreach tasks (Smith 1993).

The majority leader is the leader of the Senate. He is charged with scheduling the Senate's floor business, with coordination more broadly, and with coalition building. Yet his powers and resources for carrying out these tasks are meager. Neither party gives its leader resources sufficient to provide him with major leverage over his members' behavior. The majority leader is not the Senate's presiding officer, nor does the chamber's presiding officer exercise much power. The only procedural power that Senate precedents give the majority leader is the right of first recognition: when several senators seek recognition simultaneously, the majority leader is recognized first.

The most formidable constraint on the majority leader, or any other potential central leader, is the Senate's unique rules, which bestow enormous power on each senator. Extended debate allows any senator to hold the floor as long as he wishes unless cloture is invoked, a cumbersome procedure that requires sixty votes. The Senate's permissive amending rules enable any senator to offer as many amendments as he or she pleases to almost any bill, and those amendments need not even be germane. To the extent that senators exploit the prerogatives inherent in Senate rules, they rob the majority leader of control over the flow of issues to and on the floor; he loses his ability to manage the legislative schedule or to define the agenda more broadly (Patterson 1989).

The Individualist Senate

In the Senate of the 1950s and before, norms of restraint prevented senators from fully exploiting their great powers (Matthews 1960). The Senate of that era was a clubby, inward-looking body governed by constraining norms. Influence was unequally distributed and centered in strong committees and their senior leaders, who were most often conservatives, frequently southern Democrats. The typical senator of the 1950s was a specialist who concentrated on the issues that came before his commit-tees. His legislative activities were largely confined to the committee room; he was seldom active on the Senate floor. He was highly restrained in his use of the prerogatives that the Senate rules gave him, and he made little use of the media.

The Senate's institutional structure and the political environment re-warded such behavior (Huitt 1965; Sinclair 1989). The lack of staff, for example, made it harder for new senators to participate intelligently right away, so serving an apprenticeship prevented a new member from making a fool of himself early in his career. It also made specialization the only really feasible course for attaining influence. Restraint in exploiting ex-tended debate was encouraged by the lack of the sort of time pressures that would later make extended debate such a formidable weapon; when floor time is plentiful, the leverage that senators derive from extended debate is much less (Oppenheimer 1985). Furthermore, the dominant southern Democrats had an enormous constituency-based interest in re-stricting and thus protecting the filibuster for their one big issue—opposition to civil rights. The Senate of the 1950s was an institution well designed for its generally conservative members to further their goals.

Membership turnover and a transformation of the political environ-ment altered the costs and benefits of such behavior and induced mem-bers to change the institution. Norms, practices, and, to a lesser extent, rules gradually changed (Sinclair 1989; also see Foley 1980; Rohde et al. 1985). The 1958 elections brought a big, new class of senators with different policy goals and reelection needs. Mostly northern Democrats, they were activist liberals, and most had been elected in highly competitive con-tests, in many cases having defeated incumbents. Both their policy goals and their reelection needs dictated a more activist style; these senators simply could not afford to wait to make their mark. Subsequent elec-tions brought in more and more such members, and in the 1960s the political environment began a transformation. A host of new issues rose to prominence, politics became more highly charged, the interest group community exploded in size and diversity, and the media—especially television—played a much bigger role in politics.

This new environment offered tempting new opportunities to senators. Countless interest groups needed champions and spokesmen, and the media needed credible sources to represent issue positions and provide commentary. Because of the small size and prestige of the Senate, senators fit the bill. To take on those roles, however, senators would have to change their behavior and their institution.

From the mid-1960s through the mid-1970s, senators did just that. The number of positions on good committees and the number of subcommittee leadership positions were expanded and distributed much more broadly. Staff was also greatly expanded and made available to junior as well as senior senators. Senators were now able to involve themselves in a broader range of issues, and they did so. They also became much more active on the Senate floor, offering more amendments to a wider range of bills. Senators exploited extended debate to a much greater extent, and the frequency of filibusters shot up. The number of filibusters averaged less than 1 per congress over the period 1955–1960; in the 1970s the average was 11.4 filibusters per congress (Sinclair 1989; 1997). The media became an increasingly important arena for participation and a significant resource for senators in the pursuit of their policy, power, and reelection goals.

The Legislative Process in the Individualist Senate

The contemporary Senate is an individualist body that allows its members to pursue the highly activist, outward-oriented style that most prefer. Its day-to-day functioning is shaped by the need to accommodate the individual that stems from senators' willingness to exploit fully their prerogatives under Senate rules. Those attempting to steer legislation through it must be constantly mindful of two home truths of the contemporary Senate: anyone can cause trouble, and everyone is likely to want to participate on those issues that interest them or affect their reelection, whether or not they hold a formal position relevant to that issue.

Senators hold multiple committee assignments and usually at least one subcommittee leadership position. In the 103d Congress, senators averaged 11.8 committee and subcommittee assignments; majority party members averaged 1.9 chairmanships (Ornstein et al. 1994, 116, 118). Thus senators are stretched very thin; they treat their committees not as work groups in which to participate on a continuous basis but as arenas in which they pick and choose whether to participate depending on their interest in the issues being considered. Senators rely heavily on staff for committee work. On many committees, decisions on many issues are made by the "interesteds," who usually make up considerably less than the full committee membership.

Because of senators' workloads and the large number of subcommittees, subcommittees are usually vehicles for their chairs. The chairs can use their subcommittees to publicize problems and policy solutions, to cater to allied interest groups, to promote themselves, or all three. Under most circumstances, other senators are too busy to interfere.

Markups, however, most frequently take place in full committee (Smith and Deering 1990, 139–43). Paradoxically, Senate committees remain more centralized than House committees in this respect. However, the reason most Senate committees actually write legislation in full committee rather than marking it up in subcommittee first is not deference to full committee leaders but again the enormous workload of senators and the desire of all committee members to have the opportunity to participate in decision making should they so desire. Those senators on the subcommittee do not have time to go through two markups, and they know that any interested committee member not on the subcommittee would insist on having a say at the full committee level.

Committee decision making must be sensitive to the policy preferences of interested senators who are not members of the committee. Because any senator can cause problems and may in fact be able to block legislation from getting to the floor, committee proponents of the legislation have considerable incentive to try to anticipate other senators' views and to bargain with those with intense feelings before the committee reports the bill. Senate committees are perforce highly permeable.

In the Senate, floor scheduling and coalition building are of necessity exercises in broad and bipartisan accommodation (Davidson 1985; Sinclair 1989; Smith 1993). The Senate only runs smoothly when the majority leader and the minority leader cooperate—and not always then. Using his right of first recognition, the majority leader brings legislation to the floor by simply taking the bill to be considered off the calendar. He does so either by unanimous consent, which can of course be blocked by any senator's objection, or by a motion to proceed to consider the legislation, which is a debatable motion that can be filibustered. Because any senator could wreck his plans, the majority leader must check with all interested senators before he brings legislation to the floor. He always consults with leaders of the committee of origin and with the minority leader; effective Senate scheduling requires intensive consultation between the majority and minority leaders. Senators are expected to inform their party leadership if they have an interest. For every bill, the staffs of the majority and minority leaders keep a record of senators who have asked to be informed before it is brought to the floor, and these senators must also be consulted.

Senate party leaders contend that their only responsibility is to inform those senators when they are ready to bring a bill to the floor, and that may well be all a senator expects. He or she may simply want to be sure the legislation comes up when the senator is in town. In other cases, however, a senator objects to the legislation's floor consideration either altogether or until the bill's supporters have altered it to his liking. Such a notification by a senator to his party leader is called a "hold"; what gives holds their bite is the implicit or explicit threat to filibuster the motion to proceed. The majority leader can and sometimes will go ahead with the legislation despite a hold, but he then may face a filibuster on the motion to proceed and, if that is overcome, a filibuster on the bill itself. Especially when floor time is short—before a recess or near the end of the session, only the most essential legislation is likely to be considered worth so much time. Supporters of legislation come under increasing pressure to make concessions that will remove the threat of a filibuster. As time becomes scarcer, a hold increasingly becomes a veto.

Once legislation is on the floor, the majority leader's control over its consideration remains tenuous. Senators are free to offer as many amendments as they wish, and amending marathons are frequent. Legislation that is controversial or broad in scope or "must-pass" is likely to provoke multitudes of amendments. Thus, the 1993 reconciliation bill that implemented Clinton's economic program—legislation which had all these characteristics—was subject to twenty-five amendments that were pushed to a recorded vote. Appropriations bills and tax legislation are frequent targets; almost fifty amendments were offered and pushed to a roll call vote on the big Reagan tax bill of 1981.

Since, in most cases, amendments need not be germane, senators can use the amending process to bring issues to the floor that the majority leader would rather avoid. In 1996, for example, Majority Leader Bob Dole and most Senate Republicans did not want to vote on a minimum wage increase that most opposed but that was popular with the public. Senate Democrats were prepared to offer the minimum wage increase as an amendment to every important piece of legislation brought to the floor. To avoid a vote, Dole was forced to put off votes, bringing the legislative process in the Senate to a standstill. Eventually, Trent Lott, Dole's successor, capitulated, and the bill came to a vote and passed handily. Senate amending rules make it much more difficult for the majority party and the Senate leadership to control the agenda.

They also make the Senate floor a superb arena for publicizing issues and policy positions and speaking to and for constituencies of all sorts. Not only can a senator speak as long as he wishes but he can seem to be doing something about the problem at issue. And, often not incidentally, he can put his opponents on the spot, forcing them to take hard votes. Jesse Helms (R-N.C.) has always used nongermane amendments on hot button topics such as busing, homosexuality, pornography, and abortion to get his issues to the floor and force senators to vote on them. In the late 1980s, for example, he successfully attached an amendment outlawing dial-a-porn services (900 telephone services that provide explicit sexual messages for a fee) to a major education bill. But Helms is by no means alone; most senators use the tactic at least occasionally. Thus, in early 1993, Bob Dole attempted to attach an amendment on homosexuals in the military to family and medical leave legislation.

Obstructionism: Standard Operating Procedure

Because, with the exception of especially protected budget act legislation, a filibuster is always a possibility, a bill's supporters must think in terms of building a supermajority coalition of sixty votes; a simple majority is often not enough (see Binder and Smith 1997). Consequently, the bargaining power of minorities is much enhanced. The legislative process in the Senate is frequently characterized by bargaining to accommodate small groups and even individuals. Such negotiations take place at every stage of the process; the frequent lengthy quorum calls during Senate consideration of a bill often signal that the bill's supporters are engaged in negotiations with senators who have "a problem" with the legislation.

Even after a bill has passed the Senate, the opportunities for obstructionism are not foreclosed. Extended debate can occur not only on the motion to proceed to consider the measure, on specific amendments, and on the measure itself but also on various motions related to going to conference and on the conference report.

Table 2.1 shows just how frequent filibusters are (see Beth 1995 for some caveats concerning the data). By the mid-1990s, they were occurring at a rate of more than one a month. Attempts to invoke cloture have

Table 2.1. Filibusters and Cloture Votes in the U.S. Senate, 1951–1994

Years	Congresses	Filibusters per Congress	Cloture Votes per Congress	Successful Cloture Votes per Congress
1951–60	82–86	1.0	.4	0
1961–70	87–91	4.6	5.2	.8
1971–80	92–96	11.2	22.4	8.6
1981–86	97–99	16.7	23.0	10.0
1987–92	100–102	26.7	39.0	15.3
1993–94	103	30.0	42.0	14.0

Sources: Congressional Research Service, "A Look at the Senate Filibuster," *DSG Special Report,* no. 103-28 (June 13, 1994), appendix B; Norman Ornstein, Thomas Mann, and Michael Malbin, *Vital Statistics on Congress, 1993–1994* (Washington, D.C.: Congressional Quarterly Press, 1994), 162; Richard S. Beth, "Cloture in the Senate, 103rd Congress," Congressional Research Service (June 23, 1995).

become a routine part of the legislative process in the Senate; often several attempts are made to cut off debate on a particular measure. Although cloture votes are frequently successful, a bill's supporters must often make significant concessions to get the sixty votes required. And, especially in the last two congresses, much major legislation has succumbed to proponents' inability to muster sixty votes.

The 103d and 104th Congresses (1993–96) have seen the emergence of the filibuster-centered partisan strategy. In the past, filibusters have often been partisan in the sense that the obstructionists were predominantly of one party. In some cases, the obstructionists were directed by party leaders. Not until the 103d Congress, however, did extended debate–based obstructionism emerge as a systematic partisan strategy. To be sure, Bob Dole, as minority leader in the 100th Congress (1987–88), did pursue a filibuster strategy for much of the first year; Republicans had just lost control of the Senate, Reagan was a lame duck without an agenda, and the congressional Democrats were aggressively pursuing their own agenda. However, Dole's run for the presidential nomination distracted him and led to the strategy's demise.

The 103d Congress marked the return of united control of both houses of Congress for the first time since the late 1970s. The new Democratic president had a big and ambitious agenda in 1993, yet he had been elected with only 43 percent of the vote and in an era of popular distrust of politicians and of government. Those circumstances, combined with the increased ideological polarization of the congressional parties, made it possible and profitable for Senate Republicans under Bob Dole's leadership to pursue a systematic filibuster strategy. In the 103d Congress, about half of all major legislation encountered some extended debate–related problem identifiable from the public record (Sinclair 1997).

A Republican filibuster killed Clinton's stimulus package; Republicans used the filibuster or a threat thereof to extract concessions on a number of bills, for example, voter registration legislation ("motor voter") and the national service program. Republican attempts to kill or water down legislation via a filibuster were not always successful, of course. For example, the Republican filibuster of the Brady bill imposing a seven-day waiting period for buying a gun collapsed when a number of Republican moderates began to fear the political price of their participation.

Time pressure makes extended debate–based obstructionism an especially effective weapon at the end of a congress, and Republicans were determined to deprive Clinton and congressional Democrats of legislative victories. At the end of the 103d Congress, Republican filibusters killed campaign finance and lobbying reform bills. Although unsuccessful in the end, Republicans filibustered and tried to prevent passage of a massive crime bill, the California Desert Protection Act, and a comprehensive education bill. In some cases, filibusters were waged to prevent legislation from being sent to conference or, more frequently, to deny approval of conference reports. Republican threats of obstructionist floor tactics were major contributors to the death of important bills revamping the superfund program, revising clean drinking water regulations, overhauling outdated telecommunications law, and applying federal labor laws to Congress.

In the 103d Congress, the filibuster was used as a partisan tool to an extent unprecedented in post–World War II American history. In the 104th Congress, Democrats, now in the minority, returned the favor; about half of major legislation encountered filibusters, and Democrats had managed to block much of the "Contract with America."

Uneasy Partners: House-Senate Relations

Its status as an equal partner, its different representational base, its non-majoritarian rules, and its greater prestige shape the Senate's relationship with the House. Because they are equal, they must work together. Before a bill can become law, the Senate and the House must agree on identical language. The differences in the two chambers' memberships and rules almost guarantee that important legislation will emerge from the two chambers in different forms. Either one chamber must accept the other's version or the differences must be reconciled by bargaining. On major legislation, most often a conference committee including members from both chambers is charged with working out an agreement.

Although they must work with their Senate counterparts and many aspire to eventually join them, House members resent senators. For years, House members have derided senators as media-obsessed prima donnas, as showhorses rather than workhorses. They have complained that the senators they deal with in conference lack in-depth expertise, depend too much on staff, and often do not even show up and yet hog more than their share of the media attention and the credit.

In recent years, the tension has been exacerbated by the increase in minority obstructionism in the Senate. Even when the same party controls both chambers, relations are often hostile, especially at the rank-and-file level and especially on the House side. In the 103d Congress, House Democrats were angered by the parade of Senate Democrats who extracted concessions from President Clinton in return for their vote on his economic program, and they were furious when David Boren (D-Okla.) killed the gas tax in Clinton's economic program for which many had voted. They were irate when told they had to accept compromises tilted toward the Senate position on a host of legislation because otherwise a Senate minority would kill the legislation, and they were outraged when Senate Republicans, in fact, killed a number of major bills for which there was clear majority support.

In the 104th Congress, House Republicans were at least equally frustrated by the Senate. Within the first hundred days as promised, they voted on all of the items in the "Contract with America" and passed all but term limits. Once the legislation got to the Senate, it was as if it had dropped into a black hole, they complained. Because of Senate rules, the Senate pace was painfully slow; to get movement, major concessions to minorities had to be made and, not infrequently, minorities blocked action altogether. To House Republicans who believed the 1994 elections carried a mandate for their agenda and that, to ensure their reelection, they had to deliver on their promises, the Senate was a major obstacle to their achieving their goals. "The other party is just the adversary," members of the House say, not entirely in jest. "The Senate is the real enemy."

Although sometimes frustrated as well, House and Senate party leaders realize the importance of cooperation between the chambers. The party leaders of each chamber communicate with their partisan counterparts on a regular basis and attempt to coordinate the chambers' schedules when possible. If the same party controls both chambers, the majority leaderships have a common interest in establishing a positive legislative record. The Senate leader's more tenuous control over his chamber's schedule and greater difficulty in passing legislation does limit the extent to which coordination is possible.

Despite the differences between the chambers in rules and membership, most House-Senate conferences do reach agreement, and most of the resulting compromises are approved by both chambers. A considerable proportion of the legislation sent to conference is not highly controversial. Even when legislation is contentious and ideologically charged, the interest of members of both chambers in enacting some legislation may well make possible a compromise that both prefer to no legislation at all. After all, members of the two bodies are often subject to similar public pressures to address issues that concern voters and to get something done.

The President and the Senate

Since Franklin Roosevelt's time, Americans have expected their president to set the policy agenda and engineer the enactment of his program. Within the U.S. system of government with its division of powers, the president needs the cooperation of both houses of Congress to produce a record of legislative accomplishment. Yet the constitutional structure gives him few powers over Congress to induce cooperation. He can veto legislation, and a two-thirds vote of both chambers is required to override.

As the single executive and the only official elected nationwide, the president is by far the most visible officeholder. The weak party system that the constitutional structure fostered deprives the president of major election-based leverage over congressional members of his party. Members of Congress do not owe their election to the president. They win election, especially reelection, on their own and often run ahead of the president in popular votes. Candidate-centered elections in a decentralized party system are likely to produce an elected party membership that is heterogeneous in terms of policy views and reelection needs. With the veto and the bully pulpit as his primary resources, the president confronts two very different legislative bodies. One—the Senate—has special powers of great importance to his success and rules that make positive action difficult.

Frequent divided control and increasing partisan polarization in recent years have led to high visibility confrontations between president and Congress. In the Senate, nominations have sometimes been at issue. Thus, Democratic Senates turned down Reagan's nomination of Robert Bork to the Supreme Court and Bush's nomination of former senator John Tower to be secretary of defense. In 1995, the Republican Senate refused to allow an up-or-down vote on Clinton's nomination of Henry Foster to be surgeon general. Although a majority of the Senate favored Foster, the proponents could not muster the sixty votes necessary to invoke cloture on the nomination.

The Senate's rules make a large and cohesive minority a potent force. Thus, in the 103d Congress, Senate Republicans repeatedly extracted concessions from Clinton on legislation supported by a majority and killed a number of major bills outright. In the 104th Congress, on the other hand, Senate Democrats used the rules to ameliorate or block many bills that Clinton disliked.

Even for members of the president's party and even under conditions of united control, the incentives toward individualism that the Senate rules provide often overwhelm those toward cooperation. Senators not infrequently pursue their own agendas, even when these conflict with those of a president of their own party, and they use their power to extract concessions from their president. Jesse Helms put "holds" on nominations he did not like during the Reagan, Bush, and Clinton administrations. Sam Nunn (D-Ga.) openly opposed Clinton on gays in the military during the early months of the new Democratic president's term and thereby gained considerable media attention at Clinton's expense. When the young administration, the first Democratic administration in over a decade, worked to put together winning coalitions on its crucial economic program, a number of Democratic senators publicly held out and extracted concessions for their votes. Senators lack a strong electoral tie to the president; they function in a political environment in which public opposition to a president of their own party is likely to pay off in favorable media attention; many believe they themselves should be president and are sure they could do the job better. Under such conditions, the incentives to exploit the great powers that the Senate gives the individual, even at the expense of a president of one's own party, are considerable.

Still, the Senate approves most presidential nominations with little controversy, it ratifies most treaties that the president sends it, and it passes most essential legislation. The president and members of Congress, especially senators, do function in the same political environment and are subject to some of the same political pressures. Furthermore, when conflict between the president and Congress threatens to block legislation, the Senate is by no means always the culprit. When the House shut down the government in 1995, preemptive Senate action led to a resolution of the crisis (Sinclair 1997).

Clearly when the president's party controls both houses of Congress, the Senate is the more difficult chamber for the president to deal with. The minority-empowering rules give his partisan opponents much more clout than they have in the majority-rule House, and Senate individualism tempts his own partisans to reap political benefits at his expense. However, when the other party controls Congress, the power that Senate minorities wield can benefit the president if employed to that end by his partisans, as they were in the 104th Congress.

Furthermore, in the 1990s, the Senate has been more moderate than the House; moderates make up a larger proportion of the membership, and when partisan margins are relatively narrow as they have been, Senate rules especially empower those in the middle of the ideological spectrum. A president of the other party finds it easier to deal with a moderate chamber than one controlled by his ideological opponents. During the 104th Congress, the hard line, highly ideological House majority, not the more moderate Senate, was the primary barrier to agreement between the president and the Congress on a host of issues, most notably a comprehensive budget package.

Because of the Senate's rules and how they are employed by contemporary senators, winning coalitions are harder to put together in the Senate than in the House. When the president is the agenda setter and the coalition leader, the Senate poses a problem for him. When he is in a weaker political position and on the policy defensive, the Senate makes it harder for his opponents to construct coalitions for proposals that he strongly opposes.

The U.S. governmental system militates against nonincremental policy change. A president and two distinct legislative bodies, all separately elected by different sets of voters, must come to agreement. For better or worse, barring a crisis of major proportions, incremental change is the most that the system can usually produce. The way the contemporary Senate functions increases the system's status quo bias.

The Senate and the American Political System

The Framers perceived bicameralism as one of a number of mechanisms for guarding against a dangerous concentration of power. For the Senate to check the House, it would have to possess substantially equal power, and the Framers so endowed it. The check would be most effective if the two chambers were separate and distinct. From our vantage point, we can conclude that the Framers were successful in constructing legislative chambers that, two hundred years later, remain significantly different. The smaller size of the Senate, senators' longer terms, and the character of senators' constituencies distinguish the Senate from the House and ensure that the two chambers do in fact differ in their "principles of action." As a result of these distinguishing characteristics, especially its small size, the Senate has always been a more informal, less hierarchical body than the House. In interaction with characteristics of the American political system external to it, its small size, long terms, and statewide constituencies have made the Senate the more prestigious body, and senators have been more visible than House members and more oriented to national constituencies. As politics became more nationalized and more media-dominated after World War II, senators took on an increasingly important role in the national political debate. They publicize problems, they promote solutions, they speak for a wide variety of claimant groups, and they provide a visible and legitimate opposition view to the president. The contemporary Senate provides its members with an excellent forum for debate framing, agenda setting, and policy incubation (Polsby 1975).

However, the contemporary Senate is much less effective at legislating; its nonmajoritarian rules greatly exacerbate the problems of building coalitions that the weakness of the bond of party creates. Defenders of Senate rules argue that they reflect the Framers' intent. The Framers did hope and expect the Senate to be more temperate, more experienced, more stable in membership, and more insulated from the gusts of public opinion than the House. However, the Senate's smaller size and senators' longer terms, more advanced age, and different mode of election—not nonmajoritarian rules—were to produce the difference.

Whether the Senate, in fact, displays the character the Framers hoped for to a greater extent than the House is open to debate. With the development of congressional careers, the House membership is not the mass of inexperienced neophytes that the Framers expected, and callow youth is seldom a problem. Most House members would contend that they, more than senators, possess the expertise necessary for effective governance that Madison worried about (*Federalist* no. 62, Hamilton et al. 1961 [1788], 380). Both bodies show considerable stability in membership— too much, according to some critics. Whether the Senate is less subject to the winds of public opinion is also questionable. The six-year term provides some insulation, but the greater competitiveness of Senate than of House elections requires senators who desire reelection to remain sensitive to their constituents. By enacting the 17th Amendment, Americans indicated they did not want a too-insulated Senate.

The move to popular election of senators did not make House and Senate elections or the representational relationship for House members and senators identical. Indeed, the typical House and Senate constituencies differ sufficiently to make members of the two bodies subject to different pressures. Senators may be no less likely than House members to "yield to the impulse of sudden and violent passions," but it may well be different passions to which they respond. And, given the very different bases of representation in the two chambers, the bodies' legislative decisions are likely to be still more different.

Although time and usage have changed the Framers' scheme in many particulars, bicameralism continues to have the effect of rendering policy making difficult; two equal but significantly different bodies must come to agreement. The nonmajoritarian rules of the Senate as they have come to be employed by contemporary senators enormously exacerbate the difficulty and may threaten the entire system. If the political system cannot respond to the problems that concern the American people, it loses legitimacy. Americans' current deep cynicism about their government is the product of many factors and failings, but governmental gridlock is an important one, and the Senate's rules are a major contributor to gridlock.

Yet, because the individualist Senate is so attractive to its members as individuals and because Senate rules pose such a formidable barrier to rule changes, only intense public pressure is likely to force the Senate to change, and only a major crisis is likely to generate such pressure.

References

Beth, Richard. 1995. "What We Don't Know about Filibusters." Presented at the annual meeting of the Western Political Science Association, Portland, Ore.

Binder, Sarah. 1997. *Minority Rights, Majority Rule: Partisanship and the Development of Congress.* New York: Cambridge University Press.

Binder, Sarah, and Steven S. Smith. 1997. *Politics or Principle? Filibustering in the United States Senate.* Washington, D.C.: Brookings Institution.

Bogue, Allan G. 1994. "The U.S. Congress: The Era of Party Patronage and Sectional Stress, 1829–1881." In *Encyclopedia of the American Legislative System,* ed. Joel H. Silbey. New York: Charles Scribner's Sons.

Davidson, Roger H. 1985. "Senate Leaders: Janitors for an Untidy Chamber?" In *Congress Reconsidered,* 3d ed., ed. Lawrence C. Dodd and Bruce I. Oppenheimer. Washington, D.C.: Congressional Quarterly Press.

Fenno, Richard. 1982. *The United States Senate: A Bicameral Perspective.* Washington: American Enterprise Institute.

———. 1995. "Senate: An Overview." In *Encyclopedia of the United States Congress,* vol. 4, ed. Donald Bacon, Roger Davidson, and Morton Keller. New York: Simon and Schuster.

Foley, Michael. 1980. *The New Senate.* New Haven: Yale University Press.

Freedman, Alan. 1997. "Lawyers Take a Back Seat in 105th Congress." *Congressional Quarterly Weekly Report* 55:27–30.

Gamm, Gerald, and Steven S. Smith. 1997. "Emergence of Senate Leadership, 1833–1946." Presented at the annual meeting of the American Political Science Association, Washington, D.C.

Hamilton, Alexander, James Madison, and John Jay. 1961 [1788]. *The Federalist Papers.* New York: New American Library.

Hinckley, Barbara, and Edward Muir. 1994. "Elections to the U.S. Senate." In *Encyclopedia of the American Legislative System,* ed. Joel H. Silbey. New York: Charles Scribner's Sons.

Huitt, Ralph K. 1965. "The Internal Distribution of Influence: The Senate." In *Congress and America's Future,* ed. David Truman. Englewood Cliffs, N.J.: Prentice Hall.

Jacobson, Gary C. 1992. *The Politics of Congressional Elections.* 3d ed. New York: HarperCollins.

Matthews, Donald E. 1960. *U.S. Senators and Their World.* New York: Vintage Books.

Oppenheimer, Bruce I. 1985. "Changing Time Constraints on Congress: Historical Perspectives on the Use of Cloture." In *Congress Reconsidered,* 3d ed., ed. Lawrence

C. Dodd and Bruce I. Oppenheimer. Washington, D.C.: Congressional Quarterly Press.

Ornstein, Norman J., Thomas E. Mann, and Michael J. Malbin. 1994. *Vital Statistics on Congress, 1993–94.* Washington, D.C.: Congressional Quarterly Press.

Patterson, Samuel C. 1989. "Party Leadership in the U.S. Senate." *Legislative Studies Quarterly* 14:393–413.

Polsby, Nelson W. 1975. "Good-bye to the Senate's Inner Club." In *Congress in Change,* ed. Norman Ornstein. New York: Praeger.

Riker, William. 1955. "The Senate and American Federalism." *American Political Science Review* 49 (June): 453–69.

Ripley, Randall B. 1969. *Power in the Senate.* New York: St. Martin's Press.

Risjord, Norman K. 1994. "Congress in the Federalist-Republican Era, 1789–1828." In *Encyclopedia of the American Legislative System,* ed. Joel H. Silbey. New York: Charles Scribner's Sons.

Rohde, David, Norman Ornstein, and Robert Peabody. 1985. "Political Change and Legislative Norms in the U.S. Senate, 1957–1974." In *Studies of Congress,* ed. Glenn R. Parker. Washington, D.C.: Congressional Quarterly Press.

Sinclair, Barbara. 1989. *The Transformation of the U.S. Senate.* Baltimore: Johns Hopkins University Press.

———. 1997. *Unorthodox Lawmaking: New Legislative Processes in the U.S. Congress.* Washington, D.C.: Congressional Quarterly Press.

Smith, Steven S. 1993. "Forces of Change in Senate Party Leadership and Organization." In *Congress Reconsidered,* 5th ed., ed. Lawrence C. Dodd and Bruce I. Oppenheimer. Washington, D.C.: Congressional Quarterly Press.

Smith, Steven S., and Christopher Deering. 1990. *Committees in Congress.* 2d ed. Washington, D.C.: Congressional Quarterly Press.

Swift, Elaine K. 1996. *The Making of an American Senate.* Ann Arbor: University of Michigan Press.

3

The Very Federal House:
The German Bundesrat

WERNER J. PATZELT

In Germany, the process of state formation began with the principalities, so the country's history is marked by a long tradition of particularism and territorial divisions. Designing a sound relationship between federal and national governments has been a continuous and difficult task for German political elites.[1] All conceivable basic formulas have been tried. In the twentieth century, for example, the federal Second German Empire (1871–1918) gave way to a Weimar Republic (1918–33) in which the political dominance of the national government was constitutionally guaranteed.

This unitary state became even more centralized during the Third Reich (1933–45). The norm of some sort of federal arrangement was reestablished in 1949 with the creation of the Federal Republic of Germany. This happened partially because of foreign policy considerations important to the Western Allies: the more powers rested with the individual states, the less powerful Germany would be as a nation. After 1949, however, German federalism and its single most important institution, the German Bundesrat, developed differently than had been anticipated. The country did not move in a confederal direction, and the states, or *länder*, became central actors in shaping national domestic politics.

A Brief Overview

The German Bundesrat [federal council] is, in many ways, a unique legislative body.[2] No representatives of the "people" meet there. Rather, its members are the prime ministers and other cabinet ministers of the sixteen states forming the federal republic. This makes the Bundesrat an assembly unlike those whose members are elected directly by the people. It is also different from upper houses in unitary countries where no subnational entities are represented in their own right. Its closest institutional kinship may well be with the European Council, or Council of Ministers of the European Union, both legislative bodies composed of governmental or departmental executives. Moreover, the federal roots of the Bundesrat are much older and go much deeper than its liberal or democratic roots.

The Bundesrat is, of course, a democratically legitimized body. Its members, state prime ministers and their cabinet colleagues, are elected and retained in office by the elected members of the legislatures in the sixteen states. Depending on the size of the states, from three to six members of each state's cabinet attend plenary sessions of the Bundesrat, and chair the meetings of its seventeen specialized standing committees. Except for these committee chairs, Bundesrat members are usually represented in committees by high-ranking administrative officials who act on the basis of instructions given to them by their state governments. The composition of the Bundesrat sharply contrasts with that of the lower house, the Bundestag, whose members are directly elected and whose committee sessions are open to executive officials only as guests.

The central political actors in the Bundesrat are political parties.[3] Typically, members of parliament are regional party leaders, or are federal or state cabinet ministers who are almost always high-ranking party leaders. Party cohesiveness shapes the political process in both houses of parliament. In the lower house, the parties making up the coalition supporting the government are clearly confronted by the opposition parties, and party discipline is the order of the day. In the Bundesrat, party confrontation is less clear-cut. Ministers from state governments led by the same party or party coalition cooperate more closely in the upper house than ministers coming from competing parties. But divided party control of the two houses—when the majority party or coalition in the lower house is the minority in the upper house—means that the Bundestag opposition may, and often does, use its Bundesrat majority as an efficient "second opposition."

These political considerations are important because the Bundesrat has substantial legislative power. Slightly more than half of all bills are subject to its absolute veto after having been approved by the Bundestag. For bills not subject to an absolute veto, the Bundesrat can invoke a suspensive veto, delaying action, and an absolute majority of Bundestag votes is required to override the veto. When the two houses disagree, the Bundestag majority may gain the acquiescence of the dissenting Bundesrat by modifying a bill in the permanent conference committee composed of sixteen members of each chamber. In these infrequent but politically consequential circumstances, the Bundesrat's bargaining power is superior to the Bundestag's.

All legislation initiated by the federal government—60 percent of all proposals and 77 percent of all successful bills—must go to the upper house for a "first round of deliberations" before the lower house is formally involved. The Bundesrat's comments on these bills weigh heavily in the legislative process. For this reason, to say that only 6 percent of proposals (5 percent of successful ones) emanate from the upper house is not a valid indicator of the Bundesrat's legislative importance.[4]

In addition, the Bundesrat plays an important role in federal administration. Because the federal government has few administrative agencies of its own, most federal laws are implemented by the states, and Bundesrat consent is always secured for administrative ordinances or statutory orders. This process gives the chamber detailed control over the administrative process. Finally, the Bundesrat has considerable authority in matters of foreign and European policy, where the jurisdiction or interests of the länder are at stake. The only powers reserved exclusively to the

Bundestag concern federal elections, removal of the federal chancellor and cabinet, and the right to ask federal government officials questions in parliament.

The Bundesrat is a secure, established institution in the German constitutional firmament, and its members are powerful prime ministers of the states, successors to the former German princes. The body never has suffered from any kind of "identity crisis." Indeed, its powers have grown in the last few decades, and it has readily weathered changes taking place in the European Union. Interestingly, unlike senates in many countries the German upper house has not been subjected to calls for its reform or abolition. The strong institutional foundation of the Bundesrat can be best understood in the context of its historical predecessors.

Historical and Constitutional Legacy

The earliest roots of the Bundesrat trace to the "Immerwährende Reichstag" [Everlasting Diet] of the Holy Roman Empire that convened in Regensburg, a city in Bavaria, between 1663 and 1806 (Reuter 1983; Scholl 1982; Wilke and Schulte 1990). This was a congress of ambassadors from the estates of the Empire, consisting of the Committee of the Grand Electors [Kurfürstenkollegium], the Council of Princes [Reichsfürstenrat] with its ecclesiastic and secular members, and the Committee of the Free Cities. The tradition of the Everlasting Diet was continued in 1815 by the German Bundestag. It met in Frankfurt, the site of the Holy Empire's coronation ceremonies.

At the time, the Bundestag formed the only constitutional organ of the German Confederation [Deutscher Bund, 1815–66], being composed of ambassadors from the member states. Its executive council [Innerer Rat], chaired by Austria, was the body that met most regularly and passed its decisions without consulting the full assembly. Each of the initial 39 German states (that number was later reduced to 33) held at least one, but no more than four votes, with the total number of votes in the Bundestag amounting to 69 (later 64) votes. The votes had to be cast uniformly as block votes per state, as ordered by the respective state governments. Hence, important features of today's German Bundesrat were already shaped and predefined in the nineteenth century.

Among the predecessor institutions of today's Bundesrat was also the Bundesrat of the North German Federation [Norddeutscher Bund, 1866–71]. A political consequence of Prussia's victory in the German War of 1866, this federation constituted the first truly federal arrangement in German history.[5] With a few modifications, its constitution also became the constitution of Imperial Germany [Deutsches Reich] between 1871 and 1918.

At that time, the Bundesrat formed the highest constitutional organ of the Empire, which was a federation of kingdoms, principalities, and free cities. It had twenty-five German states as its members, and their votes differed according to their size, ranging from one to seventeen (Prussia). Again, the votes of each state had to be cast en bloc. The chancellor of the Reich served as the Bundesrat's chairman, even though he was accountable only to the emperor and neither to the Bundesrat nor to a Reichstag [Imperial Diet] that was elected by the adult male population of the Reich. From the perspective of constitutional law, the Bundesrat was more powerful than the Reichstag, but in practice it did not even come near to equaling it. In theory, bills drafted by the government had to be submitted to the Bundesrat first, and their referral to the Reichstag was contingent upon approval by the Bundesrat. Indeed, bills passed by the Reichstag could be enacted into law only if the Bundesrat approved.

The Bundesrat could also issue administrative ordinances concerning the implementation of laws, although their actual implementation was a matter for the states. Finally, if approved by the monarch, the Bundesrat even had the authority to dissolve the Reichstag. In practice, however, these comprehensive powers were never actually exercised, mainly because the chancellor of the Reich, as chairman of the Bundesrat, made sure that serious disturbances in relations between the two chambers did not arise.

The monarchical principle that, together with its federal counterpart, shaped Imperial Germany and the political role of its Bundesrat came to an end with the revolution of 1918. In both practical and normative terms, the Weimar Republic's new guiding principle of popular sovereignty shifted political authority from its federal institution—the Reichsrat—to its national legislature, the Reichstag.[6] On balance, the role of federalism was strongly diminished when the Reichsrat was stripped of its legislative veto power. Its reservations could now be overridden by a two-thirds majority of the Reichstag or by a popular referendum ordered by the president. Composed of members of the state governments or their deputies, Reichsrat committees were even chaired by members of the national government. But not all links to the past were lost. The sixty-six votes in the Reichsrat (in 1930) were assigned to the states roughly in proportion to their size, and with the exception of Prussia, bloc votes were cast.

Unlike Imperial Germany's Bundesrat, however, the Reichsrat actually exercised the powers it had and became more influential in policy making than had been anticipated when the constitution was adopted. The Reichsrat was dissolved in 1934 after the Nazis had seized power. But even before the dissolution, the powers of the states had been transferred to the Reich, state legislatures had been dissolved, and state governments had been subordinated to the national government.

The rebirth of Germany after its defeat in World War II started when its länder were created or reestablished. Most former states suffered some significant territorial changes, and some were even incorporated into "new" and "artificial" states (e.g., North Rhine-Westphalia). Still, the founding philosophy included the principle of federalism so that, much like in 1815, 1848, 1867, 1871, and 1919, a national representative institution for the states had to be created and many federal traditions were continued.[7] One of the major objections to the reestablishment of a Bundesrat, voiced mainly by the Social Democratic Party (SPD), was that the participation of state governments in the national legislative process contradicted classic principles of the separation of powers. Moreover, a Bundesrat whose members were state government appointees would hold less democratic legitimacy than a directly elected Senate. The Christian Democrats (CDU and CSU) for the most part supported establishing an upper house. They argued that state administrative expertise would allow for both more effective control of the national government and more effective representation of state interests on the national level than would a Senate dominated by party politics. A compromise was finally reached and a Bundesrat emerged that was both similar to and significantly different from its predecessors.

The Bundesrat and Federalism Today

The German states preceded the nation-state in legal as well as historical terms. When they decided to form a permanent federation, they transferred many of their powers to the national government so that the latter is not "superior" to the states, since its powers are derived from them. Article 79 (3) of the Basic Law prohibits any "amendments . . . affecting the division of the Federation into Länder, [or] their participation in the legislative process." Article 30 states: "Except as otherwise provided or permitted by this Basic Law the exercise of governmental powers and the discharge of governmental functions shall be incumbent on the Länder," and Article 70 (1) dictates that "the Länder have the right to legislate in so far as this Basic Law does not confer legislative powers on the Federation."

According to Articles 70 (2) through 75, some legislative powers rest exclusively with the states, others exclusively with the national government. In some areas, "the Länder have the right to legislate as long as and to the extent that the Federation does not exercise its legislative powers" (concurrent legislation; Article 72 [1]). In still other areas of politics, the national level of government can enact framework laws whose details the states can thereafter fill in by means of their own state laws (framework legislation, Article 75). Whenever a law is enacted nationally, the states participate in the legislative process, often with absolute and always with suspensive veto powers. Hence, the federal states are active participants in national politics and are by no means limited in their participation to merely articulating state interests.

Articles 50–53 and 76–81 of the Basic Law are the main constitutional provisions concerning the German Bundesrat.[8] It is equal in rank to the four other constitutional organs of the Federal Republic—the Bundestag, the federal government, the federal Constitutional Court, and the federal president—and has its seat in the federal capital. Constituted independently of the other constitutional organs, administering its own affairs autonomously, the Bundesrat is not, strictly speaking, the second chamber of a bicameral national parliament. Rather, composed of länder ministers, including premiers, it is the "institutional adversary" of a Bundestag that, being democratically elected, is the sole national parliament. Nonetheless, the two houses cooperate closely "in the legislative process and administration of the Federation and in matters concerning the European Union" (Article 50). This cooperation gives state governments a substantial voice in national politics in two respects. First, the länder as governmental entities (as opposed to elected representatives of the public) take part in framing legislation through the Bundesrat. Second, the states have a share in the implementation of legislation, since most of the administrative responsibilities of the national government are carried out by the bureaucracies of the states. Moreover, nearly all administrative ordinances issued by the federal government need Bundesrat approval.

However, the development of the constitution and the ongoing process of European integration have eroded länder sovereignty and changed the political role of the Bundesrat. Neither development was foreseen when the constitution was enacted. Meeting little resistance from the states, the Bundestag from the outset made such extensive use of its legislative powers that the states' ability to determine their own policies was significantly limited. State powers were even transferred to the European Union. The Bundesrat quite unexpectedly shifted its focus from preserving länder sovereignty to securing for the state cabinets an active and effective role in determining national policy. Over the last couple of years, in contrast, the states have begun to use their considerable potential for political pressure in Bonn to win back some of the powers ceded in previous decades.

The actual political role the Bundesrat plays is to a large degree shaped by the "cooperative federalism" predominant in Germany (see Fabritius 1976; Fröchling 1972; Kisker 1971; Lehmbruch 1976). This takes the form partly of institutionalized conferences and meetings between länder prime ministers, departmental ministers, heads of state chancelleries, and administrative and legislative policy experts. It also entails extensive routine cooperation between the national and state governments that far exceeds the minimum standards set by the constitution. The federal chancellor meets with the state prime ministers, and federal departmental ministers meet regularly with their länder counterparts. There are hundreds of joint committees composed of officials from both levels of government, and there is an even larger number of treaties and executive agreements between them.[9]

Thus, contrary to the expectations of the framers of the constitution, German federalism has not developed as a "dual federalism," with strictly separated rights and responsibilities for the two levels of government. Instead, it has taken the form of a system of cooperative, or even linkage, federalism characterized by an extraordinarily high degree of policy overlap [Politikverflechtung] that is extremely complex and virtually impossible to disentangle. The political evolution of the Bundesrat can only be properly understood when seen in this light since cooperative federalism worked to ease its burdensome responsibility of alone representing länder interests on the national level. Precisely this shared responsibility allowed the Bundesrat to seek to increase its influence in national politics.

Because Germany is a parliamentary system, policy debate is dominated by the clash between government and opposition, a clash that is usually cross-cut by disputes between national and state governments. Whenever an important partisan issue is on the agenda, however, the Bundesrat mimics the Bundestag's dualism as state governments take the position of the parties in government in their respective länder.[10] Hence, state governments do not always place highest priority on representing state interests in the Bundesrat. Instead, they choose to take a party position and thereby create the same alignments and disputes as are found in the Bundestag. Thus, nationwide party competition is, on average, more important than policy conflict between levels of government in shaping Bundesrat behavior. Legislative opinion formation and decision making are thereby standardized nationally, and this has made Germany a "unitary federation."

This situation hardly conforms to a simple doctrine of a vertical separation of powers. Nor does the Bundesrat fit a conventional horizontal separation-of-powers model, inasmuch as it is a legislative body formed by officials of the state governments. Because länder interests are usually different from federal interests, and more often than not the Bundestag's major opposition party is, in fact, the dominant party in the Bundesrat, the two houses may move in quite different directions. If the concept of separated powers is understood mainly as entailing checks and balances to control government, then the performance of the German Bundesrat cannot be viewed as deficient. However, the way the Bundesrat exercises its role in a system of checks and balances is not always apparent to the outside observer.

Structure of the Bundesrat

Membership

Composed of members of the sixteen länder governments, the Bundesrat knows no legislative terms; it sits permanently. Its members are appointed and recalled by their respective state governments so that the composition

Table 3.1. Distribution of Votes in the German Bundesrat

Federal State	Population in 1995 (millions)	Votes in the Bundesrat	% of Total Population	% of Votes
North Rhine–Westphalia	17.89	6	21.9	8.7
Bavaria	11.99	6	14.7	8.7
Baden-Württemberg	10.32	6	12.6	8.7
Lower Saxony	7.78	6	9.5	8.7
Hesse	6.01	5	7.3	7.2
Saxony	4.57	4	5.6	5.8
Rhineland-Palatinate	3.98	4	4.9	5.8
Berlin	3.47	4	4.2	5.8
Saxony-Anhalt	2.74	4	3.3	5.8
Schleswig-Holstein	2.73	4	3.3	5.8
Brandenburg	2.54	4	3.1	5.8
Thuringia	2.50	4	3.1	5.8
Mecklenburg–Western Pomerania	1.82	3	2.2	4.3
Hamburg	1.71	3	2.1	4.3
Saarland	1.08	3	1.3	4.3
Bremen	.68	3	.8	4.3
Total	81.81	69	99.9	99.8

of the Bundesrat changes when the partisan composition of state governments does. The number of members appointed by each state is determined roughly by both its population size and the principle that no single state should again play the hegemonic role Prussia did between 1871 and 1918. The Bundesrat is, thus, a representative body of the länder that also reflects the power constellations among the political parties in the states. The distribution of its sixty-nine votes, a number that became effective after unification, is presented in table 3.1.

The Bundesrat membership usually comprises states' prime ministers, their federal affairs ministers (sometimes called commissioners to the Federation), finance ministers, and as many others as are required to match the number of votes to which the state is entitled. The remaining state cabinet ministers usually become deputy members of the Bundesrat, and they enjoy equal rights when sitting in for the permanent members. Prime ministers attend plenary sessions when important political issues are on the agenda. Otherwise, state departmental ministers show up at the sessions when issues affecting their specialized subject areas are discussed.

The ministers for federal affairs are always present at the plenary sessions. They also cast the votes of their state if the prime minister is absent.

High-ranking administrative officials can, and usually do, represent their states in Bundesrat committees where specialized policy experts or senior officials of the state bureaucracies meet. The committee sessions are always chaired by a state minister whose competence falls within the sphere of the committee's policy area. In practice, administrative officials take turns in attending committee sessions to ensure that the most qualified to discuss the issue at hand are present. The states are regularly represented by their prime ministers only on the "political" committees of foreign affairs and defense.

Bound by the instructions of their ministers, administrative officials serving on Bundesrat committees do not exercise a free mandate. Ministers must, in turn, follow the political guidelines set by their state governments, guidelines that as members of the state government they themselves have helped to construct. Thereafter, though, their room for individual action is limited since each state's votes must be cast as a single bloc. Just as an MP cannot ignore party policy when deciding how to vote, Bundesrat members must be attentive to the decisions passed by their state government and the political parties constituting it. Only a prime minister can come close to exercising a "free mandate," because he is usually entitled to determine the policy guidelines of his state.[11] Even here, however, a premier's unannounced deviation in the Bundesrat from an agreed state policy position will usually lead to a crisis within the governing coalition in his state. Accordingly, such deviations are extremely rare and tend to occur only if overriding considerations of national party politics dictate such behavior.

Unlike their Bundestag counterparts, members of the Bundesrat are representatives not of the German people as a whole but of their states and state cabinets. Their decision-making processes can only be fully understood if account is taken of the complexity of their obligations. First, as members of länder cabinets, they play an important role within their states. Second, as members of the Bundesrat they hold national office and must pay heed to the interests of the Federation. Finally, as usually high-ranking state or even national party leaders, they take party positions and have to satisfy the expectations of party supporters. In effect, Bundesrat members have to balance and to reconcile three different, sometimes conflicting, sets of demands. Two of these are especially hard to combine. Whereas Bundestag members are obliged only to act within the framework set by their parliamentary party groups, members of the Bundesrat have to promote both state and party interests. In promoting state interests, cooperation with the federal government is required; in fostering party interests, members must cooperate with their party's parliamentary group in the Bundestag. These requirements can be hard to reconcile when the two houses are under the aegis of different party majorities.

Simultaneous membership in both the Bundesrat and Bundestag is not allowed. When such a situation arises as a result, for example, of a member of the former being elected to the latter, Bundesrat rules require the person to vacate one or the other seat "within due time." Nevertheless, each individual member of the Bundesrat has the right to attend, and to be heard at, the plenary sessions and the committee meetings of the Bundestag at any time.[12] This being an individual right, no single member of the Bundesrat exercising it can claim to represent the house as a whole. Rather, only individual state, or even party, interests may be pursued in its exercise.

For purposes of institutional representation, the Bundesrat formally delegates members to attend the Bundestag's plenary and committee sessions on a continuous basis, mainly to support the Bundesrat's own legislative initiatives. The Bundesrat can also have state administrative officials attend Bundestag committee meetings so that they can keep their ministers up to date. On special occasions, and at the request of the Bundestag committee itself, these state officials can even address it on specific policy issues. In this way, very close cooperation between the two chambers is assured.

Being composed of officials of the executive branch of state governments, the Bundesrat as a legislative body is sometimes criticized for having a lack of "democratic legitimacy." That this is overstated is indicated by the fact that the state cabinets, whose members are present in the Bundesrat, are themselves an outgrowth of democratically elected state parliaments (see Friedrich 1975; Scholz 1990). Moreover, state cabinets must remain continuously attentive to these parliaments insofar as choices they make in Bundesrat matters may jeopardize their majority support in the state legislature.[13] Criticism of the Bundesrat's lack of legitimacy has become even harder to sustain as state elections have increasingly become barometer elections for national politics and are perceived in this way by the public. At the same time, state government activities in the national political arena of the Bundesrat rarely become contentious issues in the state parliaments, largely because these bodies can only recommend Bundesrat actions to their state cabinet. Binding directives would represent interference with the latter's sphere of political competence, as defined by German constitutional law.

Institutional Structure

Like any parliament, the Bundesrat is composed of a plenary and specialized policy committees. All the chamber's important work is done by its committees during preparation for their sessions and through state government cooperation. Just as with the relationships between parliamentary groups within a legislature, cooperation in committee work is especially close between state governments supported by the same political parties. The central role of committees in the legislative process means that plenary sessions mostly involve the taking of votes and the issuance for the record of political declarations.[14] Seldom do newsworthy floor debates occur in the Bundesrat because contested issues are usually debated for the public in the Bundestag.

The Bundesrat has seventeen standing committees, essentially matching the departmental structure of the federal government. To debate very complex subjects, the Bundesrat can establish special committees. It can also form subcommittees if certain matters require extraordinarily thorough discussion. This is why a number of committees, including those on finance and agriculture, have formed standing subcommittees. Each state has only one vote per committee, so that the majority constellation within the committees may differ from that in the chamber as a whole. The plenary of the Bundesrat elects the committee chair for a term of one year. While the Committee on Foreign Affairs has a rotating chair, each of the other sixteen committees is chaired by a minister from one of the sixteen länder. The reelection of chairs leads to high levels of expertise and continuity on these committees. The downside is that committees come to be viewed as belonging to certain states, parties, or individual chairs.

The Bundesrat's EU-Chamber was established in 1988 with a view to avoiding the extraordinary plenary sessions that would otherwise be needed if the Bundesrat were to keep abreast of European Union decisions. It comprises one member from each state government, usually the commissioner to the Federation, and that person commands as many votes in it as he or she would in the plenary of the Bundesrat. Thus, the EU-Chamber acts as a "small Bundesrat," and its decisions are binding just like those of the plenary. It becomes active when the Bundesrat president sends it items for decision and its sessions are usually open to the public. In the event that an actual meeting is considered unnecessary, the EU-Chamber may canvas its members' opinions by mail. In many cases, the decisions of the EU-Chamber are prepared by more specialized committees of the Bundesrat.

The plenary, and the Bundesrat as a whole, is chaired by a president or one of three deputies; these are recruited from the ranks of the state prime ministers and, unlike the practice in Imperial Germany and the Weimar Republic, are elected by the Bundesrat itself.[15] This election has lost its political importance, however, since the 1950 decision of prime ministers to rotate the presidency among themselves, with the first vice president always being the president of the previous year and the one-year term always beginning in early November. Should a sitting president lose his position as state prime minister, his successor automatically replaces him as president of the Bundesrat.

In addition to convening and chairing plenary sessions, the president is responsible for representing the Bundesrat whenever the need arises. The president is also the employer of the Bundesrat's staff. Finally, he or she stands in for the federal president should the latter be unable to carry out the duties of his office or be removed from it before his term expires. In this case, the first vice president becomes the Bundesrat's president. The president of the Bundesrat, however, does not hold the second highest political position in Germany. This honor belongs to the president of the Bundestag, a contradiction that illustrates the complexity of the institutional arrangements needed to combine Germany's federal tradition with its democratic principles.

The actual work of the Bundesrat is prepared by an office managed by the director of the Bundesrat, who, given that there is a new president each year, has to lend nonpartisan continuity to the institution. The director heads a staff of some 180 members. The work of the committee secretaries in particular requires efficient and output-oriented work routines, since deadlines are usually tight.[16] After all, committee chairs serve simultaneously in state government and travel to the capital only for short periods to attend the sessions. Other Bundesrat offices include a parliamentary service responsible for organizing plenary sessions, a president's office providing support for his everyday administrative work, a press office, shorthand writers, and a documentation service. In contrast to the Bundestag, the Bundesrat can manage without a reference and research service because its members have unrestricted access to their specialized and highly competent state ministries.

In addition, there is a standing advisory board to the presidium of the Bundesrat, composed of the länder commissioners to the Federation. Its weekly sessions are also attended by the director of the Bundesrat and by a high-ranking representative of the federal government, normally the head of the Chancellory.[17] The first task of this board is to assist the president in preparing the plenary sessions. Its second task is to constitute a permanent institutional link between the Bundesrat and the federal government. The opportunities it provides for informal communication contribute significantly to a positive work atmosphere, enabling the Bundesrat to fulfill its role in the political service of both nation and state. This same role is also played by the permanent delegations all sixteen länder have established in Bonn. Among their main tasks is the maintenance of good relations with the other states, with the departments of the federal government, and with the Bundestag. Close and continuous contact of this kind is a crucial ingredient in the successful representation of state interests in the capital and in efforts to influence specific pieces of federal legislation.

Procedures and Lawmaking

Procedures

The Bundesrat works under tremendous time constraints. Its participation in the federal legislative process is bound by narrow time limits defined by the Basic Law. On the other hand, its members also have to fulfill their demanding state government obligations. The number of plenary sessions is therefore kept as low as possible, about fifteen per year. Separated by three-week intervals, they are normally held on Fridays, with all of the dates set in advance annually. Federal ministers participate if the issues on the agenda fall within their policy areas; the chancellor rarely shows up. Committees convene in private at least two weeks prior to the plenary session. The items they have to deal with, as well as the relevant documents and materials, are submitted to them by the president of the Bundesrat or, on order of the president, by the director. If a particular item is forwarded to more than one committee, one of them will be given principal responsibility for handling it. Unlike in the Bundestag, the role of principal does not give the committee a privileged position in terms of procedural rights. This is why it is not uncommon for different Bundesrat committees dealing with the same item to come up with different and even conflicting policy recommendations.

Even more than in the Bundestag, Bundesrat committee sessions are characterized by an atmosphere of open-mindedness and mutual trust. Committee members strive not just to represent their state or the parties forming the state government, but also to analyze thoroughly the matters before them while paying attention to both their substantive content and their political implications. Additionally, meetings are characterized by an ongoing dialogue between federal and state officials, since federal government ministers have the right (and, on demand, the obligation) to attend them, as do their civil servants. Moreover, since they attend regularly, the outcome is an ongoing, fruitful exchange of opinion and practical experience between federal and state policymakers and implementers.

The work of the Bundesrat starts with proposals that require political debate, consultation, and decisions to be distributed to members as early as possible, normally via the state delegations in the federal capital. Preparations for committee consideration then begin in the state capitals. These preparations include both coordination between the different departments affected by the proposal and coordination between states. Cooperation will be especially close between states whose cabinets are composed of members of the same political party or coalition.

These preparations are followed by committee meetings in the Bundesrat, which must result in recommendations for state government decisions at least two weeks prior to consideration in a plenary session. In contentious cases, state governments may have to reconcile divisions within their own departments or among the parties supporting the state cabinet itself. Such differences notwithstanding, they have to decide to approve, reject, or abstain when the proposal comes up for a vote in the Bundesrat. They may also, of course, decide to table amendments or discuss support-building strategies should it be felt that the proposal needs to be altered before it can be endorsed.

Two days before the plenary session, the Standing Advisory Board of the Bundesrat, or the leading officials in its secretary's office, set the rules for plenary debate. This includes the identification of the speakers, the motions to be tabled, and the sequence in which votes are taken. Frequently, intensive consultations between the state chancelleries become necessary at this stage to finalize arrangements and to ensure the desired majorities in the Bundesrat. Shortly before the plenary session, a brief and confidential meeting of the Bundesrat members is held to prevent possible surprises arising during debate. If this meeting reveals continuing differences on substantive or procedural questions, the prime ministers or their deputies, the commissioners to the Federation, will gather informally to try to iron them out.

This meticulous preparation has meant that "real" plenary debate has become a thing of the past in the Bundesrat. Indeed, given the chamber's heavily crowded agenda, for things to be otherwise would be impossible. Consequently, plenary sessions are formally required but necessarily highly staged events. In the final analysis, their purpose is not to provide a forum for debate but to pass a multitude of bills and administrative ordinances and to provide a stage for the last explanation and justification of policy proposals that are about to pass into law. This time pressure and premium on results makes for plenary sessions that are characterized by an orientation toward facts, by a pervasive lack of political passion, and by a concentration on the issues at hand. In particular, fiery parliamentary rhetoric is absent as Bundesrat members focus instead on efficiently working their way through the agenda. Applause is uncommon, and calls to order are unknown. Indeed, there are hardly any interruptions at all.

The net result is that the usual plenary session of the Bundesrat is even less attractive to the general public than its counterpart in the Bundestag. The Bundesrat's dull and routine sessions discourage media attention. Accordingly, media coverage of its plenary sessions, and of the political positions voiced there, is deficient. But the cost of reducing this media deficit would be a severe cutback in legislative output, and this is a tradeoff that the Bundesrat is even less willing to contemplate than is the Bundestag.

Legislation

In Germany, the right to initiate legislation rests with the federal government, the Bundesrat, or a group of at least 5 percent of the Bundestag membership. Since 1949, about 60 percent of all legislative proposals on average have emanated from the government, about 34 percent from Bundestag members, and the remaining 6 percent from the Bundesrat. (Quantitative data on all aspects of the legislative process in Germany can be found in Schindler 1994.) If only bills subsequently enacted into law are considered, 77 percent had their origins in the federal government, 18 percent in the Bundestag, and 5 percent in the Bundesrat. Obviously, the initiation of legislation is not one of the Bundesrat's principal legislative functions, but nonetheless the chamber's overall importance in the legislative process should not be underestimated.

Any bill initiated by the federal government must initially be sent to the Bundesrat for a "first round of deliberations." The Bundesrat can comment on the bill within six weeks, a period that can be extended to nine weeks.[18] Along with this comment and the government's response, the bill is then introduced into the Bundestag. Traditionally, the Bundesrat has paid careful attention to the comments it makes in the first round of deliberations, and takes them very seriously. Quite frequently the government will incorporate the Bundesrat's recommendations and amendments into the final version of bills. Inasmuch as most federal legislation is initiated by the government, and it can be assumed that bills are written in anticipation of comments from the states, the Bundesrat's considerable influence becomes readily apparent. Moreover, if a legislative proposal requires the consent of the Bundesrat, the comments and demands it articulates in the first round of deliberations cannot be circumvented or ignored.

The Bundesrat also has the right to initiate legislation itself. Such an action may be taken by its plenary, based on a motion from at least one federal state. Then the federal government must introduce the bill, together with its own comments on it, into the Bundestag within three months. Although Bundesrat-initiated proposals average only 6 percent of all bills, their number increases at the beginning of periods where the Bundesrat and Bundestag majority parties or party coalitions differ. This is because, like opposition bills in the Bundestag, the spate of Bundesrat activity publicly demonstrates its dissent from views of the federal government and its majority in the Bundestag. This is another reason why the number of proposals is not a valid indicator of the Bundesrat's actual impact on federal legislation. It needs to be recognized that this impact stems from the persuasiveness of the chamber's comments and from its potential for applying political pressure through its absolute or, at least, suspensive veto powers.

After three readings and passage of a bill in the Bundestag, it must be sent to the Bundesrat for a "second round of deliberations." The critical distinction at that stage is whether the bill requires consent [Zustimmungsgesetz] or whether the Bundesrat only has the right to lodge an objection [Einspruchsgesetz]. In the first case the Bundesrat's right to veto the bill is absolute; in the second case it is suspensive. The purpose of this distinction is to prevent lopsided Bundestag legislation from encroaching on the powers of the states or from altering their political competencies. According to the Basic Law, bills requiring active Bundesrat consent include those amending the Basic Law, affecting states' rights in the areas of finance and taxation, and touching on the states' administrative responsibilities.

When there is doubt, the Bundesrat has to prove that a given piece of legislation requires its consent. There have been some, but not many, disputes, even bitter controversies, between the two chambers on which of these categories a certain piece of legislation falls into. In such instances, the federal president will decide the issue as a condition of his signing the bill into law.[19] In very rare instances, the president may choose not to make such a decision at all, thereby effectively killing the bill.

Contrary to the expectations of the framers of the Basic Law, today slightly more than half of all bills turn out to require Bundesrat consent. The reason is the chamber's aggressiveness whenever a credible argument can be made that a bill affects states' rights. Moreover, consent must be obtained for the bill as a whole even if only a single paragraph of it requires consent. In particular, Article 84 of the Basic Law broadens the scope of Bundesrat intervention by making the states' implementation of federal laws their own responsibility. This is why the Bundesrat has interpreted this provision as implying co-responsibility for a bill's entire content ("theorem of shared responsibility") since 1952. Even if rooted in nothing more than partisan politics, conflicts over this issue can, and have, developed into confrontations before the Constitutional Court.

In fact, such conflicts have had important consequences. The first was a far-reaching Constitutional Court ruling in 1974. The Court held that legislation changing existing law that had required Bundesrat consent must also receive that consent. Moreover, this is required even if the amended paragraphs per se do not affect the rights of states, but contain only changes that significantly alter the meaning or the importance of affected administrative procedures that may themselves remain unchanged. This ruling strengthened the Bundesrat's legal position. Therefore successive federal governments have sought to split new and controversial legislative proposals into two parts, one containing policy details, and the other containing the procedural provisions for implementation. It is only the latter that needs consent. Hence, a political grey area has been created and no one has thus far appealed to the Court to clarify it for fear of precipitating a marked shift in the balance of power between the Bundesrat and the federal government.

If the Bundesrat refuses consent, the Bundestag, the government, or the Bundesrat itself can request that the conference committee meet in the next three weeks (Bardenhewer 1984; Niemann 1978).[20] There is only one such committee. It is composed of thirty-two members, sixteen elected by each house, serving for the duration of the Bundestag's legislative term. Proxies may not be substituted for its members, members are not bound by mandates from their states' respective parliamentary groups, and its sessions are not open to the public. Making decisions by simple majority vote, it can recommend modification or rejection of bills referred to it [Einigungsvorschlag, or settlement recommendation]. This recommendation must then be accepted or rejected by each house as a package. The Bundestag votes first on the package. If the Bundestag approves, the package must then be approved by the Bundesrat. Only then has the legislative process come to fruition.

Having a veto power generally gives the Bundesrat a weightier bargaining position than the Bundestag, but customarily a compromise agreement is reached. Such an outcome is made easier because, in contrast to committee sessions of either house, the administrative officials responsible for the first draft of the bill and the politicians who committed themselves to it in public are not present at conference committee deliberations. In practice, the conference committee has not been convened many times, tending to meet only when different majorities have prevailed in the two houses and when important government policies have been at stake. Between 1980 and 1990, the Bundesrat approved more than half of the bills submitted to it without calling for mediation. Over the same period, another 40 percent of bills passed the Bundesrat without objection, while it asked the conference committee to convene in the case of less than 3 percent of the bills adopted by the Bundestag.[21] About 70 percent of these compromise bills were then approved. Thus, the Bundesrat rejected only 88 out of a total 4,389 bills between 1949 and 1990, and there were only 40 instances of bills not promulgated despite the mediation efforts of the conference committee.

Bills not requiring Bundesrat consent [Einspruchsgesetz] are sometimes called "ordinary bills." The Bundesrat is consulted on them, and although it has no absolute veto power, it can voice its intent to object to such a bill. If the Bundesrat decides to object, it has to call for the conference committee to be convened. Seldom are objections raised, and when they are, it is most often the result of party rivalry. If the objection is then overridden by the Bundestag, the bill will be enacted into law against the will of the Bundesrat. If, however, the Bundestag fails to override the objection, the bill is defeated. Between 1949 and 1990 there were twenty-six such objections, nineteen of which the Bundestag subsequently overrode.

If a Bundesrat objection is passed by an absolute majority, it can be overridden by an equivalent majority in the Bundestag and, under normal circumstances, a government easily commands that level of support there. But if the Bundesrat majority reaches two-thirds, its objection can only be overridden by the same majority in the Bundestag. Only a "grand coalition" of the two largest parties, the Christian Democrats and Social Democrats, would normally command that kind of support. So far the need for such a majority has not arisen, but it remains possible that a hostile two-thirds majority in the Bundesrat could effectively paralyze a federal government supported by a "normal" majority in the lower house. If, under such circumstances, new Bundestag elections do not yield an appropriate majority or at least a coalition with which the Bundesrat is willing to cooperate and if the federal government or its supporting Bundestag majority remains unwilling to cede its authority to the Bundesrat, then the German political system could be faced with a severe crisis that would not be amenable to solutions provided for in the constitution.

A different kind of systemic crisis, reminiscent of those so common during the Weimar Republic, is susceptible to constitutional solution. Article 81 of the Basic Law empowers the federal president to declare a state of "legislative emergency" with regard to a specific piece of legislation when the following conditions are met: the chancellor has lost a vote of confidence in the Bundestag, the federal president has nonetheless refrained from dissolving the Bundestag, and the government has failed to win a parliamentary majority on a piece of legislation it has labeled urgent. A request for an emergency declaration must be made by the federal government and have Bundesrat approval. With these conditions met, the legislation becomes law without majority support in the Bundestag if it is approved by the Bundesrat.[22] For the next six months, this same procedure can be applied to other legislation turned down by the Bundestag. After six months, there can be no further "legislative emergencies" as long as the same chancellor is in office. Hence, the Bundesrat's role as "substitute legislature" temporarily replacing the Bundestag will be ended until another chancellor faces a similar crisis.

Foreign Policy

As an important institution in the German constitutional system, the Bundesrat has a voice in the country's foreign policy (see Bos 1977). International treaties, for example, are referred to the Bundesrat as well as to the Bundestag and, depending on the substance of the treaty, the same distinction between issues susceptible to an absolute or to a suspensive veto applies as in domestic matters. Because no line-item veto of treaty provisions is possible when the Bundesrat becomes involved in the process of debating a ratification law, it is imperative that the chamber demand detailed information from the federal government at the earliest possible stage.

Yet with the exception of European politics, where the Bundesrat with its EU-Chamber has probably become the single most active national legislative body among all EU-member countries, the Bundesrat has always practiced great restraint in the foreign policy area. Nevertheless, there have been instances when its preferences ran counter to those of the federal government. The first major controversy arose in early 1953 in regard to the ratification of the establishment of the European Defense Community. This brought the Bundesrat's significant foreign policy role to public attention for the first time. It became the same focus of public attention in the 1970s.[23] In 1974, the Bundesrat even lodged an objection to ratification of an international agreement when it opposed a treaty with Czechoslovakia.

In addition, a new Article 23 of the Basic Law, adopted in 1992, gives considerable authority to the Bundesrat in foreign policy matters, including the European Union, if the exclusive jurisdiction or interests of the German states are affected (Lang 1997; Oschatz and Risse 1995; Schede 1994; Schmalenbach 1996). Article 23(5) provides that "Where in an area in which the Federation has exclusive legislative jurisdiction, the interests of the Länder are affected, or where in other respects the Federation has the right to legislate, the federal government shall take into account the opinion of the Bundesrat." In regard to European Union decisions affecting the states' constitutionally defined legislative jurisdiction, the same article rules that "the exercise of the rights of the Federal Republic of Germany . . . shall be transferred by the Federation to a representative of the Länder designated by the Bundesrat" provided that this transfer happens "with the participation of, and in agreement with, the federal government." This constitutional provision clearly reflects Germany's strong federal tradition.

Administration

The Bundesrat also plays an important role in regard to the public bureaucracy in Germany, not least because the federal government has very few administrative agencies in its own right.[24] Instead, most federal laws are implemented by the state government bureaucracies, albeit under federal oversight. To protect the states against the potential erosion of their authority that such oversight might entail, nearly all administrative ordinances issued by the federal government require the consent of the Bundesrat, giving it an absolute veto in such matters. Of course, this arrangement considerably increases the workload of the Bundesrat. For example, between 1983 and 1990 the Bundesrat had to act on about 500 administrative regulations issued by the federal government, whereas it considered only about 350 bills during the same period.

Such regulations constitute the most important cases of administrative law with which the Bundesrat is concerned. In addition, federal statutory orders that take the form of instructions to state bureaucracies to carry out federal laws or ordinances are subject to Bundesrat approval. Their number amounted to a little over 130 between 1983 and 1990. Should the Bundesrat amend federal draft administrative ordinances or statutory orders, they can only be enacted as approved by the Bundesrat. The Bundestag is not involved in this process, so that outcomes are profoundly shaped by the administrative expertise of government departments on the state level. Theoretically, the Bundestag has the right to repeal administrative regulations that affect the budgetary process, although the need to exercise this right has not yet arisen.

Finally, the Bundesrat is consulted if one of the federal states fails to comply with its obligations as described in the Basic Law or in federal law. According to Article 37 of the Basic Law, the federal government may, under these circumstances, take the steps necessary to ensure compliance. When enforcing this so-called federal coercion [Bundeszwang], the federal government or its authorized agent even has the authority to issue binding directives to the delinquent state and its administrative agencies. However, such actions require the consent of the Bundesrat.

Other Bundesrat Prerogatives

Other prerogatives of the Bundesrat include the right to elect, by a two-thirds majority, half of the judges serving on the federal Constitutional Court. In addition, the Bundesrat takes turns with the Bundestag to elect the president and the vice president of the same court. The nominees of the federal minister of justice for appointment to the office of federal prosecutor or federal prosecutor general also need Bundesrat approval. Furthermore, the Bundesrat can file lawsuits with, and be sued before, the federal Constitutional Court. This may happen in cases of jurisdictional disputes within the federal government, of disputes between federal and state governments, and in matters of judicial review concerning the observance of constitutional norms with or without reference to a specific case. Finally, the plenary of the Bundesrat appoints from among its ranks (or from among the state governments) representatives to serve on various appointed bodies and organs, e.g., on the presidium or administrative board of the Federal Institute for Employment.

The political role of the Bundesrat becomes especially compelling when there is a national emergency. Should Germany be attacked, or threatened with attack, the federal government may request that a "state of defense" be declared by the Bundestag, with the agreement of the Bundesrat. If this action is not possible, a state of defense may be determined by the Joint Committee. It includes thirty-two members of the Bundestag (elected each legislative term, and in proportion to the number of seats held), and sixteen members of the Bundesrat (one per state). The Committee is chaired by the president of the Bundestag, with a member of the

Bundesrat serving as its first vice president. During a state of defense, the Joint Committee can even assume the functions of both the Bundesrat and the Bundestag if two-thirds or more of its membership determines that insurmountable obstacles exist to the Bundestag's convening in time, or that the Bundestag is in a state of complete disarray or disfunction. Under such conditions, the Joint Committee could even elect a successor to the federal chancellor.

Parliamentary Functions

This very federal house, the Bundesrat, has clear parliamentary functions, including passing legislation, controlling the government, and maintaining communication between the society and its political system. Parliamentary systems of government also need to provide a majority to elect and support the executive branch of government. The Bundesrat performs, or is at least entitled to play a role in performing, all these functions.

First, in a state of defense, the Bundesrat can take part, via its representation on the Joint Committee, in making or unmaking the federal government. Second, in cooperation with the Bundestag it holds comprehensive and significant powers in shaping federal legislation. It is influential in the "first round of deliberations," and can exert absolute or suspensive veto powers in the second round.

Third, and perhaps most important, the Bundesrat does exercise control over the federal government. A key weapon in its armory in this regard is the constitutional provision that the "Bundesrat shall be kept informed by the federal government about the conduct of business" (Article 53). After a hesitant start in the early years of the Republic, the routine information flow is now so smooth that the Bundesrat rarely makes use of its right to summon members of the federal government.

One mechanism of Bundesrat control is governmental anticipation of the members' policy preferences and the house's reaction to government initiatives. Additionally, leading members of the Bundesrat make frequent use of their right to take the floor in the Bundestag, especially prior to elections. Not being obliged to represent their home state or the Bundesrat as a whole, they can use this opportunity to advocate the policy positions of their parties, and this is exactly what they are expected to do. Thus, they can confront federal government leaders and hold them publicly accountable for their actions or inactions. This right to address the Bundestag directly is especially important for party chairmen or chancellorial candidates who are not themselves members of the Bundestag. Their membership in the Bundesrat as länder ministers or prime ministers provides them with access to a highly visible forum, the floor of the Bundestag, from which they can address the public. Finally, state administrators cooperate very closely with their federal counterparts in Bundesrat committee sessions, thereby effectively controlling government by influencing the decisions and actions it takes.

The fourth parliamentary function of the Bundesrat is relatively weak and underdeveloped. It is the cultivation of direct communication links with the general public (Patzelt 1996). The problem for the Bundesrat is that its members are state prime ministers or cabinet ministers. Typically they are also members of the state legislature, or they are national party leaders. But they definitely are not perceived as "members of the Bundesrat." The point is that the Bundesrat can attract national attention as an institution, but it cannot win such attention from the public visibility of its members. The institution hits the headlines only when it engages in contentious, visible, and highly partisan conflict with the federal government or supporting parties. But this kind of confrontation is not usually compatible with the Bundesrat's constitutional and political role. Indeed, it is exactly this role which is the source of its weak communicational links with the public.[25] Representing the state cabinets, it maintains no direct relations with the national electorate. As a result, the privilege of direct democratic legitimation by the nation as a whole is reserved exclusively for the Bundestag.

Informal Role in Political Decision Making

Theodor Heuss, Germany's first federal president, is said to have labeled the Bundesrat a "parliament of bureaucrats." It may be true that, compared with the Bundestag, the Bundesrat is overly preoccupied with issues of administrative and technical feasibility. But this description is unfair. From the beginning the Bundesrat has taken on an important political role as well. This has inspired the bon mot that the Bundesrat is not a "second chamber" but a "second government." It is said to provide a forum for complex negotiations between federal and state government experts and to some extent serve as a "board of internal oversight" of the federal government. Given its frequent clashes with the federal government, the Bundesrat might be better characterized as a "second opposition."

The Bundesrat's oppositional role is a function of the different structural principles at work simultaneously in the German political system. Two of them relevant to this discussion are properly expressed by the term *federal party state* (see Lehmbruch 1976). The German parliamentary system engenders a central dualism between a government camp, consisting of the federal cabinet and its supporting Bundestag majority on the one side, and the parliamentary opposition on the other side. Both camps cooperate closely with their state and national party organizations. This dualism, fostered and enforced by the electoral system of proportional representation, gives shape to all processes of public policy making. Moreover, it applies to national and state politics. However, in the states the voters often prefer parties in opposition in the Bundestag. Consequently, time and again the opposition in the Bundestag controls a majority of state governments and hence of the votes in the Bundesrat. The national-level opposition parties are readily tempted to seek and fight political battles in a Bundesrat that comes to serve as a "second arena" of national party politics.[26]

For this purpose, state prime ministers act in the Bundesrat mainly as party leaders, using the chamber's veto powers to stop, or at least modify, legislation passed by the "hostile" Bundestag majority. The strong position of the upper house in the legislative process is used to balance their party's minority position in the lower house. This is an especially attractive strategy when, as in 1997–98, federal elections loom. This strategic behavior may interdict the federal government's legislative program. If so, the Bundestag's majority can be blamed in public for losing its policy-making capacity, which might provide party contestants with convincing arguments to use in the election campaign.

Conflicting majorities of this type may be detrimental not only to the federal government and its supporting parties but also to the major opposition party in the Bundesrat. It can lead to tension within the party because policy positions appropriate to its federal role in opposition may not be reconcilable with the deals and compromises it has to accept in its länder role in government. Moreover, the confrontational tactics that parties routinely and reasonably employ in the Bundestag often do not sit easily with the effective representation of state interests in the more consensual Bundesrat. Therefore, overarching nationwide party competition is often at odds with the states' need for cooperation in the Bundesrat and with the federal government.

Indeed, a great deal of criticism has been leveled at the Bundesrat for functioning as a partisan "second opposition" to the federal government. Most of it has been motivated by considerations of political expediency as partisan groups seek to discredit competitors in the public eye. Some of it goes to the heart of the proper role of the Bundesrat in the German political system. Its essence is that the Bundesrat should serve the interest of the states and not those of their governing parties. But this argument does not stand up to close inspection since democratic elections vest the authority to define a state's interests in the parties constituting its government. Thus, it would violate the principles of democracy to seek to regulate, or otherwise restrain, state governments' oppositional behavior in Bonn simply because of a preference for "friendly conduct" in national level Bundestag-Bundesrat relations or because of a belief that such conduct better demonstrates states' allegiance to the federation. In addition, it must be remembered that Bundesrat members achieved their qualifying positions as state cabinet ministers precisely because of their party leadership functions. These party ties cannot be expected to be forgotten when individuals cross the Bundesrat threshold. In short, it misses the point to criticize the Bundesrat for its members' acting in accord with the functional logic of a federation run by powerful parties in the framework of a parliamentary system.

Party considerations cannot be the only ones, however. Partisan politics would be widely considered to have gone too far should the Bundesrat attempt to paralyze the federal government. After all, it is this government, commanding majority support in the Bundestag, that represents the German people as a whole and the Bundesrat has no legitimate right to bring it to its knees. Until now, the Bundesrat has exercised self-restraint in this regard and, despite its numerous heated exchanges with the Bundestag, it has not yet resorted to overt obstructionist tactics. Nonetheless, the internal cohesion of the governing coalition in the Bundestag has been put to the test over and over again as federal governments, faced with Bundesrat opposition, have been forced to exercise their constitutional right to impose policy guidelines. Such assertions of authority, though, have usually come at high political cost in the sense that the price paid has been far-reaching concessions to the Bundesrat's, that is to say, the political opposition's, policy demands. But compromise of this kind is to be expected in a federal system that actively practices pluralism under majority rule.

The final consideration in regard to the Bundesrat's role in the making of federal policy decisions is that its close cooperation with the federal government clearly strengthens the *concordance* (or consociational) element that has always characterized German democracy. Highly public and partisan disputes between the two houses notwithstanding, decision-making processes are managed by de facto grand coalitions whose leaders may not even hold state or federal governmental positions, but who are the leaders of the political parties whose support is needed to reach binding compromises. Frequently, their informal meetings even include policy experts or interest group representatives. Obviously, these consociational or neo-corporatist ways of securing cooperation and support entail advantages and often make the machinery of government work more smoothly. At the same time, however, they can obfuscate who is responsible for decisions and enormously undermine the fundamental democratic principle of political accountability. As a result, voters are deprived of their right to make deliberate choices between distinguishable policy alternatives. This weakening of the linkage between voters, elected representatives, and policy outputs is the main problem with the Bundesrat's frequent performance of the role of "second opposition."

Toward Reform?

In contrast to the continuous debates on reforming the German Bundestag, there have been few serious discussions of reform of the Bundesrat. The political parties' practice of utilizing the Bundesrat as a "second opposition" to the federal government has repeatedly led to public criticism, but it is a criticism that inevitably vanishes as soon as its immediate catalyst does. There having been no extreme cases of Bundesrat misuse for partisan purposes, it has not been possible to make a convincing case for reform. The Bundesrat is simply not an institution that enjoys high levels of public visibility, and in the absence of such disaffection public interest in the question of its reform cannot be stirred. Inertia is only compounded by nobody's really wanting to undermine the compromises that were agreed upon in 1948–49 and that appear to have worked reasonably well. Finally, the Bundesrat has adapted to new situations by taking preemptive measures when the clear need for reform has arisen. The best example has been the creation of its EU-Chamber in response to the growing volume and importance of European legislation. For all these reasons, the Bundesrat is a widely accepted and valued part of the constitutional setup, not being an issue even during the debates on amending the Basic Law after German unification in the early 1990s.

Being an institution much older than the Federal Republic itself, the Bundesrat has indeed stood the test of time. No one really doubts that it will also stand the challenges of the future. Certainly, it remains an open question what impact ongoing European integration will have on the German states and, hence, on the role of the Bundesrat. But experience suggests that this centuries-old institution will not change very much.

Notes

1. This challenge has been complicated by Germany's geopolitical location in the center of Europe. Time and again, a unitary Germany led by a strong central government became a political powerhouse that disrupted the European balance of power. By contrast, a divided and weak Germany allowed for an effective balance of power. The price, however, was damaged German self-esteem, which encouraged the exaggerated German nationalism of the nineteenth and twentieth centuries. The issue of German federalism and its institutional design, therefore, is closely connected with the issues of political stability in Europe and German national identity.

2. Introductory treatments of the Bundesrat are Böhringer, Büjer, and Hrbek 1991; Gorges 1992; Hrbek 1989; Patzelt 1997; and Pfitzer 1995. More comprehensive and detailed are Hanikel 1991; Herzog 1987; Laufer 1972; Limberger 1982; Reuter 1991a, 1991b; Stern 1980; and Ziller and Oschatz 1993. Selected aspects of the institution are discussed in depth in Bundesrat 1974, 1979, and 1989. Comparative analyses of the Bundesrat may be found in Heger 1990; Jaag 1976; and König and Bräuninger 1996.

3. Christian Democrats (CDU/CSU) and Social Democrats (SPD) with an average of 45 percent and 37 percent, respectively, in federal elections between 1949 and 1994; Free Democrats (FDP) with a declining average of 9 percent in the same period; the Green Party (GRÜNE) with a growing average of 6 percent since 1984; and the Democratic Socialists (PDS), successor to the former GDR's Communist Party (SED), with a national average of barely 4 percent since 1990. The PDS has a significant political basis only in the former East Germany, with percentages reaching 20 percent or more.

With the exception of the PDS, all parties, especially the FDP, are much weaker in the former East Germany than in the former West Germany.

4. The remaining 34 percent of proposals and 18 percent of bills, respectively, are initiated by members of the Bundestag. Bills emanating from the opposition usually are voted down by the governing majority coalition.

5. The main outcome of the war was Austria's exclusion from further German history and federalism.

6. The former monarchical principle remained present in the institution of a Reich president [Reichspräsident] elected by the people and endowed with considerable powers.

7. In the course of German unification later, the last East German parliament (re)established five federal states on its territory in 1990. When the GDR ceased to exist on October 3, 1990, those five states joined the Federal Republic of Germany.

8. These articles define the functions (50), the composition (51), the presidency and the rules of procedure (52) of the Bundesrat as well as the attendance of members of the federal government (53). Articles 76–78 regulate the legislative process. Article 79 deals with amendments to the Basic Law, Article 80 prescribes the way statutory orders are issued, and Article 81 defines the role of the Bundesrat in cases of so-called legislative emergency.

9. This is why the type of federalism found in Germany is also commonly described as "administrative federalism."

10. One reason states follow party lines in these circumstances is that their prime ministers are at the same time leading party politicians, sometimes even the chairs of the political parties represented in the Bundestag.

11. The exception is Bundesrat members who also belong to conference committees (usually comprising sixteen members of the Bundesrat and sixteen members of the Bundestag). These exercise a free mandate within the conference committee.

12. The same rights do *not* apply to members of the Bundestag vis-à-vis the Bundesrat. Only members of the federal government enjoy unlimited access to the Bundesrat and its committees.

13. If a state government is sustained by a parliamentary coalition, rules for voting in the Bundesrat are normally fixed in an agreement negotiated before the election of the prime minister.

14. Just as with the Bundestag, the Bundesrat meeting as a whole reserves the right to make the final decision on matters referred to it by committees. The only exception is the Bundesrat's EU-Chamber.

15. The president and his deputies form the Bundesrat's presidium, but this body seldom meets.

16. One secretary usually serves several committees.

17. In the past, some governments in Bonn have had a minister for Bundesrat affairs. At present, the head of the federal chancellory is often given the rank of a cabinet member as, for example, minister for special tasks.

18. If the federal government declares a bill "urgent," however, the Bundesrat has only three weeks to comment on it.

19. In a typical period, between 1983 and 1990, a little less than 1 percent of the laws promulgated by the federal president as requiring the consent of the Bundesrat were considered not to require this consent by the Bundestag. In the same period, the president declared 2 percent of promulgated laws not to require consent when the Bundesrat had argued that they did. Presidential decisions can be challenged in the federal Constitutional Court, and reversed. There have been a few instances where such reversals have led to the relevant law being declared null and void.

20. The Bundesrat does not enjoy equal rights in regard to the conference committee. If one of its bills is rejected by the Bundestag, it cannot demand the convening of a conference committee.

21. The government and the Bundestag have demanded mediation even less frequently than the Bundesrat.

22. The Basic Law cannot be amended, suspended, or repealed under conditions of legislative emergency.

23. The disputes in question concerned ratification of treaties with the Soviet Union, Poland, and Czechoslovakia in the context of the government's new "eastern policy" [Neue Ostpolitik].

24. Two of the more significant of them involve the armed forces and the diplomatic service.

25. In 1988, 95 percent of Germans knew about the existence of the Bundesrat as an institution, but only 42 percent gave correct answers about its composition. Thirty-two percent offered no response at all. Public knowledge of its tasks and functions was even worse, with only 32 percent giving right answers and 36 percent none at all (Noelle-Neumann and Köcher 1993, 65). While still far from perfect, Germans' knowledge of the Bundestag is clearly more comprehensive (Patzelt 1996, 1997).

26. This constellation of political forces reigned from 1969, when a Social Democrat–Free Democrat coalition government came into existence in Bonn until its demise in 1982. It also characterized German politics between July and November 1990, and again from June 1991 until today. In 1994, there was even a possibility that the federal government, led by the Christian Democrats, would face a Social Democratic Party controlling two-thirds of the votes in the Bundesrat.

References

Bardenhewer, Franz. 1984. *Die Entstehung und Auflösung von Meinungsverschiedenheiten zwischen den Gesetzgebungsorganen.* Der Ausschuss nach Artikel 77 Grundgesetz und die Stellung des Bundesrates im Gesetzgebungsverfahren (Reihe Rechtswiss. 1). Pfaffenweiler: Centaurus.

Böhringer, Anton, Joseph Büjer, and Rudolf Hrbek. 1991. *Parlamentarismus und Föderalismus im Unterricht und in der politischen Bildung.* Rheinbreitbach: Neue Darmstädter.

Bos, Werner. 1977. *Der Bundesrat als Träger der auswärtigen Gewalt.* Diss. Tübingen.

Bundesrat, ed. 1974. *Der Bundesrat als Verfassungsorgan und politische Kraft.* Beiträge zum fünfundzwanzigjährigen Bestehen des Bundesrates der Bundesrepublik Deutschland. Bad Honnef/Darmstadt: Neue Darmstädter.

———, ed. 1979. *Jahre Bundesrat, 1949–1979.* Beiträge zum dreißig-jährigen Bestehen des Bundesrates. Bonn [o.V.].

———, ed. 1989. *Vierzig Jahre Bundesrat.* Tagungsband zum wissenschaftlichen Symposium in der Evangelischen Akademie Tutzing. Baden-Baden: Nomos.

Fabritius, Georg. 1976. "Der Bundesrat: Transmissionsriemen für die Unitarisierung der Bundesrepublik?" *Zeitschrift für Parlamentsfragen* 7:448–60.

Friedrich, Manfred. 1975. "Bundesrat und Landesparlamente." *Zeitschrift für Parlamentsfragen* 6:48–76.

Fröchling, Helmut. 1972. *Der Bundesrat in der Koordinierungspraxis von Bund und Ländern: Zur Rolle des Bundesrates im kooperativen Föderalismus.* Freiburg im Breisgau: Becksmann.

Gorges, Renate. 1992. *So arbeiten Regierung und Parlament: Organisation, Zusammenarbeit und Kontrolle im parlamentarischen Regierungssystem.* Rheinbreitbach: Neue Darmstädter.

Hanikel, Andreas. 1991. *Die Organisation des Bundesrates* (Recht-Wirtschaft-Gesellsch. Recht 32). Rheinfelden/Berlin: Schäuble.

Heger, Matthias. 1990. *Deutscher Bundesrat und Schweizer Ständerat: Gedanken zu ihrer Entstehung, ihrem aktuellen Erscheinungsbild und ihrer Rechtfertigung.* Berlin: Duncker and Humblot.

Herzog, Roman. 1987. "Stellung des Bundesrates im demokratischen Bundes-staat." In *Handbuch des Staatsrechts der Bundesrepublik Deutschland,* vol. 2, ed. Josef Isensee and Paul Kirchof. Heidelberg: C. F. Müller.

Hrbek, Rudolf, ed. 1989. *Miterlebt, mitgestaltet: Der Bundesrat im Rückblick.* Stuttgart: Bonn Aktuell.

Jaag, Tobias. 1976. *Die zweite Kammer im Bundesstaat: Funktion und Stellung des schweizerischen Ständerates, des deutschen Bundesrates und des amerikanischen Senats* (Zürcher Beiträge zur Rechtswissen-schaft NF 497). Zurich: Schulthess.

Kisker, Gunter. 1971. *Kooperation im Bundesstaat.* Tübingen: Mohr.

König, Thomas, and Thomas Bräuninger. 1996. "Power and Political Coordination in American and German Multichamber Legislation." *Journal of Theoretical Politics* 8:331–60.

Lang, Ruth. 1997. *Die Mitwirkungrechte des Bundesrates und des Bundestages in Angelegenheiten der Europäischen Union gemäss Art. 23 Abs. 2 bis 7 GG.* Berlin: Duncker and Humblot.

Laufer, Heinz. 1972. *Der Bundesrat: Eine Untersuchung über Zusammen-setzung, Arbeitsweise, politische Rolle und Reformprobleme.* Bonn: Bundeszentrale fur politische Bildung.

Lehmbruch, Gerhard. 1976. *Parteienwettbewerb im Bundesstaat.* Stuttgart: Kohlhammer.

Limberger, Gerhard. 1982. *Die Kompetenzen des Bundesrates und ihre Inanspruch-nahme: Eine empirische Untersuchung.* Berlin: Duncker and Humblot.

Niemann, Helmuth. 1978. "Die bundesstaatliche Bedeutung des Bundesrates unter besonderer Berücksichtigung der Funktion des Vermittlungs-ausschusses." Diss. Göttingen.

Noelle-Neumann, Elisabeth, and Renate Köcher, eds. 1993. *Allensbacher Jahrbuch für Demoskopie, 1984–1992.* Vol. 9. Munich: Saur.

Oschatz, Georg-Berndt, and Horst Risse. 1995. "Die Bundesregierung an der Kette der Länder? Zur europapolitischen Mitwirkung des Bundesrates." *Die Öffentliche Verwaltung* 48 : 437–52.

Patzelt, Werner J. 1996. "Das Wissen der Deutschen über Parlament und Abgeordnete." *Gegenwartskunde* 45 : 309–22.

———. 1997. "Unaufgeklärte Bürger und ein unverstandenes Parlament—was tun?" *Das Parlament* 38 : 4.

Pfitzer, Albert. 1995. *Der Bundesrat: Mitwirkung der Länder im Bund.* 4th ed. Heidelberg: Huthig.

Reuter, Konrad. 1983. *Föderalismus: Grundlagen und Wirkungen in der Bundesrepublik Deutschland.* Heidelberg: Decker.

———. 1991a. *Bundesrat und Bundesstaat: Der Bundesrat der Bundesrepublik Deutschland.* 7th ed. Bonn: Direktor des Bundesrates.

———, ed. 1991b. *Praxishandbuch Bundesrat: Verfassungsrechtliche Grundlagen, Kommentar zur Geschäftsordnung und Praxis des Bundes-rates.* Heidelberg: Müller, Juristischer.

Schede, Christian. 1994. *Bundesrat und Europäische Union.* Schriften zum Staats- und Völkerrecht 56. Frankfurt: Peter Lang.

Schindler, Peter. 1994. *Datenhandbuch zur Geschichte des Deutschen Bundestages 1983 bis 1991.* Baden-Baden: Nomos.

Schmalenbach, Kirsten. 1996. *Der neue Europaartikel 23 des Grundgesetzes im Lichte der Arbeit der Gemeinsamen Verfassungskommission: Motive einer Verfassungsänderung.* Berlin: Duncker und Humblot.

Scholl, Udo. 1982. *Der Bundesrat in der deutschen Verfassungsentwicklung.* Schriften zum öffentlichen Recht 407. Berlin: Duncker und Humblot.

Scholz, Rupert. 1990. "Landesparlamente und Bundesrat." In *Der Bundesrat: Die staatsrechtliche Entwicklung des föderalen Verfassungsorgans,* ed. Dieter Wilke and Bernd Schulte. Darmstadt: Wissenschaftliche Buchgesellschaft.

Stern, Klaus. 1980. *Das Staatsrecht der Bundesrepublik Deutschland.* Vol. 2. Munich: C. H. Beck.

Wilke, Dieter, and Bernd Schulte, eds. 1990. *Der Bundesrat: Die staats-rechtliche Entwicklung des föderalen Verfassungsorgans.* Darmstadt: Wissenschaftliche Buchgesellschaft.

Ziller, Gebhard, and Georg-Berndt Oschatz. 1993. *Der Bundesrat.* 9th ed. Düsseldorf: Droste.

Generating Divided Government:
The Australian Senate

JOHN UHR

Today's Australian parliament is a late-nineteenth-century creation. The Constitution of 1901 establishes a bicameral parliament composed of a House of Representatives and a Senate with virtually equal powers. The Senate is now composed of seventy-six members elected for a six-year term, twelve for each of six states and four representing federal territories. Half of the state senators stand for election every three years. All territory senators face reelection every three years, as do the 148 members of the House of Representatives. Since 1949, senators have been elected by the single-transferable vote mode of proportional representation (PR), with each state or territory forming a multimember constituency. This mode of electing senators complements the single-member preferential voting method used in House elections. It is now characteristic of Senate party representation that neither the party of the government of the day nor that of the official opposition, both of which are determined by the strength of their relative numbers in the House of Representatives, can expect to control the Senate. PR allows minor parties and independents to hold the balance of power between the major parties, and it creates uncertainty about the fate of many legislative measures.

The formal constitutional limitations on Senate power qualify the manner rather than the might of the Senate's capacity to act independently of the House of Representatives and of the political executive based therein. At first glance, the formal provisions might seem to deprive the Senate of institutional clout. For example, the formal constitutional provisions include limiting the size of the Senate to half that of the House, prohibiting the introduction of basic money bills in the Senate, banning the Senate from amending tax bills or supply bills "for the ordinary annual services of the government," and requiring final resolution of intercameral deadlocks through a joint sitting of the House and Senate—at which stage the House's numerical strength, and the political strength of the executive based in the lower house, can be expected to win out.

But a closer look at the form and substance of Senate power reveals a remarkable parliamentary institution, unlike any other upper house in the Westminster-derived world. Although the Senate is limited in the legislative matters which it may initiate or amend, it has unlimited power to return to the lower house "any proposed law" with requests for amendments. If unpersuaded, the House's only resort is to play out the cumbersome deadlock resolution procedure, which involves a three-month interval between the initial and a second deliberate attempt by the Senate to alter a House measure, followed by a "double dissolution" for all House and Senate members, before the final convening of a joint sitting in the event that the election outcome has itself not resolved the protracted disagreement.

These facts provide the barest of bones about the Senate as an institution. Beyond these commonplaces, bicameralism in Australia allows for the emergence of divided party government, a condition often thought to be anathema to parliamentary systems of government. The constitutional design and political operation of the Australian Senate, which has proven its capacity to bring down governments and, with that power as a threat, to transform the policy substance as well as the administrative style of governments, provides the focus for this chapter. We begin the analysis with an extended example that illustrates the emerging characteristics of the Senate as a political institution. This leads to an examination of the Senate's contribution to an Australian version of what American political scientists call "divided government," which is distinguishable from the case of minority party government often found in parliamentary settings.

Constitutional design, along with the crucial adoption of proportional representation beginning with the 1949 parliamentary elections, frame the development of Senate norms of institutional behavior and the patterns of power devised by the modern Senate. Of particular institutional importance has been the development of an extensive committee system. This appraisal of the Senate as a parliamentary body concludes with a review of the range of fears that governments have expressed about the adverse effects of its power in Australian government. As we shall see, these fears confuse the virtues of the separation of partisan powers inherent in divided government with the vices of legislative and policy gridlock, to which divided government does not necessarily give rise.

Contemporary Characteristics

The most striking examples of the emerging political power of the Australian Senate are two developments of 1993: the surgical strike against the budget of the recently elected Keating Labor government, and the more general hijack of the timetabling procedures for the legislative agenda of governments. For Westminster-derived parliamentary systems, budget bills are symbolically the most important of all legislative business. A government can enjoy no greater authority than its ability to apply its voting power to the annual budget in order to stamp its mark on policy and legislative processes. Indeed, 1993 was a major turning point in the norms of Australian parliamentary government because it showed the capacity of the minor parties in the Senate to take the initiative and orchestrate parliamentary resistance to the government of the day's power to manage two of its most possessively cherished processes: the core budget process, and the timetabling of legislative processes more generally.

All subsequent governments have had to live with the consequences of the Keating government's defeats at the hands of the Senate. Upon being elected for its fifth term, the Labor government prepared its budget as an opportunity to establish the framework for its next three years in office. At no point since its original election in 1983 had the Labor government enjoyed a Senate majority. More significantly, the official opposition also failed over this time to command a Senate majority. Instead, the balance of power was held by a collection of minor parties. The 1993 election result was typical, with the government emerging from the election with thirty of the seventy-six Senate seats and falling nine short of a majority, the official opposition winning thirty-six seats, which was three short of a majority—and the balance going to the seven Australian Democrats, two Greens, and one Independent. The minor parties knew that they had no prospect of forming a government, but they had learned to extract concessions from the major parties in exchange for their support.

The combined power of the minor parties was used to pressure the government into revising not only the content of its budget package but also the very process through which this package was developed so as to widen the opportunities for constructive participation by those nongovernment parties on which the government might have to rely for passage of its budget. In fact, Westminster-derived parliaments typically facilitate the practice of strong party government, and their procedural norms reflect this preoccupation with government domination of financial initiatives. This was also the traditional Australian practice until the minor parties began to rewrite the legislative rule book. As Jackson notes of the emerging Australian practice, "By comparison, British and Canadian budgets are never amended by opposition tactics" (Jackson 1995, 12). The centerpiece of Labor's proposed budget was the so-called deficit reduction strategy, which involved a comprehensive package of legislative initiatives with many increased taxes that provoked widespread community protest for being at odds with earlier election promises. The minor parties took advantage of this wave of protest: significant elements of the government's package were withdrawn after the formal parliamentary presentation of the budget and were amended to take account of views of the nongovernment parties. Thus, the government was forced not only to reduce or delay a wide range of proposed revenue measures but also to increase outlays in social security measures—making for increases in the budget deficit of some $730 million over three years (see Senate 1994, 72–77).

The larger procedural changes heralded in 1993 are of two kinds. First, from 1994 the government undertook to include the minor parties in pre-budget consultations that included access to confidential treasury information. The idea was to co-opt the minor parties into the budgetary process, trading off early access to government information for a commitment to bring on a final Senate vote on the budget bills by a set date. The evidence from the 1994 budget was that the minor parties gained little while giving little away but that the government had broadcast its desperation and growing dependency on the goodwill of those parties (Adams 1994). Second, the Senate greatly expanded the scope of a 1986 ruling under which its consideration of government bills was conditional on government compliance with timetables for the introduction into the Senate of government bills.

The 1993 extension included a new "double-deadline" test obliging the government to meet stipulated deadlines for the introduction of bills into the lower as well as the upper house, so that parliament as a whole would have enhanced opportunities to debate and examine legislation. The government expressed outrage at the presumption of one parliamentary house laying down conditions for the internal operations of another house, and at the hubris reflected in Senate preaching about its role in protecting the capacity of parliament as a whole to act as an effective deliberative assembly (Jackson 1995, 11–14; Senate 1994, 68–69; Senate 1995, 93–94).

These events were the tip of a larger set of institutional changes consolidating in the Australian Senate. Prominent in the price that the government was having to pay for the support of votes from the minor parties was a new deal on accountability. Ministers conceded unprecedented obligations to explain and justify the conduct of government and to provide new levels of information and documentation about government decision making that would formerly have been withheld on the grounds of executive privilege. The budget battles of 1993 prepared the ground for the establishment of the accountability accord of 1994, which among other things committed the government to a code of ministerial conduct to identify standards expected of the political executive, and enhanced independence for the Auditor General as the primary instrument of the bureaucracy's accountability to parliament. As the government Senate leader ruefully observed when conceding the new intrusion of the Senate into the prerogatives of executive government, "We are talking not about any old upper house but the most powerful upper house constitutionally in the Westminster world. There are no ifs, buts or maybes about that" (see Uhr 1995, 130; Reid 1984; Blewett 1993, 11–13).

Divided Government

If one word summarizes the traditional orientation of Australian parliamentary executives, that word is *mandate*. When used in this sense, "having a mandate" means having the popular authority and hence democratic legitimacy to proceed with a promised course of action in law or policy, even over the objections of nongovernment parties in parliament. The language of mandate is normally used by political executives to argue that the defeated forces in parliament do not have the political authority to obstruct the passage of the victor's legislation. But over recent years the traditional magic has begun to wear off, especially as minor parties in the Senate have not accepted that they, unlike the official opposition, are defeated forces. They might be small parties, but to an extent their minority position is one of choice, reflecting a deliberate strategy to hold the balance of power between government and opposition.

The minor parties have developed their own version of mandate theory, which holds that they too have been returned to parliament with a mandate from electors endorsing their public commitment to subject government legislation to the closest possible scrutiny short of outright obstruction—to "keep the bastards honest," to use a slogan devised by the most established of the minor parties, the Australian Democrats.

One would suspect that the Australian electoral system, with its characteristic combination of House with half-Senate voting, especially considering the presence of proportional representation in the Senate, makes it difficult for any incoming government to claim a mandate for representing the nation. The claim makes more sense as a sign of a government's frustration with parliamentary impediments to its will. Thus it comes as no surprise that simultaneous or so-called double dissolutions for the whole Senate as well as the whole House have taken place on six occasions, when justified by the constitutional provisions regulating the resolution of disagreement between the two houses: 1914, 1951, 1974, 1975, 1983, and 1987 (Evans 1995, 75).

Australian political analysts have begun to rely on the United States concept of divided government when examining the capacity of the Senate to frustrate the policy and legislative agenda of Australian governments. Divided government refers to the division of control over the core institutions of government when opposed political parties dominate the executive and legislative branches of government (see Mayhew 1991; Cox and Kernell 1991; Thurber 1996). Divided government refers in part to the checks and balances built into the constitutional framework, and in part to the deliberate choice by the electorate to "split the ticket" and place opposed parties in control of executive and legislative branches of government. A recent example occurred after the 1996 U.S. elections, which saw the Democrats retain control of the White House and the Republicans retain their control of both houses of Congress, which they had won initially in 1994.

At the center of the divided government literature is a debate over the legislative and policy effects of divisions of partisan control between legislative and executive branches. The initial supposition was that divided government meant deadlocked government, or political gridlock, as it is sometimes called. One response to this fear of deadlock was the revival of interest in parliamentary alternatives to congressional government first articulated by Woodrow Wilson over a century ago.

This longing for the supposed capacity of decisive leadership thought to be found in parliamentary systems can be traced back to Woodrow Wilson's critique of the deleterious effect of systems of separation of powers on a nation's political leadership (Ceaser 1986). Debate ensued over possible reform of American governmental institutions along parliamentary lines in order to establish a better platform for identifiable political responsibility and democratic accountability. Although without any practical institutional consequences, this search for a parliamentary alternative reawakened interest in the serious comparison between congressional and parliamentary systems, motivated by the belief that in general parliamentary systems facilitate public accountability as well as political leadership (see Weaver and Rockman 1993).

Another response that attracted greater scholarly support was to review the evidence to determine whether the institutional separation of legislative and executive powers has really led to gridlock. Despite the worst fears of those interested in parliamentary alternatives, the evidence does not easily support the argument that legislative and policy outcomes suffer under conditions of divided government (Mayhew 1991, 175–99;

Thurber 1996). Mayhew's important attempt to demonstrate the limitations of the more extreme fears about divided government is an object lesson in the perils of loose fears about the separation of partisan power across competing political institutions.

The emerging Australian debate is comparatively poor, and it displays a confusion between the messy routines of American budget making and the larger fears about policy gridlock between legislative and executive institutions. The political debate over the Australian Senate reflects only a limited range of the issues in the original American debate that it dimly reflects (see Sharman 1990; Mulgan 1995, 190–93). This is evident in two typical examples. First, there is Adams's report of the political debate about whether the Australian budget process has begun to become "Americanized," in which he quotes former Liberal prime minister Malcolm Fraser, who has argued that the Senate "is running the risk of making Australia ungovernable . . . [by] turning the annual Budget process into a series of bargains and trade-offs similar to those which occur in the United States" (Adams 1993, 223, 225). Second, Jackson's detailed analysis of federal and state parliamentary developments leads him to ask if Australia "has entered an era of at least partially negotiated budgets and the threat of political gridlock," which is at odds with the conventional accounts of the supposed virtues of the Australian parliamentary system (Jackson 1995, 12).

The concept of divided government was not devised with parliamentary government in mind. A parliamentary approximation to this situation is the condition referred to as "minority government" when a parliament without a party or coalition in command of a clear majority is prepared to entrust executive office to a minority party or coalition, on the basis that the government has a realistic opportunity of stitching together a working majority to enable it to get on with the routine business of government. But minority government differs from divided government in that it does not refer primarily to institutional deadlocks that can divide government into two camps each possessed of the power to veto the other. One might be tempted to think of the Australian parliament as establishing a minority government, to the limited extent that most governments cannot command a majority in both parliamentary houses. But to accept this temptation would be to downplay the significance of the often huge majorities that governments can command in the House of

Representatives and of their ability to use this to their ultimate advantage in joint sittings of the parliament, which is the final phase of intercameral dispute resolution.

The relevance here of the term *divided government* is that it focuses, first, on the electorate's choice to share political power among the parties of government and of opposition and, second, on the institutional capacity of the Senate to mobilize nongovernment interests to check and balance the power of governments enjoying comfortable majorities in the House of Representatives. The Australian electoral and party system for the House has provided clear winners at every election for the past fifty years, although the same cannot be said about parliamentary government at state level, where minority governments have been far from unusual.

The challenge at the federal level is posed by the Senate, where governments have rarely secured a majority since the introduction of PR. The exceptions are 1951–55 and 1958–61, at the end of which the Menzies government faced the permanent prospect of two minor parties holding the Senate balance of power; and 1976–80 at the end of which the Australian Democrats arrived in strength. The historical description for this standard situation has been that governments have faced "a hostile Senate" where the most severe challenge to the authority of the government was likely to be Senate obstruction. This usually meant something falling far short of the 1975 situation when the opposition parties refused to pass budget bills of the Labor government and stampeded the governor general into dismissing the Whitlam ministry, which resoundingly lost the subsequent general election.

The Australian constitution provides little guidance on the distinctive political responsibilities of the two parliamentary houses, although it comes closest to articulating norms of parliamentary governance when dealing with the resolution of deadlock between the two houses. Deadlock is defined in terms of the inability of a government based in the House of Representatives to secure parliamentary passage of its legislation. The constitutional provisions relating to the resolution of a parliamentary deadlock apply only to Senate obstruction of government initiatives and not to any failure by the House to pass Senate initiatives.

Although governments have anything up to a third of their ministry drawn from the Senate and, to use the 1993–96 figures, introduce around a third of their legislation in the upper house, the rules of the constitutional game pay particular attention to Senate disagreements with government bills passed by the so-called house of government. Under specified conditions of deadlock, the government may arrange a "double dissolution," which is a fresh election for both houses. Should that fail to clear the legislative path, the government may subsequently convene a joint sitting of all senators and members (as distinct from a conference of representatives of the two houses), at which point the relative weight of house numbers will secure passage of any contentious legislation.

But even the constitution's careful recognition of the potential for institutional conflict falls short of identifying the range of particular parliamentary tasks expected of the Senate. The standard role claimed for it was that of a states' house, although it is important to note that the constitutional framers overturned an early decision to call it the "states' assembly" (Uhr 1995, 134). The fact that the Senate so early in its institutional development after federation failed to act as a states' house is less surprising than the lack of a political consensus, then or now, on a positive role for the Senate.

Australian political life has a variety of competing terms that try to identify the role of the Senate, and most do so in terms of a subordinate relationship to the House of Representatives. For example, "upper house" relates to the lower house and has all the disability of democratic preference for institutions that are closer to the people. "Second chamber" refers to the first and implicitly primary chamber. Even the term "house of review" relates to the lower house as the "house of government," implying that the Senate's role is basically reactive, checking and balancing the initiatives of the government of the day. The lower house is widely regarded as "the house of government" by virtue of the fact that the government of the day is formed from the party or parties holding a majority in it, and further that the leading minority party forms the official opposition or shadow government (Barlin 1997, 33–42, 103–6). The Senate is often regarded as the house of review, suggesting that its primary role is one of scrutiny and review of government operations, as distinct from more proactive tasks in which it might collide with the lower house over the conduct and direction of government (Evans 1995, 11–14, 117–20).

Although originally there were few doubts about the extent of the Senate's constitutional powers, over the years doubts began to surface about the appropriate role of the upper house in a federal system of responsible parliamentary government. Despite periodic proof of its constitutional clout, the Senate has never displaced the House of Representatives as the primary political arena in which governments are formed. Not even the awful events of the 1975 dismissal of the Whitlam government prove the primacy of the Senate. It is true that the governor general exercised his constitutional prerogative to dismiss a ministry enjoying a clear majority in the House of Representatives on the argument that the government failed the core test of parliamentary confidence because it could not control the Senate. But these constitutional niceties pale in comparison with the political realities, particularly the role of the leader of the opposition, Malcolm Fraser, using his base of power in the lower house to marshall his Senate party members as instruments in his quest for prime ministerial power. Few can forget the audacity of Fraser's rise to office, but few can remember any of the Senate leaders or the supposed rights of the upper house (Barlin 1997, 52–59; Evans 1995, 89–105).

The divided government thesis arose at a time when analysts in the United States were comparing the alleged gridlock of their own congressional system with the apparent virtues of Westminster-derived responsible parliamentary government. But the irony is that at around the same time as Wilson was comparing the vices of congressional government with the virtues of parliamentary government, Australian nation-builders were approaching federation as an opportunity to modify the inherited parliamentary system to move in the direction of the congressional system (La Nauze 1972, 24–28, 273–75). A further irony is that the revival of Wilsonian interest in institutional reform of the congressional system coincides with the strengthening of an Australian republican movement which displays surprising interest in adapting elements of the congressional system in order to promote more open and deliberate legislative processes (see Uhr 1993).

But before exploring the effects of the contemporary Senate on the practices of Australian government, it is important to take stock of the deeper constitutional roots of the institutional power of the Senate. Those roots find their nutrients in the original constitutional design for a bicameral parliament of approximately equal powers, and in the later establishment of an electoral system using proportional representation to break the policy and institutional domination of the established major parties and to give minor parties the chance to acquire considerable parliamentary power.

Constitutional Framework

Names of political institutions do not always provide reliable guidance to their real significance. The legal framework for Australian national government is contained in a constitution that establishes a federal polity consisting of the commonwealth or national government and the six state governments. The federal government is a parliamentary government comprising two elected houses: the larger House of Representatives reflecting the national distribution of population, and the smaller Senate in which each state is equally represented. Senators' terms are twice the length of those of House members, staggered so that half the Senate is elected every three years. The constitution provides that the House shall be twice the size of the Senate, which effectively conveys the original understanding of the relative political weight of the two bodies. But institutional developments have not always complied with that original understanding.

The formal titles are interesting for a nation with a British colonial history and an inherited system of parliamentary government at state and federal levels. Although Canada shares a similar history, its national parliament is organized around a House of Commons that explicitly draws on British precedent. Although the Parliament of Canada includes a Senate that might appear to be loosely modeled on that of the United States, the Canadian upper house is an appointed body, representing regions rather than states or provinces. In choosing the title of Senate, the Australian constitutional framers rejected the Canadian version and even revised the American original by rejecting the practice in the United States of election by state legislatures and opting for popular election (Uhr 1989; Sharman 1990).

But it is one thing to confer democratic legitimacy on a political institution; it is another thing to arrange that institution so it complements rather than competes with other democratic institutions. Although the title Senate reflects a commitment to equal state representation, the constitution does not stipulate any particular legislative tasks as the preserve of the Senate, as does, for example, the United States Constitution in relation to the ratification of treaties and confirmation of executive and judicial appointments. The Australian Constitution makes the two houses virtually equal in their legislative power, although the Senate is limited in its capacity to amend tax bills or bills "for the ordinary annual services of the government." But even matters that the Senate may not amend, it may reject outright or return to the initiating house with a request for amendments. Clearly the constitution grants the Senate enviable power, but from the beginning uncertainty has surrounded the areas of political responsibility in which the Senate might best use that power.

It is well known that the design of the Senate repeatedly gave rise to the most protracted disputes during the 1890s Conventions in which the constitution was framed (La Nauze 1972, 40–44, 140–41; Crommelin 1992, 39–43). The Convention delegates were divided over the purpose and practices associated with a federal house of review. Progressive Liberals tended grudgingly to accept the Senate as the price that had to be paid for federation and the transition to the new nation. The general contours of the Convention debates over the powers of the Senate have been well described elsewhere (Galligan 1980; Galligan and Warden 1986). But despite the attention that has been directed to the Senate's legal powers, much less attention has been given to its electoral composition.

PR in Theory

The framers' case in principle for proportional representation can be reconstructed from evidence of their approach to representation in general. Many of the framers had few illusions as to the likely place of party politics in both houses of the federal parliament; some, like Deakin and Barton, probably tolerated PR as a means of adapting the principle of party to serve a distinctively qualified Australian variant of parliamentary government (La Nauze 1972, 44, 119, 148, 188; Quick and Garran 1976, 444). The argument for an upper house conceded the case that equal state representation was the inevitable entry price being extracted by the smaller states, but it reached beyond that to issues relating to the structural requirements for effective parliamentary deliberation in a large continental federation (see Quick and Garran 1976, 386–87, 422).

Very prominent framers like Deakin and Barton went on the record predicting that parliament would probably opt for PR for the Senate. The constitutional framers were convinced that PR would realize the promise of the Senate as a house of review by establishing a different parliamentary institution capable of representing a range of community views not reflected in the House. With the inclusion of PR in the original 1902 electoral bill, where the provisions were deleted, opponents quite rightly saw the guiding influence of such philosophical liberals as John Stuart Mill. Arguably, Mill's account of the merits of a second chamber organized on proportional representation provides one of the important missing ingredients in the framers' confident recipe for a federal house of review (see Reid and Forrest 1989, 87–94; Mulgan 1995, 201–2). Mill provides the substance for the argument, advanced only hesitatingly by a few of the framers, that the primary purpose of an upper house, and of proportional representation, is to enhance the deliberative capacities of parliamentary institutions by providing new opportunities for minority voices to be heard and new accountability requirements that ministerial voices be heard at the convenience of parliament rather than the government of the day. Perhaps surprisingly, Mill can still be found as an authority on bicameralism in the contemporary Senate (see Uhr 1995, 136).

According to Mill, the aim of the second chamber was to act as "the center of resistance to the predominant power in the Constitution," which in modern democracies is the force of the majority. This "democratic ascendancy" had a proven tendency to cultivate what he, following Tocqueville, identified as the tyranny of the majority. The purpose of the review chamber is to check "the class interests of the majority" and to represent above all the interests of vulnerable minorities, ever conscious of the need to respect the political principles and institutional norms of equality and so to promote "nothing offensive to democratic feeling." The review function is one which Mill termed "the function of antagonism," by which he refers to the check or control to be placed on the unexamined power of "the ruling authority." Control in this legislative sense means open, public examination of the reasons for ruling; and proportional representation can provide the requisite "rallying point" around which "dissentient opinions" can form, facilitating review and revision of the governing strategies of the ruling majority (Mill 1991, 386, 388, 391).

PR in Practice

The first federal government attempted unsuccessfully to introduce PR for Senate elections. The 1902 electoral bill was introduced in the Senate, and after an important debate over the strengths and weaknesses of responsible party government, the Senate deleted the proposed provisions for proportional representation on the understandable grounds that they posed real risks for the stability of British-derived party government (Uhr 1995, 136–38). The proponents of PR defended it in terms of establishing the true voice of the majority, and not in terms of minority rights. They explicitly accepted that democracy means that "the majority in decision must rule" and that the minority has "a right to be heard and not to rule." The government Senate leader's case was that traditional forms of representation associated with the British Constitution had been "invested with a certain amount of sacredness" that was "altogether unsuited to modern times." Parliament must strive to become "a true reflex of the opinion of the people" by arranging political representation so that "every shade of opinion, as far as possible, may be represented."

After extensive debate, the Senate threw out the provision for PR, chiefly on the correct perception that it would introduce a war of representation into the new federal parliament, probably challenge the conventions of cabinet government (or "honest party government," as it was called) and increase the potential of the Senate to compete for popular legitimacy with the House of Representatives. The preconditions of responsible cabinet government would be eroded, in that under what the opponents cleverly called "fractional representation" political leadership would be challenged by the activity "of sections and fads," enfeebling cabinet's claim to representative leadership as "the dominant power." Opponents rightly appreciated the potential of the revamped Senate to "altogether paralyze responsible government modelled upon the British system" (Uhr 1995, 138). The 1902 electoral legislation entrenched a version of the block vote, which had the striking effect of confirming both sides' expectations and delivering Senate representation generally into the grateful hands of whichever party was about to become the government of the day, with little or no regard for minority representation. Typical government majorities in the Senate were 31 to 5 in 1914, 35 to 1 in 1919, 33 to 3 in 1934, and 33 to 3 in 1948.

The 1948 reforms to the electoral legislation that introduced PR for the Senate are well researched and require only limited comment here (Reid and Forrest 1989, 118–22; Fusaro 1968, 129–30, 135). By way of contrast to the 1902 legislation, the 1948 measures were introduced in the House, as though to suggest that this was as much a matter for government as for the house of review. Sure enough, Attorney General Evatt explained the reformed system of Senate representation as "one most likely to enhance the status of the Senate." The stated aim was to ensure that "the majority group will get the majority of seats and no more," a policy on representation long advocated by the established third party then known as the Country Party.

Opposition leader Menzies clearly identified Labor's partisan strategy, in which a Labor majority in the Senate was an insurance policy against the probability that they might lose office at the next election, as in fact happened. Menzies also foreshadowed the possibility of a government using the barely tested procedures for double dissolutions to attempt to restore parity of representation in both houses, which is exactly what he did in 1951. For Menzies as for all subsequent prime ministers, the existence of the constitutional provision for double dissolutions and subsequent joint sittings was proof enough of the subordinate place of the Senate in Australian government. The "will of the people" must trump the representation of minority groups in the Senate; and it is the people's House which "makes and unmakes governments" (Uhr 1995, 138–39; 1992, 99–102).

Forms of Senate Power

One can distinguish between two general phases of Senate reform since the introduction of PR in 1949. The first phase may be called "the age of majority" to refer to the prevailing ethos that was compatible with the norms of strong party government. This phase extended from 1949 to the late 1960s, embracing the heyday of the first minor party, the Democratic Labor Party (DLP), which broke away from Labor and effectively entered an alliance with the coalition government against Labor, doing comparatively little to transform the ways of the Senate. The second phase may be called the "age of minority" because it sees the rejuvenation of the Senate as a parliamentary chamber through the arrival of the second wave of minor parties which were less committed to shoring up the major parties in government. Between the decline of the DLP and the arrival of the second-wave minor parties, there was something of an interregnum, coinciding with the Fraser government's unprecedented command of a majority in both houses of parliament between 1976 and 1980.

The presence of minor parties holding the balance of Senate power is not the sole ingredient in the rise of a system of multiparty decision

making. The DLP was formed out of the Labor split of the 1950s. It effectively held the balance of Senate power from 1955 to 1958, and then later it
shared that balance with other splinter groups and independents from
1961 until the party's eclipse in 1974. But the relevant point here is that not
all minor parties are the same, and that the DLP made little effort to alter
the rules or procedures of Senate decision making. As Malcolm Fraser has
argued, it was not until the demise of the DLP and the arrival of the
Australian Democrats as the holders of the balance of power in 1980 that
the apple cart of convenience was overturned (Fraser 1993). As a striking
symbol of the potential docility of minor parties, consider the impact of
the DLP on the growth of the Senate committee system, which they voted
against when it was originally established at the insistence of the Labor
opposition. DLP leader Gair, drawing on his state experience in executive
office, advocated a "policy of gradualism," which would have held back
the committee system until extensive trials had been conducted. Clearly
there are major differences among minor parties, and these can spoil tidy
predictions about the modes of multiparty parliaments.

Two reservations should be borne in mind when thinking of an age of
minority. First, it is rational for minority parties to resist routine reliance
on legislative committees as a substitute for chamber consideration because the chamber is the one site in which minor parties and especially
independents can marshall their legislative power to constrict the flow of
legislative business. Thus it comes as no surprise that the age of minority gives rise to more complex rules for chamber treatment of government proposals, equal in importance to the threat of referral of bills to
committees.

Second, there is no single cutoff date separating the age of majority
from that of minority: the two overlap, with the result that the Senate can
still revert to type whenever the minor parties lose the will or interest to
hold the line against the combined ambition of the major parties. The
major reforms associated with the age of minority occurred at the end of
the Keating government, when the Democrats were joined by the Greens.
But the tone was set in the mid-1980s when Democratic senator Michael
Macklin successfully moved what became known as the "Macklin motion," which was a resolution declaring that the Senate would defer until
the next period of sittings consideration of any bills received after a specified deadline (Evans 1995, 253–55).

Recollecting the initial case study of the 1993 timetabling reforms effected by the Senate, we can see that this package of procedural reforms stands as a symbol of the arrival of the age of minority. Although the Senate may waive its right not to consider "late" legislation, the onus is on the government to convince it to lift the ban on a case-by-case basis, which is itself a time-consuming burden. In the initial period of operation from November 1994 to mid-1996, the Senate exempted 141 government bills and refused exemptions for only 15 of them, or a little more than 10 percent. The proportion might suggest that the Senate tends to cave in to government demands, but one should remember that the legislative process is now so tight that governments only apply for exemption in those cases where they genuinely believe that there is some pressing need for early consideration of nominated legislative proposals.

Characteristic of the age of minority is the procedural revolution of 1994, which broke the government chokehold on committee power. It had long been observed that although the post-1949 Senate almost never had a government majority, standing orders reflected the interests of the established parties competing for government by requiring that the power of the chair reside in the party in government. Even in the absence of procedural protection, Senate power reflected the interests of the governing party, which is nowhere better illustrated than in the convention that the presidency is a gift to the party in government, regardless of that party's proportion of Senate seats. Why not have that power shared to reflect the actual balance of the parties represented in the Senate? That traditional convention held sway until the minor parties brokered a new accord which eventually obtained Senate support (Evans 1995, 392–93).

The first manifestation of the new committee system was the division of each former committee into two new separate committees. These included (1) a legislation committee of six members with government chair and majority, and (2) a reference committee of eight members with nongovernment majorities and chair, shared between the opposition and the Australian Democrats on a 3 to 1 ratio. The two Greens and the lone Independent won no such rights of formal responsibility, but their voting power remained decisive when formal considerations reached the chamber.

The original intention was that the reference committees under opposition control would target matters of public policy and other matters referred to them, but events never turn out as neatly as the rules intend. Early in the life of the 1996 Howard government, the Senate successfully referred a number of important government bills to reference and not legislative committees, on the basis that the former but not the latter had nongovernment majorities. Thus, despite the initial logic behind the two spheres of responsibility, the Senate adopted the more sustainable logic of using its numbers to take government legislation out of the hands of government majorities and to incorporate the reference committees into the routines of the legislative process.

According to governments, the general behavior of the Senate as a legislative chamber has been obstructive, but the evidence does not support this accusation. The trend is that around 30 percent of bills passed by the Senate receive prior committee examination, and around 30 percent of eventual amendments have been examined during committee consideration (Evans 1995, 262). The 37th parliament (1993–96) provides an instructive example: the Senate record shows that the government had 482 bills passed during that 1993–96 period, 140, or 30 percent, of which were referred to committees for examination. Taking amendments to government bills as a good test of the Senate's legislative will, the record shows that 157, or 33 percent, of these 482 bills were amended. It is true that a majority of these amendments are recorded as government amendments, but a high proportion of them indicate a change of legislative mind on the part of a government as it moves to repair provisions which, to judge from the state of Senate opinion, might otherwise not pass.

The charge of obstruction only makes sense when the Senate's profile of amendments is contrasted with the ineffectual protest of the nongovernment parties in the House of Representatives where governments can expect to pass their initiatives at will. During the 37th parliament (1993–96), 157 bills attracted 1,812 successful Senate amendments at an average of 11 amendments per bill. The bills withstood many more proposed amendments that were unsuccessful, including half a dozen of the government's own proposed amendments. The distribution of successful nongovernment amendments is as follows: official opposition 267, or 15 percent; Australian Democrats 159, or 9 percent; Greens 76, or 4 percent; and Independent 2, or less than 0.1 percent. This understates the impact of the Australian Democrats, who have had many proposed amendments taken up by the government and formally moved either by the government alone or in cosponsorship with the Democrats.

Another test of the Senate's power over government is the rigor of its daily Question Time compared with that in the House of Representatives.

Australian practice in both chambers is that "questions without notice" to the ministry alternate from opposition and government, so that only half of the questions come with real surprise or are likely to carry much sting. But within the tame limits of Australian practice, the Senate process provides greater opportunity for nongovernment parties to keep the heat of accountability on the ministry, a third of which will be senators (Barlin 1997, 507–25; Evans 1995, 498–502).

Parliamentary standing orders protect the right of parliamentarians to put questions to ministers, but they do not compel ministers to answer questions, and practice in the lower house has degenerated into a parade of lengthy ministerial statements typically about the defects of the opposition parties (Blewett 1994, 6–8). But Senate and House versions of Question Time differ in fundamental ways, with the Senate version being of more value in terms of backbench opportunities to test the credibility of ministers. Following a 1992 overhaul at the instigation of the nongovernment parties, Senate Question Time now is distinguished by rules that attempt to share around as evenly as possible the exposure time enjoyed by questioners and answers. Questions are limited to one minute, answers to four, with tighter rules for supplementaries; and each day after Question Time senators have thirty minutes set aside as a kind of right of reply in which to "take note" of earlier answers, again subject to tight time limits on each speaker (Evans 1995, 498–514).

Regarding written "questions on notice," Senate rules stipulate that when ministers fail to provide answers within thirty days, they must provide "an explanation satisfactory to that senator" who asked the question, or run the risk of Senate debate on their ministerial failure to provide either information or explanation to the Senate. Related Senate rules that give the upper house a comparative advantage in extracting information from the ministry include the use of "returns to order," by which the Senate formally "orders" that specified documents be "returned" or submitted to the Senate by a certain date. Another is the use of orders directing the auditor general to investigate matters on the Senate's behalf, a relatively new practice begun in the 1990s which could signal a revolution in parliament's use of so-called parliamentary officers as investigative arms of nongovernment parties.

A final distinguishing feature of the Senate's armory of accountability is the role of estimates hearings by legislative committees during the Senate's consideration of the government's annual appropriation bills for public service expenditures. In formal terms, these hearings are meant to provide the committees with opportunities to examine the government budget estimates as contained in the two sets of appropriation bills passed twice each year. But despite this formal appearance as a legislative reference designed to help senators form a judgment on the merits of legislation implementing the government's budget, estimates hearings typically take on the substance of an open and frequently disorganized investigation into suspicions of ministerial or bureaucratic inefficiency and maladministration.

The term *hearings* accurately conveys the orientation: estimates committees approach their task as a hearing or audit of government explanations of budget and management performance. To the extent that the hearings move away from details of financial inputs to larger issues of ministerial or bureaucratic performance, the committees openly accept that they have usually lost any prospect of consensual agreement. This honest embrace of dissent is reflected in the quality of the committee reports which, unlike the hearings that precede them, frequently do little to enhance public debate about government operations. Opinions vary on the value of a model of estimates hearings that culminates in a shopping list of unresolved items in dispute, to which senators can declare their determination to return during subsequent Senate debate of the budget bills.

As instruments of accountability, estimates hearings are potentially significant because they provide regular opportunities for the Senate to take advantage of the availability of public servants who appear as witnesses to clarify and explain the extensive budget and management information prepared by each agency. Although departmental public servants appear at the direction of their ministers, the Senate's role as a small upper house means that in many cases they are accompanied by a duty minister unprepared to intervene and protect witnesses against probing lines of questioning about agency details. Better alternatives have been proposed, but one basic hurdle is the remarkable lack of interest by the House of Representatives in adopting detailed estimates processes. An experiment with estimates committees was attempted under the Fraser government, and even though this coincided with growing interest in and experimentation with legislative committees, the House dropped both practices after a few years, and estimates committees have never returned. This leaves the main estimates responsibility with the Senate, which itself tells much about

the limits of "Westminster" categories for the analysis of Australian parliamentary practices (Reid 1984; Reid and Forrest 1989, 378; Evans 1995,
323–28).

Forms of Government Opposition

In the Australian situation, proof of the pudding of divided government
is found in the escalating resentment that political executives express
over the effects of the Senate on the legislative and policy agenda of
governments, and their increasingly strained defenses of their right and
supposed mandate to unobstructed government (Mulgan 1995, 193–98).
There is ample evidence that the Senate is in the process of redefining its
representative role. The novel level of intrusion into government decision
making has been joined by a deeper transformation of the Senate's institutional understanding and norms of due process. Most importantly, this
alteration in the business of the Senate poses fundamental challenges to
the conventional model of Australian responsible government. It is not
accidental that Prime Minister Keating, a spirited defender of the established parliamentary order, should be the one to provoke this articulation
of a new system of multiparty shared responsibility.

The Senate has ensured that Keating will remain famous for his views
that senators are the "unrepresentative swill" of Australian politics and
that Australia does not really need a Senate (Uhr 1995, 129–33, 139–40).
Keating argued that precisely because of PR, especially with the current
"exceptionally low quotas," the Senate has become "unrepresentative,"
displaying the behavior of "a spoiling chamber . . . usurping the responsibilities of the executive drawn from the representative chamber" (i.e.,
the House of Representatives). Institutional conduct that the minor parties describe as part of an agenda of accountability Keating calls "simply
holding any government to ransom."

The traditional view of responsible party government has its able proponents. Senator Evans concedes that "it is all very well for minorities to
have their voice," and "it is all very nice having them chirp up from time
to time, but it is not very nice having around 50,000 votes determining
the ability of a government with five million votes to govern." Supporting
the traditional model is a concept of a government's popular mandate,
openly on display in the views of Prime Minister Keating. The mandate
concept derives from the inherited British model of responsible party

government, where it fits the institutional circumstances of a popularly elected house defending itself against the pretensions of an unelected upper chamber. But Australian institutional circumstances differ, consistent with a deliberate strategy for reshaping that inherited model—not by reintroducing the powers of an established estate, but by widening the net of political representation to implement more rather than less democracy.

Only slowly and reluctantly have the major parties begun to learn the lessons of their minority status in the Senate. PR brings to the Senate a set of institutional incentives for less hasty decision making and enhanced political deliberation across party divisions. Defenders of the old order are unlikely to alter their views on preferred institutional arrangements, but a more accurate guide to the virtues of the emerging order comes from Labor's former Senate leader John Button, who concedes that "the necessary process of conciliation and negotiation tempers the mood of the Senate considerably more than is the case in the House of Representatives." Further, Button openly concedes that the current Senate system establishes something akin to "a minority government," which while "very difficult" is also "a very salutary experience" (Button 1992, 25).

Conclusion

Most analysts of Australian parliamentary institutions assess the Senate's representative capacity in two related ways. First, they contrast the practice as a party house with the supposed original intention of an assembly representing states' interests. Second, they concede that, although the 1948 introduction of proportional representation brought a refreshing legitimacy to the Senate, that reshaping reflected very little by way of theoretical design, and can best be seen as a clever Labor scheme to retain hold of power in the upper house in the likely event, all-too-true, of an imminent loss of control in the approaching elections for the House of Representatives (see Souter 1988, 94–97, 403).

I have argued that a strong case can be made that the constitutional intention of the framers and founding generation of Commonwealth politicians was for the Senate to represent majority interests, even more accurately than the professed House of Representatives, by providing opportunities for the election of minority parties. The original design did not focus exclusively on PR as an instrument for protecting minority interests as an end in itself. The representation of minor parties was intended as an instrument to help form a broader coalition of democratic, as distinct from simply majoritarian, interests. The common rhetoric of the Senate as a (failed) states' house has got it no more than half right, and has done a disservice in suppressing the wider justification of the Senate as a brake on the misuse of majority power. The current institutional redefinition of the importance of PR should come as no great surprise; it gels with much, but not all, of the Senate's norms of committee scrutiny of government action affecting civil liberties (Sharman 1977; Reid and Forrest 1989, 141–45; 215–30; Galligan and Uhr 1990; Mulgan 1995, 201–3).

The contrast in styles and substance between the two parliamentary chambers is nicely captured in the contrasting fates of the opposed leaders of the government and the Senate at the time of the resurgence of Senate power in the late 1960s: Liberal senator John Gorton and Labor senator Lionel Murphy.

In 1968 Gorton was promoted from the office of leader of the government in the Senate to that of prime minister when elected leader of the governing Liberal Party upon the death of Prime Minister Holt. Gorton knew that he could not lead a government or more particularly a governing party from the Senate, from which he resigned to take up a lower house seat. His conduct has been followed in spirit by many ambitious leaders of the government in the Senate who have resigned and taken up House of Representatives seats as part of a strategy to position themselves for the highest political office. His story illustrates that peak political power is located in the House of Representatives, and that ambitious parliamentarians who want to be considered for prime ministerial office eventually have to make their way in the larger and more public world of the lower house.

Gorton's opposite number in the Senate was Lionel Murphy. Prompted by the legendary Senate clerk J. R. O. Odgers, Murphy saw the opportunities for the Senate as a house of review with an extensive committee system. Almost as Gorton departed for his prime ministerial office, Murphy began his move to establish a fresh institutional capacity to review government operations, which was set in place in 1970 through a system of estimates and general purpose committees (Reid and Forrest 1989, 178–79; 375–80). Murphy's interest in civil liberties led him to push the Senate into the sphere of scrutiny of government operations and the cultivation of an institutional ethos as the watchdog protecting the community against the bureaucratic pretensions of big government. The establishment of the Senate committee system in 1970 brought a new sense of legitimacy to the upper house, which within a few short years was to find expression in the confident assertion of its will against that of Murphy's own Labor government.

Murphy himself escaped the trauma of the 1975 dismissal, since he moved on in 1974 from Gorton's old position as leader of the government in the Senate to the High Court. But not even the separation of powers between judiciary and legislature could protect Murphy from Senate scrutiny. In the 1980s, Murphy triggered a series of Senate inquiries that marked the beginning of impeachment proceedings against him for alleged misconduct. Murphy's affairs were the subject of two inconclusive Senate committee inquiries in 1984 and a further inquiry by a specially established parliamentary commission in 1986. Murphy died before the 1986 parliamentary commission could complete its inquiry (Evans 1995, 538–50).

Nothing better illustrates the power of the Senate than this determination to bring even the highest court within the orbit of its scrutiny. Opinions naturally differ on the capacity of the Senate to make responsible use of this vast power. For too long, Australian political analysts have simply presumed that the Senate was an anomaly in terms of the conventions of responsible parliamentary government. Only now are observers learning to take seriously the Australian version of divided government, which is challenging the traditional model with its implied right to untrammeled rule by the party holding power as the government of the day.

References

Adams, David. 1993. "Political Review." *Australian Quarterly* 65:217–34.
———. 1994. "Political Review." *Australian Quarterly* 66:101–16.
Barlin, Lyn, ed. 1997. *House of Representatives Practice.* 3d ed. Canberra: Australian Government Printing Service.
Blewett, Neal. 1993. "Parliamentary Reform." *Australian Quarterly* 65:1–14.
Button, John. 1992. "The Role of the Leader of the Government in the Senate." In *Parliamentary Perspectives 1991,* 20–30. Papers on Parliament, no. 14. Canberra: Department of the Senate.

Ceaser, James. 1986. "In Defence of Separation of Powers." In *Separation of Powers—Does It Still Work?* ed. R. A. Goldwin and A. Kaufman. Washington, D.C.: American Enterprise Institute.

Cox, Gary, and Samuel Kernell, eds. 1991. *The Politics of Divided Government.* Boulder, Colo.: Westview Press.

Crommelin, Michael. 1992. "The Federal Model." In *Australian Federation: Towards the Second Centenary,* ed. G. Craven. Melbourne: Melbourne University Press.

Evans, Harry, ed. 1995. *Odgers' Australian Senate Practice.* 7th ed. Canberra: Australian Government Printing Service.

Fraser, Malcolm. 1993. "Senate Risks Overstepping the Mark." *Australian,* 29 September.

Fusaro, Anthony. 1968. "The Australian Senate as a House of Review: Another Look." In *Readings in Australian Government,* ed. C. A. Hughes. St. Lucia, Brisbane: University of Queensland Press.

Galligan, Brian. 1980. "The Founders' Design and Intentions Regarding Responsible Government." In *Responsible Government in Australia,* ed. P. Weller and D. Jaensch. Melbourne: Drummond.

Galligan, Brian, and John Uhr. 1990. "Australian Federal Democracy and the Senate." *Public Law Review* 1:309–28.

Galligan, Brian, and James Warden. 1986. "The Role of the Senate." In *The Convention Debates, 1891–1898: Commentaries, Indices, and Guide,* ed. Greg Craven. Sydney: Legal Books.

Jackson, Robert. 1995. "Executive-Legislative Relations in Australia." *Political Theory Newsletter* 7:1–18.

La Nauze, John A. 1972. *The Making of the Australian Constitution.* Melbourne: Melbourne University Press.

Mayhew, David R. 1991. *Divided We Govern: Party Control, Lawmaking, and Investigations, 1946–1990.* New Haven: Yale University Press.

Mill, John Stuart. 1991. "Considerations on Representative Government." In *On Liberty and Other Essays,* ed. J. Gray. Oxford: Oxford University Press.

Mulgan, Richard. 1995. "The Australian Senate as a 'House of Review.'" *Australian Journal of Political Science* 31:191–204.

Quick, John, and Robert Garran. 1976 [1901]. *Annotated Constitution of the Australian Commonwealth.* Sydney: Legal Books.

Reid, Gordon S. 1984. "The Westminster Model and Ministerial Responsibility." *Current Affairs Bulletin,* June, 4–15.

Reid, Gordon S., and Martyn Forrest. 1989. *Australia's Commonwealth Parliament, 1901–1988.* Melbourne: Melbourne University Press.

Senate. 1994. "Procedural Digest 1993." *Papers on Parliament,* no. 22. Canberra: Department of the Senate.

———. 1995. "Procedural Digest 1994." *Papers on Parliament,* no. 25. Canberra: Department of the Senate.

Sharman, Campbell. 1977. "The Australian Senate as a States' House." In *The Politics of New Federalism,* ed. D. Jaensch, 64–75. Adelaide: Australian Political Science Association.

———. 1990. "Parliamentary Federations and Limited Government: Constitutional Design and Redesign in Australia and Canada." *Journal of Theoretical Politics* 2: 215–30.

Souter, Gavin. 1988. *Acts of Parliament.* Melbourne: Melbourne University Press.

Thurber, James A., ed. 1996. *Rivals for Power: Presidential-Congressional Relations.* Washington, D.C.: Congressional Quarterly Press.

Uhr, John. 1989. "The Canadian and Australian Senates: Comparing Federal Political Institutions." In *Federalism in Canada and Australia,* ed. B. Hodgins et al. Peterborough: Trent University Press.

———. 1992. "Prime Ministers and Parliament: Patterns of Control." In *Menzies to Keating: Development of the Australian Prime Ministership,* ed. P. Weller. Melbourne: Melbourne University Press.

———. 1993. "Instituting Republicanism: Parliamentary Vices, Republican Virtues?" *Australian Journal of Political Science* 28:27–39.

———. 1995. "Proportional Representation in the Australian Senate: Recovering the Rationale." *Australian Journal of Political Science,* special issue, 127–41.

Weaver, R. Kent, and Bert A. Rockman, eds. 1993. *Do Institutions Matter? Government Capabilities in the United States and Abroad.* Washington, D.C.: Brookings Institution.

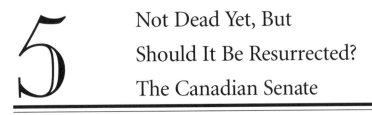

Not Dead Yet, But
Should It Be Resurrected?
The Canadian Senate

C. E. S. FRANKS

The Canadian Senate is both the most written about and the least studied of Canadian political institutions. It is the most written about because reformers look to a reformed Senate to resolve problems of federalism (e.g., Burns 1977; Cody 1995; Crommelin 1989; Galligan 1985–86; Janda 1992; Lusztig 1995; McConnell 1988; McCormick 1991; Sharman 1987; Stillborn 1992; and White 1990). It is the least studied because academics have been satisfied with the accepted image of the Senate as a dusty, obscure Arcadia filled with aged and retired political war horses—once characterized by former prime minister Mulroney as "has-beens and never-weres"—whose main concern, apart from enjoying a good, comfortable, life, is to preserve private wealth and the interests of big business, the "lobby from within" (Campbell 1978; Zolf 1984). In fact, Canada has two Senates. One is the real, working, but little understood Senate as it actually exists; the second is the imaginary Senate reformers propose. There is no relationship or resemblance of the one to the other. There has been no major study conducted of what the Senate actually does for nearly twenty years, even though between 1984 and 1997 the Senate was more active and influential in Canadian politics than at any other time in its history. This renewed activism was highly partisan, and the feisty opposition majority in the Senate much of the time saw itself as the true opposition to the government in the Commons, which it alleged had been emasculated and rendered ineffective by government control (Frith 1990).

This recent Senate activism raises important questions about Canadian democracy: What did the Senate really do after 1984; was it only a minor change, or did it in fact become more aggressive and influential? Should an appointed upper chamber try to become the "real" opposition and defy and obstruct a government supported by a majority in the lower house? What has gone wrong with the House of Commons to allow the Senate to claim this role? What does this tell us about the legislative process in Canada and the state of Canadian democracy? In the first part of this chapter I will relate the little known story of what the Senate has actually done since 1984 and examine these broader issues. The second and shorter part will examine the issue of Senate reform, this most written about aspect of Canadian parliamentary government.

The Canadian Senate

At the time of confederation in 1867, the Canadian Senate had 72 seats. Ontario and Quebec had 24 members each, and 24 were equally apportioned between New Brunswick and Nova Scotia. Prince Edward Island got 4 seats when it joined the confederation in 1873, and the western provinces were given seats as they joined Canada, becoming a third region of 24 seats divided equally among the four western provinces in 1915. Newfoundland was given 6 seats when it joined, and the northern territories later were assigned 1 each. This gives the present total of 104. The greatest disparities between population and Senate seats are in the west, where two provinces, British Columbia and Alberta, each now have more citizens than the four Atlantic provinces combined. Prince Edward Island, with under 150,00 people, still has four senators. Senators are appointed by the Governor in Council, in effect the prime minister, and unless they resign, they retain their seats until the compulsory retirement age of seventy-five.

In these two factors, regional representation and method of appointment, lie most of the sources of criticism of the Senate. The western provinces in particular complain that they are drastically underrepresented in the upper chamber, as indeed they are. As a remedy, Alberta in particular proposes a Senate in which all provinces would have equal representation. However, because of the huge variations between provinces, this would create even more severe imbalances in representation than exist at present. Under equality, for example, each citizen of Prince Edward Island would have roughly one hundred times the representation in the Senate as citizens of Ontario, the largest province. Canada, more so than most other western democracies, has been ruled by long-lived governments and government parties. Prime ministers have been equally long-lived in power, and the effect of this on the Senate has been a preponderance of senators from the government side—the Liberal Party for most of this century—and frequent accusations (often valid) that the prime reason for a senatorial appointment is the senator's support of the party in power, or friendship with the prime minister. The method of appointment of senators and the imbalance in party representation were recurring issues during the post-1984 period of Senate activism.

In legislation, the Canadian Senate has coequal powers with the House of Commons, with the exception that bills for appropriating public revenues, or for imposing any tax (commonly referred to as "money bills") must originate in the Commons. The Senate has the constitutional right to amend, but not to increase, money bills sent up from the House of Commons. Any other legislation, public or private, government or private member's, may be introduced first in the Senate, or, if introduced first in the Commons as most major bills are, may be amended by the Senate as it sees fit, though these amendments must subsequently be agreed to by the Commons. The Senate can also reject legislation. These powers are greater than those of the British House of Lords, whose only sanction is now a suspensive or delaying veto.

Despite these formal constitutional powers, the Senate's role traditionally was, at the most, to make minor amendments to legislation passed by the House. Often it would pass bills grudgingly but unchanged in the last days of a session, when a rush of bills from the Commons gave the upper chamber more than it could examine. An unwritten, self-denying convention kept the Senate from interfering with legislation passed by the Commons (Heard 1991, 87–100). As Senator Keith Davey observed, "Although we are not elected, we can block any and all legislation passed by the duly elected House of Commons. Not that we would ever use our powerful veto, given our unelected status. If we did, it would immediately be taken away from us; and so it should be" (Davey 1986, 306). There was, most of the time, little difference between the Senate's activities on bills whether the majority in it was from the government side or not (Heard 1991).

There were some notable exceptions to this habitual docility. In 1875, in its first major legislative confrontation with the Commons, the Senate rejected a bill for the construction of a railway from Esquimault to Nanaimo in British Columbia. In 1913 the Senate defeated the Naval Assistance Bill, arguing that it could not give its assent until the country had given its judgment in an election. These and other public confrontations were the exception, however, and for the most part the Senate either approved bills passed by the Commons with little discussion or made minor amendments.

In his pioneering 1947 book on Canadian government, MacGregor Dawson observed that "Canada is slowly developing some institutions of government which, if they cannot yet be placed in the vestigial class, are in danger of attaining that questionable distinction." The Senate was one of these: "It would be idle to deny that the Senate has not fulfilled the hopes of its founders; and it is well to remember that the hopes of its founders were not excessively high" (Dawson 1970, 282). The Senate, according to Dawson, had "become so sluggish and inert that it seemed capable of performing only the most nominal functions" (279). Its end as an effective component of Parliament seemed imminent. Senate committees performed useful work in revising ill-drafted legislation coming to it from the House of Commons and in making investigations, but these could not justify the costs of the institution (Kunz 1965; MacKay 1963; Franks 1987; O'Neal 1994).

A few observers suggest that the real Senate was something quite different. "Of course one of the clichés is that the Senate is just a bulwark for the rich and their interests," Senator Eugene Forsey complained. "But the journalists, with few honourable exceptions, possess convictions that are above and beyond being shaken by anything so trivial as mere evidence.

Perhaps the saddest thing about it all is that many of those who simply reel off the ancient clichés are on other subjects well informed—clear, logical, and sensible. Is this a case of what the Roman Church calls invincible ignorance?" (Forsey 1990, 168–69). But a more recent study of the Senate's role in defense policy supported the critics. It found that, even including committee work, "Canada's 'upper house' is more of a constitutional anachronism than a legislative assembly" (Sokolsky 1989, 15). Whatever the validity of these received truisms, all was to change after the general election of 1984.

Not Dead Yet: The Senate as Opposition

By the time of the general election of 4 September 1984, the Senate was composed largely of appointees of the Liberal governments which had been in power virtually without interruption since 1963. Of its 99 members, 73 were Liberals, 25 were Conservatives, and 4 were independents. At the same time, the new House of Commons reflected the public's strong rejection of the previous Liberal government: Prime Minister Brian Mulroney's Progressive Conservative government held 211 seats, the largest majority a Canadian government has ever enjoyed, while the Liberals were reduced to 40, with the New Democratic Party at 30, and 1 other.

The conjunction of a Senate dominated by one party and a Commons dominated by another had occurred before in Canadian history, but never so overwhelmingly. This time there was also another crucial difference. John Turner, leader of the opposition in the Commons, announced on October 10 that Allan MacEachen would become opposition leader in the Senate. MacEachen, formerly a very senior Liberal cabinet minister with a reputation as a cunning political tactician, lost neither his cunning nor his ardent partisanship on his elevation to the Senate and to his new role. His appointment as Senate opposition leader began a series of confrontations between the two Houses the like of which had never been seen before, and which continued until 1997.

The Borrowing and Drug Patent Bills

Under a practice that, though it had begun earlier, became much more widespread after 1971, when it was used to handle extremely complex tax legislation, the Senate engaged in "prestudy" of legislation introduced in the Commons by referring the subject matter of legislation to committee before it had been formally passed by the Commons. Previously, the Senate had often been faced with a rush of legislation toward the end of a session and "had almost always dutifully swallowed their pride and passed legislation no matter how late it was received, while complaining of the indignity of being taken for granted" (Dobell 1988). Prestudy had been introduced when the Senate and Commons were dominated by the same party.

Critics of the Senate often ignored prestudy and overlooked the low-key and serious work done in Senate committees before bills had passed the Commons. MacEachen dropped the practice of prestudy, giving the Senate both more prominence and stronger tools for resistance to the Commons. In MacEachen's opinion the Senate is a legislative body, not an advisory one, and should act consecutively with the Commons, not in conjunction with it. To replace prestudy MacEachen proposed reviving the use of joint conferences between representatives of the two chambers to resolve disputes. The Mulroney government rejected this proposal, presumably because they did not wish to encourage the exercise of independent Senate power. This set the stage for serious, prolonged, and continuing disputes between the two chambers.

The first skirmish in the subsequent long-running battle occurred in January 1985, when the upper chamber delayed passage of Bill C-11, a $19.3 billion borrowing bill that had been passed unanimously by the House of Commons. Twelve billion dollars of the total was for the 1985–86 fiscal year, and Liberal senators objected to this "because the government had failed to tell how the money would be spent. It was like a request for a post-dated blank cheque!" (Davey 1986, 315). Bill C-11 was finally passed by the Senate after the tabling of the 1985–86 estimates, and was given royal assent on February 27, 1985, but not before the press had strongly criticized the Senate's actions (Franks 1987, 193). The defense that the Senate was constitutionally entitled to act independently on legislation, even money bills, was given less weight than the argument that the government's finances were properly the business of the Commons, and the Senate's action was seen as mischievous partisan meddling. Heard views the Senate's actions on Bill C-11 sympathetically, noting that it was roundly criticized for delaying the bill because it quite properly "said that Parliament should not approve funds for which the government had not presented any spending plans" (Heard 1991, 93).

Prime Minister Brian Mulroney reacted strongly. On February 28 he let it be known that the federal government was shaping legislation intended to curb some of the powers of the Liberal-controlled Senate. Discussions were already under way with the provinces for a constitutional amendment that would remove the Senate's right to veto money bills adopted by the House. Mulroney said that he had decided to act on Senate reform because a "bunch of Liberal rejects" in the nonelected Senate delayed passage of the borrowing bill for a month after it had been passed without opposition by the House. The Senate, the government claimed, had cost the taxpayers many additional millions because of its obstruction. The government introduced its constitutional resolution to amend the Senate's powers into the Commons in May. It was debated briefly and then allowed to die. The governments of Manitoba and Quebec refused to support this Mulroney proposal, Manitoba because it wanted the Senate abolished, Quebec because it did not recognize the 1982 constitution. Senate reform did not die in the minds of the government, however, and was a recurring theme during the Mulroney years. But because discussions of Senate reform inevitably raise questions of the imaginary Senate as well as the real one, these efforts became part of later cumbersome and disastrously unsuccessful efforts at broader constitutional reform.

Parliament was recalled from its summer adjournment in July 1986 to pass legislation aimed at keeping dangerous offenders behind bars longer. This bill too had been an issue of contention between the two Houses, with the Senate refusing to be a rubber stamp, and making amendments to which the government objected. This minor skirmish was, however, simply a preliminary to a massive battle between Senate and Commons later that year.

In November 1986 Consumer Affairs Minister Harvie Andre introduced legislation in the Commons, Bill C-22, to amend the Drug Patent Act. The amendments were to give the patent holders of brand-name drugs ten years of freedom from competition for most of the products they brought to market in the years to come. The Patent Act, a policy of the previous Liberal government, had encouraged competition by producers of generic or no-name drugs, which could make inexpensive copies of brand-name drugs upon payment of nominal fees to the patent holders. Critics argued that, because the prices of patent drugs would rise, the bill would be more damaging to consumers than the government was prepared to admit. The minister, on the other hand, argued that benefits would include increased spending on research in Canada by the drug companies. The drug companies on this legislation lobbied universities, doctors, provincial governments, and, of course, the various actors in the federal government, often in a lavish manner new to Canada (Robinson 1996).

Bill C-22 had been debated in the House of Commons for nearly ninety hours. It had been studied by a Commons committee that heard hundreds of witnesses in twenty-two separate sessions. Nevertheless, the Senate decided to hold its own hearings on it, and established a committee of five Liberal and three Conservative senators. After three months of intensive work, the committee submitted reports introducing significant amendments to the legislation, including reducing the period of exclusivity from ten to four years, eliminating a proposed Patented Drug Prices Review Board, and increasing the royalty fee from 4 to 14 percent to finance research and development in the Canadian pharmaceutical industry. In its deliberations, the Senate committee divided along party lines, with Conservative senators defending the government and Liberals supporting the proposed amendments.

The government-controlled Commons rejected most of these amendments, and the bill was returned to the upper chamber, where Senate Government Leader Lowell Murray declared, "The moment of truth has arrived for the Senate. It is up to the Senate now to decide whether to exercise its undoubted constitutional right, which has been exercised rarely, if ever, in modern times, to insist on its amendments, or whether the Senate will bow to the will of the elected House" (*Debates*, 2 September 1987, p. 1776). Conservative senators argued that the Senate had reached the limits to its political legitimacy, and that once the Commons had made its voice heard it was time to yield to the will of the lower house. Liberal senators argued that the reasons given by the Commons for not accepting the Senate's amendments deserved further investigation. They were not stonewalling the bill, they claimed. They were encouraged by public demonstrations and protests against the bill, by the lobbying efforts of the generic drug industry, and by provincial departments of health.

The Senate sent the bill to the Standing Committee on Banking, Trade, and Commerce, which was to answer the question of whether there was a possibility of compromise with the Commons and Harvie Andre, the minister responsible. Two months later, on October 21, the committee reported back that Mr. Andre was not willing to compromise or alter any of the fundamental principles of the bill. "I think after the House of Commons has had five votes on [the bill] we've got a little more than a mandate to negotiate," the minister observed, in claiming that the Prices Review Board and the ten-year period of exclusivity were essential and rejecting further changes (*Globe and Mail,* September 3, 1987, A4). In his presentation of the Senate Banking Committee's report, the chairman, Liberal senator Ian Sinclair, quoted Sir John A. Macdonald to the effect that the Senate should never set itself against the deliberate and understood wishes of the people. The wishes of the people on this bill were easy to determine, according to Sinclair. They were apparent in the opinions and evidence presented by various witnesses and briefs and in the reports of the two Senate committees, each of which had concluded that there was no public mandate to pass the bill (*Debates,* 29 October 1987, p. 2095). And they were also evident in the number of public demonstrations and protests held on Parliament Hill.

Conservative senator Jacques Flynn complained that "in this case the Senate, or rather the Liberal majority in the Senate, has tried to use its powers in a spirit of confrontation . . . and partisanship. The background of Bill C-22 illustrates the longest filibuster I have ever seen in my 30 years in Parliament . . . it is a record of time spent to actively debate a bill in this house" (*Debates,* 29 October 1987, p. 2096). The bill bounced back and forth between the two houses until November 19, 1987, when the Liberal senators retreated and allowed it to become law. Most Liberal senators followed the advice of John Turner that the will of the Commons must prevail "at the end of the day" and let the Conservative minority pass the bill in the Senate by a vote of 27 to 3, with 32 Liberals abstaining (*Maclean's,* August 24, 1987, 18–19; November 30, 1987, 19).

The Drug Patent Bill, though the most important of the Senate's acts of opposition to the decisions of the lower house, was far from being the only one during this period. In August 1987 Parliament was again recalled to deal with the Drug Patent Bill and two bills deregulating the transportation industry that Senate committees were considering over the summer. In 1988 a copyright bill and two controversial immigration bills were disputed, on quite reasonable grounds, by the Senate. After a prolonged struggle, the Senate dropped its demands for amendments to the copyright bill, and the immigration bills were passed after the government acceded to amendments demanded by the Senate. The Progressive Conservative government, with its huge majority, could, and did, force legislation through the Commons by using closure and timetabling instruments (Sealey 1995), but the Liberal-dominated Senate had become a much more difficult and contrary obstacle. Prime Minster Mulroney continued persistent but unsuccessful efforts to reach agreement with the provinces on Senate reform.

The Senate and Free Trade

The Senate achieved its greatest importance in history in 1988, when it refused to pass legislation for a free trade deal with the United States. This time Liberal Opposition Leader John Turner reversed the position he had taken on the drug patent bill and asked the Senate to stall the free trade bill until Canadians could vote on the issue. "Call an election and let the people decide," Turner told the prime minister as the Commons passed the legislation under strict closure and timetabling. For his part, Prime Minister Mulroney brushed aside calls for an immediate election and accused the Senate of "hijacking the fundamental rights of the House of Commons" by refusing to pass the legislation. He attacked Turner for abandoning his leadership and handing it over to the unelected Senate. But Turner rejected the suggestion that the Senate and not free trade could become the issue in the next election. "I am the issue," Turner told a press conference. "I have asked the Senators to do this and I will take the responsibility." Senate Liberal Leader Allan MacEachen said he supported the position of Mr. Turner, "and we're working on how to carry through that position." Here, the Senate was following in the tradition of 1913, when it had refused to approve the controversial naval aid bill until the government had won support in a general election. The government at the time was in the fourth year of its mandate, and an election was drawing near in any case.

Trade with the United States has been a perennial issue in Canadian politics. Traditionally the Progressive Conservative Party had opposed free trade, while the Liberals supported it. This time around, the first major proposal for free trade came during the previous Trudeau Liberal government from a Senate committee chaired by Liberal senator George

Van Roggen. A royal commission on the economy and federation established by Liberal prime minister Trudeau also supported free trade. But in the topsy-turvy world of Canadian parties and platforms, the Liberals were now opposed, and the Conservatives were in favor. Turner's first disappointment in this battle came when Senator Van Roggen broke ranks and resigned his chairmanship of the Senate's Foreign Affairs Committee, saying that he supported free trade.

Editorial coverage of Turner's move was mixed, with western newspapers by-and-large being critical and eastern ones laudatory. The *Winnipeg Free Press* called Turner's move "a final gasp by a ruined politician," while the *Calgary Herald* observed that "the man who stayed just long enough for a cup of coffee as prime minister had finally demonstrated his total contempt for the parliamentary tradition of government of the people by the elected representatives of the people." On the other side, the *Toronto Star* said that with "this risky but bold move, Turner has not only shown great personal courage, but also the integrity to insist that this fundamental issue be resolved by Canadians."

On September 15, the Senate gave approval in principle to the free trade bill in a 19 to 0 vote, but only because Liberals unanimously abstained to avoid killing it and to show their support for Turner. The legislation moved to the Senate Foreign Affairs Committee, where it languished until the federal election was called. In the 1988 general election the Mulroney government was returned, though with a much-reduced majority, becoming the first Canadian government to win back-to-back majorities since the Liberals under Prime Minister St. Laurent in 1953. The Liberals stood by their commitment to allow the free trade legislation through if the country supported it in a general election, and free trade became law on December 24, 1988, just in time for Parliament to recess for Christmas and for free trade to come into effect at the beginning of the new year. Randall White accurately describes the mixed reactions to the Senate's role in the free trade issue: "When Brian Mulroney's new Progressive Conservative government came to office, it complained, with at least some justice, of harassment by the continuing Liberal majority in the Senate. . . . On the other hand, there are Canadians who still believe that the unreformed Senate, with its unelected Liberal majority, did indeed live up to its highest responsibilities as a body of sober second thought in 1988, when it helped precipitate a federal election over the Canada-U.S. Free Trade Agreement" (White 1990, 220).

The GST Battle and Others

A $33 billion supply bill became the first subject of contention between the two houses in 1989. The Senate proposed an amendment which implied that the cabinet had acted illegally by passing a governor general's special warrant to spend $6.2 billion on April 1, before Parliament had reconvened.[1] Treasury Board President Robert De Cotret expressed alarm: unless the bill was passed by midnight May 15, the government would have no cash to pay immediate expenses such as Royal Canadian Mounted Police wages, government suppliers, and veterans' pensions. But Liberal senators countered by criticizing the use of special warrants and claiming that they were defending the right of Parliament to approve government spending. They complained that the use of special warrants (the Conservative government had used three in 1989) was a step toward presidential government. On May 17, the Senate backed down and passed the supply bill unamended. It immediately received royal assent.

Senate activism did not go unnoticed, however. In December a spokesman for the National Pensioners and Senior Citizens' Federation, representing 500,000 seniors across the country, urged the still Liberal-dominated Senate to block a bill that would allow the federal government to tax back (claw back) old-age pensions from well-off seniors. The Conservative majority in the Commons had limited final debate on this contentious bill to two days and rejected amendments.

The year 1990 was more contentious. The problems began in December 1989, when the Senate established a special committee to consider amendments to the Unemployment Insurance Act, Bill C-21. These amendments were designed to curtail expenditures on unemployment insurance through several provisions affecting the eligibility of seasonal workers, training programs, and the shifting financing of the program toward employers and employees. The government had forced the bill through the Commons. Senator MacEachen, not entirely innocently, alerted his colleagues to the possibility that, if senators were properly to complete their examination of the bill, it would take longer than the government hoped. He said he wanted to avoid a situation of crisis or confrontation that might arise if the Commons suspected that the Senate was using delay as an instrument to block, slow, or frustrate the bill. The Senate committee asked for permission to meet during sittings of the Senate because pressure was coming from government members, and it did not want to be accused of delaying the legislation. Prime Minister Mulroney was having none of these professions of good faith, and denounced the Liberal majority in the Senate (Stewart 1989).

The Senate committee heard from groups that had been denied the opportunity to testify before the Commons committee. Senator Mac-Eachen, stating a principle to which the Senate had only paid lip service during much of its history, argued the need for a thorough and independent review of the legislation: "If we were to accept the work of the House of Commons, if we were to take the view that we have received the bill now from the House of Commons, that they have done the work, then it would question very seriously the validity of the Senate. We are supposed to do our own work when the bill comes here, and if we cannot do that then we should not put up the pretence—if it is a pretence—that we are a chamber of sober second thought" (*Debates*, 19 December 1989, p. 938). Since many of the changes being urged on the Senate involved increasing appropriations, the Senate's power to make amendments was limited. Conservative senators expressed frustration that the bill was being delayed, while an "angry" prime minister urged the committee to speed passage of the bill (Toulin 1989).

The battle over unemployment insurance took many curious twists, including the passage by the Senate of a bill inspired by MacEachen, S-12 (the *S* indicates that it was first introduced in the Senate rather than the Commons, where it would have been designated by a *C*), in which money provisions were "red-lettered," an arcane and archaic procedure which involved leaving money clauses in red ink, and not as part of the provisions actually passed. The Senate special committee reported that it agreed:

with the great majority of witnesses before it who condemned the changes to the entrance requirement and benefit structure. The motivation behind these changes appears to be not simply to divert funds to new training programs, but to promote what one witness euphemistically described as, the 'adhesion' of workers to their jobs. The government would seem to believe that many of the unemployed are in a position of their own making, and that, with proper 'incentives,' they would find work or remain in their jobs longer. This, of course, fails to recognize that what is needed is jobs, not incentives to find jobs, or training for jobs that simply do not exist. (Third Report, *Debates*, 14 February 1990, pp. 1146-47)

Regardless of its other merits, this report was a thinly disguised commentary on Mulroney's earlier election promise of "jobs, jobs, jobs." The committee's recommendations were criticized by Conservative senators for containing money provisions, and the government continued this criticism in the Commons. "We're not going to have this unelected coterie of Trudeauites decide what the policy of Canada is to be in 1990," declared John Crosbie, a senior minister in the Mulroney government (Delacourt 1990). The government house leader in the Commons, Doug Lewis, accused the Senate of "harassment."

Senator MacEachen defended the committee's report by expressing concern about the attitude of the government. He was "somewhat worried that the Minister [Employment Minister Barbara McDougall], by this bill, has taken a somewhat—maybe bureaucratic, maybe mechanical approach to peoples' problems, namely unemployment and unemployment insurance. . . . We attempted to understand the problems of the Government, and, as well, those of the unemployed. It is in that spirit that we have made the amendments" (*Debates,* 20 February 1996, p. 1224).

Unquestionably, ideological differences between senators appointed by the Trudeau Liberal government and the Mulroney Conservatives underlay much of this battle over unemployment insurance. At the same time, the Mulroney government was trying to come to terms with both a massive deficit in current spending and the burgeoning public debt; the Liberal Chrétien government, which succeeded it, had to deal with the same problems and was, if anything, harsher in its reductions to spending on social programs. But these ideological concerns were mixed with a strong dose of partisanship, and subsequently the Liberals in the Senate under Jean Chrétien's Liberal government have shown no comparable zeal for disputing the government's cuts to welfare, unemployment insurance, and other social programs. The Senate's opportunities to dispute cuts, like those of the Commons, were somewhat limited, because the cuts came to Parliament in the form of appropriations in Supply, which Parliament cannot unilaterally increase, rather than in the form of legislation, as the cuts of the Mulroney government had done. This contributed to the lack of parliamentary discussion of these very important changes.

Meanwhile, two other important items of business from the Commons were occupying the Senate. In May 1990 legislation requiring women to obtain the consent of a single doctor for abortion, and retaining other abortions as crimes within the criminal code, narrowly passed the Commons in one of its rare "free votes," 140 to 131. This abortion bill was a compromise. After the Supreme Court had declared the then-existing legislation unconstitutional, the government had proposed five choices to the Commons, ranging from virtually free access to abortion at one end to strict limitation and control at the other. In free votes, the Commons had rejected each of the options. Opinions on abortion were too polarized to allow the compromises and coalitions necessary for a majority to form (Flanagan 1997). Ardent antiabortionists in the Liberal and Conservative ranks, as well as pro-choicers led by the New Democrats, had campaigned vigorously against the government's bill and hoped to form an alliance to scuttle it. But cabinet ministers solidly supported the legislation and managed to hold the loyalty of enough Conservative backbenchers to push it through the Commons. As it passed from Commons to Senate, lobby groups on both sides of the issue said they would turn their attention to the upper chamber.

Even as the Senate was battling the government on unemployment insurance, and the contentious abortion issue went to the upper chamber, a third issue, far more central to the government's economic and fiscal policies, had been the major issue facing the Commons. This was the Goods and Services Tax (GST)—a measure designed to replace outdated taxes on manufacturing with a tax of the sort economists like but taxpayers detest, in effect a general sales tax, or tax on consumption. On April 10, 1990, the Conservative government, after nine months of rancorous debate and committee hearings, forced the GST bill through the Commons. It too went to the Senate, where Liberal senator Sidney Buckwold, chairman of the Senate Banking Committee, said they would probably hold cross-country hearings on it. On June 27 Parliament adjourned for the summer. Three major bills—the 7 percent GST, abortion, and unemployment insurance—were left in the Liberal-dominated Senate with no hope of becoming law before the fall. When Parliament reconvened, the battles recommenced. On September 25 the Senate Banking Committee, still Liberal dominated, recommended that the GST be scrapped, and despite a Conservative filibuster the committee's report was tabled the following day.

Prime Minister Mulroney took drastic and unprecedented action. On September 27, unfazed by rising public furor against the new tax, he enlarged the Senate by eight members, claiming that the Liberal senators were undermining the principle of responsible government by blocking the GST and other bills. The move raised the number of senators to 112, giving the Conservatives a majority which would eventually get the stalled GST and other bills moving. He had already added fifteen Tory senators to fill vacancies since August. And over the years since his government was first elected in 1984, time, retirement, and attrition had reduced the Liberal majority in the upper chamber to the point where the appointment of eight new Conservative senators would tilt the balance.

In stacking the Senate, Mulroney took advantage of a never before used article in the 1867 Constitution Act, section 26: "If at any time on the Recommendation of the Governor General the Queen thinks fit to direct that Four or Eight Members be added to the Senate, the Governor General may by Summons to Four or Eight qualified Persons (as the Case may be), representing equally the Four Divisions of Canada, add to the Senate accordingly." No new senators could be appointed until the Senate returned to its membership quota of twenty-four for the relevant region. Only once before, in 1873, had a Canadian government attempted to use this provision, and then the British Colonial Secretary, observing that the Senate had not yet defeated Commons business, refused to advise Queen Victoria to approve the additional appointments. This time Queen Elizabeth granted approval.

Mulroney's decision to "swamp" the Senate drew angry responses from opposition leaders and most of the provinces. British Columbia and Alberta challenged it in the courts. But "it seems clear that the original intent of section 26 was to provide a 'deadlock' mechanism in the event of an irreconcilable clash of wills between the two Chambers," a study by the Library of Parliament had observed the previous month, and "the fact that no such clash occurred in the first 120 years after Confederation invalidates neither the purpose nor the use of section 26 in the appropriate circumstances" (Dunsmuir 1990). This time there was a serious deadlock between the two houses, and the Mulroney government's claim that these were "appropriate circumstances" was upheld by the courts. The Conservatives now, for the first time since they had come into power, enjoyed the support of a majority in the Senate.

The battle over the GST was not yet over, however. Liberal senators, taking advantage of procedural rules much less stringent than those in the Commons, began a filibuster, which at times degenerated into rowdy name calling and whistle blowing. There were renewed calls for Senate reform in the press. Mulroney accused the Liberal senators of "legislative terrorism." By October 24 the Liberal Party had sunk below the New Democrats, the perennial third party, in the polls, and Liberal Leader Jean

Chrétien admitted that the hijinks of Liberal senators in fighting the GST may have contributed to the Party's drop in support. An apparent truce negotiated between Liberals and Conservatives in the Senate to timetable the GST and other bills began to unravel, but on October 25 the GST cleared a major hurdle when the Conservatives, aided by three independents, defeated the Senate committee report calling for the bill to be killed.

A *Globe and Mail*–CBC poll found that 75 percent of Canadians remained opposed to the GST, and this massive rejection was matched by opposition to Mulroney's stacking the Senate to get it passed. Still, representatives of seventeen business groups called on the Liberal senators to stop their opposition so that the GST could be implemented as planned by January 1. The Senate finally passed the bill on December 13, and it was given royal assent the following Monday, the Liberals having succeeded in one last delay by adjourning for the weekend before assent could be given the Friday before. The Senate sat over the Christmas break to catch up on the backlog of work, including the unemployment insurance bill, which had accumulated during the prolonged battle over the GST.

In June 1991 the Conservative majority in the Senate ensured passage of a package of new rules that gave the government more control over the Senate agenda and reduced the opportunities for filibustering and other delaying tactics (Robertson 1991). The Liberal senators had boycotted the committee that drafted the rules. These were the first real changes to Senate procedure since 1906. Until the post-1984 confrontations, the Senate had traditionally operated on a "gentlemanly" basis; its procedural rules had not been "adhered to with any degree of rigidity and a considerable portion of the Senate's business [was] in fact conducted under suspended rules" (Kuntz 1965). To Liberal senator Royce Frith, "The emasculating surgery was completed. The House of Commons had already been taken care of by further amendments to its rules. No worry about effective opposition there. Now the Senate, having shown what was possible under its rules by its fight against the GST had [been] taken care of. The only effective opposition left to the government is the media, and perhaps academia, but neither of them seems to have noticed. Or if they have, they don't care" (Frith 1990, 109–10).

But that was not the end of the Conservative government's difficulties with the upper chamber. On January 31, 1991, the controversial abortion bill came to a vote. The result was an unusual tie, 43 to 43. Cheers went up on both sides of the chamber when the acting speaker explained that the tie meant defeat of the bill. It had been a free vote, but most Conservatives had voted for it, most Liberals against. Key to the government's defeat was the defection of Senator Pat Carney, a former Conservative cabinet minister who had been expected to support the government. Government Senate Leader Lowell Murray said that it would be some time before the government tried again to fill the void left three years earlier when the Supreme Court of Canada had thrown out the earlier law, and this was echoed by Justice Minister Campbell's observation that this was the government's best shot at achieving an acceptable compromise that could pass the constitutional test, and they would be hard pressed to find an alternative.

Defections from the government side caused the defeat of another item of Conservative legislation in 1993. This was an act to implement provisions of the budget that proposed reducing the number of government agencies by eliminating some, amalgamating others. Contention focused on the proposal to amalgamate the Canada Council, which nurtures cultural and artistic activities, with the Social Sciences and Humanities Research Council (SSHRC), a grant-giving agency that administers funds for research and scholarship, and the international programs of the Department of External Affairs. Both the arts groups and the academic community objected to the amalgamation. The two granting agencies had been separated in 1978 because of their different concerns and needs. Discussion in the Senate was acrimonious, as often happened after the trauma of the GST battle. Some senators opposed to the bill pointed out that it was a cosmetic change that would generate no savings, while others argued that it was flawed in substance and political in purpose. Senator Frith proposed that the bill be divided into two, so that the noncontentious issues could be passed while the Canada Council–SSHRC merger was examined more closely, but the Conservative majority defeated this motion.

The chairman of the Senate Committee on National Finance, Liberal senator H. A. Olson, reported on May 27 that his committee had heard from over thirty groups of witnesses, many of whom had been refused appearance before the Commons committee. Most testimony was critical of the merger. Witnesses argued that the distinct voices of the arts and social sciences and humanities research communities would be lost. Conservative senator Finlay MacDonald agreed with these concerns: "The opposition to this legislation is heartfelt, intelligent and of a very non-partisan stripe. This is by no means frivolous or ideological opposition. The appeals to the Government have been extremely reasonable, patient, and circumspect. That kind of democratic intervention should be recognized and applauded, not ignored" (*Debates*, 31 May 1993, p. 3315).

He offered a spirited defense of the Senate's traditional role:

> There is a sufficient amount of confusion, incredulity, and opposition to justify the government to say, 'Okay, we will pause. We will have a second look.' In that way, they would win public confidence, and that is the way to win an election. If ever there was an opportunity, a duty, or a responsibility for the Senate of Canada to make a small contribution to political stability by acting as a counterweight to the House of Commons, today is one day we should reflect upon the reason for our existence. There would be no use for a Senate, if it did not exercise, when it thought proper, the right of opposing or amending or postponing the legislation of the House of Commons. We would be of no value at all, if we were a mere chamber for registering the decrees of the lower house. (*Debates*, 3 June 1993, p. 3368)

The government refused to accept Senator MacDonald's amendment to remove the merger from the bill. But to its surprise, the vote in the Senate on June 10 was a tie, resulting in defeat of the entire bill. While Senator MacDonald had worked quietly to gain the support of four other Tory senators in voting against it, and others in abstaining, the government whip had not done his homework. He had underestimated the strength of the revolt, and as a result the entire omnibus bill was lost. A reporter claimed that many other senators would have voted against the bill except that it would have angered Prime Minister Mulroney, "who values loyalty more than independence. . . . As many as a dozen other Tory senators wanted to vote against C-93, but refused to because they would have angered Mulroney" (Cohen 1993).

This important event showed once again that senators are less vulnerable to pressure from party whips than are members of the House of Commons, and senators have correspondingly greater freedom to dissent from party positions. Several senators on the government side asserted their independence, and because the sanctions that the government can impose on them are much weaker than those to which MPs are liable, they could act on the basis of their studies and beliefs and defeat their own government's legislation. The period of Conservative rule was draw-ing to a close. Prime Minister Mulroney resigned to be replaced by Kim Campbell, who called a national election for October 25. The Progressive Conservative government received the most resounding defeat of any government in Canadian history in this election, with all its sitting mem-bers but one being defeated, and this member, Jean Charest, being joined by only one other new member. The Liberals now formed a massive majority with 172 seats, while the New Democratic Party, reduced to 9 members, like the Conservatives lost their status as a recognized party in Parliament.

This sweeping public rejection of the Progressive Conservative govern-ment proves that they must have done a lot of things wrong. The GST was one of these, and Liberal Leader Jean Chrétien made an election promise, which he later found he could not honor, to get rid of it. Without doubt the Senate's obstruction, public hearings, airing of differing viewpoints, and constant questioning of government policies contributed to the de-feat. But how much, it is impossible to say. The Senate, far from being "so sluggish and inert that it seemed capable of performing only the most nominal functions," as Dawson had described it, was lively and influential during the Mulroney years. And contrary to Senator Davey's views, the unelected Senate had used its powerful veto more than once. Senate ob-struction had led Prime Minister Mulroney to demand not once but many times that the Senate be reformed. But Senate reform got lost in the broader and unsuccessful efforts at constitutional amendment.

For much of this period, the Senate was the more interesting house, though the lack of media coverage obscured this from the general public. Parliamentary government, particularly when the party lines and disci-pline over the private member are as rigid as they are in Canada, requires checks on the government through a vigorous opposition. The rules of the House of Commons had changed enough by 1998 that the capacity of the opposition to delay, to expose faults, and to instigate public discussion on contentious issues had been drastically curtailed. The time spent on debate of each item of legislation in the chamber itself was reduced (Sealey 1995), and committee investigation became more virulent, partisan, and superficial than before (Franks 1997).

In this 1984–93 period the Senate was, in many ways, the real focus of opposition to the government. On many crucial issues, both debate and committee investigation in the upper chamber were freer, more extensive, and more interesting than in the lower house. The Senate fulfilled its role as a chamber of sober second thought. On the other hand, much (though certainly not all) of the motivation for its scrutiny of government proposals came from partisan considerations, and the Senate found itself in the position of receiving more criticism for its partisanship and the method of appointing senators than it did praise for its investigations and arguments on principle. The practice of exclusive prime ministerial control over appointment to the Senate, and the perceived public image of the Senate as a refuge for superannuated party workhorses and has-beens, prevented its very good work from receiving the attention and support it deserved.

The Senate under Prime Minister Chrétien

Like Brian Mulroney before him, Prime Minister Jean Chrétien was faced with a Senate whose majority was from the opposition, though this time the Senate majority party was backed by only two members in the Commons. But there was an important difference between 1993 and 1984. The MacEachen Liberal senators had been part of the expansion of government, especially of social programs, during the sixties and seventies. They had been ideologically on the opposite side of the fence from the Mulroney Conservative government, and their battles with the Commons had always mixed in with partisanship a measure of fundamental disagreement over the role of government and the vision of the good society. The new Chrétien Liberal government placed a much higher emphasis on reducing government expenditures than had even the Mulroney Conservatives. Because many of the reductions had to come from the biggest items of expenditure, the social programs, the Chrétien government was, on this score, in practice at least as "conservative" as the Mulroney government, and arguably more so. Consequently, on the key issue of reductions to major social programs, the Conservative majority in the Senate was in sympathy with the actual, if not professed, policies of the Chrétien government. Further, financial constraints meant less major legislation reached the Senate from the Commons.

The opposition in the House of Commons was vastly different from previous parliaments. The *Bloc Québécois,* a separatist party exclusively drawn from Quebec, became Her Majesty's Loyal Opposition with 52 seats, while the Reform Party, western-based and more to the right politically than the Progressive Conservatives, nearly matched them in size. In the sessions that followed, the *Bloc* proved a perceptive and intelligent critic of the Chrétien government's cuts to social and cultural programs. Unfortunately, the fact that they spoke almost entirely in French, and retained an aura of being anti-Canada, meant that the English media largely ignored them. Canadians outside Quebec mistrusted them, even when the *Bloc* attempted to speak on behalf of a broad spectrum of Canadians. All the members but one of the Reform caucus were new to Parliament, and the party had come to Parliament with a program deeply critical of how government and Parliament operated. The Reform Party did not have much success in making its mark on Parliament or winning public support. With the *Bloc* and Reform parties laboring under these handicaps, the Commons after 1993 did not have an effective opposition.

John Lynch-Staunton, the Conservatives' new Senate leader, at first proposed a much less ambitious role for the Senate than the MacEachen Liberals, saying that the Conservative senators would not use the upper chamber as a government-in-exile to defeat legislation, but would do what they could to change bills they felt to be flawed. Jean Charest, the interim Tory Leader, and the only sitting member of his party to be returned to the House, agreed that there were limits to how far the party could push its agenda in the upper house: "The bottom line is that the House of Commons makes decisions." Nevertheless, some Conservative senators, observing the weakness of the opposition in the Commons, concluded they had to become the real opposition.

The distribution of seats in the House of Commons, and the revision of the boundaries of electoral districts, have always been thorny issues in Canadian politics, not only because governments, and for that matter sitting members in general, tend to want to ensure that both are carried out so that their chances of reelection are preserved if not improved, but also because Canada, as a growing country, experiences large demographic changes that affect the size of ridings. The process of redistribution following the 1991 national census was well under way by 1994, with commissions in each province, established by the Mulroney government, managing the process. Partly under pressure from the substantial number of Liberal members who were apprehensive over the possible outcomes, the Liberal government introduced a bill to suspend and amend the process. This delay would have meant that redistribution would likely be delayed until after the next election, due in 1997 or 1998.

In April 1994 the Conservative Senate majority said they would challenge the Liberal government's bill. After a long and vigorous fight in the Senate, the objections of senators forced the government to abandon its legislation. Redistribution then proceeded under the old act. Many members of Parliament had concerns about the proposed changes to their districts. The Commons's committee on procedure held hearings at which these and other concerns were expressed, and in the end, some modifications were made to boundaries proposed by the various provincial commissions. The new boundaries were in place before the general election of June 1997, allowing the distribution of seats and the electoral map to reflect demographic changes recorded in the 1991 census. A majority of members were satisfied with the new district boundaries, with complaints largely centered in Ontario, where the demographic changes and consequent readjustments had been greatest, and in New Brunswick, where the redistribution commission appeared to be somewhat sympathetic to Conservative concerns. The unelected Senate in this instance found itself in the curious position of opposing both the government and the House of Commons in defending the principles of political equality of citizens.

Receiving more notoriety was the issue of privatization of Toronto's Pearson International Airport, the largest and busiest airport in Canada. The Conservative government had approved a contract to privatize Pearson Airport in its last months, just before the 1993 election. By this time, the Mulroney government had become so tainted with allegations of patronage that, regardless of whether this contract made good business sense and had been awarded in a fair manner, suspicions of patronage were strong. The airport deal had become a symbol of the partisanship and influence of lobbyists that voters connected with the Mulroney regime, and Jean Chrétien had made an election promise to scrap it. On July 7, 1994, Conservative senators started a showdown with the new Liberal government by blocking a bill passed by the Commons that would have killed the privatization deal. The Tories used their majority in the Senate to delete clauses of the bill which stripped the Pearson Development Corporation, the winners of the contract, of the right to go to court to sue the government for more compensation than the $30 million provided by the bill. Tory senators argued that the bill violated the corporation's constitutional rights. The Liberals claimed that the Tories were trying to protect their friends who had signed the contract.

In September, Transport Minister Doug Young escalated this confrontation between the houses. "Tory Senators don't want us to settle for out-of-pocket and reasonable expenses," he told the House Commons (*Debates,* 28 September 1994, p. 6268), declaring that the bill would go back to the Senate as it was. He charged that the Pearson Development consortium wanted to sting the Canadian public for over $400 million. A spokesman for the consortium claimed that they were actually only claiming $173 million in compensation. In December the Liberal government accepted some of the changes demanded by the Senate, and increased the compensation they were willing to pay to $80 million, but still included the prohibition against suit for lost profits. Conservative senators were not satisfied, however, and in May 1995 the Liberal government reluctantly agreed to allow the Senate to hold an inquiry into the Pearson Airport deal. When the session prorogued in February 1996, the Senate and Commons remained deadlocked over the bill.

Early in the new session the Liberal government introduced a bill identical to the one that had died at prorogation. But on June 19, the Senate defeated this bill. The Liberals at the time held one more Senate seat than the Conservatives, but illness and absence, and the key defection of one Liberal senator to the Tory side created a tie vote, 48 to 48, the Senate's third tie on important legislation in five years, and caused the defeat. Transport Minister David Anderson said that he was determined to protect taxpayers from footing the bill for "millions of dollars of unearned and undeserved profits in an unacceptable deal," and would not rule out any options, including stacking the Senate with more government supporters, as Mulroney had to get the GST passed. Within a few weeks the government and the Pearson Development Corporation settled on compensation far lower than the many hundreds of millions that had been rumored, though allegations persisted of hidden benefits.

This Pearson Airport bill was unusual, not only in that it was introduced by the government to honor an election commitment but also in that it was highly controversial and based on dubious legal and commercial principles. In the end it was defeated by the defection of senators from the government's own side.

These were by no means the only bills that the Senate delayed. A major revamping of unemployment insurance and a new transportation act died in the Senate at the 1996 prorogation. The Senate also was accused of dragging its feet on a constitutional amendment on secularizing schools in Newfoundland, on amendments to the copyright act, on a child support bill, and on a sales tax law designed to replace the GST in three maritime provinces. Many of the Senate's concerns over these bills were reasonable and deserved consideration on their own merits. But these merits got drowned in the flood of criticism of an unelected Senate thwarting the will of the elected House of Commons. In April 1997 Prime Minister Chrétien appointed two women to the Senate, both strong Liberal supporters, giving the government a clear majority in the upper chamber. However, the era of Tory obstruction was not entirely at an end.

When Parliament was dissolved for the June election, many bills passed by the Commons remained unpassed by the Senate. A deal between Conservative senators and the government allowed some bills, including antigang legislation, a ban on the gasoline additive MMT, changes to the Income Tax Act, the Canada-Chile free trade agreement, an antitobacco advertising law, and two budget bills, to pass and receive royal assent. Left unpassed by the House of Commons were many other important bills dealing with endangered species, an Environmental Protection Act, amendments to the Canada Labour Code, and a bill to hive off Canadian ports and "commercialize" the St. Lawrence Seaway, amendments to the Competition Act, and many other issues. Almost all of this backlog was caused by the government's haste in calling the election. But it was the Senate, not the government, that was blamed by the media for failing to pass these bills.

The Senate and the Legislative Process

The least that can be said about the Senate since 1984 is that it transformed its role from what was previously accepted understanding, and defied most of the previous norms and unwritten rules governing its behavior. It became an intensely partisan chamber, and in many ways was a more effective opposition to the government than the House of Commons was. The Senate precipitated an election by refusing to pass the free trade bill, and though the Senate had done this before, in 1913, it was nevertheless a striking deviation from its behavior in the seven decades between then and 1984. It rejected many government bills. It protracted arguments with the Commons over others. It obstructed the important GST legislation to the point that the prime minister had to resort to a previously unused clause of the 1867 British North America Act of the British Parliament (Canada's founding statute) to create a Senate majority of supporters.

Senator Keith Davey's view that the Senate would not use its "powerful veto, given our unelected status," seemed by 1993 like a remark from another age, about a quite different Canadian Senate. The Senate left far behind its image as a sleepy pasture for retired party workhorses. Nor was it the lobby within protecting the rights of privilege and wealth. For the nine-year period of the Mulroney government the Senate was a voice in favor of social programs and active government redistribution of wealth. Only in the Pearson Airport affair, in the succeeding Chrétien administration, could it be argued that the Senate, now dominated by Conservative Mulroney appointees, acted as the lobby within. But even on this issue there were questions of fairness and legality that were at least as important as business lobby concerns.

Since 1993, and even more so since the Liberals regained their majority in the Senate in 1997, the period of Senate activism seems to be over, and the Senate for the most part has reverted to its traditional less visible and less overtly partisan form of behavior. However, this period of Senate activism after 1984 poses important and disturbing questions about the legislative process and responsible parliamentary democracy in Canada. In particular, it highlights the problems of and the legitimacy of a powerful Senate appointed exclusively by the prime minister. Two factors have masked this incompatibility for most of Canada's history. First, the Senate has normally not been as visibly activist and confrontational as it was under Senator MacEachen. Second, for most of its history Canada has been governed by long-serving government parties—in the nineteenth century the Conservatives, in this century the Liberals—and as a result, most of the time the party with a majority in the House of Commons has also had a majority in the Senate. The reasons for the post-1984 confrontations lie in the 1984 election of a Conservative government with a massive majority, after virtually uninterrupted Liberal rule since 1963. If Canada were to have more frequent changes of government in the future, the likelihood of more confrontations between the two houses, like those seen in the 1984–97 period, would increase. This in itself suggests that some sort of Senate reform is necessary.

In the Canadian system of responsible parliamentary government, the crucial control over the use of power is that the government must enjoy the support of a majority in the elected House of Commons. In practice this support is ensured by government control of the majority party in the Commons. The key agent in making accountability and responsibility to Parliament work is not the individual members of Parliament, for almost without exception they vote according to their party's wishes, but Her Majesty's Loyal Opposition, to whom falls the task of criticizing and debating the government's proposals, and of presenting themselves as a credible alternative to the government, so that they in turn will win an election and replace the governing party in power, as happened in the general elections of 1984 and 1993.

Effective parliamentary democracy demands both an opposition that can present itself as a credible alternative to the government, and parliamentary processes that enable the opposition to criticize government policies effectively and hold the government accountable for its stewardship. These core activities are highly partisan in nature, and their legitimacy derives from their support through the democratic election of members to the Commons. The Senate is appointed, not elected. For most of its history it has been largely non-partisan in its approach to government business and at best peripheral to the core democratic processes. After 1984 it acted in such a way that it appears to have a new and more influential position as both a legitimate opposition and as a voice of the people.

The bulk of the battles between Senate and government, though not all, pitched a majority of one party in the Senate against a majority of the other party in the Commons. Partisanship was a huge motivating factor. Liberal senator Jacques Hebert, a strong supporter of the Trudeau government's social programs, during the contest over the Mulroney government's unemployment insurance reforms, remonstrated over claims of partisanship: "I was disappointed that in her speech in the House of Commons the minister accused us of political theatrics and of playing games. She said that because of our political games it was difficult to believe that our amendments were a sincere attempt to improve this bill.

I hope that we can convince the minister that, indeed, we are serious and sincere in our attempts to improve the bill, and that we do not want simply to defeat it, as we have been requested to on many occasions" (*Debates*, May 16, 1990, p. 1639). No doubt Senator Hebert and many of his colleagues, like many other Canadians, felt that the bill needed improvement, and that the improvements they would like to see were either complete rejection of the bill or a drastic reversal of its fundamental policies and intent. Hebert's own sincerely felt ideological convictions would have led him to this conclusion. But the traditional role of the Senate has not been to alter the main thrust of legislation. Rather it has been what is termed "technical amendments," improving the clarity and wording of bills without affecting policies.

What the MacEachen-inspired Senate Liberal leadership did was replace the technical with an ideological thrust. Liberal senators no doubt were sincere, but they were also, despite what Hebert and others claimed, highly partisan. So also was the Conservative-dominated Senate's opposition to the Chrétien government's legislation restricting compensation for cancellation of the Pearson International Airport development contract. On the GST issue, the partisan motivation dominated. Some sort of tax like that was necessary, as the Chrétien government later found when it discovered that it could not abolish the tax. The quiescence of the Liberal senators when faced with cuts to social programs by the Chrétien government reinforces the conclusion of partisanship.

The House of Commons is supposed to be the battleground between the parties. Was the Senate reinforcing its allies in the Commons, or did it see itself as replacing the Commons? Both views have some validity. When John Turner explicitly requested Liberal senators to obstruct the free trade legislation until a general election could be called, he was asking Liberal senators to be the allies of the Liberal Party in the Commons in its contest with the Mulroney Conservative government. But much of the time, although the battles the Senate fought repeated arguments heard in the Commons, senators like Hebert emphasized the "justice" of their arguments rather than their partisan content. The senators often claimed to be acting independently of the Commons. Sometimes they argued that they had to do this because the Commons itself lacked an effective opposition or because opposition was muzzled in the Commons.

Senator Frith defended the Senate's activist role by arguing that government control over the Commons had reached the point where the lower House was ineffective:

> In Canada democracy has become an illusion. In reality Canadians are ruled by one person. The Parliament of Canada has become nothing more than a vehicle for the election of a new despotic government in cycles of four or five years. . . . The resulting totalitarian system has evolved in a most remarkable manner: no armed revolution or military coup was required. It has sneaked up on us because Parliament has been doing nothing to stop it from doing so. Indeed, Parliament has been encouraging its own evolution into impotency by quietly lying down and holding still for a slow and painful emasculation process, a process masquerading as the 'streamlining' of the parliamentary system. The objective of all streamlining is to increase speed by eliminating resistance. When applied to the parliamentary process it means changing the rules so as to reduce Parliament's resistance and thus increase the government's speed in having its own way. And in our system the word government now means Prime Minister. . . .
>
> So successive governments have found Parliament, and the need to listen to parliamentarians, a damned nuisance. And governments have been able to persuade the media and electorate that that is just what Parliament is—a damned nuisance. Especially when parliamentarians went 'too far' in partisan resistance to 'efficient' government. (Frith 1990, 7, 10)

There is more than a little truth to Frith's contention. By 1990 the Mulroney government had used closure and timetabling in advance more times than all previous Canadian governments (Sealey 1995). They limited debate, even on major bills, to twenty hours. The opposition was no longer able to delay and argue to the point that a headstrong government could be slowed down and forced to listen to criticism.

Parliamentary government is as much about accommodating minorities as allowing majorities to have their way. The Commons was no longer working in a way that allowed these slow processes of vision and revision to work. In the last analysis, this heavy-handed domination of Commons business did not help the Mulroney government. No other Canadian government has by the measure of electoral outcomes failed so drastically to mobilize consent for its programs. A close connection exists between the Mulroney government's excessive limiting of Commons debate and its failure to win support for its policies from the general public. Good government needs a strong opposition. This the Canadian parliamentary system has not always provided, whether because of government domination, as in the Mulroney period, or electoral fortunes, as in the Chrétien. But an appointed Senate is an unlikely and unconvincing remedy for this deficiency.

Much of the time, senators defended their activism by saying that they were responding to public opinion as expressed by witnesses before committees, in letters and phone calls, or in public opinion polls. The government, they claimed, was at fault in not heeding these voices. This argument must be rejected. Governance involves making unpleasant as well as pleasant decisions, and the only true test of public opinion is its expression in a general election on the aggregated performance of the government during its tenure in office since the previous election. Senator MacEachen had it right when, as the final vote on the drug patent bill approached, he told the Senate, "Defeating the bill would relieve the government of its commitments, which it steadfastly refused to put into legislation, to provide additional jobs, investment in research, and to safeguard the population from the harm arising from future increases in drug prices. These are the burdens of government. The defeat of the bill today could become a victory for the government. . . . It is much more appropriate that the government take the responsibility for the impact of the legislation rather than that the Senate should do so" (*Debates*, November 19, 1987, p. 2224). In the last analysis the elected government, not the appointed Senate, must be responsible. Only a government responsible to the House of Commons can be held accountable by the electorate. In 1988 the electorate disagreed with the Senate on free trade; in 1993 the electorate supported the Senate on the GST. The Senate was not, and could not be—despite the claims of some senators—a voice of the people confronting an autocratic government. Only the people or their elected representatives can do this.

The activism of the Senate since 1984 offers a cautionary lesson to would-be Senate reformers. Much of the argument for a "Triple-E" Senate—Elected, Effective, and Equal—lies in the claim that it will be nonpartisan and will represent the interests of provinces rather than parties. But if an appointed Senate not accountable to the voters can act in as partisan a manner as the present Senate, then there is not much hope that an elected Senate will be any less partisan. The party organizations will be needed to recruit Senate candidates and whip up voter support. Senators will be identified by their party labels, especially if they are elected proportionately from lists. Quite likely, an elected Senate will be as partisan as the Commons. That certainly has been the experience of the Australian Triple-E Senate, which, when its majority differs from that of the lower house, has been more than willing to carry on its share of the party battles and confront the government. The Australian Senate is more the voice of party than of region (Sharman 1987). A Triple-E Senate in Canada is not likely to be different on this score from the Australian.

Concerns over the legitimacy and appropriateness of the appointed Senate in Canada obstructing and defying an elected House of Commons could be alleviated if its powers were to be limited to a suspensive veto of, say, six months. After that time had elapsed, passage of a bill once again by the Commons would be deemed as passage by the Senate as well. This sort of procedure would give the government an opportunity to rethink contentious legislation, muster its forces for a new attempt to win over public opinion, or withdraw gracefully if that path proves advisable. The Senate as well would benefit because it would have more freedom to disagree with the Commons, as would individual senators when they want to diverge from party lines, without these actions causing calamitous results. Less formal power would likely, in the long run, produce a more influential and valuable Senate.

Should It Be Resurrected? Reforming the Canadian Senate

The British magazine of the rural upper classes, *Country Life,* in a recent discussion of the British House of Lords, observed that reform of this venerable institution should not stop at merely abolishing hereditary peerages, for that "would leave an Upper House filled entirely by appointment by prime ministers—the worst of all worlds. There is no other democracy on the planet whose second chamber is filled only by this means" (January 9, 1997). Obviously *Country Life* has never heard of the Canadian Senate, which since its creation in 1867 has lived in this worst of all possible worlds, with all appointments at the discretion of the prime minister.

There have been innumerable proposals for reform of appointment procedures, and at least as many about the functions and powers of the Senate. Senate reform proposes a whole new upper chamber, which bears little if any relationship to the existing Senate. The main concerns of reformers have been, first, to broaden and improve the base for appointment and, second, to identify a useful role for the Senate and give it powers appropriate to this role. The Canadian Senate was originally conceived, somewhat like the American, to be a forum for the representation of regional interests in federal politics. But from early on, regional and provincial interests were more powerfully represented in the Canadian cabinet than the Senate. Since the Second World War, with the growth of government and the extension of the social safety net, which involve the two levels of government in both policy formation and execution, executive federalism, in effect negotiations between the provincial and federal governments, has become a major national policy-making forum. Executive federalism bypasses both the House of Commons and the Senate, leaving a problem in integrating the federal Parliament with the increasingly important federal-provincial relations (Olson and Franks 1993; Franks 1998; Smiley 1978; Watts 1988). This lacuna, the absence of a role or forum for Parliament in executive federalism, has been the focus of most recent proposals to alter the role and functions of the Senate.

Senate reform has also become a more acute issue in recent decades because of the pressures that threaten to pull Canada apart. The most powerful of these, the Quebec separatist movement, has little interest in Senate reform. But western alienation, the sense in the western provinces that they are left out of government and that central Canadian interests take advantage of the west, finds a strong expression in proposing a reformed Senate that would give the provinces a greater voice in national policy making, and in particular would prevent the federal Parliament from unilaterally legislating on revenues from the rich resources of western provinces.

A concrete expression of these concerns in terms of Senate reform can be found in the wide-ranging provisions for constitutional amendment in the *Consensus Report on the Constitution* (or Charlottetown Agreement), which was agreed to by the provincial premiers and the federal government in August 1992 (Canada 1992). Though this comprehensive proposal for constitutional reform was later rejected in a nationwide referendum, its proposals for the Senate embody all recent major streams of criticism and reform, and provide a useful pathway for identifying the streams of thought on why and how the Senate should be reformed.

Sections VII to XV of the Charlottetown document deal with the

Senate. Article VII proposes changing the method of appointment from prime ministerial prerogative to election, though with many twists and turns:

> VII. The Constitution should be amended to provide that Senators are elected, either by the population of the provinces and territories of Canada or by the members of their provincial or territorial legislative assemblies.
>
> Federal legislation should govern Senate elections, subject to . . . constitutional provisions requiring that elections take place at the same time as elections to the House of Commons and provisions respecting eligibility and mandate of Senators. Federal legislation would be sufficiently flexible to allow provinces and territories to provide for gender equality in the composition of the Senate.

Three strands of Senate reform coexist in these proposed methods of appointment. First is an Elected Senate. This is one of the three E's of the Triple-E Senate reform proposals of the Alberta government, the western province most concerned with Senate reform because of its perceptions of injustice and discrimination against it by the federal government (Lusztig 1995; McConnell 1988; McCormick 1991; White 1990). The other two E's— Equal provincial representation and an Effective Senate in protecting provincial rights—are addressed later in the Charlottetown document.

This proposal for popular election is qualified, however, by allowing provincial or territorial assemblies to elect senators. This provision was put in at the insistence of the government of Quebec. Because of the domination of elected legislatures by premiers (prime ministers) and cabinets in Canada, election by provincial legislatures would mean, in effect, ratification by the legislature of nominations by the premiers. In other words, instead of powers of senatorial appointment residing in the federal prime minister, they would reside in the premier of whichever provinces chose to exercise this option, in particular the key province of Quebec. This would not, in any real sense, be popular election of senators.

Appointment by provincial governments harkens back to a pre-Triple-E strand for Senate reform based on the German Bundesrat (Burns 1977; Janda 1992), which proposed that the upper chamber should provide direct representation for provincial governments in the federal legislature. In the Bundesrat version of reform, the Senate would become an extension of, or even a focus for, federal-provincial relations and executive federalism, and would be a key part of policy making in the Canadian amalgam of parliamentary and federal institutions.

The third strand, gender equality, was put in at the insistence of the premier of Ontario, Bob Rae, who then headed the first NDP (social democratic) government of Ontario. The Rae government, which was soundly defeated in the Ontario election of 1994, had a strong concern with equity and minority representation. In Senate reform, this was to be translated into two lists of candidates, one male, one female, from which equal numbers would be elected.

The combined result of these different strands would have meant that senators from Quebec and Ontario, the two largest provinces, containing well over half the country's population, would have been selected under different rules from the rest of the country. The divergence from the norm of Quebec would have been the most severe, leaving the French-speaking province in this, as in many other areas, a "province not like the others."

Articles VIII and IX dealt with composition and equality. Article VIII dictated that "The Senate should initially total 62 Senators and should be composed of six Senators from each province and one Senator from each territory," while Article IX proposed that Canada's aboriginal peoples should be guaranteed Senate representation. Equality of the provinces in Senate representation was thus to be enshrined in the constitution. The model here was the United States and, to a lesser extent, Australia. At least one provincial premier, Clyde Wells of Newfoundland, a strong proponent of the Triple-E Senate, believed that upper chambers throughout the world were based upon equal representation of the second level of government. The examples of countries like India or Germany, where the number of members of the upper house varies with the population of the state or province, were ignored by Wells and other proponents of equality. The vast differences between Canadian provinces and the American states were also ignored. Canada has only ten provinces, giving each one much more prominence than any of the fifty American states. The smallest province, Prince Edward Island, has roughly 1 percent of the population of the largest, Ontario. Article IX would have given each citizen of Prince Edward Island one hundred times the influence of citizens of Ontario in the revitalized Senate.

Quebec also presented particular problems in terms of equality. Quebec is clearly different from the other provinces, with its majority French-speaking population and its strong nationalist and separatist movements.

Equal representation of the provinces ignores the uniqueness of Quebec, and in particular its strongly held view that Canada was built by two founding peoples, the French and English, who should be represented through dualism rather than equality of ten provinces. The Charlotte-town document proposed to resolve the special position of Quebec partly through guaranteeing it, in Article XXI, 25 percent of the seats in the Commons, regardless of demographic changes—since 1867 Quebec's proportion of the Canadian population has steadily decreased, and con-tinues to do so as the west in particular grows. The combination of Articles IX and XXI elevated provincial equality in representation in the Senate to a higher status than equality of the citizens in representation in the House of Commons. No argument was presented in the document or by its drafters to explain or justify this dubious deviation from fundamen-tal democratic principles.

Articles X to XV dealt with the powers of the Senate. To eliminate the problems faced by the Mulroney government with a Senate dominated by the opposition party, the Senate would have to dispose of legislation other than revenue and expenditure bills within thirty sitting days of the House of Commons (Article XII). Revenue and expenditure bills would be sub-ject to a thirty calendar day suspensive veto; if such a bill were defeated by the Senate within this period it could be repassed by a majority vote in the Commons. Bills affecting French language and culture would require the approval of a majority of senators, and a second majority of Franco-phone senators. The Commons could not override the defeat of such a bill. Senate defeat of bills involving tax changes relating to natural re-sources also could not be overridden by the Commons. Defeat or amend-ment of ordinary legislation by the Senate would trigger a joint sitting process with the House of Commons, in which a simple majority vote would determine the outcome. Article XV gave the Senate, like its Ameri-can counterpart, the power to ratify key appointments, including the Governor of the Bank of Canada, the heads of national cultural institu-tions, and the heads of federal regulatory boards and agencies.

These proposals would have reduced the powers of the Senate over ordinary legislation by giving it a relatively short period to consider bills and permitting the decision of a joint sitting to override Senate defeat. Powers over natural resource legislation were increased, a concession to the western provinces, as were Senate powers over legislation dealing with language and culture, a recognition of Quebec's concerns.

With the defeat of the Charlottetown proposals in the nationwide referendum, this particular phase of Senate reform came to a halt. The proposals for Senate reform had not satisfied the ardent believers in a Triple-E Senate, nor had the reforms won much support elsewhere. Comprehensive constitutional reform in Canada faces such enormous problems in, first, getting agreement of premiers and federal government to a reform package, and, second, in winning assent through referendum in all provinces, and there are such harmful consequences to failure in terms of damaged expectations and frustrated hopes, that Canadian governments are unlikely to be eager to engage in the process again in the near future (Russell 1993; Franks 1995).

However, two of the E's of the Triple-E Senate, election of senators and a definition of the Senate's powers of the sort proposed in the Charlottetown document (Effective), could be made through ordinary legislation of the Parliament of Canada because they do not require constitutional amendment. Changing the composition of the Senate to achieve provincial equality or some other goal, on the other hand, would require constitutional amendment. Whether a government will undertake Senate reform, either with or without constitutional amendment, depends on the political pressures of the times. So far, the present federal government has shown no eagerness to engage in the comprehensive sort of reforms embodied in the Charlottetown document or in less ambitious incremental reforms that might not involve so much political capital and so many daunting obstacles and penalties.

Meanwhile, the Canadian Senate remains as it has for 131 years, an anomaly, a peripheral institution of government, sometimes a nuisance, occasionally of value, and, if *Country Life* is to be believed, the worst of all possible worlds. It is worth cautioning that even a Senate reformed along the lines of the Charlottetown document would not likely alter to any great extent the practices of federal-provincial relations in Canada. Because of the dominance of the executive, executive federalism seems to be an inescapable part of the amalgam of parliamentary and federal institutions (Watts 1988). Experience with the Australian Senate (Sharman 1987), and that of the post-1984 Canadian Senate, indicates that the Senate proposed at Charlottetown would have remained highly partisan, and that its main concern would be to support party, not region or province. The variety of bases for representation might have produced complex and conflicting purposes within the Senate that would have detracted from the priority of provincial representation. In any case, these proposals are now lost in the sands of time, and the Canadian Senate remains much as it always has been, awaiting, unreformed, the proposals of a new generation of reformers and reforms.

The three key issues in Senate reform are, first, how senators are appointed; second, what the powers of the Senate should be; and third, what balance in the representation of provinces or regions it should have (Franks 1998). On the first, it is clear that appointment by the prime minister from among party supporters has by now reduced the legitimacy of the Senate to the point where it harms not only the Senate but also Parliament as a whole and even the government. It is not good for the country to have the bulk of news stories and other coverage of one of the chambers of the national legislature to be primarily criticism of appointments for having no merit other than service to the party in power or, worse, to the prime minister personally. Either the Senate could be elected, or a portion of appointments chosen by the opposition in Parliament or by provincial legislatures or governments.

An elected Senate would have more legitimacy than the present one, but at a cost of potential tensions within parliamentary institutions that would be unacceptable without drastically reducing the powers of the Senate from what they now are. The same problem exists for most other reforms that would give the Senate more legitimacy, leaving the inescapable conclusion that reduction in the Senate's powers is a necessary part of any reform package.

Equality of provincial representation is less important, and probably more potentially damaging, than its proponents believe. Canada is marked by formidable inequalities between the provinces, ranging from the tiny size of Prince Edward Island, and the poverty of most of the maritimes, to the unique character of Quebec's language and culture, the large population and wealth of Ontario, the enormous government revenues from oil and gas in Alberta, and British Columbia's immense resources and potential as part of the Pacific rim. Provincial equality would give the smallest six provinces, which together contain only about 10 percent of Canada's population, a majority in the Senate. Some form of redistribution is desirable, but not provincial equality.

Whatever the proposals for reform, the Canadian Senate remains an anachronism, and an anomaly. For the most part, its work is better than is appreciated, but lack of legitimacy damages both itself and Canadian parliamentary institutions generally. At present, proposals for reform are mired in the seemingly intractable problem that they must be part of a broader constitutional reform package. Recent efforts (Meech Lake, the Charlottetown Accord) have been unsuccessful and extremely damaging to Canadian unity. The method of selecting senators can be altered by Parliament itself through statute—by binding the prime minister to appoint senators nominated through some new process—and similarly a self-limiting statute could restrict the Senate's powers. These very real possibilities for Senate reform exist as yet untried within the present constitution.

Notes

I am very grateful to the Social Sciences and Humanities Research Council of Canada for their support of my research into parliamentary government in Canada. Stephanie Robinson performed invaluable service as research assistant for my work on the Canadian Senate. I am also grateful in particular to Senators Gildas Molgat, Lowell Murray, John Stewart, and Donald Oliver for their invaluable comments on a draft of this paper and for their insights in further discussions into the work of the Senate and parliamentary government in Canada. Charles Robert provided immensely useful comments and criticisms, as did many others.

1. Governor general's warrants allow the government to spend money without appropriations having been voted by Parliament. In some years in the 1960s the entire expenditure of the Canadian government was made under governor general's warrants because opposition obstruction and elections had prevented Parliament from voting supply. The rules of the House of Commons were subsequently amended to ensure passage of supply. The Senate, however, remained "unreformed" and immune to these Commons rules.

References

Barnhardt, Gordon. 1990. "Administrative Relationship of the Clerk of the Senate to the Committee on Internal Economy, Budgets, and Administration." February. Unpublished.

Burns, R. M. 1977. "Second Chambers: German Experience and Canadian Needs." In *Canadian Federalism: Myth or Reality?* ed. J. Peter Meekison. Toronto: Methuen.

Campbell, Colin. 1978. *The Canadian Senate: A Lobby from Within.* Toronto: Macmillan.

Canada. 1992. *Consensus Report on the Constitution, Charlottetown, August 28, 1992.*

Canada. Senate. Committees Directorate. 1993. *A Legislative and Historical Overview of the Senate of Canada.* Rev. March 31.

———. 1989. *Third and Final Report of the Special Committee of the Senate on Bill C-21.*

Charbonneau, Guy. 1985–86. "A Second Chamber; Not a Secondary One." *Canadian Parliamentary Review* 8:16–18.

Cody, Howard. 1995. "Lessons from Australia in Canadian Senate Reform." *Canadian Parliamentary Review* 18 (2): 19–25.

Cohen, Andrew. 1993. "Renegade Senators Deserve Accolades." *Financial Post,* June 18.

"Confronting the Red Chamber." 1987. *Maclean's,* August 24, 18–19.

Crommelin, Michael. 1989. "Senate Reform: Is the Game Worth the Candle?" *University of British Columbia Law Review* 23 (2): 197–213.

Davey, Keith. 1986. *The Rainmaker: A Passion for Politics.* Toronto: Stoddard.

Dawson, R. MacGregor. 1970. *The Government of Canada.* 5th ed. Revised and edited by Norman Ward. Toronto: University of Toronto Press.

Delacourt, Susan. 1990. "Liberal-Led Senate Throws UI Reforms Back in Tories' Lap." *Globe and Mail,* February 15, A1.

Dobell, Peter C. 1992. "An Elected Senate: Relations with the House of Commons." *Parliamentary Government* 41 (June): 18–21.

———. 1989. "The New Senate." *Parliamentary Government* 15 (April): 21.

———. 1988. "The Senate: New Found Levers of Power?" *Parliamentary Government* 14:14–17.

Dunsmuir, Mollie. 1990. *The Senate: Appointments under Section 26 of the Constitution Act, 1867.* Ottawa: Research Branch, Library of Parliament.

"Ending a Bitter Stalemate." 1987. *Maclean's,* November 30, 19.

Flanagan, Thomas. 1997. "The Staying Power of the Status Quo: Collective Choices in Canada's Parliament after *Morgentaler.*" *Canadian Journal of Political Science* 30 (March): 31–54.

Forsey, Eugene. 1990. *A Life on the Fringe: The Memoirs of Eugene Forsey.* Toronto: Oxford.

———. 1991. "No More than a Triple E Senate Is Needed." In *Politics: Canada,* 7th ed., ed. Paul Fox and Graham White. Toronto: McGraw-Hill Ryerson.

Franks, C. E. S. 1998. *Parliament Intergovernmental Relations and National Unity.* Kingston, Ont.: Institute of Intergovernmental Relations, Queen's University.

———. 1997. "Constraints on the Operations and Reform of Parliamentary Committees in Canada." In *The Changing Roles of Parliamentary Committees: Working Papers on Comparative Legislative Studies II,* ed. Lawrence D. Longley and Attila Ágh, 199–207. Appleton, Wis.: Research Committee of Legislative Specialists, International Political Science Association.

———. 1995. "Representation and Policy-Making in Canada." In *Canada's Century: Governance in a Maturing Society,* ed. C. E. S. Franks et al. Montreal: McGill-Queen's University Press.

―――. 1987. *The Parliament of Canada.* Toronto: University of Toronto Press.

Frith, Royce. 1990. *Hoods on the Hill: How Mulroney and His Gang Rammed the GST Past Parliament and Down Our Throats.* Toronto: Coach House Press.

Galligan, B. 1985–86. "An Elected Senate for Canada? The Australian Model." *Journal of Canadian Studies* 20 (Winter): 77–98.

Greene, Richard. 1986–87. "Information Explosion and the Senate." *Canadian Parliamentary Review* 9 (Winter): 19–21.

Heard, Andrew. 1991. *Canadian Constitutional Conventions: The Marriage of Law and Politics.* Toronto: Oxford University Press.

Jackson, Robert J. 1984. "Remarks to the Special Joint Committee of the Senate and House of Commons on Senate Reform." In *Contemporary Canadian Politics: Readings and Notes,* ed. Robert J. Jackson, Doreen Jackson, and Nicholas Baxter-Moore, 178–82. Scarborough: Prentice Hall.

Jackson, Robert J., et al. 1986. "The Senate." In *Politics in Canada: Culture, Institutions, Behaviour, and Public Policy,* ed. Robert J. Jackson, Doreen Jackson, and Nicholas Baxter-Moore. Scarborough: Prentice Hall.

Janda, Richard. 1992. *Re-Balancing the Federation through Senate Reform: Another Look at the Bundesrat.* Background Studies of the York University Constitutional Reform Project, no. 11. Toronto: York University Centre for Public Law and Public Policy.

Johnson, Brian D. 1984. "Lessons of the Red Chamber: Inside the Senate." *Equinox* 16 (July–August): 26–47.

Kent, Tom. 1988. *A Public Purpose: An Experience of Liberal Opposition and Canadian Government.* Montreal: McGill-Queen's University Press.

Knowles, Valerie. 1988. *First Person: A Biography of Carine Wilson, Canada's First Woman Senator.* Toronto: Dundurn.

Kunz, F. A. 1965. *The Modern Senate of Canada: A Re-appraisal, 1925–1963.* Toronto: University of Toronto Press.

Landes, Ronald G. 1983. "The Legislative Branch of Government: Representation and Legitimation." In his *The Canadian Polity: A Comparative Introduction,* 150–95. Scarborough: Prentice Hall.

Lapointe, Renaude. 1975. "The Role of the Canadian Senate." *Journal of Parliamentary Information* 21 (October–December): 596–606.

LeClerc, Wilbrod. 1978. "A 'Useless' Senate Rebuffs Transport in Examination of the Maritime Code Act." *Optimum* 9 (Summer): 46–50.

Lemco, Jonathan, and Peter Regenstrief. 1984. "Let the Senate Be: There Is Not Enough Support for the Effort or Cost of Reforming or Abolishing the Senate, Which Gives Some Useful Public Service and Usually Knows Its Place." In *Contemporary Canadian Politics: Readings and Notes,* ed. Robert J. Jackson, Doreen Jackson, and Nicholas Baxter-Moore, 183–87. Scarborough: Prentice Hall.

Lijphart, Arend. 1987. "Bicameralism: Canadian Senate Reform in Comparative Perspective." In *Federalism and the Role of the State,* ed. H. Bakvis and W. M. Chandler. Toronto: University of Toronto Press.

Lusztig, Michael. 1995. "Federalism and Institutional Design: The Perils and the Politics of a Triple-E Senate in Canada." *Publius* 25 (Winter): 35–50.

McCauley, Janet Marie. 1983. *The Senate of Canada: Maintenance of a Second Chamber through Functional Adaptability*. Ann Arbor, Mich.: University Microfilms International (Ph.D. diss., Pennsylvania State University).

McConnell, R. 1988. "The Case for a 'Triple E' Senate." *Queen's Quarterly* 95 (Autumn): 683–97.

McCormick, Peter. 1991. "Canada Needs a Triple E Senate." In *Politics: Canada,* 7th ed., ed. Paul Fox and Graham White, 435–39. Toronto: McGraw-Hill Ryerson.

MacKay, Elmer. 1963. *The Unreformed Senate of Canada*. Rev. ed. Toronto: McClelland and Stewart.

Marsden, Lorna R. 1991. "Doing Its Thing—Providing 'Sober Second Thought': The Canadian Senate, 1984–1990." In *Politics: Canada,* 7th ed., ed. Paul Fox and Graham White, 446–54. Toronto: McGraw-Hill Ryerson.

Massicotte, Louis, and Françoise Coulombe. 1988. *Senate Reform*. Ottawa: Research Branch, Library of Parliament.

"New Labour, Old Prejudices." 1997. *Country Life,* January 9, 19.

O'Brien, Gary. 1995. "Legislative Influence of Parliamentary Committees: The Case of the Senate of Canada, 1984–1991." Paper presented at the Annual Meeting of the Canadian Political Science Association, Montreal.

Olson, David, and C. E. S. Franks, eds. 1993. *Representation and Policy Formation in Federal Systems*. Berkeley: University of California, Institute of Governmental Studies.

O'Neal, Brian. 1994. *Senate Committees: Role and Effectiveness*. Ottawa: Research Branch, Library of Parliament.

Pawelek, Nancy. 1984. "The Conscience of Parliament: The Second Chamber Contemplates Its Future." *Parliamentary Government* 5:1–2.

"Reluctance in the Red Chamber." 1985. *Maclean's,* March 4, 34.

Robertson, James R. 1991. *The Rules of the Senate: 1991 Amendments*. Ottawa: Research Branch, Library of Parliament.

Robinson, Stephanie. 1996. "The Senate of Canada during the Mulroney Years: The Red Chamber Playing the Part of the Loyal Opposition." B.A. thesis, Queen's University, Kingston, Ont.

Russell, Peter. 1993. *Constitutional Odyssey: Can Canadians Become a Sovereign People?* 2d ed. Toronto: University of Toronto Press.

Sealey, Ellen. 1995. "Mobilizing Legislation, Losing Consent: Treatment of the House of Commons under the Mulroney Conservatives." B.A. thesis, Queen's University, Kingston, Ont.

"Senate Showdown on Drug Patent Bill Is Delayed." 1997. *Globe and Mail,* September 3.

Sharman, Campbell. 1987. "Second Chambers." In *Federalism and the Role of the State,* ed. Herman Bakvis and William M. Chandler, 82–100. Toronto: University of Toronto Press.

Smiley, Donald V. 1978. "Federalism and the Legislative Process in Canada." In *The Legislative Process in Canada: The Need for Reform,* ed. William A. W. Neilson and James C. MacPherson. Toronto: Butterworth.

Smith, Jennifer. 1988. "Canadian Confederation and the Influence of American Federalism." *Canadian Journal of Political Science* 21 (September): 443–63.

Sokolsky, Joel. 1989. "Overload and Marginality: Parliament and Defence Policy in the 1980s." Paper presented at the biennial meeting of the Association of Canadian Studies in the United States, San Francisco.

Stewart, Edison. 1989. "PM Slams 'Non-elected' Senate for Tardiness on Jobless Bill." *Montreal Gazette,* December 14, A5.

Stillborn, Jack. 1992. *Senate Reform Proposals in Comparative Perspective.* Ottawa: Research Branch, Library of Parliament.

Toulin, Alan. 1989. "Quit Stalling on UI, Mulroney Tells Senate." *Financial Post,* December 15, B2.

Watts, Ronald L. 1988. *Executive Federalism: A Comparative Analysis.* Research Paper 26. Kingston, Ont.: Institute of Intergovernmental Relations, Queen's University.

White, Randall. 1990. *Voice of Region: The Long Journey to Senate Reform in Canada.* Toronto: Dundurn.

Wirick, Gregory. 1988. "Of Warhorses, Pastures, and Power: An Interview with Allan J. MacEachen." *Parliamentary Government* 7:11–13.

Wudel, D. 1986. "A Job Description for Senators." *Policy Options* 7 (April): 22–23.

Zolf, Larry. 1984. *Survival of the Fattest: An Irreverent View of the Senate.* Toronto: Key Porter.

6

A Problem of Identity:
The French Sénat

JEAN MASTIAS

The French Senate is in search of its identity. Heir to a long and contradictory history, it seemed to take on a new life in the 1958 Fifth Republic constitution. But did it? Designed to support the head of state, it quickly found itself opposing him and was even threatened with elimination in 1969. A bastion of parliamentarism, it came to operate in a presidentialist regime where, anxious to stand aside from the to-and-fro of partisan politics, it nevertheless became enmeshed in a majoritarian political system.

Its ability to intervene in the legislative process is real but limited. A "chamber of reflection," it exercises influence by engaging in dialogue with the lower house and suggesting amendments to legislative proposals, but deputies in the National Assembly have the last word. It cannot wholly control the government because it cannot vote it out of office. Nonetheless, it remains ever vigilant and intent on scrutinizing government actions and protecting individual rights and freedoms. In a changing world, it is a symbol of stability. More, as both the representative of the country's local communities and a force for moderation, it generates controversy by sustaining a political order and type of society rooted in France's rural past. A brake on hasty action in the eyes of its supporters, it is accused of immobilism by its detractors.

The question is whether the sense of security and responsibility that the Senate inspires is sufficient foundation for its legitimacy in the eyes of the French people.

Historical Background

The Senate has long been part of the French political landscape, although its political character and role have varied substantially over time. Bicameralism first emerged in France in 1795 as a result of the excesses of the single house and the weariness of a 1789 revolution in its final days. Under the Monarchy and the Empire, it became an aristocratic body and a force for moderation in national political life. It retained this character so that, by 1875, democrats in the newly established Third Republic wanted nothing to do with it, accepting its existence only in return for monarchist support of a republic widely anticipated to be very short-lived. The monarchists dominated the new republic's constituent assembly, but the pretender to the throne's excessive demands prevented them from reinstating a monarchist regime. Negotiation became necessary and the "conservative Senate" was part of the compromise. It gained important powers and, as the mouthpiece of the localities (communes and departments), it became synonymous with a rural France hostile to progressive ideas.

Royalist aspirations for the Third Republic did not last long. Republicans won the 1879 Senate elections and took control of an upper house of the Parliament that was to remain politically moderate and socially conservative, making extensive use of its political powers and institutional prerogatives and even going so far as to force several governments to resign. The Republican Left became lastingly hostile to the institution and took advantage of its majority status in the Fourth Republic's constituent assembly in 1946 to launch a referendum on a return to unicameralism. The French people said no in May, and in October they endorsed a new constitution that created a Conseil de la République alongside a lower house elected by direct, universal suffrage. Limited bicameralism was re-established. Showing skill and resolution, the new "councillors" gradually increased their influence in the legislative process, and the measure of their hard work and growing prestige was the increased powers they received in the 1954 revision of the constitution.

Although never discussed in principle, the Senate's changed role in the 1958 constitution appeared to be a public recognition of, and tribute to, its Fourth Republic achievements.[1] Its title was restored, as was its standing in government after the Fourth Republic interlude. It could no longer be dissolved, and its members were to be elected for nine years, with one-third of them standing for reelection every three years to make for institutional stability and continuity. Its president was given the right to nominate three of the nine members of the Constitutional Council, as well as the right to be consulted on important decisions affecting the nation. Most notably, the Senate president was to be consulted should the president of the Republic decide to dissolve the National Assembly or to take on himself the exercise of emergency powers in times of exceptional difficulties for the nation. He was also constitutionally mandated to assume the presidency when the office fell vacant, as it did, for example, when Charles de Gaulle resigned in 1969 and when Georges Pompidou died in 1974. The indirect election of senators through an electoral college was carried over directly from the Fourth Republic. Indeed, it was also the method adopted to choose the new head of state, the keystone of the Fifth Republic's constitutional edifice.[2] Finally, under exceptionally important circumstances, for example, revision of the constitution or organic laws relating to it, the Senate was granted powers equal to those of the lower house. In short, the upper house of the Fifth Republic was not, in principle, the minor player its immediate predecessor had been.

But at the same time it was not the major player it had been in 1875. Its constitutional elevation in 1958 is not an accurate measure of the power and influence it has actually come to enjoy. Its problem has been that it operates in a bicameral framework that is both constitutionally unequal and tightly orchestrated by the executive power. The Senate is equal to the lower house (National Assembly) or subordinate to it depending on whether or not the government chooses to intervene in disputes to give the last word to the lower house. In addition, having only a mandate to control the actions of ministers, the upper house is not empowered to censure the government of the day. It advises, it oversees, and it warns, but it does not override. Stated succinctly, it has "power without so much as exercising it" (Baguenard 1990, 19). Its influence derives from the political experience and local power bases of its membership.

An Element of Continuity

The Senate was designed to ensure that reason prevailed over passion and time and reflection over immediate action. It was to represent the deep and the lasting in French political life, while the National Assembly would voice the political concerns and anxieties felt in the country at any given moment. In this sense, the Senate would institutionalize the political moderation and wisdom accumulated over the years. Thus, unlike a lower house whose life was brought to a premature end in 1962, 1968, 1981, 1988, and 1997, it cannot be dissolved, and it does its job without serious interruption. The partial renewal of its membership every three years, for example, means that legislative proposals and parliamentary reports do not fall into a void as a new house is elected. It can also remain in session when the lower house has been dissolved. Senators enjoy a greater sense of security as well. At nine years, their term in office is the longest of any French elected official, lasting almost twice as long as the five years for which deputies are elected. Deeply rooted in their local communities, senators also frequently have their mandates renewed, which gives them a feeling of detachment from the day-to-day demands of running for office, a pride in their own independence, and a concern with the issues facing them currently. Lastly, the shared experience of participation in public life and the historical and calming atmosphere of the Palais du Luxembourg (the location of the Senate) promotes mutual courtesy and restraint.

The replacement of roughly one-third of senators every three years limits the scope for innovation. It is rare for more than one-sixth of its membership to be new recruits, even when the oldest members decide not to stand for reelection. It is not unusual for former deputies, ministers, and other leading personalities to end their political career in the upper house.

The two-stage method of electing the Senate has a conservatizing effect. The first stage is the election of the country's municipal councils for a period of six years. The second stage is the appointment of delegates to the senatorial electoral college in each department that elects members of the upper house. An example of the results of this process is that the one-third of senators elected in 1980 (just before the Socialist victory in the 1981 presidential election) by municipal councillors who themselves took office in 1977 remained in place until 1989. By this time, François Mitterrand's first term as president was already over.

Another force for conservatism is the age requirement. Senators must be at least thirty-five years old, whereas deputies need be only twenty-three. The result is not an assembly of the very old, since the average age today is sixty-one. Nonetheless, deputies are about ten years younger on average. More than by electoral law, however, this age difference is explained by the need to have proven oneself in public life before election to the Senate.

The Senate is thus the institutional expression of what is deep and long-standing about France, an upper house designed to remain calm regardless of the political forces buffeting the presidency and the lower house. But does this quality contribute to its effective oversight of government? It depends. The difficulty in giving a definitive answer to this question is that in the Fifth Republic the powers of legislative initiation and arbitration passed early from the Parliament to the president. The government may be theoretically responsible to the lower house, but in practice it answers to a head of state who is the nation's chief policy maker. The regime became presidentialist in its infancy and has remained so since. The constitutional elevation of the Senate has been counterbalanced to some degree by the effective political demotion of both houses.

Deputies have adjusted to this new political reality with little resistance, whereas senators have balked at it, seeking instead to strengthen their position by defining and reinforcing their institutional identity and tailoring their behavior to changed circumstances. Their dream has been to play their constitutional role to the fullest in a balanced parliamentary system of government. But the relationship between the government and the Senate has in fact been unequal, since it has been based on the presumption of common goals and excluded all notion of serious rebellion on the Senate's part. A more balanced relationship can only come into being if the Assembly is riven, partisan, and fragmented and thus unable to use its constitutional supremacy to lord it over the Senate. But in the event of a presidential or governmental majority in the lower house, the Senate automatically becomes less useful to the political executive, and this is precisely the situation that came about early in the life of the Fifth Republic. The Senate's political role, behavior, and actions have thus become deeply influenced by its immediate political context and institutional environment. Its place and role in French political life is defined by decisions over which it has little control.

A Checkered History

The French upper chamber has had a checkered history since its contemporary inception at the outset of the Fifth Republic. The pattern of its development as a parliamentary institution is highly relevant to its present-day operation and performance.

The Difficult Years, 1959–1974

At the beginning of the Fifth Republic, all indications were that the Senate would perform the traditional upper house functions of overseeing and moderating the directly elected lower house. First elected in 1959, it immediately scotched this expectation. Far from acting as an appendage of the government, it distanced itself from it as the centrist groups dominant in the Senate rejected the Gaullist policies passed in the Assembly. The Left, well represented in the Assembly, defended the actions of a "republican Senate" standing against the encroachment of that other French political tradition, one-man rule in the form this time of President de Gaulle. How the constitution was to be interpreted proved a particular bone of contention. The Senate upheld a parliamentarism favoring both houses even while presidential preponderance increased. A clear sign of who was winning in the struggle came when the Constitutional Council struck down important provisions that the Senate had proposed in order to strengthen its hand vis-à-vis the government. The Senate took it upon itself in particular to establish controls over government that went beyond the strict provisions of the constitution, to manage its own parliamentary agenda better, and to intervene more effectively at the initiation stage of the legislative process. With failure, disillusionment set in.

The divorce finally came in autumn 1962. President de Gaulle announced his intention to hold a referendum revising the constitution to allow for the direct election of the head of state. Senators were furious not only that Parliament was to be bypassed but also that the referendum had been called in an unconstitutional manner. Senate President Gaston Monnerville went so far as to speak of abuse of authority. The stakes were high, and the successful passage of the referendum reinforced the presidential character of the regime, ending the situation where president and senators were accountable to similar electoral colleges. Widening the rift, the parliamentary elections held at the same time returned a Gaullist government with a clear majority in the National Assembly. The Senate was no longer needed by an executive allied with a lower house whose unremitting hostility it had previously taken for granted. Slipping from its position of conflict (and sometimes compromise), the Senate became politically isolated and marginalized.

Sidelined, the Senate lived through seven dark years. Its legislative proposals came to nothing, its leader was no longer received at the Elysée (the presidential palace), and government ministers practically never attended its public sessions. Procedural devices for ignoring an angry Senate were multiplied, and deputies were at last able to proceed with legislation. Relations sank to an appalling low. Moreover, to add insult to injury, the government mounted a public relations campaign depicting the upper house as serving no useful purpose and being systematically hostile to the government of the day.

Soon the very existence of the Senate was under threat. De Gaulle believed that no political system could accommodate a part that was dysfunctional for the whole and that no institution hostile to the principle of majoritarianism could be left in place. His aversion to the Senate finally crystallized with the referendum of April 27, 1969, asking the French people to approve his plans to "renew" (perhaps more accurately eliminate) the Senate. His proposal was to turn the upper house into a consultative council of mixed membership. Included in its ranks would be locally elected representatives, individuals nominated by social and cultural organizations, and delegates of French citizens living overseas. The local representatives were to be elected under a regionally based proportional system for a six-year term. The categories of socioprofessional senators were specified, but the question of who would choose them was left for future presidential decree. Most importantly, though, the reformed upper house would lose all its political power. It would give preliminary advice to deputies who would eventually enter into dialogue with it. But politically emasculated, it would be only a technical and consultative institution.

Alain Poher, the Senate president elected only in 1968, campaigned actively against de Gaulle's referendum, helping to defeat it and save the upper house. It is impossible to say whether it was the Senate issue that determined the people's negative vote, since the referendum encompassed several issues. What is certain, though, is that the referendum was effectively a personal vote of confidence in General de Gaulle and, on losing, he resigned immediately, although he was not constitutionally required to do so. Analyses of public opinion at the time show a Senate little known to the French people and widely perceived as archaic. Individual senators, though, were valued for their local ties and services. Bicameralism afforded the French a sense of security, and from that day the Senate's right to exist has never again been brought seriously into question. Nonetheless, its future guaranteed, the upper house still needed to define its own identity and find a place for itself in the political process.

Safe, the Senate gradually normalized its relations with the other institutions of government. Official contact with the new president, Georges Pompidou, was resumed, relations with the government became less tense, and legislative procedures that had tied the Senate's hands were relaxed. Dialogue with the lower house also increased, even if disagreement persisted on important issues.

The Senate emerged from its dark years in 1969. It was not, however, the legislative chamber envisioned in the 1958 constitution, the thorn it had been in the executive's flesh in 1962, or the shadow of its former self proposed in the 1969 referendum. It remained anxious to affirm its uniqueness, its positive role in government. Thus, to strengthen its legitimacy, it adapted to France's changing demography and, in 1976, expanded its number of members to accommodate increased population size in a number of departments.[3] To increase its authority, it diversified and enforced more rigorously the means at its disposal to control the actions of government. In particular, it took on itself the defense of individual rights and freedoms and successfully brought cases before the Constitutional Council. To improve its own effectiveness, it reorganized both its operational procedures and its administration, increased the resources and personal assistance available to its members, improved its public relations, and opened itself up to the outside world through public meetings, press conferences, information bulletins, and the like.

Its aim was clear. By reforming itself, it intended to change its image and play a distinctive role in the political process as an independent chamber operating on the fringes of the majoritarian system of government. But this role assumed that it would not soon be called upon to become a key cog in the workings of that same system.

The Pitfalls of Majoritarianism, 1974–1988

With the election of Valéry Giscard d'Estaing as president in 1974, presidential and senatorial majorities coincided for the first time. Indeed, still dominated by centrists, the Senate was better disposed to the new president than was the National Assembly with its continuing right-wing majority. From the outset, tensions existed between the centrist president and his Gaullist prime minister, Jacques Chirac. When Chirac resigned to be replaced by Raymond Barre, an economics professor with no strong partisan ties, tensions in the lower house intensified and the Senate went from being useful to the president to being indispensable. The government simply could not do without its support.

The upper house was overwhelmed with attention, and on the anniversary of its centenary in May 1975, the head of state publicly sang its praises. Three times in succession, and in accordance with Article 49.4 of the constitution, the Senate was invited unprecedentedly to give its opinion on the government's legislative agenda. It was also given the privilege of being informed about important governmental initiatives and legislative proposals before the National Assembly was. The Senate, for its part, was not sparing in its support for the government. When, for want of a majority, Prime Minister Barre ran into difficulties in the National Assembly and called for a vote of confidence on a bill, senators supported the prime minister's action in large numbers.[4] When, at the end of 1978, a majority of deputies ignored government advice and voted in favor of state financing for European election campaigns, the Senate failed to place the measure on its legislative agenda, so the proposal died for not being enacted before the elections in question took place. Sometimes the Senate even contradicted itself by acceding to government requests to reject bills it had previously corrected.

This period of Senate-government cooperation was fruitful in terms of the passage of laws and the acceptance of Senate amendments. Inquiries were held on topics that above all else demonstrated to the French public the high levels of senatorial competence and effectiveness. Still, all was not well. The heightened workload and its unequal distribution gave rise to outbursts of bad temper and heated denunciations in President Poher's biannual public speeches. Moreover, the Senate's independence of the government was regularly proclaimed in speeches. The truth of the matter was that in effectively giving up its role as critic, the Senate took on the appearance of a rubber stamp legislature caught in the trap of the majoritarian system, especially when the stakes were high or the risk of conflict with the right-wing majority in the Assembly loomed.

Then, in mid-1981, the political circumstances in which the Senate found itself were transformed when a leftist majority was returned in the Assembly, a majority that supported the equally newly elected Socialist president, François Mitterrand. The Senate was implacably opposed to both and found itself on the horns of a dilemma. How could it avoid lapsing into being entirely peripheral to the political process? Should it cultivate obstructionism, or should it retreat from the majority-opposition confrontation and speak with its own voice? Its solution was to acknowledge its fundamental political opposition to the new majority, while not entering into an opposition of principle characterized by blanket hostility. It opted instead for moderation and compromise. Taking on itself the detailed reading and amendment of legislative proposals largely initiated by the government, its measured response helped to enact into law bills it valued highly and dealing with issues like the abolition of the death penalty and the elimination of military security courts. Yet later on its behavior changed, as it could not disguise its complete disagreement with the lower house, and its refusal to compromise resulted in its outright rejection or disruption of legislative proposals coming before it.

This political disagreement had very real practical consequences. The nature of the dialogue between the two houses changed, and the hostility between them crystallized. The government increasingly resorted to procedures designed to expedite the passage of legislation, procedures that served to limit Senate involvement in the legislative process and the opportunities it was afforded to express its opinion. The Assembly ignored established conciliation procedures, and the Senate turned to previously little-used devices to assert its authority. It made particularly abundant use of the "preliminary question" and the "inadmissibility provision."[5] Relations grew ever more polarized, and the National Assembly took more and more decisions that the Senate then rejected, particularly on budget bills.

Even if the breakdown in relations was not total, Senate opposition to the government was even more comprehensive than it had been in the 1962–69 Gaullist era. The tense relations between them reached their climax in summer 1984 over a bill concerning state support for private schools. The Senate cleverly played for time, counted for support on public opinion hostile to the proposal, and argued bitterly with the president over plans to submit the issue to a referendum. The upper house's show of strength and determination paid off, and the bill was withdrawn. To be sure, such incidents did not threaten the existence of the Senate itself, but norms of behavior took a sharp turn for the worse. Systematic resort to delaying tactics became routine, relations between senators deteriorated, debate took on a more confrontational tone, bitter quarrels broke out between government supporters and opponents, and rules of procedure became weapons. Issues that it was widely agreed needed to be looked at carefully were not subjected to detailed political scrutiny, and recourse to the Constitutional Council became automatic when legislation was adopted against the advice of the Senate.

The 1986 legislative elections brought this unhappy period to an end. The right won a majority in the National Assembly, and Jacques Chirac became prime minister. His relations with the president during this period of cohabitation were heavily strained, and the consequences for the Senate were two. First, with the prime minister professing his high esteem for the Senate, the passage of legislation once again became a cooperative effort. Alain Poher, president of the Senate, even spoke of a "reactivation of bicameralism" at the same time as protesting against the government's tendency to declare all its bills urgent and the consequent overcrowding of the legislative calendar. In general, though, the Senate no longer sought systematically to hinder government decision making.

Second, the Senate became an active and partisan participant in the conflict between president and prime minister. Its traditional calmness and slow pace was the first casualty. Its work rate speeded up, and its skill at standing back from the fray when appropriate was seriously impaired, as was its ability to debate issues, to engage in constructive dialogue, and to improve bills.

Looking to help the government in innovative ways, the Senate even accelerated (and cut short) debate on opposition-inspired preliminary questions designed to sabotage government proposals of which the Senate as a whole approved. The opposition, for its part, delayed the adoption of government bills as long as possible, especially when it was of the impression that the relevant committee was not fully satisfied with how the bill was written. But regardless of whether it be as victim or accomplice, the Senate was again caught up in the turbulence of the majoritarian political system. Could it ever hope to find a middle way?

Missed Opportunities, 1988–1997

The 1988 legislative elections brought a minority Socialist government to power and, not being in the majority, it had to be more subtle in its relations with the Senate. According to circumstance, concessions were encouraged or held back. Even so, successive prime ministers differed in the kind of relations they established with the upper house. The Senate suffered an identity crisis.

A climate of mutual respect prevailed during Michel Rocard's premiership. His demonstration of symbolic and political respect for the Senate was deeply appreciated. Six senators were appointed to his cabinet, and unprecedentedly the prime minister attended a president's conference setting the weekly agenda for the upper house, breaking with the tradition whereby the government was represented by the minister in charge of relations with Parliament. In addition, he dutifully solicited Senate approval of his policies (Article 49.4) and made clear in a memo circulated to ministers the importance he attached to free parliamentary discussion. The effect on policy making was positive since, even during difficult times, dialogue was the norm and compromise was often sought.

But this interlude was brief. Rocard's successors neither used the same methods nor obtained the same results. Dialogue between the chambers hardened, agreement became less common, and resort to urgency procedures became ever more frequent. Senatorial oversight tightened up, especially on European questions. Action and reaction were widely perceived as being motivated by mutual hostility. Thus, the government did not appreciate Senate endorsement of a preliminary question to reject its 1993 proposed budget. The Senate in its turn reacted equally badly to a December 1991 bill altering its representational base.[6] Taking advantage of a proposal to revise the constitution (for which its support is necessary), it even increased its powers in regard to the passage of an organic law.

But this increase and its return to a confrontational relationship with the government could not hide the fact that the Senate was experiencing its own internal crisis. Numerous criticisms had been made of its method of recruitment, its ways of operating and carrying out its responsibilities, its failure to reflect adequately on the legislative proposals coming before it, its membership, and its lack of originality. These criticisms came from across the political spectrum, papering over substantial differences in opinion about how best to coordinate the senatorial majority and whether to oppose the government through constructive dialogue or intransigent opposition. Rules of procedure were modified to increase effectiveness, and some innovative proposals were introduced by young senators, only to be watered down and lead to no more than limited reform. With a divided majority and suspicious opposition, agreement could be reached on nothing more. A problem was that some ideas, like increasing the powers of committees, were before their time.

A right-wing majority then carried the day in the 1993 parliamentary election, and two years later Chirac succeeded Mitterrand as president. Initially, therefore, the political context of the new parliament was one of cohabitation (Gicquel 1996) and the Senate generally took advantage of the situation without experiencing too many drawbacks as a result of it. Faced with a massive but largely inexperienced right-wing majority, it was able to play a more prominent role in mediating conflicts that did not set president and prime minister poles apart. Sometimes it played a moderating role, sometimes it improved the text of bills, sometimes it held debates that were less harsh and polarized in tone than their counterparts in the National Assembly, and sometimes it turned to good account its experience, its local roots and its independence.

The period was reminiscent of its successes in the 1970s as all laws but one were passed by agreement in both houses. Eighty-five percent of Senate amendments were upheld in the Assembly, and the high quality of a number of debates in the upper house was publicly recognized. Still, the period was not without its problems. One bill out of five was examined under conditions of urgency, the workload became heavier and heavier, the number of extraordinary sessions multiplied, and the rules governing the debate of a number of bills did not allow a calm and measured examination of their provisions and generated heated rejoinders from the opposition. Scrutiny relaxed a little except on European bills, where a new procedure enabled both houses to examine directives affecting French legislation.

The internal reform of the Senate continued apace. René Monory, its president newly elected in October 1992, wanted reflection to be aimed not only at correcting existing problems but also at anticipating the future. He opened the institution to the outside world, developing international exchanges, welcoming foreign heads of government, and generally communicating a more attractive portrayal of what the Senate did. But on all these points, the Senate found itself in competition with a National Assembly also engaged in enhancing its parliamentary role. Thus, a 1995 constitutional revision broadened the scope of the referendum, put in place a system of parliamentary immunity, and increased the length of the parliamentary session from six to nine months. Moreover, priority is now given in one sitting per month to the legislative agenda set by each house and not the government, each now determines the days and hours of its own sittings, and the rights to initiate legislation and to control the government have been made easier. The Senate's reputation as a careful and valuable lawmaker has benefited from the originality of some of its innovations in the area of controlling the government.

A Chamber of Reflection

Legislation is shaped by iterative negotiations between the two houses of Parliament under government direction. After two readings of the bill (one if it is declared urgent), the government can appoint a conference committee drawn in equal numbers from both houses to hammer out a mutually acceptable final version of the bill. These are officially called *Commissions Mixtes Paritaires* (CMP). Each CMP is made up of seven deputies and seven senators who strive to produce a bill all can support when the government submits it to each house. The government alone has the right to propose or accept amendments to this bill. When agreement cannot be reached, the government can declare the National Assembly version of the bill to have carried the day once it has received a new reading in each chamber. Such is the philosophy behind Article 45 of the

Constitution. The Senate's role in this process is one of reflection; it suggests textual modifications and amendments to legislation in its discussions with the government and the lower house. But is it effective and influential in this role?

The Aim: To Amend Bills

The right to initiate laws is shared between parliamentarians and a government that introduces legislative proposals into the house of its choice. The exception is financial bills, which deputies have to see first. Parliamentarians introduce their own legislative initiatives in the house to which they belong, although these rarely become the law of the land. As in most European countries, virtually all legislation originates with the government. From 1959 to 1995, 89 percent of the laws passed were government initiated, 8 percent started life in the National Assembly, and 3 percent began in the Senate (112 of a total 3,522 bills). Deciding which of its legislative proposals survive is often the work of the upper house itself. Of every 100 of them, less than 10 are considered and lead to a report from the relevant committee. To succeed, the proposed bill must be able to win majority support in the Senate, it must be legally admissible, and the parliamentary timetable, which is controlled by the government, must not be too congested. This means that no more than four or five Senate-initiated bills are adopted each year.[7]

The Senate has no means of making the National Assembly take its legislative initiatives seriously, especially when the government is not on its side. The Senate deplores its helplessness since it feels that deputies ought to look at its suggestions, if only to reject them. Overall, its record is not strong, although it must be said that the number of Senate-initiated bills to become law has doubled to 6 percent of the annual total under favorable political circumstances. Moreover, others of its initiatives show up later in government-sponsored bills so that the true measure of the Senate's legislative influence is not this 3 percent figure alone. In fact, it is the amendment, not the legislative proposal, that is the Senate's stock in trade, and it is in its suggesting amendments that reflection finds its reward thanks to the quality of the upper house's scrutiny of bills and its open discussion of them.

The number of senatorial amendments has been growing rapidly since 1970. Nearly 5,000 are put down each year, and about 2,000 of these are accepted. They mostly reflect the opinion of the majority, although the opposition is not altogether without success. Above all, however, the amending process attests to the influence of the permanent committees. These are the authors of one-third of the amendments proposed, but of 80 percent of those accepted. Other amendments are sometimes withdrawn before being put to the vote because the ministerial promise of concessions obviates the need for them. Thus, depending on political circumstances, the National Assembly accepts 50 to 85 percent of the amendments adopted by the Senate, and many of them find their way in some form or other into the final bill.

Senatorial amendments vary in character. Some correct inaccuracies, others improve the wording of drafts, and still others fill in gaps—all of which are important contributions when legal documents are involved. At bottom, the amendments often attest to an interest in the principles of law and a practical concern with putting the written texts into practice. That is, Senate amendments aim to make the content of legislation precise and broadly applicable. They affect all areas of legislation, but the most significant ones involve matters relating to local communities, to agriculture, to legal frameworks (individual law, commercial law, and so on), and to improving financial rectitude. When Senate amendments overturn the initial provisions of a bill and form a coherent package of their own, they amount to real counterproposals, and it is not unusual for senators to rewrite a bill of which an administration far removed from the French people or deputies pressed for time were the original authors or first readers. Thus, if the purpose of a second chamber is to perfect legislation technically, then the Senate serves this purpose. But it is able to do so only in consultation with other political actors.

A Constructive Dialogue

The goal of interaction between the two houses of Parliament is reconciliation through dialogue. Working together guarantees a higher quality legislative process. Each house checks the other, the contemplation of problems is more profound, ideas are made more precise, and compromises are sought. The more readings of bills there are, the more an influence for the Senate is ensured. Indeed, contrary to received wisdom, harmony between the houses is the norm. The consensual adoption of legislation is the rule, recourse to the CMP is rare, and never more than a third of them fail to produce legislative proposals that pass into law. It is political circumstances that produce the variation. Except in moments of high tension, the Senate obstructs only if basic principles are at issue or if it sets a high value on a provision under negotiation. Its more normal role is to correct and regulate.

The Senate can be presumed to be influential to the extent that bills are passed into law only after agreement between the two parliamentary houses has been reached. From 1959 to 1980, such was the case 85 percent of the time, although this figure fell in later years. Between 1981 and 1985, the period of the Senate's liveliest opposition to the government, it was 62 percent, rising again to 73 percent during the cohabitation between President Mitterrand and Prime Minister Chirac. The upper house's return to an opposition role between 1988 and 1992 then brought it back down to 63 percent and it rose again to 76 percent in the 1993–95 period. The evidence is conclusive.

The CMP has been used more and more often since 1974, but it is an ambivalent device. For senators, it can promote conciliation if committee members are chosen to reflect faithfully the different shades of opinion in the two houses, if it does not divide into opposing camps at the first sign of difficulty, if the need for reciprocal concessions is widely accepted, and if the government does not change its recommendations. If these conditions are met, it becomes a useful parliamentary tool, since it allows negotiated agreements to be reached as long as disagreement on principles is not absolute. The government, by contrast, sees the CMP as a device for speeding up the legislative process and for stimulating dialogue within the majority. According to the times and the individual cases at hand, it is a device that fulfills perfectly one or the other of these political roles. The bottom line is that when the Senate is in accord with the government, it gets something out of the CMP, but finds this to be far less the case in times of disagreement.

This means that the final decision has rested with deputies only rarely. Indeed, it did so with only 60 (or about 3 percent) of the 2,121 bills passed into law between 1959 and 1980. At the height of the 1962–69 crisis, the same unilateral action was taken on only 6 percent of successful bills. This figure fell below 1 percent from 1974 to 1980 and to one single bill in the 1986–87 session and one more from 1993 to June 1996. During these last three periods, senatorial and presidential majorities were the same, but this has not always been the case. When the Socialists held the presidency and the Left enjoyed a majority in the lower house between 1981 and April 1, 1986, unilateral Assembly action occurred on 26 percent of the bills passed and on 18 percent of them from 1988 to 1992.

The difficulties in the relations between Senate and National Assembly in these two periods do not mean that the Senate played a lesser role in the legislative process. Rather, insurmountable disagreements were encountered on profoundly important legislative proposals concerning nuclear armament, civil liberties, the organization of the social security system, several finance laws, and, not least, a number of large-scale reforms undertaken by the Left after 1981 (nationalizations, and so on). The increase in disagreement, in other words, reflected political differences rather than institutional decay. With the exception of the occasions when the Senate was tempted to play the role of political advocate, dialogue between the two houses was not useless. Disagreement was persistent but often partial, and a number of important Senate amendments were kept in bills that became law without direct approval of the upper house being sought. All in all, then bicameralism seems to be working well. Nonetheless, the balance achieved remains fragile, since obstacles to its proper functioning remain ever present.

Two Obstacles: The Government and Time

The Senate's strength lies in calculated delay and compromise, yet it is the government that decides whether it should have the opportunity to exercise fully its powers of reflection. Do the constraints that it can impose in the form of overloading the parliamentary timetable and setting its agenda limit the Senate's contribution to legislative outcomes? One of its presidents, Alain Poher, argued in a speech in December 1981 that free and open discussion "can only take place in an atmosphere of mutual respect, understanding, and tolerance," and the upper house itself has vehemently denounced externally imposed constraints of any kind. It is a body that has traditionally interpreted its own rules of procedure flexibly and liberally. The length of debates has often been unlimited, delegations of competence have infrequently been extended, and the rights of individual senators have been widely taken for granted. However, the emergence, most notably in 1986, of obstructive practices inspired by National Assembly hostility and part of a more general deterioration of relations between majority and opposition led to the reform of Senate rules of procedure. The number and length of interventions from the floor was limited, proposed amendments and subamendments could be rejected more easily, and the president was strengthened in his power to direct proceedings.

But despite having become less tolerant with their own minorities, senators protested no less when the government took advantage of its constitutional powers to dictate to them. The working conditions it imposed were a particular source of discontent. In recent years, the volume of parliamentary work has increased constantly, and at a considerable rate, and the principal cause has been the multiplication of the number of legislative texts needing to be examined. The problem has been compounded, however, by the election of new senators with energetic young aides, competition among senators active in debate, desire on their part to speak longer, and even the occasional desire to delay proceedings. The length of time debates took doubled between 1976 and 1986, and they were distributed unevenly over the year. To make matters worse, a balanced allocation of bills to the different chambers for their first reading was established only recently. The number of special sessions multiplied and debate on the floor of the house, often marked by absenteeism, gave too many opportunities for technical interventions more appropriately discussed in committee. It is still too early to judge how the August 1995 constitutional change introducing a single, nine-month session affected these problems, but there does seem to have been some improvement. The timing of sittings is better, while their number has not increased. The parliamentary week is also better planned and night sittings have been minimized.

However, the archaic and ineffective framework of the budget debate has not been changed. Debates on the floor of the Senate and in committee meetings sometimes take place simultaneously, and the same ground is covered in both venues. The daily timetable is still not known any more than three weeks in advance. Similarly, the government retains its right to declare a matter urgent without justification. The effect of this declaration is to limit the time for discussion to one reading of the bill in each chamber before it proceeds to the CMP. The Senate often receives the bill second so that its proposed amendments become known only to the seven deputies who, together with seven senators, make up the CMP. The Senate thus appears less as an important participant in the legislative process and more as a simple giver of advice that is immediately open to negotiation.

This recourse to the declaration of urgency appears to be meant less to encourage ill-considered discussion and more to bring debates to a quicker conclusion. Since 1978, its more frequent invocation has gone hand in hand with a heavier parliamentary workload, which would indicate that it is but one facet of the race against time.

To rush does a disservice to the Senate. Often legislation will better stand the test of time if it has received careful and extensive deliberation. Haste is all the more unwelcome to senators, since it is the direct result of the government setting the order of parliamentary business. It controls the administrative preparation of legislative proposals, it sets the parliamentary agenda and the convening of CMPs, and ultimately it writes the decrees putting laws into practice. The Senate does not appreciate abuse of this position of power because it stands in a special relationship to time. It is not only its responsibility to symbolize stability, to look to the long rather than short term, but also it needs to take its time if it is to maximize its influence on legislation.

Moreover, it finds every opportunity to give itself time for reflection. The government may control the daily parliamentary agenda, but the Senate sets its own meeting hours and can, according to its own rules, limit its sittings to three days a week. It knows how to manage its own time and has the freedom to organize it, which obliges the government to negotiate with it how it is used and on which issues. It sometimes chooses its moment to strike and, as in the 1984 conflict over private schools, it knows how to mobilize public opinion behind an issue. Politically, calculated slowness can allow it to win concessions when the government is pressed to bring another bill before it for consideration. Institutionally, it strengthens the Senate because it can be used to calm tensions, to accelerate the passage of legislation, to delay it, and even to obstruct it. Procedurally speaking, time is essential to the in-depth study of government proposals, to the holding of hearings, and to judging proposals for change against past experience.

Having the ability neither to block nor to impose, never mind to take the initiative, the Senate polishes bills by amending them and making skillful use of interhouse deliberations. Supporters interpret senatorial reflection in terms of maturation, while opponents see it as an almost insurmountable obstacle to legislative effectiveness. The same disagreement is sometimes seen in judgments about the way in which the Senate performs its oversight function.

Parliamentary Oversight

Since 1969, the Senate has been particularly anxious to exercise and develop its oversight function. In this regard, it enjoys all the same rights as
the National Assembly but one, the ability to dismiss the government.
Both chambers have comparable resources, although each tends to use
them differently. Both have similar rights to investigate and to question,
but they differ with respect to the areas they choose to investigate and
scrutinize as well as to the means they bring to bear on this task.

The Investigative Function

The Senate cannot veto government bills, nor can it censure the government or pass a vote of no confidence.[8] The prime minister alone has the
option of asking it to approve a general policy declaration, and he values
the opportunity to test the water at his discretion, since he is not obliged
to resign if the Senate vote goes against him. He resorts to this procedure
solely to enhance the legitimacy of his government by demonstrating to
the public and to the lower house that the majority in the Senate is favorable to his policies. It can also serve as a public expression of the respect
the prime minister has for the upper house, a gesture of goodwill that
has the advantage of entailing no political risk. Such a gesture was made
for the first time only in 1975 when relations between the Senate and governmental authorities were normalized under President d'Estaing. It then
became the norm whenever the right was in power. Cleverly, however,
the left-wing Rocard government resorted to it on issues, like the 1989
collapse of communism in Eastern Europe and the 1991 Gulf War, where
consensus already existed. The Senate was more gratified by this consultation than it was influential over policy.

Such might also be the case in instances of the upper house questioning
government intentions and actions. To be sure, the means for it to inform
itself about them are not lacking. In addition to the abundant information
they receive from a variety of sources, individual senators, just like deputies, have the right to question the government, and both groups of parliamentarians avail themselves of this right to much the same extent. The
problem, however, is that written questions (more than 5,000 a year), oral
questions (recently on the rise), and question time (televised twice a
month) do not provide the opportunity for a real dialogue. Rather, the

Senate has shown more inventiveness in the exercise of its scrutiny function when it acts collectively. In its desire to place government actions under the microscope and to defend individual rights and freedoms, it has developed some unusual oversight mechanisms.

Investigation requires a request originating within Parliament asking to find out more about something than the government has voluntarily divulged in response to questions (Duhamel 1995, 284). The request can involve big issues of governmental policy direction as well as smaller scale, more topical ones; it inevitably leads to a debate and to the house taking a public position on the issue. Several permanent organs of the Senate combine to perform its general oversight function. Here are some examples. One, at the request of one committee or another, ministers frequently appear to explain and defend their policies. Two, the budget debate, held in public session, allows senators to scrutinize proposals in detail and, where necessary, to demand explanations on individual provisions. Specialists from the Finance Committee may also at any time after the vote verify the uses of the sums requested in the budget of the ministry under scrutiny. The administration of the publicly owned enterprises is subject to similar scrutiny. Three, the Senate's European Union Delegation keeps track of the Union's activities, and the government refers to it community policy or spending proposals that fall within the domain of law constitutionally reserved for the Parliament. The Delegation can thus play a role in preparing the resolutions the Senate adopts to alert the government to unusually far-reaching community decisions. Fourth, the Parliamentary Office for the Evaluation of Scientific and Technological Decisions, which is shared by both houses, provides experts to help parliamentarians make informed decisions. In the same manner, the recently created Office for the Evaluation of Legislation and Office for the Evaluation of Public Policy should serve as useful investigative tools.

Any senator can oblige the government to discuss a matter publicly. Oral questions that engage it in debate force it to accept an exchange of viewpoints pertaining to matters that it itself may not have broached. Grouped by theme, questions offer the opportunity to examine some aspect of government policy from every angle. Usually specific but of general interest and sometimes aimed at specifically European issues, the oral question was long a great success in the Senate at the same time that it had been abandoned in the National Assembly. It would involve the government in some twenty involuntary debates a year. Its importance is now on the decline, however. Its utility as an oversight tool was always limited by the fact that such debates never ended in a vote. More recent developments have diminished its utility still further. These include a lack of time, competition from other forms of interrogation, and a general increase in the number of public hearings in the Senate.

Other bodies can intervene at short notice. Thus, for example, the Senate can focus on a current problem and create a committee of inquiry with special powers. These committees are convened to gather information on specific questions or on the running of public services and the nationalized industries with a view to submitting their conclusions to the chamber that created them. They cannot address or pursue inquiries on matters already under judicial investigation, and their work cannot last longer than six months. Their powers are extensive, including control over the committee's terms of reference and the place of the hearing, the ability to hold it in public, and the ability to summon documents and persons deemed necessary to its successful conduct. Though not having the prestige of their longer-established American counterparts, these committees nonetheless have an impact. Their reports are published, and they often contain criticisms and concrete proposals for action, thus serving as a reference document that others can use.

For a long time after 1960, the Senate made this kind of committee its specialty. Then, the National Assembly imitated it, and the two houses have sometimes even been in competition on matters being investigated. During its periods in opposition, the Senate has made extensive use of the committee of inquiry to embarrass the government in sensitive areas. Today, it is used less. To address technical questions or reflect on societal problems, recourse to more flexible arrangements is preferred. Depending on the specifics of individual cases or on the practical advantages of specific arrangements, information gathering groups are formed from the membership of the relevant permanent committees. Examples are the commissions on decentralization in 1983 and on the state of school buildings in 1973. Study groups are another option, and individual parliamentarians have even been deputed to write reports on special topics. But common to all these efforts to increase senatorial influence and better inform the French is that they are meaningful exercises only if they remain rigorous, nonpartisan, and accessible to minority groups. As instruments wielded by the majority, they have less significance. Overall, though, their balance sheet is positive and the reports produced clearly reflect Senate initiative and thoughtfulness.

Finally, its control over the implementation of laws has effectively enlarged the means through which the Senate can assert itself. The separation of the domain of law from executive rule making (Articles 34 and 37 of the constitution) means that, in the absence of implementation decrees ("décrets d'application") not all provisions of a bill can always be put into practice efficiently. It is the government that dictates the contents and the timing of the publication of these decrees so that parliamentary recommendations do not always make themselves immediately felt. To limit and expose governmental abuses of this power, senators keep close track of the implementation of bills that have been voted upon. At the beginning of every session, each of the Senate's six standing committees checks that enabling legislation has been passed in the desired time. The results of their inquiries are published and, in cases of delay, conveyed to the prime minister. He is not bound to act on this report, but it can be persuasive enough to influence his behavior. Delays are now rarely of scandalous length.

Protecting Rights and Freedoms

For many observers it is the upper house's defense of civil liberties that is one of its most valuable and characteristic activities. It also occupies a central position in its own self-image, being evident in the rejection of legislative proposals and, still more, by referring them to the Constitutional Council. For the Senate to reject a legislative proposal is a serious matter for three main reasons. These are the political conflict it generates, the protection of social groups favored by the Senate, and a concern for rectitude in financial and legal matters, especially as they relate to legal principles and the protection of individual and collective freedoms. Rejection by the Senate does not in and of itself prevent a bill from becoming law, since the government and National Assembly can pass it without upper house consent. By appealing to the Constitutional Council, however, the Senate can have a say in whether the bill is constitutional or whether it respects the jurisdictional boundaries between lawmaking and rulemaking. As long as the Council is seized of the matter, this is a useful weapon for the Senate and has become frequently used by it.

Prior to the 1974 constitutional revision, only the president of the Republic, the prime minister or the presidents of the two houses of Parliament could refer a bill to the Constitutional Council. Since then, however, sixty deputies or the same number of senators acting together have enjoyed the same right. The appeal floodgates were opened. The president of the Senate was initially reluctant to risk the prestige of his office by taking advantage of this new opportunity, but ordinary parliamentarians were another story. They resorted to it not only to show their concern for the law but also to win partisan points against the government. But more interesting than motivations is the object of appeals from the Senate. Until 1969, the Senate was anxious above all to protect the rights of Parliament. Since then, it has taken on itself more the defense of the rights of citizens.

Breaking sharply with the past, the 1958 constitution curtailed the policy areas in which Parliament had the right to make law. The Senate took this change badly. Rule- and lawmaking each had its own domain, and the apportionment of competences between them gave rise to various legal disputes between the upper house and the government. The Senate president referred these disputes on several occasions to the Constitutional Council in order to get an authoritative interpretation of the scope of the legislature's field of competence. He got no satisfaction until 1968 when the Council recognized the Senate's lawmaking character with its endorsement of a bill guaranteeing the status of veteran to soldiers who had fought in North Africa. For eight years afterwards, governments gave up defending the regulatory character of provisions challenged as not being so by either house. Three further decisions favoring Parliament reinforced this behavior. One such decision followed a Senate initiative and was handed down on May 8, the anniversary of victory in the Second World War. The symbolism was powerful.

Preoccupied with parliamentary rights and still ambivalent about the Constitutional Council, the Senate had shown little confidence in challenging the constitutionality of laws. After all, this same Council, when approached by Senate President Monnerville in 1962, had declared itself not competent to judge the constitutionality of the proposed referendum on the direct election of the president. The attitude of both the Senate and the Council began to change only in 1969. The former wanted to revive its political role and the Council to enlarge its. The Senate president referred two new pieces of legislation, both concerning individual freedoms, to the Council. As well as the Preamble to the Constitution, his argument invoked the 1789 Declaration of the Rights of Men and Citizens and fundamental principles of French law. The Council decided in his favor in both instances, thereby both expanding the principles to which laws must conform beyond the articles of the 1958 constitution and condemning governmental challenges to freedom of association (January 16, 1971) and the principle of equality before the law (December 27, 1973).

Senators have embraced this right to appeal with great enthusiasm, referring seventy-three cases to the Council between 1981 and 1986, for example. Their rate of success, however, has not been uniform. When the disputed bill has raised serious legal questions and Senate argumentation has seemed to derive from first principles, it has frequently carried the day. But when it has been overtly partisan, as in the cases of nationalization and the question of the state's role in private education, success rates have been patchier and defeat more common. The Council's deafness to partisan argument has also been apparent in its unresponsiveness to opposition senators when governmental and senatorial majorities have overlapped.

The existence of a meaningful avenue of appeal has strengthened the Senate as well, more generally, as the opposition to the government of the day. Dialogue between the two chambers and with governments has become more the norm. The threat of appeal, evoked by senators, has made the three partners to the legislative process more realistic for fear of the debilitating effects of reversal.

Senatorial oversight has thus taken a variety of forms and, regardless of who holds political power, is particularly necessary in the political system that is the Fifth Republic. More than in other forms of government, power tends to flow to power in a system that is presidentialist and majoritarian because in it ideas and goals are shared by the head of state, the government, and the majority in the lower house. In this context, the principal role of the Senate is to block or moderate the actions of deputies. It is not just also to control the possible abuse of power by those at the helm of government. The Senate's role is to be the voice of criticism, and it is not enough to show evidence of reflection in the improvement of legislative proposals or vigilance in the oversight of government actions, if it is to be performed effectively. Public attention and respect must also be won. It must therefore function as a nationally representative body, but the method of its election, the social role it sets for itself, and the steadfastness of its political orientation all provoke debate, questions, and sometimes polemics.

A Controversial Representational Base

The Senate reflects the geography of France, its land and communities, whereas the National Assembly represents its demography and the current state of public opinion. Article 24 of the Constitution sets this difference in stone: "The Senate shall be elected by indirect suffrage. It shall ensure the representation of the territorial units of the Republic. Frenchmen living outside France shall be represented in the Senate."[9] In keeping with tradition, the Fifth Republic grants privileged status to intermediary bodies deeply rooted in the localities. Senators therefore are indirectly elected by departmentally defined colleges made up for the most part of local elected officials.[10]

Pronounced Inequalities

The constitutional provision allowing for the parliamentary representation of French citizens living overseas is novel and places their representatives in a Senate that has often shown a special concern for their problems. The Higher Council of French People Overseas appoints twelve senators by proportional representation and, since 1982, has itself been directly elected by French adults living permanently abroad and registered with their embassy or consulate. The 309 other senators are chosen by electoral colleges comprised of officials holding elected office within departments. Favoring the department in this way is no accident; it is a unit seen as being sufficiently small to sustain close contact between candidates and electors. Each college is composed of several hundred people. Election campaigns are muted and incumbents have the advantage of already knowing personally all those whose support they need to win. Colleges themselves are made up of deputies (elected nationally), departmental councillors, councillors from regions of which the department is part, and municipal councillors or their delegates.[11] All these people are directly elected by universal suffrage, although the different categories of local communities are not equally represented in the college. In fact, the communes virtually monopolize its membership. They provided, for example, 95.5 percent of those taking part the last three times the colleges have met to elect senators. The Senate, therefore, is first and foremost the creature of the communes.

Moreover, the way the representation of communes within the college is determined generates further serious inequalities. The problem is that the number of representatives enjoyed by each commune is not always proportional to its population size, and the smallest, i.e., most rural, communes are most advantaged by this disparity. Those with fewer than 1,000 inhabitants are overrepresented, while towns with more than 20,000 inhabitants, making up 40 percent of the country's total population, are seriously underrepresented. Department-by-department analysis shows that representational distortions are the norm (Grangé 1988, 1990). In 38 departments, delegates from communes with fewer than 2,000 inhabitants are in the majority, while the population of these same communes constitutes less than half the total population of the department. More generally, half of those responsible for electing senators represent only one-third of the French population. This distortion is aggravated by the fact that the relatively few departmental councillors that there are in the colleges tend to overrepresent rural areas.

The magnitude of the distortion is a function of the relationship between each department's urban and rural populations. If their demographic structure is more or less the same, then, as in Paris and its suburbs, distortion is nonexistent, just as it is in departments that are almost exclusively rural. By contrast, rural overrepresentation is especially marked in the one-third of departments that are part urban and part rural. Moreover, contrary to what apologists for these inequalities claim in order to justify them, it is not the poorest or least inhabited departments that are the least well represented in senatorial electoral colleges. With the exception of a few mountain regions, this honor falls on the towns and villages of regions where agriculture is quite prosperous and the economy is in fundamentally good shape (Grangé 1988, 1990). Thus, the indirect election of the Senate acts as a prism that severely distorts its sociological and demographic representational base.

This distortion is worsened by communal delegates to the electoral college being chosen by different electoral systems. In communes of less than 3,500 inhabitants, they are elected by majority vote by municipal councillors themselves elected on the same basis. In more populated communes, municipal councillors are chosen according to an electoral system that combines proportional representation and majoritarianism, but up to the point of communes having 9,000 inhabitants, their electoral college delegates are still chosen on the majoritarian principle. Indeed, only the extra delegates allotted to towns with more than 30,000 people are chosen by proportional representation. Thus, in the smaller communes (those with less than 9,000 inhabitants), the delegation to the Senate electoral college is chosen wholly by the majority in control of the municipal council. In urban communes, by contrast, political minorities can win delegates thanks to proportional representation. The system works, therefore, to increase the representation of political majorities in small and average-sized communes already advantaged by boasting a number of delegates disproportionate to their population.

A separate provision of the electoral law distorts the distribution of seats between departments. The number of seats per department is not, as in the U. S. Senate, equal regardless of population size. Equally, it is not proportional to population size. Each department with less than 150,000 people returns one senator. A seat is then added for every extra 250,000 inhabitants or fraction of that number. Discrepancies between population size and number of seats inevitably follow. Lozère, for example, has 75,000 inhabitants and one seat, whereas a department with twelve times as many inhabitants is entitled to only four seats. Departments with heavy population densities are thus penalized, and redistricting, which last took place in 1976, is not written into the law, so population movement since then has been ignored. The result is that if the last census, taken in 1990, were used to redraw the boundaries of the 304 metropolitan seats on the basis of population size, 20 rural departments would lose a representative to the benefit of more urbanized departments.

Finally, the electoral system varies with the number of seats to be filled in each department. Most common is majoritarianism with two rounds of voting, and it takes place in departments not returning more than four senators. Candidates present themselves as individuals or as a member of a list, vote splitting is allowed, and the two ballots take place on the same day. An absolute majority is required to win on the first ballot, but a plurality suffices to win on the second. An alternate is elected with each victorious candidate.[12] The fifteen departments with five or more seats return ninety-eight, or one-third of, metropolitan senators. In them, proportional representation is used, and neither vote splitting nor preferential voting is allowed. Seats are awarded to candidates in accordance with their placement on party lists. The preponderance of majoritarianism only serves to aggravate the representational distortions described earlier. The political majority in the most rural departments guarantees itself a monopoly or quasi-monopoly of representational opportunities in the Senate, while a proportional system, in promoting minority representation, ensures that the more populated departments will not have the same opportunities.[13]

Notables and Mediators

The electoral system, indirect election, and the composition and departmentally based character of the electoral college all lead to the choice (one might say, co-optation) of local notables experienced in public service. Above all else, senators are citizens active in civic and local life. They have proved themselves at the grassroots level. Not surprisingly, therefore, electoral college delegates are not distributed uniformly across socio-professional groups. The agricultural professions or professions closely tied to peasant life are heavily represented in the upper house, constituting 17 percent of its metropolitan membership as opposed to nearly 4 percent of that of a National Assembly that is more representative of the French population at large. Educators and professionals in the fields of commerce and industry are also numerous, while lawyers, a traditionally important group, are declining in number, currently constituting 12 percent of senators. Practitioners in the medical professions are constantly growing in number and now constitute 16 percent of members. Wage earners, and notably workers, are underrepresented.

Being knowledgeable and experienced mediators, senators act as two-way channels of communication between the central government and the localities. Rooted in the latter, they claim to be their voice in Paris and their authoritative mediators. They preside over the main associations of elected local officials, of French mayors, of presidents of the departmental councils, and numerous other specialized bodies. Their local roots and popular election allow senators to speak for the institutions whose main concerns and interests they share. The senator is not a locally elected official sitting in Parliament, but a parliamentarian chosen by locally elected officials. Thus, many of them remain locally elected officials while sitting in the Senate. This was the case for more than 90 percent of all senators in September 1993. Their ranks included 171 mayors, 66 municipal councillors, 34 departmental council presidents, 124 departmental councillors and 32 regional councillors (including three presidents). Some of these statistics are similar to those found in the National Assembly. The big difference, though, is that the deputy seeks to consolidate his position in national political life by holding local office, whereas accession to the Senate is recognition of distinguished achievement in local affairs and the crowning point of an individual's public career. It is rare for it to represent a starting rather than a finishing point.

Given these circumstances, it is not surprising that the Senate holds detailed debates on problems affecting local life and claims the right to be the first to consider bills touching on such matters. Senators thus accord a threefold significance to their representative mission: (1) to reiterate that the Senate is the natural advocate and defender of France's local communities; (2) to maintain that this role is its constant preoccupation; and (3) to show through its actions that it ensures the defense of these communities and the values (liberty, community, and tradition) they uphold.

This frame of mind results in a desire to keep the institution as it is. Senators reject the notion that other forms of collective representation, notably one that is socioprofessionally based, can replace or be combined with its territorial character. Change thus becomes suspect and reforms are kept to a minimum because senators feel comfortable with what is. The commune and the department are valued for what they are, and restructuring proposals entailing combining them, introducing new ones, or promoting the virtues of the region over the longer established departments and communes are distrusted. Developments in the overseas territories are followed attentively, and local elected bodies, their legal standing, and spheres of competence are protected by avoiding local referendums or any other form of direct citizen participation in the life of the community. The Senate's goals are instead to enhance local autonomy, to change fiscal policy in the localities' favor, and to reinforce the authority of mayors.

Championing representative democracy in this traditional form, senators effectively defend the local system in force and the local elected officials in place. System of government and rural civilization are seen as one and the same thing. This is not to argue that the Senate is a chamber of unbending agricultural defense. Rather, it gives institutional expression to the deliberate choice of a way of life. Stability, caution, and experience are all values that it honors and respects. The problem is that, based on a rural, artisan, and declining society long symbolized by the politico-administrative units of commune, canton, and department, the Senate does not capture the complex reality of French society as it is today.

Rather, it is sliding quietly into the role of protector and champion of social groups and forces that, more marginalized than oppressed, are threatened by the way the country is evolving. The association between the upper chamber and an out-of-date social order is well reflected in the small number of female senators. While growing in number, there are still only 18, or about 6 percent. Their numbers in the National Assembly are barely higher, having varied between 2 percent and 7 percent up until 1997. But more to the point, women senators are almost all elected on PR party lists and usually belong to parties of the Left. Thus, sexual equality is far from having been achieved, largely because the Senate has set itself up as the defender of a social order that belongs to the past.

An Unchanging Political Orientation

Perhaps unsurprisingly given the Senate's self-image, its political majority displays political orientations that have remained constant since the first wave of Fifth Republican senators took office in 1959. Little has changed as the result of the turnover of either individual senators or of generations of them. Moderates dominate the chamber, largely because parties distant from the political center are only weakly represented in it. The Ecologists and far-right National Front do not have a member between them, and the Communist contingent has never been more than 8 percent of the total body. The Socialists have done better, often constituting about 20 percent of the membership and boasting 24 percent of it today. Despite being the dominant group in the National Assembly, the Gaullists claimed only between 10 and 13 percent of the total membership. Since 1983, however, the party has reaped the benefits of having built itself up both as a grassroots organization and as an influence in agricultural circles; it is now the single largest group in the Senate with 29 percent of the seats.

It is the parties at the center and center-right of the political spectrum that have always formed the majority in the second chamber and provided its president. In former times, they claimed about three-fifths of the seats, a figure that has fallen to a little above 40 percent now. Split into various groups with ever-shifting identities, they nonetheless display enduring characteristics that tie them to traditional political families. Thus, for example, the Independent Republicans (RI) practically absorbed a "peasant group" that had remained autonomous until 1980. Even so, the once preponderant RI has declined in recent times to the benefit of a centrist group whose name has varied but whose members come for the most part, although not always, from the ranks of Christian Democrats. The Democratic Left (renamed the Democratic and European Social Rally) aspires to unify the heirs of radicalism (which was very influential in the Third Republic) and moderates, some of whom belong to the government majority and some to the opposition. Unlike the Union for the Democratic Center in the National Assembly, in other words, no single group unifies centrist forces under a single banner. Rather, there is a simple system of liaisons and agreements whereby political groups are united by shared affinities and behaviors that themselves set the Senate apart in the French political system. These include most clearly courtesy, restraint, and individualism.

The limited change in the Senate is highlighted by the changing pattern of election outcomes in recent years. A few shifts in the distribution of seats have taken place to the benefit of the Centrist Union and then of the Gaullists; even the Socialists have experienced a slow growth in their numbers. Nonetheless, the general character of the Senate has remained unchanged because the Center and the Right have always commanded two-thirds of the seats and remained firmly in control of an institution that has withstood the changes that shook and transformed the National Assembly in 1962, 1968, and 1981. Indeed, the insulation of the Senate from the sometimes radical changes following from other electoral outcomes has been a constant of French political life. This insulation is particularly apparent in departments, where Senate elections continually return monolithic majorities of the right, while the National Assembly vote is more evenly distributed. The alternation of political ideologies in power is unknown in the Senate.

But does the Senate's being shielded from the pendulum swings of French political life not prevent it being the force for balance and accommodation that many see as its political role? Is it not instead a partisan institution protecting a particular sociopolitical order?

Conclusion: An Uncertain Identity

To be sure, the Senate's legitimacy is widely accepted. Time has done its work and it has become part of the French political landscape. In spite of its limited opportunities for action, of operating within the constraints of a rationalized parliamentarism, of the emergence of presidentialism, of a majoritarian and bipolarized regime, and of occasional deep conflict with the government actors running the country, it has made skillful use of longevity and compromise. Combining persuasion and amendment, negotiation and accommodation, pressure and retreat, reflection and imagination, it has managed to carve out a place for itself in the new political regime that is the Fifth Republic. Still, it has not always taken full advantage of the political opportunities available to it. Nor has it been constant in the political role it has chosen for itself. Depending on who formed the majority and the circumstances of the time, it has either moderated the actions of a regime in which power is concentrated or tried to swim against the political tide. But the way it is recruited has frozen its partisan composition, and its consequent failure to produce alternating majorities has limited its ability and its will to adjust to changing political circumstances.

However, this is not its image in public opinion. Better known, appreciated by locally elected bodies, esteemed for the quality of its work, it is perceived to symbolize calmness, vigilance, and security as it moderates, corrects, humanizes, and protects. Given this image, the Senate's calling is always to be the chamber in which dialogue takes place, in which different points of view are expressed, and in which original contributions to political debate are made. Its specific role must be adversarial both to complete the work of the lower house and to set itself apart from the government of the day. But this role can be too demanding for this Senate. As it has found, it is not always possible to fulfill tasks that are to some degree at odds with each other, while at the same time conforming to the image that the public has of it. The Senate is still searching for its identity.

Notes

This chapter was translated from French by Anthony Mughan.

1. The form the Senate would take remained vague for several weeks. At Bayeux on June 16, 1946, General de Gaulle made a famous speech on the form of government he preferred for the Fourth Republic. In 1958, he envisioned dividing the Senate into three groupings—two territorial (metropolitan, overseas) and one economic and cultural. But he soon renounced this plan, although it was to reappear in another form in 1969.

2. The principle of election of the president by direct, universal suffrage was adopted in 1962. Prior to that time, the constitution allowed for his appointment by a national electoral college of about 80,000 people. The composition of this body was similar to that choosing senators on a department-by-department basis. This is the method by which de Gaulle was elected president in 1958.

3. The organic law of December 28, 1976 added 33 seats in 29 of France's 100 departments in order to take account of an increased population shown in the 1975 census. The existing number of seats was not redistributed because the Senate was anxious not to reduce the representation of the two departments, Paris and la Creuse, that had lost population.

4. Article 49.3 of the constitution sets up a novel procedure: the National Assembly has to accept a legislative proposal in its entirety or pass a vote of no confidence in the government. If there is no censure vote, the legislation is accepted without being voted upon any further. This procedure could not be invoked in the Senate since that body does not have the right to dismiss the government by a vote of no confidence. It was often used in the Assembly by Raymond Barre as a means of bypassing Gaullist obstructionism. It was particularly effective because, although the Gaullists may not have liked certain legislative proposals, they did not want to give the Left an opening by censuring d'Estaing's centrist government and precipitating new elections.

5. The "preliminary question" is intended to determine whether there is any justification for proceeding with consideration of a bill. The "inadmissibility provision" involves Senate recognition that a legislative proposal is inconsistent with some constitutional provision. The Senate's acceptance of either claim entails automatic rejection of the bill.

6. The government presented three proposals intended to correct representational inequalities. These were (1) the election by each municipal council of delegates whose number was to be determined by the population size of the commune (one delegate for each 500 inhabitants or fraction of that number), (2) the designation of municipal council delegates by proportional representation in communes with 3,500 inhabitants or more, and (3) election of senators by proportional representation in departments with at least three Senate seats. The Senate rejected these proposed changes by voting in favor of a preliminary question on the issue, and refused to discuss further reforms of the Senate.

7. One of the early effects of the August 1995 revision of the Constitution was that the Senate examined eleven such initiatives between October 1995 and June 1996, suggesting a possible revival of its legislative initiative.

8. Reserved for the National Assembly, the prerogative to dismiss is considered to be compensation for being liable to dissolution. The Senate cannot be dissolved.

9. These broad constitutional principles are fleshed out by more easily modified laws concerning the composition of the Senate and the elections and terms of office of its members. Election disputes and the constitutionality of each chamber's rules are determined by the Constitutional Council.

10. The Senate comprises 321 seats: 304 of them are allocated to departments (296 in metropolitan France, and 8 overseas); 3 to overseas territories (New Caledonia, Polynesia, and the Wallis and Futuna Islands); 2 to communities with special standing (Mayotte and Saint-Pierre-et-Miquelon); and 12 are reserved to French people living outside France.

11. The presence of deputies in these colleges is somewhat incongruous, since they are the only national political figures in them. Departmental councillors are elected by majority ballot held in cantonal districts. Regional councillors are elected within departments, but represent the whole region of which their department is a part. Municipal councillors run France's communes.

12. The alternate takes up the seat most commonly if the person elected to it dies or assumes a cabinet position, but not if the senator resigns. In departments where proportional representation is used, it is the leading unsuccessful candidate on the senator's party candidate list who replaces him or her.

13. When its existence was threatened, the Senate adopted a proposal in 1968 to bring departmental representation up to date, and foresaw a subsequent reform of the composition of electoral colleges to reflect population changes in the department. The National Assembly did not get around to considering this proposal, however, and it has now lapsed.

References and Sources

Avril, Pierre. 1988. "Les innovations sénatoriales." *Pouvoirs* 44:111–18.

Avril, Pierre, and Jean Gicquel. 1996. *Droit parlementaire*. 2d ed. Paris: Montchrestien.

Baguenard, Jacques. 1990. *Le Sénat*. Paris: Presses Universitaires de France.

Bécane, Jean-Claude. 1988. "Le règlement du Sénat: A la recherche du temps maîtrisé." *Pouvoirs* 44:79–85.

Cluzel, Jean. 1990. *Le Sénat dans la société française*. Paris: Economica.

Delcamp, Alain. 1991. *Le Sénat et la décentralisation*. Paris: Economica.

Duhamel, Olivier. 1995. *Le pouvoir politique en France*. Paris: Seuil.

Georgel, Jacques. 1988. *Le Sénat dans l'adversité, 1962–1966*. Paris: Cujas.

Gicquel, Jean-Eric. 1996. "Le Sénat sous la seconde cohabitation." *Revue du Droit Public* 4:1069–94.

Grangé, Jean. 1981. "Attitudes et vicissitudes du Sénat." *Revue Française de Science Politique* 31:32–84.

———. 1984. "L'efficacité normative du Sénat." *Revue Française de Science Politique* 34:955–87.

———. 1988. "Le système d'election des sénateurs et ses effets." *Pouvoirs* 44:35–57.

———. 1990. "Les déformations de la représentation des collectivités territoriales et de la population au Sénat." *Revue Française de Science Politique* 40:5–45.

Huber, John D. 1992. "Restrictive Legislative Procedures in France and the United States." *American Political Science Review* 86:675–87.

Luchaire, François, and Gérard Conac, eds. 1987. *La Constitution de la République française.* 2d ed. Paris: Economica.

Marichy, Jean-Pierre. 1969. *La deuxième chambre dans la vie politique française depuis 1875.* Paris: Librairie Générale de Droit et de Jurisprudence.

Mastias, Jean. 1980. *Le Sénat de la Ve République: Réforme et renouveau.* Paris: Economica.

———. 1988. "Histoire des tentations du Sénat de la Ve République." *Pouvoirs* 44:15–34.

———. 1997. "La place du Sénat dans le système politique français." In *Le bicamérisme.* Association française des Constitutionnalistes. Paris: Economica.

Mastias, Jean, and Jean Grangé, eds. 1987. *Les secondes chambres du Parlement en Europe occidentale.* Paris: Economica.

Maus, Didier. 1995. *Les grandes textes de la pratique institutionnelle de la Ve République.* 7th ed. Paris: Documentation Française.

———. 1996. *Le Parlement sous le Ve République.* 3d ed. Paris: Presses Universitaires de France.

Money, Jeannette, and George Tsebelis. "The Political Power of the French Senate: Micromechanisms of Bicameral Negotiations." *Journal of Legislative Studies* 1: 192–217.

Poher, Alain. 1993. *Trois fois président.* Paris: Plon.

Pour mieux connaître le Sénat. 1993. Paris: Documentation française.

Tsebelis, George, and Jeannette Money. 1995. "Bicameral Negotiations: The Navette System in France." *British Journal of Political Science* 25:101–29.

7

To Revise and Deliberate:
The British House of Lords

DONALD SHELL

The House of Lords is a most surprising institution. Its survival as a largely hereditary and politically lopsided body in a democratic state is paradoxical. Proposals for its substantial reform have been legion, but little structural change has taken place. It remains true in the 1990s that not a single member of the House derives a seat from any kind of election. Most have inherited the right to be there, and the others owe their appointment to the exercise of prime ministerial patronage. This peculiar basis of membership is reflected in the permanent preponderance enjoyed by the Conservative Party in the House. Regardless of which party is in government, the Conservatives always enjoy a majority over all other parties in the upper house.

Predictions that the House of Lords would wither away have long been heard, but in the past few decades the House has actually become more significant. Governments rely on it to scrutinize draft legislation, as does the House of Commons, which frequently dispatches bills to the upper house in a decidedly ill-digested condition. The House of Lords stands as a blatant contradiction of democratic principle, yet it remains an active second chamber in a supposedly democratic political system. How is this paradox sustained?

The key to understanding the House is to recognize that it is all of a piece with the British Constitution. Because there has never been sufficient occasion to oblige Britain to reformulate its constitution, this has evolved gradually over many centuries. It is the product of incremental change made in response to changing attitudes and altered circumstances rather than the outcome of any deliberate design. Neither defeat in war, nor successful revolution, nor federal union of any kind has imposed the need for a fresh start. The Cromwellian interlude of the seventeenth century was followed by a "Restoration" and a "Glorious Revolution." Former institutions which had been abolished, including both the House of Lords and the Monarchy, were reinstated. Had these upheavals taken place a century later, then a full written or codified constitution would probably have been devised. But in the late seventeenth century there was neither the aptitude nor the desire to do this. Instead, there was a recognition that while the future would see a different relationship between the Crown and Parliament, the precise nature of that relationship would be better worked out in political practice than defined in formal principle. And that preference has remained as a guiding light in subsequent constitutional developments.

In the nineteenth century the House of Commons gradually adapted to the demands of democracy as the franchise was extended from 1832 onwards. The junior status of the House of Lords became clearly recognized many years before the passage of the 1911 Parliament Act, which imposed for the first time a limitation on the power of the House to veto legislation. It was only the failure of the upper house to abide by the convention not to overturn the clearly expressed will of the Commons that precipitated the constitutional crisis of 1909–11, a crisis eventually terminated by the passage of the 1911 Act.

Change continued throughout the twentieth century, but the process of change has never been the outcome of carefully considered and deliberately designed reform. Instead, change occurred in response to events and expectations. For example, at the turn of the century the prime minister and half the cabinet sat in the House of Lords, but without any formal declaration or change of written rule it soon thereafter became accepted that the political ascendancy of the House of Commons was such that the prime minister must be a member of the lower house. By the 1990s it had become difficult to imagine more than two or three cabinet ministers sitting in the Lords and thereby excluded from the Commons.

This preference for an uncodified constitution along with a capacity to adapt ancient institutions to modern roles, and to generate reasonably clear understandings about the relationship between them, is characteristic of the British. There remains a reluctance to think deeply about fundamental constitutional principles, or to attempt to formulate precise rules about the extent of power or the limitations upon its exercise. To some this is an infuriating weakness, exposing the British to the accusation of failing to consummate the principles of democracy. To others these features are the hallmark of a sophisticated system, one only possible in a highly mature political society. The continuation of a House of Lords as a real working second chamber in the British Parliament can only be understood in this wider context of constitutional understanding.

The Twentieth Century: Change but Not Decay

Since the passage of the 1832 Reform Act, the anomalous character of the House has been widely accepted. Schemes for reform have abounded. Yet actual reform has been tardy and tentative. In opposition, parties have tended to espouse the cause of reform, but in office they have almost invariably found their priorities have lain in other directions. Legislation has brought two significant changes in the twentieth century and two relatively minor adjustments, affecting the powers and the composition of the House.

First was the formal curtailment in the power of the House. The absolute veto the House had possessed over legislation was replaced by a suspensory veto in 1911, initially set for two years but in 1949 cut to one year. However, any bill certified by the speaker of the House of Commons as a money bill could be passed within one month, notwithstanding opposition from the Lords. When the Parliament Act was passed in 1911, politicians expected the House of Lords to use its newly prescribed delaying power with some regularity. Indeed, in the first three years that is exactly what happened (Bromhead 1958, 136–40). But thereafter expectations changed, and since the First World War only two bills have been enacted despite resistance from the House of Lords, and both were unusual. The first was the 1949 Parliament Act, where the House used its delaying power to delay the proposed further reduction in its delaying power. The second was the War Crimes Act of 1990, a bill introduced by the Conservative government but one which was not in any normal sense of the term a party measure. Opposition to this bill, which permitted the prosecution of individuals who had committed war crimes in German-held territory in Europe during the Second World War, came from within all parties and from the judiciary. This became the first bill which had ever been passed using Parliament Act procedure under a Conservative government (Shell 1992, 132–33).

On two other occasions under the Labour government of the 1970s, the upper house declined to pass bills in the form the government and the Commons wished. Both times the bills concerned were reintroduced in the following parliamentary session under Parliament Act procedures. But before they had run their course, agreement was reached. One concerned the position of journalists in relation to possible trade union "closed shop" arrangements, and the other concerned the nationalization of ship repairing in the context of a bill that nationalized shipbuilding (Baldwin 1995).

Although the House retains the right to delay legislation, this is a power it has been most reluctant to use. In 1945, the leader of the Conservative peers, the fifth marquess of Salisbury, articulated a view that the House should not use its power to resist bills that had been foreshadowed in the governing party's previous election manifesto, though it would reserve the right to propose amendments to such bills. As originally defined, this was a precise and limited restriction on the powers of the House. But the tendency has been for such understandings to be extended over the years, for example, to cover all Queen's Speech bills, irrespective of any foreshadowing of the bill concerned in an election manifesto, or any significant amendment to a manifesto bill, notwithstanding the fact that election manifestos are hardly written in the precise terms found in a government white paper.[1] Although secondary legislation was not covered by the Parliament Acts, leaving the House with an absolute veto over statutory instruments, this is a power which the House has in practice virtually relinquished. It has been used only once in the postwar period—when the Conservative majority vetoed the S. Rhodesia (UN Sanctions) Order of 1968 (Morgan 1975, 137–51).

The caution the House has displayed in regard to the use of power may be considered understandable in the context of its anomalous character and lack of democratic legitimacy. To have acted otherwise might well have resulted in the forfeiture of its remaining powers. Indeed, the unreformed composition of the House has suited successive governments well because it has enabled them to ensure the House remains comparatively docile. For the House of Lords, the price of continuity has been restraint, perhaps to such a degree that some would say the House has embraced a voluntary impotence.

But composition has not been entirely ignored. The second major change of the twentieth century was the introduction of life peers in 1958. Prior to that date all new peerages (save for those given to senior judges) were hereditary. The case for life peerages had long been acknowledged; Bagehot writing in 1867 bemoaned the failure of a recent proposal to bring about such a reform (Bagehot 1963, 144 – 46). Only with the advent of life peerages could the House regularly receive newly created members without inexorably swelling its total size. Again, this might have seemed a small reform, but it was accompanied by a continued change in the notion of the sort of person to whom a peerage might be given. The House became more representative, at least of the professional classes. The balance of membership shifted, with an increasing proportion being those who had accepted a peerage rather than those who had inherited a peerage. The rate at which new peerage creations took place doubled after the passage of the 1958 Act. A larger number of practicing politicians found their way into the upper house, mostly those who were approaching retirement. And, for the first time, women were admitted.

This was followed in 1963 by a minor legislative change that allowed peers by succession to renounce their peerages and so escape the obligation to sit in the Lords. This enabled those who wished to continue to sit in the House of Commons to do so. The need for this change arose because an able and ambitious young Labour MP (known since as Tony

Benn) inherited a peerage and was in consequence instantly disqualified from sitting in the Commons. His campaign to secure a right for peers by succession to renounce their peerages found some support among prominent Conservatives, two of whom—Quintin Hogg and Sir Alec Douglas Home—became, along with Tony Benn, the first to take advantage of this change (Crick 1964, 139–46). But since 1963 only fourteen other individuals have followed their example.[2]

Apart from these changes, ideas for reform have frequently been considered. The Parliament Act of 1911 was seen as temporary; it actually contained a prologue to this effect. Following its enactment, a commission was established under Lord James Bryce to consider the second house question. This recommended considerable change in the composition of the House, but nothing was done (Bryce 1918). In 1949 all party talks produced a wide measure of agreement, but a gap remained between the Attlee-led Labour government and the Conservatives over the appropriate powers that a reformed second chamber should have. So Labour carried out its own adjustment to the 1911 Parliament Act, but did nothing about the composition of the House (Crick 1964, 122–31).

Labour in office again in the late 1960s produced an elaborate scheme for reform, which would have phased out all hereditary peers and brought into being a house of nominees, who—providing they were regular attenders—would have retained their right to membership until they reached a retirement age fixed at seventy-two. The scheme appealed to many in both major parties, and the upper house itself expressed clear support. But the Conservative Right disliked the removal of hereditary peers, and others in all parties disliked the idea of creating a house the membership of which in the long run would be entirely the result of prime ministerial patronage. Many MPs were apprehensive about doing anything that would potentially strengthen the legitimacy of the second chamber. Although legislation to bring about these changes gained a second reading in the Commons, at committee stage the bill sank in a sea of hostility bereft of sustained commitment from a government that never seemed more than lukewarm in support of the proposals that ministers had devised (Morgan 1975, 169–220).

In the 1970s and early 1980s, Labour flirted again with the idea of abolishing the Lords before settling on a policy of reform. The Conservatives in opposition in the 1970s gave serious consideration to House reform; a Conservative Party committee recommended a two-thirds elected and one-third nominated chamber shorn of all hereditary peers (Home 1978). But back in office under Margaret Thatcher, the Conservatives pushed constitutional reform off the agenda; Thatcher preferred governing to thinking about the machinery of government. In opposition since 1979, Labour supported first the removal of the second house altogether, then its replacement by a nominated house almost devoid of power, and then a proposal simply to remove the peers by succession with the promise of further reform at a later date.

Meanwhile, the House of Lords itself underwent something of a renaissance. The average daily attendance of peers increased from a little over one hundred in the late 1950s to almost four hundred in the mid-1990s. No doubt the introduction of a daily expenses allowance in 1957, and its steady increase since then, has encouraged higher attendance.[3] Twice as many peers contributed to debates in the 1990s compared with the 1950s, and the number of hours the House sat more than doubled over the same period. The legislative work of the House grew as it passed seemingly ever more amendments to bills. At the same time its select committee work expanded, mainly through taking up roles which for various reasons the Commons appeared to eschew, not least the scrutiny of draft proposals from the European Community. The record of the House in securing adjustments to bills against the wishes of government appeared to grow; peers themselves gave evidence of quiet satisfaction when their House, still Conservative dominated, was described as the "other Opposition" (Shell 1992). The place of the House seemed more secure than it had been for decades.

House Membership

With around 1,200 individuals having the right to a seat, and over 800 attending at some point in the year, the House of Lords has a very large membership (see table 7.1). Over 60 percent are peers by succession, of whom some 450 attend the House, about half doing so on over one-third of the sitting days. Peers by succession are the aristocracy, still divided into five ranks (dukes, marquesses, earls, viscounts, and barons), although these rankings have no significance in the work of the House. Despite their presence, it is wrong to think of the House in practice as a predominantly aristocratic institution. The aristocratic nature of the working

Table 7.1. Membership in the British House of Lords, 1996

Membership Categories	Total	Women	Conser-vatives	Labour	Liberal-Democrats	Cross-bench	Others
Peers by succession	760	17	332	12	26	161	70
Hereditary peers	15	0	6	0	1	5	3
Life peers	386	62	143	104	31	92	8
Life peers (Law Lords)	20	—	—	—	—	20	—
Bishops	26	—	—	—	—	—	26
Total	1,207	79	481	116	58	278	107

Note: Included in columns one and two above, but excluded from figures for party strength, are peers without writs of summons ($N = 85$) and peers on leave of absence ($N = 82$).

house has been diluted by the arrival of life peers in plentiful numbers and their generally higher level of activity. At the same time, aristocracy has become a less potent force in the nation. The highest ranking aristocrats may remain a small and exclusive group, but they are no longer the great magnates of wealth and power that they were a century ago (Cannadine 1990).

Hereditary peers as a whole may have been educated predominantly at exclusive "public" schools (over half went to Eton), but the claim that from within their ranks the ordinary person's point of view is frequently articulated should not be ignored. It could certainly be argued that to attain membership in a parliamentary chamber does require today very special ambition and commitment; those who display these qualities are far from usual. This would also be true of most of those who reach the House of Lords as life peers. They are people of very distinctive achievement. At the same time, hereditary peers do simply arrive there through the accident of birth and death. Some are opulent to an astounding degree; most are wealthy. A few are virtually penniless. Some live comfortably off their private resources, but many earn their living in the professions and in business, and where they do this they are probably more typical of the ordinary working members of these professions than are the luminaries who become life peers. Taken as a whole, the hereditary peers do bring to Parliament a range of experience which otherwise would be absent from its counsels.

Those who do not owe their seats to the accident of birth may be divided into four categories. First are the twenty-six senior bishops of the Church of England. These are members of the House only while they hold their offices; they are the only group who do not remain in the House for their lifetime. Senior bishops are busy, and attending the Lords is only one of many demands upon their time. Seldom does a bishop attend more than 10 percent of the sittings, but collectively they take their responsibilities to the House seriously, and by means of a rota seek to ensure an episcopal presence whenever the subject matter of a debate seems to warrant this. Bishops do not feel obliged to avoid politically controversial areas; sometimes they are among the government's most determined opponents in the Lords, especially where they discern moral issues underlying legislative proposals, as for example on the 1996 Asylum and Immigration Control Bill.

Second are the senior judges who, once promoted to the House to undertake its judicial work, remain members for life. Legal learning is characteristic of the membership of many legislative chambers, but the presence of the most senior members of the judiciary as full speaking and voting members is yet another unusual feature of the House of Lords. These two dozen or so serving and retired "law lords" invariably sit on the cross-benches, indicating their independence from political party ties. This does not inhibit them from taking an active part in the work of the House and at times robustly attacking the government, especially concerning the administration of the judicial system or the sentencing powers of the courts. Third, there are a few individuals who have been awarded hereditary peerages, though since the introduction of life peerages in 1958 the award of new hereditary peerages has become unusual, and hence the number in this category is small.[4]

Finally, there are those individuals who have been created life peers, almost four hundred, or just over 30 percent of the total membership. A life peerage may be given as an honor, the first and highest category of honor in the regular honors lists that appear in the United Kingdom. But a life peerage may also be given to an individual specifically to enable that person to become a working member of the House of Lords. All new peerages are given by the Crown on the nomination of the prime minister. Persons distinguished in public life or in the business, financial, or professional worlds may receive peerages. Alongside these and receiving the same "honor" are individuals whom party leaders wish to see as working members. Sometimes lists of so-called working peers are now announced separately from the regular honors lists, but there is no formal distinction between such working peers and those whose peerage is announced in an honors list, nor are there any particular obligations imposed on working peers, some of whom quickly cease to be active in the Lords.

About one-third of all life peers have been members of Parliament. These include former senior cabinet ministers who arrive in the Lords as their distinguished careers draw to a close, as well as MPs who lose their seats in the Commons at the hands of the electorate. Other life peers may be drawn from the ranks of party supporters in business, the trades unions, or the professions, while some are distinguished former public servants, authors, and religious leaders.

Generally, in parliamentary chambers the great majority of members approximate to a very similar level of activity. This may be recognized as one of the consequences of the increased professionalism of legislators. But in the House of Lords this is emphatically not the case. Although over 1,200 individuals have the right to take part in the activities of the House, many are relatively inactive. Some members attend virtually every sitting of the House, vote in almost all the divisions, and regularly contribute to debates and to committee work. Others do so spasmodically, perhaps attending only a few times a year and rarely if ever making speeches. But it would be wrong to think of those who attend much less frequently as not making significant contributions to the work of the House. One of the characteristics of the House is that it does allow individuals who are emphatically not politicians to contribute to the work of Parliament. At a time when the House of Commons has become increasingly dominated by professional politicians and career politicians, the House of Lords retains some members who are definitely amateur politicians and others who are not politicians at all. These include some who have had highly successful careers elsewhere. There is a mingling of politicians with non-politicians which is unusual in contemporary parliamentary chambers.

A further feature of House membership is the relatively small number of women. Until 1958 the House was an entirely male preserve, but in that year women were made eligible for life peerages. The 1963 Peerage Act removed the previous prohibition that the House itself had placed on women who inherited peerages. But very few women do inherit peerages, because even if this is possible under the terms of the original peerage, a male heir will always take precedence over a female. It is worth noting that attempts to remove this gender discrimination by creating a general right for the firstborn to inherit have been actively resisted by the House of Lords itself.[5] Thus at a time when much public concern has been focused on how to increase the proportion of women in politics, it is an irony that the House of Lords maintains an active discrimination against women.

The House is also a rather elderly institution. Very few people are created life peers before the age of fifty, and most must wait until they are past sixty. A few peers by succession inherit while young, but most do not until they are at least middle-aged. The average age of the entire House is sixty-five; the average age of Labour peers (very few of whom are peers by succession) is over seventy. For many peers, House membership is associated with a kind of semiretirement. Perhaps the opportunity to go to the House of Lords does encourage some MPs to retire earlier than they otherwise would. It is after all a very congenial place to spend the eventide of a political career. Indeed, the sheer attractiveness of taking a place on those red leather benches should not be underestimated. Such a position brings status, dignity, friends, and the possibility of doing a little useful political work along the way. The House is a very comfortable institution. To be a member does not require extensive commitment; it need not be demanding of time. Yet if a peer is eager to work hard on behalf of some cause, it is possible to do this without the distraction of constituents or the preoccupation of electoral campaigns.

There is a continuous gradual turnover of members in the House of Lords in contrast to the sudden transformation in membership that occurs in the Commons following a general election. On average, some twenty new peerages are given every year; a slightly smaller number of hereditary peers die each year and are succeeded by heirs. Following a general election or a change of government, there may be an influx of new peers, but this is never comparable in scope to the changes an elected House can expect to undergo after a general election. The continuity in membership contributes to the experience the House can call upon, and probably also makes the House as a whole hesitant to precipitate change in its ways.

Diverse elements within the membership of the House are drawn together through the influence of political parties. Nationally organized, centrally controlled, programmatic parties dominate British politics, and it is not surprising that most peers accept political party discipline—they take a party whip (see table 7.2). The parties organize themselves as they do in the Commons, with front bench spokespersons and with varied levels of whipping to urge attendance. But though party whips may seek to persuade peers to support the party line, there are no effective sanctions

Table 7.2. Attendance by Peers in the British House of Lords by Party and Peerage Type, 1994–1995

Party and Peerage Type	Frequency of Attendance (days per year)				
	0	*1–46*	*47–94*	*95+*	*Total*
Conservative					
Created	4	50	33	59	146
Succeeded	61	127	44	98	330
Total	65	177	77	157	476
Labour					
Created	5	15	17	59	96
Succeeded	1	3	1	8	13
Total	6	18	18	67	109
Liberal Democrats					
Created	0	4	12	14	30
Succeeded	1	8	5	8	22
Total	1	12	17	22	52
Cross-bench					
Created	18	50	19	21	108
Succeeded	92	101	21	31	245
Total	110	151	40	52	353
Bishops	1	21	1	0	23
Law Lords	2	18	1	3	24
Total					
Created	30	158	83	156	427
Succeeded	155	239	71	145	610
Total	185	397	154	301	1,037

Note: Excludes peers who died during the session, bishops who resigned, peers on leave of absence, or peers without writs; includes peers who sat first, were introduced, or translated.

that whips can employ against the rebellious. Party cohesion as measured by voting behavior is high; typically more than 98 votes out of every 100 cast by peers in the two main parties are in conformity with the wishes of the party whips (Beamish 1993).

On the government side, in recent years there have usually been some twenty to twenty-five ministers and whips. The leader of the House and the lord chancellor may be joined by another peer as cabinet ministers drawn from the House, but even the Conservatives have only had two cabinet members in the Lords. A half-dozen or so ministers of state representing different departments and a similar number of junior ministers act as the main spokesmen for the government. Every area of government activity is spoken for in the House by one of these or by one of the half dozen or so whips, who unlike their Commons counterparts are not bound to remain silent but speak regularly for departments.

All government ministers and whips in both houses are appointed by the prime minister, but in opposition Labour elects its senior officers in the House. Although the Conservative leader in the House is appointed by the party leader, it is then the responsibility of the leader in the House to decide the membership of the front bench opposition team. Shadow spokespeople in the House are nominated for every area for which ministers take responsibility. Front-benchers wind up debates and take responsibility for piloting bills through the House, just as they do in the Commons, while opposition front-benchers provide liaison with their Commons counterparts. Because the government is answerable in the House, and because it must secure passage of its business in the House, party is a necessary feature of the life of the House. The parties hold regular weekly meetings, and some peers attend the backbench party committees that meet in the Commons.

But though the influence of party is very real, its dominance is less than in the Commons. The obvious reason for this is that peers owe neither their seats nor their continued House membership to election. Those whose party loyalty weakens may either keep quiet and abstain in divisions, or they may move to the cross-benches; they need have no fear that they may thereby lose their seat. The force of party is also muted because of the enormous imbalance that exists in party strength in the House. Within what has been seen as a classic two-party system, the Conservatives outnumber Labour in the Lords by four to one. If the two main parties were more evenly balanced in the House, it seems very likely that competition between them would become more intense.

The presence of a substantial number of cross-bench or nonparty peers further moderates the impact of party in the House. The cross-bench peers are a recognized element in the House; in some ways they act like a party, electing a convener, holding meetings, and seeking representation on House committees. Though they issue no whip, some cross-bench peers have been acknowledged within the House as being liable to swing opinion on subjects on which they are recognized to be particular authorities. Taking account of all cross-bench peers and all other parties and groups in the House, the Conservatives do lack an overall majority among those who attend the House; in recent years this has resulted in government defeat being likely where opinion on the cross-benches has swung decisively against the Conservatives.

The Work of the House

The House of Lords has both a legislative and a deliberative role. All legislation must pass through the House, which thereby has the opportunity to amend bills as they make their way to the statute book. House members also have the right to ask questions of the government and to initiate debates on motions calling the government to account over its stewardship. In its recent sessions, a little over half the time of the House has been spent on legislative work. Mostly this is a matter of revising draft legislation brought to Parliament by the government, but a few bills are initiated by private members in one or the other house. Some legislative work in recent sessions has been taken off the floor of the House and put into committees, but debate on bills in the Lords, including detailed committee stages, is still generally taken on the floor of the House, in contrast to the practice of the Commons. The rest of the time is spent on deliberative work; various procedures exist to provide opportunities for peers to debate motions and to ask questions of government spokesmen. In addition, a growing aspect of the work of the House over the last twenty years has been select committee activity; these are committees which take evidence and make reports to the House on various subjects.

Legislative Work

The value of the legislative work of the House is frequently emphasized. But, before trying to assess this, it is necessary to say something about the overall context within which this activity takes place. The legislative process in the British parliamentary system is dominated by the government. Members who are not part of the government—backbench members—have opportunities to introduce bills, but in the Commons such opportunities are very limited. The procedures ensure that only bills which are brief and either devoid of controversy or viewed favorably by the government are ever likely to pass (Natzler and Millar 1993). While about a third of all bills enacted are introduced by backbenchers, these represent typically only about 2 percent of the total number of new pages of legislation passed each year; the remaining 98 percent is government-introduced legislation.

In determining its legislative program, the government must consider the various pressures that act upon it, including parliamentary pressures. Typically, draft legislation is decided upon within government departments, after consultation with relevant organized groups, though the extent of such consultation varies considerably. In recent years the whole legislative process has been heavily criticized on several grounds (Rippon 1992). One has been the allegedly poor level of consultation, resulting in draft legislation that often needs extensive revision during its parliamentary stages simply to avoid problems that come to light after a bill has been published and publicly scrutinized. Another problem has been the growth of what has been referred to as a "legislate-as-you-go" mentality, with ministers not thinking their proposed legislation through carefully enough, resulting in the need for numerous amendments perhaps extending the scope of a bill after it has been introduced or fundamentally altering its provisions.

There are important distinctions between the two houses in respect to their activity of revising legislation. The lower house is intensely competitive in a party political sense; all activity in the Commons tends to be subordinated to the demands of competitive party politics. Bills receive many hours of scrutiny in Commons standing committees, but frequently this is less a collective effort to improve the technical quality of the bill (making it more likely to achieve the purpose as defined and accepted by the House at second reading), and more a continuation of the political trench warfare begun at second reading. The House of Lords at least offers the possibility of scrutiny of a different form. It is less party political; ministers know that if their defense of some point fails to convince the House, then there is at least a possibility of defeat in the division lobby where members' votes are counted. Such reverses can usually be overcome when a bill returns to the party-controlled House of Commons, but there may be a price to be paid by the government for doing this in terms of giving the opposition a further opportunity to expose a weak argument, or in arousing unwelcome publicity for doubts and divisions within the ranks of the governing party.

Some confirmation that the legislative work of the House of Lords is significant is found in a comprehensive study of pressure group activity made in the 1980s. Baldwin (1990) found that organized groups gave almost as much attention to the House of Lords as to the House of Commons when seeking to secure adjustments to government legislation. From the point of view of outside groups, it may be at least as easy to find a peer with the right kind of expertise and perhaps inclination to press amendments as it is to find a suitable member of the House of Commons. Precisely because the Lords is less dominated by party politics, and perhaps subject to less public attention, it may be a forum in which proposed amendments are given a more detached and objective hearing.

All this helps to explain why it is not difficult to cite impressive statistics about the number of amendments made to bills as they proceed through the House, usually between 1,500 and 2,000 per year. However, closer examination reveals that the overwhelming majority of these are government-initiated amendments (Drewry and Brock 1993). They represent the government itself having second thoughts about the draft legislation it has introduced. True, such second thoughts may be prompted in part by debate in the House, but equally they may result from influence brought to bear on government from elsewhere, perhaps the House of Commons or from lobbyists and organized pressure groups of all kinds. The most thorough recent study of the work of the House examined the sources of all amendments made to bills in the 1988–89 session and concluded that very seldom had the government given way to pressure from the House of Lords (Miers and Brock 1993).

Where the government suffers a defeat in the division lobby on an amendment to a bill, which has happened on average some fifteen times a year under Conservative governments since 1979, the outcome has most often been a compromise of some kind. But where compromise does not take place, government defeats in the upper house are more often overturned in the Commons than accepted by the lower house. There have been some notable examples of the government giving way to the House of Lords, but these have been unusual and rarely involve matters of real substance (Shell 1992, 1993a).

Because of the specific limitations on the powers of the House of Lords in relation to taxes and public spending, peers generally spend little time debating legislation in this area. Most notably, the annual finance bill implementing the budget frequently takes considerable time in the Commons but makes very little demand on the time of the upper house, where following a second reading debate all remaining formal legislative stages have usually been taken. Almost all bills are debated for fewer hours in the House of Lords than in the Commons. Party competition is more muted in the upper house. In addition, most major bills go through the Commons first, and the House of Lords conceives its role as essentially revisory. It can, therefore, be more selective in the way it uses its time.

Bills that deal primarily with law reform, or other bills about which there may be considerable cross-party agreement (though perhaps sharp disagreements that cut across party lines) are more likely to be introduced into the House of Lords. The House has at different times developed a reputation for giving especially careful consideration to bills dealing with certain subject areas, such as so-called issues of conscience, environmental concern and conservation. The relationship between central and local government has been of particular concern to the House in recent years, and because of their constitutional implications, bills impinging on this area have attracted particular attention there.

The presence of law lords, together with the fact that the lord chancellor always sits in the Lords, has ensured that the House takes a particular interest in law reform bills. In 1990 the House began expressing concern at the government's failure to introduce bills drafted by the Law Commission, a publicly financed body established in the 1960s to report on areas of law where the need for reform appears pressing. For many years reports made by this body were followed reasonably quickly by legislation, but in the late 1980s pressures on the parliamentary timetable, arising mainly let it be said because of the demands of government ministers ever eager to enact more legislation, led to Law Commission bills being squeezed out of the legislative program.

Some peers became increasingly outspoken in pointing to the failure of government and Parliament to implement law reform measures that had been carefully investigated and where expert drafting of bills had already taken place. This led to the House of Lords establishing a special procedure for consideration of such bills, the aim of which was to allow for thorough examination of what was involved, with select committee-type opportunity for interested parties to put their views to the House, before such bills would be sent on to the Commons, where hopefully their passage could be the more expeditious precisely because of the degree of scrutiny they had been given in the Lords.[6] This affords a good example of how the House has sought to develop its role in a manner complementary to the Commons.

Another such example concerns the scope of subordinate legislation. Many bills contain powers to allow government ministers to issue statutory orders which can become law with only very limited opportunity for parliamentary scrutiny. Several peers have expressed concern at the failure by Parliament to scrutinize primary legislation with the aim of identifying and systematically giving consideration to the secondary lawmaking powers contained in such bills. So the House of Lords established a Select Committee on Delegated Powers, which has reported on primary legislation and recommended changes that have been incorporated into the bills concerned (Himsworth 1995). Yet more recently the House has established special select committees to deal with some Scottish bills, and these have met and taken evidence in Scotland.

It is easy to see that the work the House does can be useful to the various groups involved in the legislative process. The government frequently needs the relative calm that the House provides and the parliamentary time it affords to tidy up much of their own legislation. To be able to do this in a forum which can bring a little influence to bear but has no real power is a bonus from the government's point of view. Organized groups outside Parliament find the House valuable in giving them a further opportunity to try to secure amendments to bills or at least to clarify their detailed provisions. The House itself has shown both diligence and restraint in discharging its legislative responsibilities. It has also been innovative in seeking to develop its procedures to accommodate changing demands. It may, of course, be argued that the work the House does in revising legislation is more a symptom of the need for reform of the legislative process as a whole than it is of the value of the House of Lords. But as long as the legislative process remains in anything like its present form, there seems little doubt that a second chamber will be necessary.

Nonlegislative or Deliberative Work?

When we turn from the House's legislative to its deliberative work, it is again the comparison and contrast with the Commons and the complementarity with the lower chamber that is noteworthy. In the House of Commons, debate is bound up with the exercise of power. The result of almost all votes may be a foregone conclusion, given the tight party control that exists, but significance may attach to abstention or rebellion in the division lobbies by a small number of MPs. Ultimately a minister who appears to lose the confidence of his own party in this way will have to resign, and a motion of no confidence can bring a government down. Such sanctions are not available in the upper house. Debate is not about the exercise of power; rather, it is about the possible exercise of influence.

Opportunities for initiating debates are shared between front and backbench peers. Although many debates are on subjects similar to those that take place in the Commons, the priorities of the upper house are somewhat different, and for individual peers the opportunities that arise to initiate debates are slightly greater than are the opportunities for MPs. The diverse membership of the House is reflected in the choice of subjects for debates. The archbishop of Canterbury recently initiated a debate on moral values in the life of the nation, while motions dealing broadly with such varied topics as the role of the judiciary or the impact of technology may be debated. Alongside authoritative speeches, some contributions may appear ill-informed, idiosyncratic, or even eccentric. But that is inherent in the nature of the House. The style of debate is different from that of the Commons; in the House of Lords most speeches show signs of careful preparation, and almost all are heard in respectful silence. Debate is almost a misnomer; rather, a series of speeches are made in which speakers may answer, or may avoid, one another's points. But every debate does receive a speech in reply from a government spokesman, and this fact distinguishes debate in the Lords from, say, debate in a university or a think tank. But who listens to debate in the House of Lords? Peers themselves frequently express in a plaintive kind of way great satisfaction with the quality of debate in their House, perhaps hoping that by singing their own praises others will be moved to take more notice of their utterances.[7]

Peers may ask questions of the government, just as MPs can. But oral question time is very different in the two houses. In the Commons, questions have become very much a matter of rapid repartee dominated by ministers and opposition shadow spokespersons. The time spent thus may be useful as a guide to the prevailing condition of the political climate. But if the object of question time is to hold government to account by extracting information from ministers, then the House of Lords may possibly achieve as much as the Commons. Certainly the handling of oral questions in the Lords is very different from that of the Commons. More time is spent on each question, giving the opportunity for more supplementary questions from all corners of the House. For ministers in the Lords, their question time ordeal is different from that faced by their colleagues in the Commons, but it may be just as searching. Well-informed supplementaries may rain down on a minister who will not find it so easy to escape simply by criticizing political opponents. Question time in the Lords undoubtedly lacks the high drama of Commons question time, at least as seen in the twice weekly bouts between prime minister and opposition leader, but questions in the Lords may in their own way be as effective as the very different question time in the Commons. At least some former MPs now in the Lords take this view (Shell 1993b).

Select Committees of the House

Select committees appointed to investigate and report on areas of government activity or public concern have developed greater significance within the British Parliament in recent years. Once again, we may note how the House of Lords has sought to complement the work of the Commons rather than rival it. Most notable has been the House of Lords Select Committee on the European Communities. When Britain joined the European Community (EC) in 1973, the desirability of providing some form of parliamentary scrutiny of EC draft legislation was evident. Yet the whole subject was fraught with political tensions because within both major parties there were significant elements opposed in principle to U.K. membership in the EC. This made for nervousness about establishing select committees for the scrutiny of EC policy in the Commons.

Furthermore, given the nature of national engagement with the EC policy making process, it could be argued that the House of Lords was better suited to this than the Commons. The upper house had no pretensions to be other than a chamber of influence, whereas the Commons still saw itself as exercising power. Another reason for peers' readiness to become heavily involved in this new role was quite simply the fact that the upper house had by the early 1970s sufficient members available to take on extra work. The arrival of many life peers with a more professional approach to their parliamentary work meant that the House had some spare capacity. A select committee was established in 1975, and over the next two decades this was the primary means by which parliamentary scrutiny of EC policy proposals took place. At times a hundred peers were involved, operating through up to eight subcommittees, each covering a defined policy area.

Reports from these committees earned a reputation for their thorough and dispassionate analysis of issues (Shell 1996). In the early 1990s the Commons established a new committee structure of its own, which enabled the lower house more adequately to address draft EC legislation. But the House of Lords continued to devote much time and effort to this task. Its reports rarely hit the headlines; frequently they are published virtually unnoticed. But within European Community institutions many were certainly given attention, and the House became known for its expertise and diligence in relation to EC policy.

Other developments in select committee work followed. In 1979, when the House of Commons amidst a general reorganization of its select committee work abolished its Committee on Science and Technology, the upper house established just such a committee. It has continued as a standing select committee, with a remarkable galaxy of talent at its disposal drawn from within the membership of the House (Grantham 1993). From the 1970s onwards, the House has regularly established select committees to examine particular issues or specific private members' bills. The impact of these has varied, but some have helped push policy along and shown how legislation could be drafted to tackle particular problems.

For example, a committee on charity law in 1984–85, chaired by a senior judge in the House, was the precursor to legislation in this complex field. A committee that examined Britain's balance of trade deficit in manufactured goods produced one of the most widely debated of all select committee reports of the 1980s. The possibility of the House of Lords exercising a more active role in reviewing constitutional matters was raised by the response to a committee that examined the relationship between central and local government in 1995. Some peers find committee work more congenial than legislative work or debate on the floor of the House. It is not just the expertise the House commands within its own membership, but the considerable detachment from party politics that select committee activity permits, which attracts many peers, especially life peers who sit on the cross-benches. Furthermore, select committee meetings can be arranged well in advance and fitted into busy schedules more easily than many debates. And a well-researched select committee report has a potential for influence well beyond the confines of the House.

The House of Lords sits for almost a thousand hours every year. In addition, its expanding system of committees sit for many more hours. This makes it one of the busiest parliamentary chambers in the world. That fact alone tells us nothing about the significance of its work. But it seems reasonable to say that in the context of the British Parliament the role of the House is of considerable importance (Shell 1993a).

Conclusion: What Future for the House?

The House of Lords is a profoundly peculiar institution. It is not difficult to recognize the case for its radical reform. It is offensive in principle because it can make no claim to being democratic. It is also offensive in practice because the Conservative Party enjoys such a dominant position within the House. Nevertheless, it is also not difficult to recognize both the practical usefulness of the House and the practical difficulties that stand in the way of its reform.

The practical usefulness of the House must be underlined. Bagehot's 1867 observation that beside an ideal House of Commons a House of Lords would not be necessary may remain true, but—as he commented then—beside the actual House of Commons the desirability of a second chamber rapidly becomes apparent (Bagehot 1963, 133–34). Support for unicameralism has never been strong in Britain, and as public respect for the Commons has been eroded in recent years, so the desirability of retaining a second chamber has been confirmed. To remove it altogether would be to reinforce the elective dictatorship against which the prominent Conservative politician Lord Hailsham spoke in 1976. The changes associated with Thatcherism have underlined not only the centralizing tendency of British government but also the vulnerability of institutions throughout society to politicization. It was suggested Prime Minister Thatcher "handbagged" British institutions, exerting far-reaching influence over them. For what it is worth, the House of Lords must be seen as an exception to this process.

Because Britain is a unitary state, there is not the same justification for bicameralism as would be the case for a federal or quasi-federal system. Rather, the justification for the House of Lords is historic. The House of Lords owes its origins as part of Parliament to a conception of society that has long since faded into history, to a time when aristocracy and church

demanded separate representation. The House owes its continued existence to a capacity to adjust and adapt, exchanging power for influence
traded within a constitutional system that has never sought formally to
consummate the principles of democracy. In the nineteenth and early
twentieth centuries, rather than stand and fight, the House accepted its
relegation to being the junior chamber within Parliament. Had it not
done so, it would have been radically altered or swept away altogether.
Today, its justification lies chiefly in the simple fact that it is already there,
and that being in existence it does usefully perform the task of revising
legislation as well as offering its wisdom to government and society
through its varied deliberations.

In a democratic society, a lively debate about reform of the House is to
be expected. Of the reforms that have taken place, most have been initiated by Conservative governments. These have essentially been modest
changes designed to remove anomalies or modify in some way the membership of the House rather than fundamentally restructure the place. The
1958 Life Peerages Act and the 1963 Peerage Act both helped to make the
House less indefensible. When the continued existence of the House was
perceived as coming under serious threat in the 1970s, the Conservatives
responded by proposing quite sweeping reform. But since then the Conservatives in government have lost interest in such reform. The House
of Lords seems secure, and the need for its work is recognized, so leave
it alone.

In the past, Labour has aspired to wholesale reform of the House. But
lack of agreement over quite how this should be done and recognition of
the fact that legislation to achieve this end would be very time-consuming
have conspired to give the subject low priority with Labour governments.
Furthermore, Labour has felt inhibited from introducing modest changes
because such alterations would in practice merely serve to strengthen an
institution that would remain fundamentally undemocratic and objec-
tionable. In the early 1990s, Labour appeared to alter this stance, and in
its 1997 manifesto, the party stated that a Labour government would, as
an initial self-contained reform, exclude hereditary peers from the House
and then initiate a review leading to further comprehensive reform at a
later stage. However, it would appear that the new Labour government
elected that year has placed House of Lords reform lower on its agenda
than other constitutional reform, notably the introduction of a devolved
parliament for Scotland.

The rationale for such further reform can be recognized in proposals to introduce devolved parliaments and regional assemblies within the United Kingdom. The membership of the second chamber could then be based on a regional structure, perhaps part elected and part appointed. The Liberal Democrats advocate introducing a single measure of constitutional reform dealing with regional government and the second chamber question together. This may be logical, but it is doubtful whether it is practical politics. In the absence of a substantial interparty consensus about such change (of which there is little sign), the ability of any government to carry the necessary legislation through Parliament must be very doubtful.[8]

The difficulty for Labour is that the interim House would be one entirely composed of the nominees of successive prime ministers. Had such a House existed in Mrs. Thatcher's day, she would have found it much easier to "handbag." And who is to say how long such an interim arrangement might endure? The 1911 Parliament Act was intended as an interim measure, but it has still not been replaced. The House of Lords remains an enduring monument to both the conservatism and the pragmatism of the English.

Notes

1. The House of Lords debated the "Salisbury Doctrine" on 19 May 1993; see *HL Debs.* cc 1780–1813.

2. Of the total of seventeen disclaimers, six have done so in order to remain or to seek membership of the House of Commons. Disclaiming is for life, and by 1996 four of the seventeen disclaimants had been succeeded by heirs who had taken up their peerages again and their seats in the House of Lords. Disclaiming has not caught on.

3. Travel expenses were first introduced in 1946. A daily out-of-pocket expenses allowance up to a maximum of £3.15 was introduced in 1957, since increased to £141.50 per day (to include overnight accommodation). Apart from government ministers, only four other peers receive salaries on account of their offices in the House; these are the leader of the opposition, the opposition chief whip, and the chairman and principal deputy chairman of committees.

4. From 1964 to 1983 no new hereditary peerages were awarded. In 1983 and 1984 under Mrs. Thatcher three such peerages were created, but none since then.

5. Lord Diamond, a former Labour minister, twice introduced such a bill, but it was voted down on both occasions; see *HL Debs* 26 Nov 1992 cc 1118–66 and 7 Mar 1994 cc 1283–1330.

6. See proposals made in the *Report from the Select Committee on the Committee Work of the House, HL 35 (1991–92)* and first report from the Select Committee on Procedure.

7. See, for example, debates on the constitutional role of the House, *HL Debs* 13 Apr 1994 cc 1540–75 and 4 July 1996 cc 1581–1690.

8. See two reports from the Constitution Unit, *Delivering Constitutional Reform* and *Reform of the House of Lords*, both 1996.

References

Bagehot, Walter. 1963. [1867] *The English Constitution.* London: Fontana.

Baldwin, Nicholas D. 1990. "The House of Lords." In *Parliament and Pressure Politics,* ed. Michael Rush. Oxford: Clarendon.

———. 1995. "The House of Lords and the Labour Government 1974–79." *Journal of Legislative Studies* 1:218–42.

Beamish, David. 1993. "Divisions in the House of Lords, 1988–89." In *The House of Lords at Work,* ed. Donald Shell and David Beamish. Oxford: Clarendon.

Bromhead, P. A. 1958. *The House of Lords and Contemporary Politics.* London: Routledge.

Bryce, Viscount. 1918. *Report of the Conference on Reform of the Second Chamber.* Cmd. 9038. London: Her Majesty's Stationery Office.

Cannadine, David. 1990. *The Decline and Fall of the British Aristocracy.* New Haven: Yale University Press.

Crick, Bernard. 1964. *Reform of Parliament.* London: Weidenfeld and Nicolson.

Drewry, Gavin, and J. Brock. 1993. "Government Legislation: An Overview." In *The House of Lords at Work,* ed. Donald Shell and David Beamish. Oxford: Clarendon.

Grantham, Cliff. 1993. "Select Committees." In *The House of Lords at Work,* ed. Donald Shell and David Beamish. Oxford: Clarendon.

Hailsham, Lord. 1976. *Elective Dictatorship.* BBC.

Himsworth, C. M. G. 1995. "The Delegated Powers Scrutiny Committee." *Public Law,* 34–44.

Home, Lord. 1978. *Report of the Review Committee on the Second Chamber.* London: Conservative Political Centre.

Miers, David, and J. Brock. 1993. "Government Legislation: Case Studies." In *The House of Lords at Work,* ed. Donald Shell and David Beamish. Oxford: Clarendon.

Morgan, Janet. 1975. *The House of Lords and the Labour Government, 1964–70.* Oxford: Clarendon.

Natzler, David, and Douglas Millar. 1993. "Private Members' Bills." In *The House of Lords at Work,* ed. Donald Shell and David Beamish. Oxford: Clarendon.

Rippon, Lord. 1992. *Making the Law: The Report of the Hansard Society Commission on the Legislative Process.* London: Hansard Society.

Shell, Donald. 1992. *The House of Lords.* 2d ed. London: Harvester Wheatsheaf.

————. 1993a. Conclusion to *The House of Lords at Work,* ed. Donald Shell and David Beamish. Oxford: Clarendon.

————. 1993b. "Questions in the House of Lords." In *Parliamentary Questions,* ed. Mark Franklin and Philip Norton. Oxford: Clarendon.

————. 1996. "The House of Lords and the European Community: The Evolution of Arrangements for Scrutiny." In *Westminster and Europe,* ed. Philip Giddings and Gavin Drewry. London: Macmillan.

8 Parliamentary Autonomy: The Italian Senato

CLAUDIO LODICI

The institutional design of the contemporary Italian Parliament was shaped following World War II (Cazzola 1974; Cotta 1979; Manzella 1977; Sartori 1963). Today, Parliament is a fully bicameral institution consisting of a Chamber of Deputies [Camera dei deputati] and a Senate [Senato della Repubblica]. The Senate, composed of 315 elected members and some others appointed by the president of the Republic, is among the larger upper chambers of today's parliaments. The two parliamentary chambers are coequal in legislative powers and in their role in approving the appointments of prime minister and cabinet ministers. In the family of representative assemblies, the Italian Parliament is among the more powerful bodies, even in some respects comparable to the U.S. Congress (see Cotta 1990, 1994, 60–63).

The purpose of this chapter is to lay a foundation for understanding the institution of the Italian Senate. It is important to elaborate the historical development of Parliament and its upper house, to explain the institutional structure of the Senate, to characterize the Senate's lawmaking role and functions, to focus on legislative-executive relations, and to consider proposals for Senate reform. We take up these tasks in turn.

Early Days: The Albertine Statute

The year 1848 marked a turning point in European history. The wave of revolution that washed over that part of Europe lying between the Pyrenees and the czarist empire substantially spared only the Spanish peninsula and Scandinavia. Italy was still divided into several states, and it became directly involved in the uprisings that led to its passage from an absolute to a constitutional monarchy through the concession of statutes—that is to say, constitutions—by the sovereigns of Naples, Tuscany, Piedmont, and the Holy See (the pope).

From a historical and juridical point of view, the Piedmontese Statute (otherwise known as the Albertine Statute, after King Charles Albert) is particularly relevant. This charter, based on the French Constitution of 1830 and the Belgian one of 1831, was adopted in 1861 by the—at last—unified Kingdom of Italy. It was the constitution in force until Benito Mussolini took power in 1922.

The statute reserved a broad field of action to the king, with ministers being responsible to him and not to the two parliamentary assemblies (thus introducing a constitutional though not a parliamentary system). Furthermore, the statute accorded fairly ample freedom of association and of the press, and even if Article I did declare Catholicism the state religion, it ensured religious tolerance both to the Waldenses (a Calvinist congregation especially numerous in Piedmont) and to the Jews (rendered equal to other citizens and no longer discriminated against by the obnoxious "interdictions").

However, it must be noted that the word *parliament* was not expressly mentioned in the Albertine Statute. There was mention of a Chamber of Deputies, elected by a very restricted suffrage, which exercised legislative power alongside the king. There was also mention of the Senate of the Kingdom, conceived along the same lines as the British House of Lords or the French Chamber of Peers, as a body for moderation and stability, whose members were to be selected by the king on the basis of specific titles and for lifelong tenure. Furthermore, the term *senate* evoked deep and ancestral memories. Since the seventeenth century, special senates exercising judicial powers and control over government had been active in Piedmont and in the Savoy region. They were right and proper pillars of the Savoy state and, as such, were completely hostile to reform.

Nevertheless, on May 8, 1848, "the first session of the national parliament" (so defined by the king's deputy) was inaugurated in Turin. Charles Albert himself was not present, being engaged as he was in the ill-fated war against Austria, the first of three Italian wars of independence (the other two being in 1859 and in 1866). Prince Eugene of Savoy Carignano, the king's lieutenant and cousin, addressed the "senators and deputies," as the chronicles of the day relate, "in a timid but clear voice." Two months after the concession of the statute "octroyé" by the sovereign, still a symbol of royal condescendence, the constitutional design was complete (Ungari 1971). The two branches of the legislative power stemmed from the same legislative tree. From that tree sprouted the first Italian parliamentary regime, which thirteen years later Prime Minister Camillo Benso di Cavour would deliver intact to a united Italy.

The Kingdom of Sardinia (as the Piedmontese state was actually called) took upon itself the task of guiding the process that has been recorded in history as the Risorgimento, the political unification of the Italian peninsula completed in 1870 by the conquest of the Holy See and the transfer of the capital to Rome. Sardinia itself was quite weak, having slightly under five million inhabitants in 1848. Turin, its capital, had 136,000 inhabitants, not many more than Genoa or Florence. In that small kingdom, only 82,369 people were registered to vote in the April 1848 election of members of the Chamber of Deputies. Of these, only 53,924 actually voted, 65 percent of the entire electorate. Only large landowners, academicians and graduates, top military, and government officials had the right to vote and, consequently, the right to run for election. Some constituencies had as few as thirty electors; in the September–October 1848 by-election, Giuseppe Garibaldi was elected in Cicagna (Liguria) by only eighteen votes.

"An electorate prevalently composed of landowners, but with a strong representation of merchants, manufacturers, and professional men," wrote Rosario Romeo, the eminent chronicler of Prime Minister Cavour, principal architect of Italian unification. "The result," said Romeo, "was a Chamber composed mainly of lawyers, magistrates, and officials, with a rather moderate majority, but also a rather vivacious democratic representation to whom political developments over the following years would attribute a growing influence." Political distinctions of right wing and left wing were unknown in a parliament that had had no previous authentically revolutionary experience. Members sat haphazardly in the parliamentary chamber, inattentive to ideological differences. This was true at least until 1920. Benedetto Croce always sat on the right with the Neapolitans, and Luigi Einaudi would sit on the left with the Piedmontese.

The Senate of the Kingdom

The Senate held its sessions in Turin at the old Palazzo Madama, where it remained until 1864, when Parliament voted to adopt Florence as the capital city. Here, the high chamber was installed on the top floor of the Galleria degli Uffizi, annexed to Palazzo Vecchio. Giovanni Spadolini, historian of the Risorgimento and speaker of the Senate from 1987 to 1994, remarked, "Almost a cruel joke on the venerable senators who had to climb one hundred and twenty steps, often having to lean on their canes—the reason for the rigorous but often deserted sittings of the 'House of Lords' of the newly born unitary state, which had all the acerbity of adolescence."

Upon being moved to Rome in 1871, the Senate of the Kingdom was installed in adequate offices in Palazzo Madama, the old quarters of Pope Pius IX's Ministry of Finance. A curious and bizarre historical coincidence had it that there was also a Palazzo Madama on the shores of the Tiber River, although the two "madamas" represented two different stories and centuries. In Turin, the madama was Christine of France, duchess of Savoy, who was promised in marriage to the Prince of Wales but instead married Victor Amadeus in 1619. (As King Charles I, her first fiancé married her sister Mary Henrietta in 1625.) In Rome, the madama was Margaret of Austria (1522–86), illegitimate daughter of Emperor Charles V, who was given in marriage to Alessandro de' Medici, duke of

Florence, in 1536 at the age of fourteen. After his assassination a year later, she married Ottavio Farnese, duke of Parma. She later became regent of the Netherlands under her son Alessandro Farnese.

Thus, two different "madamas," but enough to contribute to the psychological background of the nation and to ensure a minimum continuity in the common imagery of a population that had endured an articulated, tormented, and diversified history. The institution seated in Margaret of Austria's Palazzo Madama was one of the two branches of Parliament provided for by the Albertine Statute. That statute established the exercise of "legislative power" by a bicameral parliament, according to Montesquieu's classical triple distinction. Alongside the elected members of the Chamber of Deputies was the Senate of the Kingdom. The Senate's members—an unlimited number, nominated for lifelong tenure by the king—had to be chosen from among the twenty-one social categories defined by Article 33 of the statute. Last but not least came the royal princes, who were members of the assembly by right of privilege.

The legislative power of the two houses was the same in all respects but one: all laws referring to taxation or to budget approval involved an order of precedence in favor of the Chamber of Deputies. In this regard, the Senate lacked every right of initiative and, consequently, of amendment in financial matters, due to its nonelective, census-based, and aristocratic origin.

Judicial functions were reserved to the Senate. Whenever convened as the High Court of Justice, its jurisdiction included crimes of high treason, threats to state security (a power it never exercised), and accusations by the Chamber against ministers (proceedings were held against Prime Ministers Giovanni Giolitti in 1895 and Francesco Crispi in 1897; and the minister of education was condemned in 1908 to eleven months of detention for embezzlement). Moreover, the Senate exercised exclusive power over offenses charged against its own members.

The great limitation of the life tenure chamber as against the elective chamber was not defined by the statute but came to be identified with the internal logic of the system. Contrary to the letter of the statute ("the king nominates and revokes his ministers"), common practice elaborated the dependence of government upon its majority in the elective assembly, the only one sensitive enough to catch the ebb and flow of popular support for the political parties.

The Senate also undoubtedly had the power of political control and censure over the government. But within what boundaries? The so-called political question or matter of confidence lay within the purview of the Chamber of Deputies. Accordingly, control over parliamentary life and, consequently, over the government's tenure in office crossed over to the other Palazzo—Palazzo Montecitorio, seat of the Chamber of Deputies. This logic became perfectly clear, after an initial and natural uncertainty, to all those members who passed through the halls of Palazzo Madama. Thus, tension between the two branches of Parliament never ran high, except on the presentation of bills of secular origin, such as provisions concerning civil marriage.

The Senate of the Kingdom became fully aware of its lesser political influence in the lawmaking process. Moreover, senators understood their minimal role in determining the government's life, an investiture that derives from the legitimacy conferred by popular representation. On the other hand, senators were conscientious enough to provide a fundamental element of balance and moderation, an institution for necessary meditation, in times of national strife and uncertainty.

Culture, political wisdom, administrative experience, military skill, specific competence, and a profound attachment to king and country were distinctive features of the assembly in the years following unification, years in which the Senate had among its members such luminaries as the writer Alessandro Manzoni, the poet Giosuè Carducci, and the composer Giuseppe Verdi. A logic of cultural aristocracy would survive to the end, up to the rise of the irrational and totalitarian Fascist regime, when the Senate housed the last voices of Italy's liberal Risorgimento tradition.

The history of the Italian monarchy records the Senate as an institution of moderation in the legislative process. It represented a guarantee against sudden change, its very existence being an insurmountable obstacle to excessive and hasty decisions that could derive from occasional majorities in the Chamber of Deputies. A negative vote of the Senate did not precipitate the automatic resignation of the government, but it did sound out a warning to the country and to the other chamber whenever the latter was compelled to pass bills of which, in all conscience, its members entirely or partially disapproved.

Fascism and the Crisis of Democracy

The takeover of power by Mussolini was not followed immediately by a complete institutional break with the old liberal state. But in 1925, the Fascist dictator went before Parliament to assume "full political, moral, historical responsibility" for the assassination of the secretary of the Socialist Party, Giacomo Matteotti, a criminal act courageously denounced by the liberal-constitutional leader Giovanni Amendola. From that time until 1928, institutional reform in a dictatorial direction took place. In particular, two laws marked the Fascist regime's complete break with the political system introduced by the 1848 statute. The first, an electoral law, definitively subordinated the Chamber of Deputies to fascism by the establishment of a single list of four hundred candidates, drawn up by the Grand Council of the Fascist Party from nominations by the Fascist Trade Unions' and Employers' Confederations and presented en bloc for unanimous approval. The second law assigned a constitutional power of sanction to the Grand Council, called upon not only to nominate the top leadership of the Fascist National Party but also to express a compulsory opinion on the succession to the throne and the designation of those fit to assume the role of prime minister. These laws represented a decisive break in the continuity of the constitutional order: the Albertine Statute was not abolished, but it was violated in several parts and voided in spirit.

There followed the full-scale establishment of the totalitarian regime, the invasion of Ethiopia, which resulted in international isolation, and an approach toward Nazi Germany. By the summer of 1938, the degenerative process had culminated in the promulgation of the notorious laws against the Jews. On June 10, 1940, with the declaration of war against France, Italy entered a conflict from which it emerged only after five years of moral and material suffering on the part of its population. However, the last two years of World War II were marked by the Italian resistance to the German Nazi invaders. In fact, it was the resistance that contributed vitally to the civil and political maturity of Italians, paving the way for a new, democratic Italy. From that moment on, political power definitively ceased to be the exclusive property of a restricted and privileged group, and it became the object of competition and conflict. This meant that ordinary citizens, the working population, could participate in democratic politics again, with their associations, their organizations, and their political parties. Parliamentary democracy had been given another chance.

Return to Freedom: The Constitution of the Republic

On June 2, 1946, a referendum was held at the same time as elections for an assembly to draw up a new constitution. King Victor Emmanuel III had abdicated on May 10 in favor of his son, Humbert II. This was a transparent attempt to influence the electorate in favor of the monarchy through the ascent to the throne of a less discredited sovereign and, above all, one not compromised by association with fascism. In this election, women voted for the first time. Voter turnout was an extraordinary 89 percent, much higher than in prefascist elections. This participation level has remained more or less constant.

In the referendum, voters narrowly came down in favor of establishing a republic, even if only by a 54 percent majority. On June 13, Humbert II went into exile in Portugal. Victory for the republic was mainly due to support in the northern and central regions (64 percent pro-republic), since the majority in the southern regions and the main islands (Sicily and Sardinia) favored monarchy. On December 27, 1947, following a debate that took up 170 sessions, the Constituent Assembly approved the new Italian Constitution, still in force today, by a huge majority (433 votes to 62). The new constitution provided for a democratic, parliamentary, and representative republic based on the principle of separation of powers.

A central governing role was accorded to Parliament. It was given the legislative power, and it was to consist of two houses, the Chamber of Deputies and the Senate to be elected, respectively, every five and six years, and its members were to be elected by universal suffrage. The central role of Parliament was reinforced by the method adopted to elect the president of the Republic, who as the head of state is responsible for promulgating laws, nominating the prime minister and other ministers, and dissolving Parliament and calling new elections. The Constituent Assembly opted for the election of the president by Parliament in joint session, rather than by universal suffrage. The fundamental role attributed to Parliament and thus to the political parties represented in it is also expressed by the subordination to Parliament of the government which, entrusted with executive and administrative functions, issues from the parliamentary majority and is called upon to interpret and implement its political guidelines (see Cotta 1990; Sartori 1963).

The judicial power was given to the magistrature. The independent judiciary is self-governing, controlled by the Superior Council, two-thirds of whose members are chosen by the magistrates themselves, with the other one-third selected by Parliament. The Superior Council is presided over by the president of the Republic. A constitutional court was also established, composed of members partly nominated by the president and partly selected by Parliament and by the magistrature. It was assigned the task of guaranteeing constitutional legality by judging the behavior of governmental institutions and assuring the conformity of laws to the constitution. It was, by express desire of the Constituent Assembly, a "rigid" or "higher law" constitution, so that ordinary laws would be considered subordinate to its provisions. However, in recognition of the people's sovereignty, the institution of the referendum was introduced to allow the presentation of proposals to modify the constitution or to partially or totally repeal ordinary laws. A request by at least 500,000 voters, or by one-fifth of the members of Parliament, is required to call a referendum.

Finally, the constitution defined the political-administrative division of the state, adding to the traditional independent local administrations—the municipality and the province—a new body, the region, whose council was to be elected by universal suffrage, like those of the municipality and the province. Regions are assigned a degree of financial autonomy and legislative power in a broad spectrum of policy areas. Because of their historical traditions, an even broader degree of autonomy was accorded to Sicily, Sardinia, the Aosta Valley, Friuli–Venezia Giulia, and Trentino–Alto Adige.

The Senate of the Republic

The Constituent Assembly did not achieve unanimity in relation to the Senate. The Italian Communist Party (PCI) had firmly favored a unicameral system. The PCI had gone into opposition in 1947, but it continued to carry out an important role in the elaboration of the Constitution. Its rejection of the idea of two parliamentary assemblies mirrored developments in the East European satellite countries of the Soviet Union. A majority of the other political and cultural forces present in the Constituent Assembly favored bicameralism, notwithstanding their differing concepts of the shape the bicameral Parliament should take. Opinions ranged from the idea favored by the Christian Democrats of a senate representing social classes or regions, to the idea of a senate directly representing the people, which was favored by the Republican Party, the Action Party, a large part of the Socialist Party, and all of the nondenominational Democratic Left (Aimo 1977).

In the wake of the liberation from fascism, and after the institutional referendum, there were signs of opposition to the establishment of an upper house. Nevertheless, bicameralism prevailed in the Constituent Assembly, both in the preparatory proceedings and in general debate in the Assembly. Once bicameralism was agreed on in principle, the contest then concerned the particular institutional design of the upper house, with proposals offered for a "second house," a "chamber of senators," a "chamber of the regions." Not by chance, the name Senate of the Republic was adopted by an amendment presented by two Republican Party members of the Constituent Assembly. This extraordinary initiative came through the political party that was both ideologically and psychologically most distant from the previous Senate of the Kingdom.

Thus the republican Senate was born. It was to be a senate different from the upper house originally established by the Piedmontese legislators in 1848, a body which actually had involved a form of "attenuated bicameralism." The transformation from a monarchy to a republican parliamentary state had been interrupted by the rise of fascism. The constituent assembly's preoccupation was to protect the constitutional guarantee of popular sovereignty in creating the new parliamentary institutions. It rejected all proposals involving the direct representation of interests, references to "power," or allusions to Fascist-type corporatist design.

The Senate retained its name, its glory, and that rather exclusive aura of a club, as well as its mission to smooth out conflicts and its propensity for moderation and mediation. But it became an entirely new body, framed in a radically different design of integral and popular democracy. The only exceptions to popular election were the life tenure of senators nominated by the head of state and the designation of senators by right afforded to former presidents of the Republic. It was a complex structure of differences, attentively calculated and assessed: different ages to elect and be elected, different electoral systems.

On April 18, 1948, the first republican senate was elected. Along with the popularly elected members, its membership also included 106 former parliamentarians who had been persecuted by the Fascist regime and nominated by the president of the Republic. This first senate should have remained in office until 1954, considering that the constitution originally fixed the Senate's term at six years. However, it was dissolved prematurely by President Luigi Einaudi when the Chamber of Deputies' term ended, so members of both houses could be elected at the same time. In the same way, the Senate elected on June 7, 1953, was dissolved in advance in 1958 by President Giovanni Gronchi, upon expiration of the Chamber of Deputies. Finally, in 1963 a constitutional law was approved reducing the length of senators' terms from six to five years to coincide with the terms of deputies. By the same law, the constitution was modified to raise the number of elected senators to the fixed number of 315. Previously, the constitution had assigned each region a senator for every 200,000 inhabitants, so that the number of senators elected had varied (237 in 1948, 237 in 1953, 246 in 1958). In addition, the Senate's rules have been revised and reformed a number of times, most recently in 1993 (see Senato della Repubblica 1949, 1988a).

Perfect Bicameralism

Within the perfectly bicameral system established by the constitution, the two assemblies nevertheless differ in their composition and election criteria. Senators are elected by citizens over twenty-five years of age, and they must be over forty years old in order to be elected; the corresponding age limits for deputies are eighteen and twenty-five years old. Members of the Senate, like those of the Chamber of Deputies, are elected for five years. In exceptional cases, the term of a legislature may be shortened should the president of the Republic decide, after consulting the speakers of both houses, to dissolve Parliament and call early elections. However, in practice the exception has become the norm in the last ten years. The early dissolution of Parliament is now an almost mundane fact of political and parliamentary life. This is borne out by the fact that only five legislatures (1st, 2d, 3d, 4th, and 10th) out of thirteen completed their five-year term. The others were interrupted in midterm by a call for early elections. In any case, the term of a parliament cannot be extended except during war and only by law. New elections must be held within seventy days of either a normal or an exceptional termination of a parliament.

Parliament's powers include (1) the power to revise the constitution

(Article 138); (2) the exercise of the legislative power, that is, the power to pass laws (Article 70) and among these, specifically, those that set fundamental principles for regional legislation and those that integrate constitutional laws involving fundamental rights; (3) the power to declare war (Article 78); (4) the power to elect the president of the Republic (Article 83); (5) the power to concede or deny confidence in the government nominated by the president, thus conditioning its juridical existence (Article 94); (6) the power to establish the administrative machinery of government (Article 81); (7) the power to investigate matters of public concern (Article 82); and (8) the power to coordinate autonomous social initiatives (Article 41) and the autonomous territorial bodies (Articles 117 and 127).

As can be seen from this litany of powers, the Italian parliamentary system is organized according to bicameral principles, tempered by unitary moments provided for by the constitution (Tosi 1974, 43–49). As a complex institution, Parliament has its structural and functional unitary expression in the joint sittings of the two houses to elect the president of the Republic and to receive his oath of allegiance (Articles 85 and 91); to elect five judges to the Constitutional Court and to vote on the list of citizens who will serve as "aggregate" members of the Court to pass judgment on constitutional matters (Article 135); to elect one-third of the members of the Superior Magistrates' Council (Article 104); and, finally, to impeach the president of the Republic for high treason or breach of the constitution (Article 90). Alongside these unitary moments, however, ordinary parliamentary activity takes place in the normal functioning of the two chambers.

The Composition of the Senate

Italian bicameralism is known as "parity" or "perfect" bicameralism, and it stands out with respect to other so-called differentiated or imperfect bicameral systems in which the two houses have a different representational legitimacy and unequal powers (Cotta 1979). We have already observed that the Senate has 315 elected members. Its membership also includes a small number of nonelected members (nine at the present time), either nominated by the president for life tenure, and selected among "those citizens who have honored their country by distinguished merits acquired in the social, scientific, artistic, and literary fields," or former presidents of the Republic who have life tenure unless they waive the right (provided by Article 59).

The number of senators tenured for life varies, since it is impossible to determine in advance either the number of former living presidents or the number of life-tenured senators to be nominated by the president. Previously the total number of lifetime senators was limited to five, but now each president is allowed to nominate five senators. This gives rise to a variable number of lifetime senators because of both the overlapping of nominations by succeeding presidents and the impossibility of naming substitutes for any of the five nominees in the case of death or resignation once the president has made his five choices. Parliamentary development since the inception of the republic has produced a generous interpretation of the regulations concerning life-tenured senators. This has led to a more marked differentiation between the two assemblies that the Constituent Assembly was not able to create at the outset.

The Senate membership is apportioned on a regional basis. None of the twenty Italian regions can have less than seven senators (except for Molise, which has two, and the Aosta Valley, which has one). In each region, three-quarters of the Senate seats are single-member constituencies in which senators are elected on a winner-take-all basis. One-quarter of seats are assigned on a proportional basis. It must be remembered that from 1945 until the general elections of 1992, the Italian electoral system was a fully proportional one. This means that there was a substantial overlap between the percentage of popular votes obtained by the various parties and the percentage of seats won in Parliament. In May 1993, in a referendum held on the Senate's electoral system, a majority of Italians voted in favor of completely abandoning the proportional system (Longi 1993, 45–61).

In the following months, the two houses were involved in the difficult task of translating this popular sentiment into law. The new electoral law for the Senate clearly adopted the principles deriving from the referendum. In the first place, it established that a candidate may run for office in only one constituency (this is not so for the Chamber of Deputies), and that a petition for candidacy must be signed by no fewer than 1,000 and not over 1,500 electors in the constituency. Independent, nonparty candidates can run for election but "do not . . . participate in the proportional allotment of seats." The law specifies the election criteria: a simple

Table 8.1. Regional Composition of the Italian Senate

Region	Majority Seats	Proportional Seats
Aosta Valley	1	0
Piedmont	17	6
Lombardy	35	12
Trentino–Alto Adige	6	1
Friuli–Venezia Giulia	5	2
Liguria	6	3
Veneto	17	6
Emilia-Romagna	15	6
Tuscany	14	5
Marche	6	2
Umbria	5	2
Abruzzo	5	2
Molise	2	0
Latium	21	7
Campania	22	8
Puglia	16	6
Basilicata	5	2
Calabria	8	3
Sardinia	6	3
Sicily	20	7

Note: According to Italian convention, regions are listed geographically, from north to south.

majority vote for about three-quarters of the constituencies in every region, and proportional voting for the remaining quarter. The seats, first majority and then proportional, are allocated region by region, as shown in table 8.1.

In each constituency, the candidate who obtains the most votes wins the seat. The proportional allotment is made after having subtracted the votes used up by the parties for the election of their candidates in the various single-member constituencies. Therefore, assuming that the candidates of only one party have won all the majoritarian seats in that region, that party will not take part in the allotment of the proportionally assigned seats. This provision does away with the inconvenience of parties that are geographically concentrated being able to cancel the representation in Parliament of other parties able to register a presence across the regions. Having summed up all the votes not used by the various parties, the proportional seats are assigned to party candidates who have a right to them on the basis of the highest individual quota. Thus, if party X has a right to two seats in Latium, proportional allotment will elect, in this order, candidate Julius Caesar who, though beaten by party Y's candidate, obtained 37 percent of the votes in constituency #8, and candidate Mark Anthony who obtained 31 percent of the votes in constituency #2. When a vacant seat is to be assigned by the majority system, a by-election is held. When a vacant seat is to be assigned by proportional allotment, the candidate of the same party with the most votes will succeed the outgoing senator. Finally, the electoral law provides for elections lasting only one day, with polling booths open from 7 A.M. to 10 P.M. Previously it had been possible to vote until 2 P.M. on the day after the opening of the polls.

The Organization of the Senate

Like the Chamber of Deputies, the Senate must convene within twenty days of the elections. This session is led by the eldest senator and is given over to the election of a presiding officer. The speaker represents the Senate, regulates all its activities, directs and moderates discussions, proposes issues for consideration, establishes voting procedures and proclaims the outcome, is responsible for maintaining order, and on the basis of Senate rules ensures that correct procedures are followed (Tosi 1974, 131–42). The speaker is expected to direct the Senate's activity impartially, which is underscored by candidates for speaker having to win an absolute majority of senators' votes on the first two ballots. Should there be no winners, the majority of the votes is sufficient for the third ballot; should even then no one obtain the required majority, the Senate proceeds on the same day with a ballot between the two candidates who obtained the most votes on the previous ballot, and the one who wins a simple majority is then elected. In case of ties, the eldest is elected. Only once, in 1994, has there been an effective contest between two candidates: incumbent speaker Giovanni Spadolini, supported by the liberal and radical senators, was challenged by Carlo Scognamiglio Pasini, supported by conservative members. Until the last vote was counted, the result of the contest was uncertain. But ultimately Scognamiglio prevailed by one vote, 162–161. Had there been a tie vote, Spadolini, the older of the two candidates, would have become speaker.

Having elected a speaker, the assembly proceeds to elect other officers of the house (Tanda 1987). These include four deputy speakers, who stand in for the speaker to moderate debates and perform ceremonial duties; three questors, who supervise services, protocol, Senate security, and budget; and eight senator secretaries (the number can be increased to include representatives of all parliamentary groups), who assist the speaker during sessions by reading the bills, verifying voting results, and overseeing the minutes of the sessions. The deputy speakers, questors, and secretaries make up the Speaker's Council, which makes decisions concerning house administration and discipline. The Speaker's Council, amongst other tasks, nominates the secretary general of the Senate, the highest official of all the Senate offices (Senato della Repubblica 1988b). The election of the speaker and the Speaker's Council does not end the preliminary procedures at the beginning of the political and legislative activity of the assembly. The next step is the setting up of the parliamentary groups, the select committees, and the standing committees.

The Parties in Parliament

According to the Italian Constitution, the people have two ways of taking part in the political life of the Republic: by organizing themselves politically, and by exercising their sovereignty directly. Citizens may vote in elections in which the membership of the two houses is chosen (Article 58). Alternatively, they may join a political party and "contribute toward determining national policy by democratic means" (Article 49) (Nocilla and Ciaurro 1987). Thus, the Italian political system is based on several linkages; the elaboration of national policy comes about through the concurrence of political parties and through parliamentary resolutions (see di Palma 1977). The link between the parliamentary institutions and the wider political system is provided by the association of their members in "parliamentary groups" (Massai 1996, 17–26). It is no accident that, in House and Senate rules, the regulations which concern these groups come immediately after those which regulate the structure of the houses.

However, the link between parties and parliamentary groups is not absolute. In fact, parliamentary regulations do not establish any relationship between being elected on a particular party list and then joining a corresponding parliamentary group. The rules only establish that senators, within three days from the first sitting, must declare which group they intend to join; deputies have only two days to decide (Rescigno 1965).

MPs make their own choices in selecting political group membership, and they may establish groups that do not correspond to any political party. Consequently, if a certain number of deputies or senators (respectively, twenty and ten) decide to form an official group independent of their formal party allegiance, they can do so freely. Article 14 of the present Senate Regulations permits the formation of groups comprising fewer than ten senators, with the authorization of the Speaker's Council, "on condition that they represent an organized party or movement in the country which has presented lists of candidates under the same token in at least fifteen regions for the Senate elections and has elected representatives in at least three regions, and on condition that at least five senators, even if elected under different labels, join the said group." Political representation organized by parties is certainly preferred. But if a group reaches the prescribed number of ten senators, no reference to any political party is necessary. In any case, it can be said that the groups are an integral part of the parliamentary structure (see Cazzola 1974).

In both the Chamber of Deputies and the Senate, the so-called mixed group unites those members of Parliament who declare they do not belong to any political party or other group or who do not make a choice. This group also hosts those members of Parliament from parties or movements which, not having achieved the prescribed number of members, have not been authorized by the speaker's office of their respective house to form a group.

The Formation of the Agenda

Each group elects a chair and a chair's council. The chairs of the Senate parliamentary groups join together in a special conference with the deputy speakers to assist the speaker with the organization of sessions by preparing bimonthly programs and, usually, monthly schedules. The standing committees formed on the basis of nominations by the single groups examine the bills and various topics before they are discussed and voted on in the assembly and, in certain cases, may even deliberate on these in lieu of a final vote in the assembly.

The preliminary object of contention between majority and opposition in Parliament is the importance to be attached either to the monitoring or the implementation of the government's agenda. This is also true of the efforts by minorities (or single members of the majority) to include their own pet topics alongside or as substitutes for those proposed by the government and the majority. The organization of the sessions is a testing ground for the capacity of conflicting groups to reconcile their differences and enable the government of the day, which has received the confidence of Parliament to govern, along with the opposition, to get on with parliamentary business.

Until 1990, the Italian system was dominated by the old warranty principle by which the houses were "masters of their order-of-the-day" (Senato della Repubblica 1988a). This institutional arrangement generated inadequate coordination of parliamentary sessions, along with a marked incapacity of governments to elaborate programs, and it weakened political cohesion in the governing majority (Modugno 1979). However, between 1988 and 1991, some important changes were made in Chamber and Senate rules by which, with the agreement of the speakers of both assemblies, a priority role has been assigned to the government in setting parliamentary agendas.

The 1971 Parliamentary Regulations had established the organization of proceedings based on the principles of "program" and "unanimity" (Di Ciolo and Ciaurro 1994, 51–54). The latter aimed at making all the parliamentary groups, including groups in the opposition, jointly responsible for decisions made during the chairs' conference. Actually, the 1988–91 rules had to do with a change of course that reflected the political need to associate the Communist Party with the government's decisions in a period of serious national and international emergency. This political operation would be remembered in history as the "historic compromise." These principles still constitute the basis for decisions concerning parliamentary proceedings. First, the speakers of the assemblies try to gather the unanimous consensus of the groups on a program outline, bearing in mind the priorities of the government and the proposals of the groups in relation to the numerical size of their constituencies. If unanimity is not reached, the rules allow the speakers to intervene. In the Senate, the speaker may draw up a program for one week only, "based on the indications which emerged during the Conference" in which the conflict arose. This outline is then communicated to the assembly, which has the power to change it. The same situation arises with the calendar, the monthly document which sets ways and times for the deliberation of the program. In the Chamber of Deputies, whenever unanimity is not reached during the group chairs' conference, the power to draw up the calendar passes entirely to the speaker, without any interference from the assembly, whereas the Senate's calendar prepared by the speaker is subject to amendment by the assembly.

The approved calendar contains the number and dates of dedicated sessions for each subject. This is made possible by means of time-sharing, which consists in the distribution of time among parliamentary groups in light of their numerical constituency and their political interest in the proceedings. In the Senate, time-sharing is decided by a majority vote in the group chairs' conference.

At their initial meeting, called by the speakers of the respective houses, parliamentary groups elect their representative bodies. The rules of these groups must be deposited with the speaker's office as a condition of access to public funding. At the same time, the parliamentary groups are not the integral parts of the houses that the standing and the select committees are. In other words, when we speak of the will of the Senate or the Chamber of Deputies, we are referring to their exercise of constitutional authority. This can be expressed only by the standing committees and, at times, by the select committees, not by the parliamentary groups. The groups may be responsible for leadership initiatives, or for the desire to act, but never for the official acts of the legislative houses. It is only in the programming of sessions, a task entrusted to the chairs of the parliamentary groups, that they contribute directly to the formation of the will of the houses. But in this circumstance it is not the groups or their chairs who directly form the will of one of the two houses. Rather, it is the chairs' conference, which is itself an institution presided over by the speaker of the Senate or the Chamber of Deputies. The groups simply designate, in the persons of their chairs, the members of this body, just as they designate the members of the standing committees and bicameral committees, in accord with the house rules. Therefore, it can be said that the party groups are independent instrumental entities within the ambit of the parliamentary system.

Standing and Select Committees

The committees set up within each house are a fundamental feature of parliamentary organization. The standing committees are so called because they are not set up from time to time for the examination of single provisions, but have a predetermined jurisdiction in the various fields of Senate activity. Their composition reflects the size of the parliamentary groups, so they tend to mirror the composition of the assembly as a whole. Palazzo Madama has thirteen standing committees, each of which has jurisdiction over the subject indicated next to its number: (1) constitutional affairs, the presidency of the Council of Ministers, the interior, and public administration; (2) justice; (3) foreign affairs, emigration; (4) defense; (5) economic programming, budget; (6) finance and the Treasury; (7) public education, cultural assets, scientific research, entertainment, and sport; (8) public works, communications; (9) agriculture and food production; (10) industry, commerce, tourism; (11) labor, social security; (12) hygiene and health; and (13) territory, environment, and environmental assets (Chimenti 1977, 85–89).

In addition, the Senate may establish committees of inquiry to look into matters of public concern. Again, special committees may be created, upon decision of the assembly, to examine particular bills. Finally, joint Chamber-Senate committees may be established, including bicameral committees of inquiry and for direction and control. Members of the Select Committee for Regulations and the Select Committee for Elections and Parliamentary Immunities are chosen by the speaker of the Senate. Although these latter committees are largely technical and required to act impartially, the speaker takes into account the size of the parliamentary groups when determining their composition.

The ten-member Select Committee for Regulations is led by the speaker of the Senate. Its number can be expanded by no more than four additional members so as to increase its range of representation. It is responsible for all initiatives or the examination of every proposed modification concerning house rules, and it responds to requests for advice on the interpretation of rules submitted by the speaker. The Select Committee for Elections and Parliamentary Immunities has twenty-three members and is called upon to verify senators' titles for admission and all causes for ineligibility. It is also charged with examining any request for authorization to proceed to arrest a senator, and any request to authorize action on ministerial offenses involving the Senate as an institution. The Select Committee for European Union Affairs includes twenty-four senators, and it has general jurisdiction over matters directly related to the activity and the affairs of the European Union and the implementation of EU agreements. The Committee for the Library has three members and is responsible for monitoring the Senate Library.

One of the practical complications faced by the bicameral system concerns the bicameral committees, comprised of both deputies and senators. These committees represent an effort to overcome the rigid Chamber-Senate dualism and to articulate Parliament's desires in matters where there is no need for the redundancy of a double decision and where there is a stronger need for a univocal exercise of parliamentary power. Some bicameral committees are provided for in the constitution (Article 126 indicates the formalities regarding the Committee for Regional Affairs) or in ordinary legislation. Much more numerous are those established by ordinary law, including the Committee for Direction and Control of Broadcasting Services; the Committee for Control over Intelligence and Security Services and on State Secrets; a committee to control the activity of agencies for social security and assistance; and several committees of parliamentary inquiry. At times, bicameral committees have been activated by nonlegislative action, through simple motions approved by the two houses of Parliament (e.g., some committees of inquiry and, in 1983, the Committee for Institutional Reforms).

The Lawmaking Process

The process for passing laws is specified in Article 71 and subsequent provisions of the constitution. The legislative function is exercised jointly by the two houses. Both houses must approve exactly the same text of a law before it can be promulgated by the head of state and published in the

Official Journal. Although consensus between both houses is required for the final approval of a law, it does not matter which house takes the legislative initiative.

Parliamentary committees may, in appropriate circumstances, exert the ultimate lawmaking decision, without recourse to the plenary of either house. The attribution to committees of such sweeping powers in legislative matters is entirely peculiar to the Italian Parliament and should make possible (unfortunately only in theory) a certain speeding up of the lawmaking process. It is up to the Senate speaker to determine whether a bill is only to be considered by a committee or given a final vote by the committee to which it has been assigned before it becomes law (Ciaurro 1982, 33–48). Exceptions to this rule are those bills which, as the constitution requires, must always be presented for discussion and vote by the full house—bills concerning constitutional and electoral issues; matters involving legislative delegation; ratification of international treaties; and the approval of budgets and statements. Furthermore, when one-tenth of the members of the Senate, one-fifth of committee members, or the government request it, bills must be presented to the assembly for resolution.

Bills come before the parliamentary houses in the version adopted by the committee that reports on it. This committee text is printed alongside the version of the bill's sponsor so that the assembly may assess any committee changes. The bill is also accompanied by a committee report or by the separate reports from majority and minority committee members. The first stage of the house's deliberative process is a general discussion in which all senators may participate, and it is intended to uphold or reject the validity of the ends or purposes which the legislation proposes to meet, including its probability of meeting them. Then, the *rapporteur* and the government representative speak. There follows an examination of the single articles, which are discussed and voted on individually, after any amendments have been accepted or rejected. The bill is then voted on in its entirety. A bill approved by one branch of Parliament is immediately passed to the other. Should the second house approve exactly the same text, the law has completed its parliamentary "iter" (that is, its passage) and can be promulgated and published.

If the text is modified in either house, a bill must be returned to the other house for a resolution of the changes approved by the first chamber. The process of passing bills back and forth between Chamber and Senate until both have approved an identical text is the "shuttle." If one house rejects the bill, further consideration is terminated. Finally, prior to the promulgation of a law, the head of state may, by means of a special message, request that Parliament examine it again. This applies particularly to laws that are fully financed by the government but that do not indicate where the money is coming from. Any imperfections in the constitutionality of a law can also be brought to the attention of the Constitutional Court during any legal action before the magistrates or by the direct initiative of a region should it consider its competence impaired by the new law. Moreover, the electorate may express itself through a referendum, requesting repeal of a law approved by Parliament (excluding proceedings on matters of taxation and budget, amnesty and pardons, and ratification of international treaties).

Parliament and Government

The constitution mandates that the government must obtain a vote of confidence from both Chamber and Senate. This prescription (Article 94) sums up what is currently considered the most important political activity of Parliament. It exercises direction and political control to oversee, press, and check the activities and performance of the government, supporting or censuring it whenever necessary and even, in the extreme, expressing a vote of "no confidence" and obliging the government to resign. Moreover, the president of the Republic can call for the early dissolution of Parliament when a new parliamentary majority willing to give its confidence to a government cannot be found.

The president of the Republic nominates the president of the Council of Ministers—in other words, the prime minister—and then nominates ministers upon his or her advice. The government must go before the houses to obtain a vote of confidence within ten days of its formation, which is sealed by the swearing-in ceremony presided over by the president. The call for a vote of confidence is made after a declaration is read by the prime minister, giving an outline of the programs and general policy guidelines for domestic and foreign affairs that the government intends to implement. This policy declaration, promulgated first in one house and then in the other, is followed by a debate culminating in a vote on a "motion of confidence" in favor of the government. If the vote is positive in both Chamber and Senate, the government is definitively formed. However, if the vote is negative, or if it is positive in one house but negative in the other, the government must resign.

Once the political guidelines proposed by the government are approved, Parliament contributes to their implementation by means of its legislative activity. This contribution comes about not only through the approval of bills proposed by the government (which represent the great majority of bills approved by the houses) but also by conferring on it the power to approve laws (by legislative delegation) on certain subjects, always for short periods and with prior indication of the broad principles to which the laws must conform. Furthermore, Parliament devotes a good portion of its time to the conversion into law of any urgent provisions (decree laws) adopted by the government (Ciaurro 1982, 42–102).

In this context, the yearly approval of the national budget is very important (Camera dei deputati 1992, 171–97). It is the accounting document prepared by the government where public revenues and expenditures are forecast for the following financial year, together with the financial law and the other related provisions. The financial law and the budget law provide the basis for the government's fiscal planning to attain the economic policy objectives to which it aspires. Indeed, the budget law must be accompanied by the presentation of a "report on estimates and programs" by the ministers responsible for the Treasury and the budget. Such presentations provide the houses extensive information on revenues and expenditures for the previous fiscal year, which allows for informed budgetary consideration by the two chambers of Parliament.

Equally important is Parliament's role in the field of foreign policy. The constitution states, in fact, that both houses of Parliament must ratify international treaties and declare war. Cooperation between government and Parliament is most readily obtained when the government has reported to the houses regularly, giving deputies and senators briefings on matters ranging from budget estimates and programs to the country's general economic situation. Often ministers testify before the assembly and appear before the appropriate committees on subjects for which they are specifically competent. At the same time, the houses may adopt motions defining their opinion on specific topics; carry out inquiries through special committees or through standing committee research; or approve resolutions on policy matters and request that ministers report to Parliament concerning their activities. Finally, each member of Parliament may put forward questions, which are requests for information to ministers on specific items or subjects, and which are a typical expression of parliamentary control over the government's activity.

The "Big Bang" of 1994

The year 1994 symbolizes the end of an era in Italian politics. It is irrelevant that in that year the Polo delle Liberta [roughly, the Alliance for Liberties] won the election and captured a bare majority in the Twelfth Parliament. The alliance was a conservative coalition headed by television and media tycoon Silvio Berlusconi. His was a heterogeneous majority whose nucleus comprised middle-class moderates, ambitious "yuppies" tied to Berlusconi's extensive economic interests, and large numbers of Berlusconi's employees turned militant and united in Forza Italia [Go Italy], the new party created ad hoc with the money and television networks of the Milanese millionaire. But it was also a majority that ranged from the former Fascists from the Alleanza Nazionale [National Alliance], headed by Gianfranco Fini, to the separatists of Lega Nord [Northern League], captained by Umberto Bossi and made up of Margaret Thatcher–type free traders and old Christian Democrats tied to a clientelist, paternalistic conception of politics. Unsurprisingly, this fragile majority fell to pieces eight months after taking over, and Berlusconi had to resign as prime minister.

There followed a more or less neutral government headed by Lamberto Dini, formerly a top-ranking official of the Bank of Italy turned politician only a few months previously. It was an administration made up of nonpoliticians chosen mostly from among university intellectuals and government bureaucrats, and it was trusted by the president of the Republic.

It had nothing to do with the beginning of a "second republic," aping the institutional journey of the French republic. Neither was it the much vaunted renewal of national leadership. Quite the contrary, other parties, both liberal and conservative, were established with the transparent purpose of assuring the reelection of politicians of the old establishment who otherwise risked political extinction. The new parties served as laundries to recycle politicians who had survived the wreckage of the previous months. No doubt even Forza Italia performed this service. The old Communist Party (PCI) managed to preserve its membership and organization almost intact, both outside and inside Parliament. The old PCI became the Partito Democratico della Sinistra [Democratic Party of the Left], or PDS. Ironically, PDS is an acronym in vogue with the ex-Communist parties of Eastern Europe.

If there was no "second republic," certainly the party system that had rebuilt Italy from 1945, and even more from the time the country joined NATO at the height of the cold war, was no more. The Christian Democratic Party, the hub of the postwar Italian political system, split into three pieces—the Partito Popolare [People's Party], greatly weakened and moving toward center-left, and the smaller CCD and CDU groups leaning center-right. The minor secular parties, such as the Republicans, the Social Democrats, and the Liberals, had practically been annihilated. The Socialist Party [Partito Socialista] had been blown away by the scandals exposed by investigations conducted by the so-called Tangentopoli [Kickback City] of the Milanese judges. Its leader and former prime minister, Bettino Craxi, is wanted by the police and self-exiled in Tunisia.

By this time the fall of the Berlin Wall had swept away the balance of power established at Yalta after World War II, and with it the *conventio ad excludendum* that was its corollary (no government with the Communist Party). Italians were no longer forced by the cold war or by considerations of international politics to accept a savage spoils system in which many parties participated—where the leading role was played by the parties in power and their friends and also, although to a lesser extent, by the parties of the opposition like the PCI, today the PDS. The Christian Democrats, its centrist allies, and since 1960 the Socialists could no longer justify their actions by the need to defend Italy from Soviet and Communist subversion. Under these conditions it was inevitable that a liberated Italian electorate would become extremely mobile and volatile.

Nevertheless, a mature democracy characterized by alternation in government is still a long way off. The most recent general elections gave a narrow parliamentary majority to the Olive Tree [Ulivo], a liberal and radical alliance whose hard core is the PDS, and to which the People's Party, the Greens [Verdi], and new minor groups of secular and centrist orientation have contributed. Also supporting the new majority, but not part of the Olive Tree coalition, is the Communist Refoundation Party [Rifondazione Comunista], a radical movement that blatantly proclaims its Marxist-Leninist ideology. The largest political party in the Olive Tree coalition is led by former Communist Massimo D'Alema, but the prime ministership fell to Romano Prodi, a former University of Bologna economics professor, former Christian Democrat, former cabinet minister before the "big bang," and former president of the IRI, the powerful holding company that controls the greater part of the country's state-owned industry.

Despite a reformed electoral law, the Italian party system has not assumed bipolar form. Bipolarity does not require a system of only two political parties; it only requires that serious contention for governmental offices fall to two leading parties or coalitions. Paradoxically, inside the two houses of Parliament fully forty-four political movements are represented, twenty-six of which have only one member. This kind of fragmentation results, above all, from the controversial and bizarre law on public financing of political parties that was approved in 1996.

Fewer political groups are represented in the Senate than in the Chamber of Deputies. In the upper house, assembled under the banner of the Olive Tree are the Democratic Left [Sinistra Democratica] mostly made up of members of the PDS, joined by a few independents and a handful of former Republicans, the People's Party, Italian Renewal [Rinnovamento Italiano], a group founded by the foreign minister and former prime minister Lamberto Dini, the Greens, and, in a strategic position given its freedom of movement, the Communist Refoundation Party. On the opposition side is the Alliance for Liberties, composed of Go Italy, the National Alliance, the Christian Democratic Center (CCD), and the United Christian Democrats (CDU). The Northern League also opposes the government, though its attitude is largely one of filibustering and hostility to national unity.

The future consequences of post-1994 parliamentary developments are not easy to predict. Italy is the same country that in recent years witnessed the maneuvering of the largest Communist party in the West as it learned, little by little, to abide by the rules of liberal democracy. Italy, devastated by World War II, decided to embrace parliamentary democracy, a free market, and free international trade. The same country only twenty years ago endured relentless, widespread terrorist activities that threatened the security of the nation. These bloody attacks were conducted by extreme leftist groups that considered the Communist Party traitorous. The mortal threat of terrorism was stifled without introducing draconian laws abolishing civil liberties. Fortunately, the democratic forces in the country, including the vast majority of political parties, gave continued strong support for democratic institutions, demonstrating that even though chaotic, Italian democracy was working.

Today, this same Italy is facing a deep crisis regarding its form of government, a crisis that is compounded both by transformations in Italian society, and by national and international economic realities. Despite lingering uncertainty and ambiguity, Italy has changed. Most important is the growing recognition, in a rapidly changing world, that the government must acquire new and effective decision-making tools, and recognize that unworkable institutions must be changed with the utmost possible haste. To move in this direction, early in 1997 Parliament established a bicameral committee to hammer out institutional reforms (Piciacchia 1997). Members of this new reform committee were nominated by the speakers of both houses according to the recommendations of the parliamentary groups, based on proportional representation. Its membership includes thirty-five senators and thirty-five deputies, and the committee elected PDS leader Massimo D'Alema as its chairman. Of course, this is not the first time a committee on reform has been created; it had been done in 1983, and then again in 1993.

The constitutional law that established the bicameral committee also endows it with its powers. Article I affirms that the seventy-member committee may hammer out proposals regarding that part of the constitution providing for the establishment of governing institutions (e.g., administrative agencies, Parliament, local government). Although fundamental principles cannot be infringed, in principle the committee recommendations can range from American-style presidentialism, to French semipresidentialism, to a Westminster parliamentary model, to German federalism. The committee's final recommendations must be taken to Parliament for consideration and, inasmuch as revisions of the constitution are involved they must be approved by both chambers in two successive sessions separated by no less than three months. If Parliament were to approve, the reforms it proposes must be submitted to a popular referendum.

Predictably, strong differences of vision and equally strong difficulties in reaching compromises emerged right from the start. The American presidential alternative never was considered; there was some support for the French model on the part of conservatives, and some support for a prime ministerial structure vaguely along British Westminster lines preferred by liberals. The German federal model, with devolution of power to the subnational units [länder], aroused widespread discussion. The issue of "perfect bicameralism" has also been considered extensively, mainly along two lines: a senate representing the regions; or a senate confined to oversight of the executive, with the lower house exercising the legislative power and charged with giving direction to the nation. The alternatives remain under discussion, and will not be soon resolved.

Bicameralism: Conclusions and Future Prospects

It is now possible, fifty years after the approval of the constitution, to draw some conclusions and trace an outline for the future. In 1947, it was right and proper for the requirements of Italian society to adopt the term *parliament*, which, as decreed by Article 55, is composed of the Chamber of Deputies and the Senate of the Republic. It was a highly innovative choice considering the nature of the pre-Fascist system, precisely because it underscored the unity of the electorally based and democratic parliamentary system. However, today no one in Italy doubts the existence of a serious institutional problem that directly involves Parliament (Di Ciolo 1994, 47–72).

What is the problem to be tackled and solved? Basically, the problem is the need to speed up the process of parliamentary decision making so as to enable a quicker and more timely response to government initiatives. Put differently, a lawmaking process must be established that can keep pace with a rapidly changing world and respond in a timely way to the new demands and needs of an advanced industrial society in continuous and profound transformation.

It might be inappropriate to question the suitability for this goal of a parliamentary system in bicameral form. The reason is not so much a blind faith in the 1947–48 constitutional model or a particular attachment to the Senate of the Republic, the parliamentary house that would be sacrificed in a unicamerally oriented constitutional reform. Rather, it is because daily practice in Palazzo Montecitorio, and more particularly in Palazzo Madama, demonstrates time and time again that the meditation allowed by double deliberation in considering bills can be useful. Redundancy has its virtues.

The Italian Parliament is called upon to do a great deal of legislating. Statistically, the average number of laws passed annually by the two houses is 240–280, as compared to 80 or so passed in France and Germany, and the 60 passed in Britain. But there is a growing gap between excessive lawmaking on minor matters and lack of regulatory legislation on matters of primary concern, for example, the crucial law on the national broadcasting system, and the inadequacy of the various provisions accompanying the annual budget.

To sum up, too few major laws and too many trivial laws. This shortcoming was observed as early as the 1960s by such distinguished scholars as Giovanni Sartori and Alberto Predieri (Sartori 1963, 205–76). Excessive preoccupation with minor legislation was encouraged and even favored by the ability to pass laws in the committees and without the approval of the full houses. This is why it is necessary to ponder making some changes in the constitutional model drawn up by the 1947–48 Constitution. In this sense, there has been an ongoing debate for most of the past twenty years on *delegificazione,* the necessary and unavoidable restriction of the lawmaking purview and powers of Parliament.

In Italy, the sternest criticisms of bicameralism have stemmed from its having come to be identified as one of the major causes of the malfunctioning of the whole institutional system, whereas the real roots of the institutional problem are in the country's extreme multipartism. In addition, the presumed defects of bicameralism were long attributed almost exclusively to the Senate, so that debate on the workings of Parliament has often given rise to proposals for its abolition. There is an interesting law of nature in politics that applies to the institutional domain: very lively, dynamic, and public debate of the great issues in politics tends to flourish in the popular house of Parliament. Thus, the major influences on Italian public opinion come from the Chamber of Deputies, which prefers a senate whose role is one of mediation, wisdom, and moderation, and not a senate with coequal legislative or government-making power.

Since the early 1970s, the vision of Parliament as a unitary institution has continued to loom large, serving to highlight how a debate about bicameralism should involve consideration of the working methods of both houses. This unitary vision is particularly important because it makes comprehensible the reality that Italian bicameralism is substantially procedural in nature and that the double-reading system can be compared to the guarantees offered by double-tier jurisdiction in criminal trials. The "parity bicameralism" in which both legislative houses are coequal, provided in the constitution, is far from being a major reason for the mal-functioning of the Italian parliamentary system. To argue otherwise only serves to distract attention from the serious political problems that jeopardize the working of Italian representative democracy.

Some Possible Reforms

Proposals abound to reform the structure and the functions of both houses of Parliament (Caretti 1981). One proposal calls for the election of senators by regional council members. However, this proposal in favor of a chamber of the regions meets with objections centering around the difficulty that the Senate could not long lay claim to the same legislative powers as the lower house if it were not directly elected. Moreover, inasmuch as Italy is not a federal state, there are reservations about the idea of one chamber representing the regions, while the other one represents the electorate as a whole (Occhiocupo 1990). At the same time, federalist urges reverberate in some forms, witness the upsurge of separatist sentiment, of which the Northern League is the loudest and most controversial advocate. In fact, it has not yet been clarified by either the majority or the opposition parties whether a federal form of local government is the chosen option. Nor is it clear whether they prefer some form of administrative decentralization through the devolution of broader powers to the regions and more consistent administrative authority to the municipalities and provinces. Such devolution, although it might signify a strong decentralization of powers, cannot be considered the same as federalism.

On the other hand, a reform proposal that has been debated for some years would allow both houses of Parliament to maintain their representative basis, but would reserve lawmaking to the Chamber of Deputies, and it would assign to the Senate the functions of controlling and monitoring the government, as well as the responsibility for setting general guidelines in certain sensitive areas of national life, such as information, security, or nomination of public agency heads. In relation to this, it may be noted that the history of control of government and the public bureaucracy in Italy does little to justify the need for an ad hoc chamber. Moreover, the distinction between legislation and control obscures the fundamental activity of setting guidelines that the Italian system expresses by means of the foremost legislative activity—that of implementing the government's program through a vote of confidence. In fact, the two functions of legislation and control are intended to reinforce one another.

A reform of this nature would also be unbalanced because it would make the Chamber of Deputies the majority group's house, and the Senate would be where the opposition would prevail. For these reasons, the greatest caution must be used regarding proposals tending to attribute specific powers to the upper house. It would also be right to ask oneself what could have been the basic motive for the constitution's implementation of parity bicameralism. The reason for bicameralism is that it provides for reconsideration of one house's actions in the other house so that decisions can be confirmed or modified. Such reconsideration is only made possible by the institution of reexamination in another assembly, especially if it is convened by a different electoral system and it operates on the basis of at least partially different regulations. In this sense, assuming that Italian bicameralism is essentially procedural, it can be said that procedural reform is called for. Such reform could ensure responsibility, clarity, and speed to the work carried out by the two branches of Parliament. In this context, reform can be foreseen that will define two categories of legislation, one consisting of proposed laws to be determined jointly by the two houses, and the other including legislation for unicameral passage (Senato della Repubblica 1990).

Accordingly, the Chamber and the Senate would remain equal components of a unitary Parliament with identical powers and equal dignity, while unnecessary duplications, procedural delays, and incomprehensible and unjustifiable repetitions would be eliminated. Thus, parity bicameralism rather than perfect bicameralism would prevail. In this sense, it would be necessary to define a limited number of necessarily bicameral laws that would have to be approved by both houses. These would be laws concerning constitutional and electoral matters, legislative delegation, authorizations to ratify international treaties of a political nature or involving important territorial variations, the elaboration and approval of budgets and statements, and the conversion of decree laws.

In every other case, a bill approved by one house would be passed to the other and would be considered definitively approved unless, within a certain time, a majority in the second house were to express a preference that the bill should be submitted to it for approval. Any late requests for reexamination by each house would then need to be presented, again within a certain time, by the absolute majority of its members. And the government would have similar powers to recall a law.

It would also be necessary to define who should have the right to assign the first reading to one or the other house without sparking a conflict between them. It is very clear that an efficient coordination of the workload between the two parliamentary houses could save time with respect to the legislative activity assigned to or initiated by only one house. Making a sharp distinction between research activity and decision making would also enable the former to be carried out jointly by the committees of the two houses or at least produce a rapid joint use of its results. The tendency to specialize could also be developed usefully for purposes of control. And a general rationalization effort involving both houses could better define the positions of majority and opposition in relation to the various matters being examined, allowing voters to acquire a clearer picture of what is going on and thereby guaranteeing an effective link with society at large.

Another matter requiring a solution concerns the propensity of Parliament to get involved, almost lost, in the approval of laws of little or no importance on extremely specific topics and items, thereby allowing itself to lose sight of the "general and abstract" nature which the Italian Constitution requires of every law. It would be simpler for any matter not expressly reserved to the law by the constitution if the government were to exercise its regulatory power. Parliament would then be left free to decide on major issues unburdened by lightweight problems such as the intonation of musical instruments, or the reconstruction of a single crane that collapsed in a certain port, or the concession of a quality brand for a special kind of ham.

These reforms would neither represent radical changes in the constitution nor provide a remedy for all the ills of the Italian system. They would require legislation limited to a series of mediated adjustments of the complex rules that lie at the core of the system. But, above all, democracy requires patience, tolerance, and gradualness. Having these properties, a democracy need not become immobilized. On the contrary, Italy needs to see concrete results issuing from its political, institutional, and juridical debates. It needs to move over from the realm of proposals and possibilities to the terrain of concrete legislative decisions. This is also necessary in order to alleviate the antiparliament prejudice so evident in Italian public opinion.

References

Aimo, Piero. 1977. *Bicameralism e regioni.* Milan: Edizioni Communità.

Camera dei deputati. 1992. *Il Parlamento della Repubblica: Organi, procedure, apparati.* Rome: Camera dei deputati.

Caretti, Paolo. 1981. "Funzionalità del Parlamento e proposte di riforma." *Democrazia e diritto* 3:65–79.

Cazzola, Franco. 1974. *Governo e opposizione nel parlamento Italiano.* Milan: Giuffré.

Chimenti, Carlo. 1977. "Per un bilancio dei primi anni de attuazione del nuovo Regolamento del Senato." *Aspetti e tendenze del diritto costituzionale* 2:73–105.

Ciaurro, Gian Franco. 1982. *Le istituzioni parlamentari.* Milan: Giuffré.

Cotta, Maurizio. 1979. *Classe politica e parlamento in Italia, 1946–1976.* Bologna: Il Mulino.

———. 1990. "The 'Centrality' of Parliament in a Protracted Democratic Consolidation: The Italian Case." In *Parliament and Democratic Consolidation in Southern Europe,* ed. Ulrike Liebert and Maurizio Cotta. London: Pinter.

———. 1994. "The Rise and Fall of the 'Centrality' of the Italian Parliament: Transformations of the Executive-Legislative Subsystem after the Second World War." In *Parliaments in the Modern World: Changing Institutions,* ed. Gary W. Copeland and Samuel C. Patterson. Ann Arbor: University of Michigan Press.

Di Ciolo, Vittorio, and Luigi Ciaurro. 1994. *Il diritto parlamentare nella teoria e nella pratica.* Milan: Giuffré.

di Palma, Giuseppe. 1977. *Surviving without Governing: The Italian Parties in Parliament.* Berkeley: University of California Press.

Longi, Vincenzo. 1993. *Elementi di diritto e procedura parlamentare: Quinta edizione aggiornata a tutto il 1993.* Milan: Giuffré.

Manzella, Andrea. 1977. *Il parlamento.* Bologna: Il Mulino.

Massai, Alessandro. 1996. *Dentro il Parlamento.* Milan: Il Sole 24 ore Libri.

Modugno, Franco. 1979. "Il sistema parlamentare è al tramonto?" *Il Mulino* 263: 469–78.

Nocilla, Damiano, and Luigi Ciaurro. 1987. "Rappresentanza politica." In *Enciclopedia del diritto,* 38:543–609. Milan: Giuffré.

Occhiocupo. Nicola. 1990. "La camera delle regioni oggi." *Studi parmensi* 39:179–203.

Piciacchia, Paola. 1997. "Dal dibattito sulle riforme all'istituzione della Commissione Bicamerale." *Il Politico* 62:47–90.

Rescigno, Pietro. 1965. "L'attività di diritto privato dei gruppi parlamentari." *Studi in memoria di Guido Zanobini* 3:557–76.

Sartori, Giovanni, ed. 1963. *Il Parlamento Italiano, 1946–1963.* Naples: Edizioni Scientifiche Italiane.

Senato della Repubblica. Segretariato Generale. 1949. *Il Regolamento del Senato e i lavori preparatori.* Rome: Senato della Repubblica.

———. 1988a. *I Regolamenti del Senato della Repubblica.* Rome: Senato della Repubblica.

————. 1988b. *Servizi e uffici del Senato della Repubblica.* Rome: Senato della Repubblica.

————. 1990. *La riforma del bicameralismo in Senato.* Rome: Senato della Repubblica.

Tanda, Anton Paolo. 1987. *Le norme e la prassi del Parlamento italiano.* Rome: Colombo.

Tosi, Silvano. 1974. *Diritto parlamentare.* Milan: Giuffré.

Ungari, Paolo. 1971. *Profilo storico del diritto parlamentare in Italia.* Rome: B. Carucci.

9

A House in Search of a Role:
The Senado of Spain

CARLOS FLORES JUBERÍAS

Today's Spanish Parliament, the Cortes Generales, is a bicameral body consisting of a lower house, the Congreso de los Diputados, and an upper house, the Senado. Both are large: the Congress of Deputies presently includes 350 directly elected representatives, and the Senate has 256 members. All representatives serve four-year terms. The basis of representation in the Senate is territorial. About four-fifths of senators (208 members) are elected directly, with each province electing four senators. The rest are elected indirectly, selected by the legislative assemblies of the autonomous communities. With this parliamentary configuration as the end product, the aim of this chapter is to recount the historical development of bicameralism in Spain. Further, the constitutional standing of the Spanish Senate will be analyzed, the processes of electing senators and the nature of election outcomes will be described, the structure and dynamics of Senate organization will be characterized, and the constitutional and political powers of the body will be considered. Finally, efforts to reform the Senate will be presented and appraised.

Bicameralism vs. Unicameralism in Spain

Spanish constitutional history is a story of struggle between unicameral and bicameral visions of Parliament. The first one-house Parliament, the Cortes, was established in the Spanish Constitution of 1812. The constitution makers reacted against precedents dating back to the Middle Ages that involved summoning representatives of the nobility, the church, and the burgers separately. Closely following the ideological premises of the French Revolution, they forged a Parliament whose members were intended to represent the entire Spanish nation in a single body (Flores Juberías 1990). The old triangular representational system no longer suited national needs, and it seemed axiomatic to the founders that only a unicameral Parliament would have the strength to enact legislation from a more liberal agenda and deal with a king whose loyalty to the new constitutional principles was dubious (see Argüelles 1981, 82–84).

The rather liberal Constitution of 1812, and the fact that it became one of the most powerful myths of Spanish liberalism, helped shape the conventional wisdom that unicameralism was essentially a liberal invention (see Martínez Sospedra 1978). Moreover, with the 1812 Constitution granting the legislature unprecedented prominence in the Spanish governing constellation, unicameralism came to be widely associated in the public mind with a strong legislature (Coronas Gonzáles 1989). Therefore, as the liberal cause lost its momentum, and more or less conservative governments acceded to power, bicameralism came to be preferred in Spanish constitutions for the remainder of the nineteenth century. These conservative governments turned to upper chambers for ideological reasons, to establish a counterweight to the popularly elected lower chamber, and to divide and weaken Parliament as a whole.

The Birth of the Spanish Senate

Following the traumatic experience of absolutist rule in the last years of the reign of King Ferdinand VII, Premier Francisco Martínez de la Rosa reintroduced constitutional government with the Royal Statute of 1834 (see Tomás Villarroya 1968), which created a bicameral legislature. However, the partly hereditary upper house, fittingly called the "Estate of the Grandees," was short-lived, since a new constitution was put in place in 1837. Closely following French precedents from 1830 and Belgian precedents from 1831, it too embraced bicameralism and introduced the names by which the parliamentary houses are known today (Tomás Villarroya 1985). Congress was to be an entirely elected house—its members chosen by direct popular vote, its constituencies formed from the nation's provinces, and its members free to run for reelection. The Senate's composition was more controversial; senators would be chosen by the king from a list of names proposed by the voters of each province, so as to give each province representation roughly in proportion to its population and renewed by thirds every three years. This arrangement satisfied nobody, and senators were not able to win sufficient prestige and political influence to sustain the institution (see Bertelsen 1974, 170ff.).

Yet another bicameral constitution followed in 1845. Persistent negative perceptions about the regulation of the Senate in the previous constitution led the new constitution makers to focus on this issue. Senators were now to be appointed for life and without restriction by the Crown from a pool of aristocrats—those with substantial wealth and qualified by previous service in the government, the church, the military, or the upper echelons of judicial service (see Sánchez Agesta 1964, 249; Tomás Villarroya 1982, 69). These arrangements were intended to reinforce the political position of Queen Isabel. Appointment of senators for life would provide stability, the open-ended size of the Senate would allow for changing the ideological leanings of the house, and limits on recruiting senators would serve as a safety valve, permitting a conservative membership whatever the partisan composition of the house.

Formally, the 1845 Constitution was in force for almost twenty-five years, until the eruption of the so-called Glorious Revolution of 1868 and the subsequent Revolutionary Sexennium of 1868–74, when politics was taken to the streets. Queen Isabel II was overthrown, free democratic elections took place, a new dynasty was enthroned, and a republic existed briefly when the new, and foreign, king abdicated. The Constitution of 1869 was by far the most radically liberal—and even democratic—constitution of the century, proclaiming the principles of national sovereignty and universal suffrage, and recognizing citizens' rights more pervasively than ever before (see Carro Martínez 1952). The question of a unicameral versus bicameral structure for the Cortes was part of the constitutional debate. But deputies were interested in much more sensitive issues, and the question was resolved quickly in favor of maintaining the upper chamber (Bertelsen 1974, 393).

The 1869 constitution makers sought to create a federal senate in lieu of the now unacceptable aristocratic chamber, based loosely on practices developed from the example of the United States (see Oltra Pons 1972). That Spain remained a unitary state largely frustrated the attempt, providing a Senate with an eclectic and even contradictory membership. Although each province was awarded four senators regardless of their disparate population sizes, the Constitution required that senators would represent "the entire Nation, and not exclusively the voters who named them," thus breaking one of the basic principles of a federal chamber. Its democratic nature was limited in addition by suffrage and eligibility restrictions. To be sure, suffrage was universal, but senatorial election was indirect. Ordinary voters chose delegates in each municipality who, along with provincial assemblymen, elected the senators. To be eligible for election to the Senate, individuals had to belong to exclusive categories— deputies, mayors, generals, ambassadors, magistrates, clergy, professors, or major taxpayers. Obviously, although liberalized, the Senate continued to be an elitist body.

Many of the ideas anticipated by the 1869 Constitution resurfaced in the draft republican federal Constitution of 1873 (see Ferrando Badía 1973, 250ff.). Although its enforcement was interdicted by military intervention, this document stands as the sole example of a federal and republican arrangement for Spain, and it introduced an unprecedented structure for the upper chamber. It provided for semisovereign states and a Senate whose members would be elected by state legislatures, along with a popularly elected lower house. As practiced in many other federal systems, the new Cortes would have a lower house representing the nation as a whole and an upper house representing the specific territories. This federal senate would have possessed rather peculiar powers of control—not over the government but over the lower house. The Senate had no legislative initiative; its role lay in its constitutional power "to examine whether bills passed by Congress ignore the rights of human personality, the powers of political bodies, or the attributions of the federation or the fundamental code" (Trujillo 1967, 194).

From Bicameralism to Unicameralism

In the remarkable family of Spanish constitutions, the record for longevity was won by the Constitution of 1876, which survived until the dictatorship of General Miguel Primo de Rivera began in 1923. Its longevity was largely due to the ways in which it took advantage of previous experience to embrace effective constitutional principles, institutions, and mechanisms and to eschew problematic or ineffective ones. In sum, the new constitutional architecture married provisions from the 1845 Constitution, admired by the moderates, with those of the 1869 Constitution, favored by progressives (see Sánchez Férriz 1984, 438).

In the 1876 Constitution, the Senate included three kinds of senators: senators in their own right, senators appointed for life by the Crown, and senators elected by the corporations and the major taxpayers of the State. The third group consisted of 180 elected senators, and the first two groups of members were not to exceed 180 in number. As a consequence, during the almost fifty years of the Restoration, the Senate provided an essential constitutional guarantee of control of the legislative branch by privileged minorities who used it to immobilize the political revolution initiated in 1868 (see Martínez Cuadrado 1973, 37). This conservatism, along with the Senate's lackluster political performance, lay at the root of the political decision to suppress the Senate in the Republican Constitution of 1931.

This decision was neither immediately apparent nor unanimously supported during the debates leading to the formulation of the 1931 Constitution (see García Valdecasas 1983). In fact, in early constitutional drafts, a bicameral solution was proposed that envisioned a corporatist upper chamber under the influence of the leading intellectuals of the day (like De los Ríos or Posada). But the agenda of the leftist republican majority in the constituent Parliament did not include bicameralism, and proposals for a corporatist Senate were thrown out at the committee stage. The argument was that the Senate was an old-fashioned institution, a device for weakening Parliament, an obstacle to progressive legislation, a denial of the essential unity and equality of the people, and an incentive for the resurrection of antiegalitarian positions (see Tomás Villarroya 1982, 127–28). Even President-elect Niceto Alcalá Zamora's defense of a territorial chamber could not counterbalance this argument. The unicameral alternative was finally imposed at the plenary session of Parliament.

This institutional arrangement persisted until republicanism was overthrown in 1936 by Franco. Just as his predecessor, General Primo de Rivera, had attempted to do in 1929 (see García Canales 1980, 141), in 1942 General Francisco Franco created a kind of corporatist assembly, with representatives elected by the official trade union, local governments, married men and women, and an endless number of cultural and professional entities (Zafra Valverde 1973, 274–80). In a strongly centralized regime in which party pluralism was strictly forbidden, this sort of assembly provided as much pluralism as the regime could accept, and it effectively rendered bicameralism a meaningless device. If parliamentary representation of regional interests was deemed unnecessary, so too was improvement in the quality of legislative outputs. After all, the head of state was the main legislative source, and social pluralism was said to be reflected sufficiently in the existing house. Thus, an upper chamber appeared outdated and entirely useless.

Emergence of the Modern Spanish Senate

Nearly half a century of unicameralism, embedded in an authoritarian regime, foretold little about parliamentary development in post-Franco Spain. Calls for the restoration of the Senate did not take long to emerge, however. In May 1976, Francoist Prime Minister Carlos Arias announced his plan for reforming the Cortes, which entailed the creation of a popularly elected Congress and a Senate with limited democratic characteristics. This second chamber would comprise forty senators for life, twenty-five appointed by the king for each legislature, twenty designated by various corporations and public institutions, and two hundred—four per province—elected by universal suffrage from among candidates nominated by local governments and by workers' and employers' associations (see Fernández Segado 1986, 738–39). The Arias proposal was soon forgotten in the national preoccupation with deeper democratization, but the notion of restoring the bicameral principle to Spanish constitutional practice remained very much alive.

Late in 1976, the new centrist prime minister, Adolfo Suárez, proposed a bill for political reform that included restoration of the Senate. Quickly approved by the Francoist Cortes and ratified by a national referendum, this basic legislation served as the schematic for transition from an authoritarian to a democratic regime (see Lucas Verdú 1976; Fernández Segado 1986, 743). Very succinctly, the law set forth six basic traits of the new democratic Senate: (1) it was to be composed of 207 elected members, 4 from each of the forty-eight peninsular provinces, 5 from each of the three insular provinces, and 2 from the African cities of Ceuta and Melilla; (2) the king was authorized to appoint additional senators for each legislature, up to a fifth of the overall number; (3) Senate elections would be based on a majoritarian electoral system and held every four years by universal, direct, and secret suffrage; (4) representation in the Senate was declared to be territorial in nature; (5) in lawmaking, the Senate would be inferior to the Congress of Deputies, lacking both a role in parliamentary control of the government and any initiative on constitutional reform bills; and (6) senators were empowered to govern their own house, electing a presiding officer and adopting their own operating rules.

This framework law was soon followed by additional legislation that provided implementation guidelines, specifying particularly the electoral system to be employed for the election of deputies to the constituent assembly to be held in June 1977. For Senate elections, the electoral procedure entailed a one-round plurality system with limited vote in mostly multimember districts. Individual candidates could run as independents or be nominated by parties, coalitions, or voters' collectives. The plan allowed voters to cast multiple ballots, depending on where they lived. They could cast three votes in the peninsular provinces, where four senators were to be elected; two votes in the larger islands, where three seats were at stake; and just one in Ceuta and Melilla (which elected two senators each) and the smaller islands, which each elected one senator.

Although the framework Law for Political Reform and its implementation were intended to apply only to the constituent assembly and its election, many of its initial provisions, particularly bicameralism and the specific configuration of the Senate, were carried over into the 1978 Constitution. But this transition did not occur easily. Because of a lack of consensus on the nature and political role of the Senate, the new constitutional provisions emerged only after protracted discussion in both houses in which many proposals, some quite unrealistic, were debated.

The debate moved "from a Senate characterized as the house of the autonomous communities ... through an intermediate stage ... to an upper house devoted to the representation of the provinces in which only subsidiarily is the representation of those communities having attained autonomous status attended. Throughout this complex evolution, we have finally and quite exactly arrived at a point rather close to the departure point ... , a Senate practically identical to the one featured by the Law for Political Reform" (Fernández Segado 1984, 90). The only substantial difference was that senators would be appointed by autonomous communities rather than by the king.

Understandably, the Senate's structure was linked to the autonomous system intended to transform Spain from a fiercely unitary state into a fairly decentralized one (Aja and Arbós 1980, 38). Debate over the future territorial arrangement of Spain had a very direct impact on deliberation about the structure of the upper chamber. Fernández Segado (1985, 64) summarized the winding road leading to the constitutional outcome for the Senate in four stages. At the outset, the Senate was conceived as a house for the representation of "the different autonomous territories integrating Spain." In a second stage, debate shifted toward a Senate for the representation of territorial entities, but leaving undefined the specific territorial units—provinces, autonomous communities, municipalities, islands—to be represented and to what extent. This line of thinking jelled at the third stage of debate, when the Senate was envisioned as exclusively representing the provinces, a striking departure from the initial conception of Senate representation (Sánchez Férriz and Sevilla Merino 1980, 432). At the fourth stage, during which many amendments to the draft constitution were proposed and discussed, a hybrid model for the Senate was agreed to in which provinces would be equally represented by four senators (three senators for each major island province, and two each for Ceuta and Melilla), and regional communities—the newly created "autonomous communities"—would be represented roughly in accord with the size of their populations (Fernández Segado 1984, 94–120).

The compromise Senate was ultimately accepted as part of the new constitution, partly because of pervasive uncertainty about the ultimate establishment of autonomous communities and partly because the two major political parties of the day—the Union of the Democratic Center (UCD) and the Socialists (PSOE)—found the compromise solution acceptable. To a large extent, the conflicting goals of the various forces in dispute canceled each other out. Therefore, the existing structure of the upper house provided for in the Law for Political Reform appeared to everyone to be a safe, acceptable solution, confirming the classic assumption that inertia is a powerful force for the perpetuation of political institutions and electoral systems (Fernández Segado 1984, 124).

Election of the Senate

As anticipated, the formation of the Senate follows two very different sets of procedures, since roughly four-fifths of the senators are directly elected and the rest are designated by the legislative assemblies of the autonomous communities (see Sevilla Merino 1987). Provincial senators are elected every four years by all Spanish citizens who are eighteen or older and who retain their full political rights. The suffrage is universal, free, equal, direct, and secret and is to be expressed as prescribed by an organic law (Article 69.2 CE). The eligible voting population, qualifications for office, and the duration of the legislature are identical for both houses of Parliament, which helps to explain why, despite the fact that the Constitution allows for the dissolution of only one house of Parliament, in actual practice elections have been called for both houses simultaneously. And, to a large extent, this practice has prevented the upper house from acquiring a partisan profile different from that of the Congress. In all seven parliamentary elections conducted since democracy was established, the majorities in both houses have shown the same political orientation.

Following constitutional rules, the boundaries of Senate election districts coincide with those of the existing provinces except for the two island provinces. Each island or grouping of islands with a cabildo (municipal council) becomes a voting district, while the African cities of Ceuta and Melilla each form a district. As far as district magnitude is concerned, each province elects four senators, regardless of its population, while each major island—Grand Canary, Majorca, and Tenerife—elects three, Ceuta and Melilla are awarded two senators each, and the smaller islands or groupings of islands—Ibiza and Formentera, Menorca, Fuerteventura, Gomera, Hierro, Lanzarote, and La Palma—elect just one each (see table 9.1).

Unlike the Congress of Deputies, the basic formula for Senate elections is not embedded in the Constitution. But the fact that the constitutional text remained intentionally silent on such a key issue did not mean that

Table 9.1. Composition of the Spanish Senate, by Autonomous Communities

Autonomous Community	No. of Provincial Senators	Senators Designated by Autonomous Parliaments	Total No. of Senators	% of All Senators	Population	% of Population
Andalusia	32	7	39	15.2	6,940,522	17.9
Catalonia	16	7	23	9.0	6,059,494	15.6
Community of Madrid	4	5	9	3.5	4,947,555	12.7
Valencian Community	12	4	16	6.3	3,857,234	9.9
Galicia	16	3	19	7.4	2,731,669	7.0
Castilla-León	36	3	39	15.2	2,545,926	6.5
Basque Country	12	3	15	5.9	2,104,041	5.4
Castilla-La Mancha	20	2	22	8.6	1,658,466	4.3
Canary Islands	11	2	13	5.1	1,493,784	3.8
Aragón	12	2	14	5.5	1,188,817	3.1
Principality of Asturias	4	2	6	2.3	1,093,937	2.8
Extremadura	8	2	10	3.9	1,061,852	2.7
Region of Murcia	4	2	6	2.3	1,045,601	2.7
Balearic Islands	5	1	6	2.3	709,146	1.8
Cantabria	4	1	5	2.0	527,326	1.4
Navarre	4	1	5	2.0	519,277	1.3
La Rioja	4	1	5	2.0	263,434	.7
Ceuta	2	0	2	.8	68,867	.2
Melilla	2	0	2	.8	58,052	.1
Total	208	48	256	100.1	38,874,980	99.9

the options available to the legislators were unlimited. Rather, the simple and uncontroversial thing for lawmakers to do was to maintain the limited vote system in use since the first multiparty elections of 1977. It was widely viewed as a plurality system not entirely hostile to minorities (Lijphart, López Pintor, and Sone 1986, 163). What has changed in the last two decades is the way candidates' names appear on the ballot. Initially, they were listed alphabetically and accompanied by their party label and logo. This meant that loyal party voters had to search through the ballot to find the candidates of their party, which translated in turn into both a clear alphabetical bias in voting patterns and a considerable degree of cross-party voting. Because both these outcomes were unacceptable to the larger parties, the ballot structure was changed to a party column arrangement in which candidates are listed alphabetically below the name and the logo of their party, with party location on the ballot being randomized. This system may not prevent voters from casting their votes across party lines, but it does incline them toward straight-ticket party voting.

The result is that candidates belonging to the same party get very similar numbers of votes, a factor which—if combined with a strategy of "prudent nomination" (nominating as many candidates as each voter has votes) and a very low degree of interparty cooperation among minority forces—usually means that the party winning the congressional election in a province gets three of the four senatorial seats at stake as well, while the remaining seat goes to the second most supported party, and the other parties win no seats at all. Only when two or more parties obtain very similar results may another seat distribution take place, but the frequency of this phenomenon certainly is low. After the 1982 elections, in forty-three of the forty-seven four-member districts, the seat distribution followed the 3 to 1 pattern, while only three saw an even distribution of seats between the two major parties, and in only one of them was an independent candidate elected (Lijphart, López Pintor, and Sone 1986, 162–63). Most recently, in the March 1996 election, all forty-seven peninsular districts followed a 3 to 1 pattern in the distribution of seats.

The end product of this system is that, broadly speaking, parties get very similar percentages of votes at congressional and senatorial elections; the ones winning the largest percentage of the popular vote get a significantly larger share of the seats in the Congress of Deputies and then an even larger percentage in the Senate. Parties coming in second still receive bonus seats in the lower house, but they cannot count on it in the Senate.

The remaining national parties suffer heavily at the congressional level and are usually not represented at all in the upper house, with the larger nationalist parties roughly breaking even in both houses.

For example, in the 1996 election the conservative People's Party (PP) won about 39 percent of the national popular vote (based on votes cast for the parties in the election of members of the lower house, the Congress of Deputies). That proportion of the popular vote for the PP yielded it nearly 45 percent of the seats in the Congress of Deputies and about 53 percent of the directly elected Senate seats. Thus, it may be said that the electoral system magnified the popular vote results in Senate seats by a difference of 14–15 percent. In some cases since 1977 the third-strongest parties in terms of the popular vote for lower house candidates won no Senate seats—witness the Communists (PCE) in 1977 and 1979, or the United Left (IU) in 1993 and 1996 (see table 9.2).

The most interesting feature of this system is how politically biased it is. Whenever a party in the center or to the right of center (UCD, or the People's Party, PP) has won the most votes, its advantage in seats has been much larger—in absolute terms, but especially in relative terms—than when the winner has been a leftist party (PSOE). This contrast shows up most strikingly when it comes to the results for parties coming in second or third. As the second most supported party, the PP has enjoyed a seats-to-votes bonus of up to 11.7 percent, while the major opposition party, the PSOE, has never exceeded 1.5 percent, and it even suffered serious under-representation in the 1977 and 1979 elections (see tables 9.2 and 9.3). The main explanation is, of course, apportionment; the Right has traditionally fared better in the less populated, rural provinces of the interior, while the Left has been stronger in the more populated, urban, peripheral provinces. With Senate seats being apportioned equally among the districts, the Right thus finds it easier than the Left to transform votes into seats.

The Constitution is somewhat more precise in specifying the conditions governing the designation, or selection, of the so-called autonomous senators (see García-Escudero Márquez 1995). The legislative assembly or higher collective body in each autonomous community is required to designate one senator, plus an additional one for each one million inhabitants in the community, thereby ensuring the communities' representation in proportion to their population size (see table 9.3). In practice, all autonomous communities except Ceuta and Melilla (the last to be designated autonomous communities, and the only ones not provided

Table 9.2. Directly Elected Senators in Spain, 1977–1996

Political Party Group	Elections Held on						
	June 15, 1977	Mar. 1, 1979	Oct. 28, 1982	June 22, 1986	Oct. 29, 1989	June 6, 1993	Mar. 3, 1996
AP/CD/CP/PP	2	3	53	62	78	93	111
PSOE	44	71	135	124	107	96	81
PDC/CiU	1	1	7	8	10	10	8
PNV	0	8	7	7	4	3	4
AIC/CC	1	0	1	2	4	5	2
HB	—	1	0	1	3	1	0
PCE-PSUC/IU-IC	0	0	0	0	1	0	0
CDS	—	—	0	3	1	—	—
UCD	109	118	4	—	—	—	—
Democratic Senate	15	—	—	—	—	—	—
Autonomous Front	7	—	—	—	—	—	—
Independents	16	4	1	0	0	0	0
Others	12	2	0	1	0	0	2
Total	207	208	208	208	208	208	208

Note: The party groups in the Senate include: AP = Popular Alliance; CD = Democratic Coalition; CP = Popular Coalition; PP = People's Party; PSOE = Spanish Socialist Workers' Party; PDC = Democratic Pact for Catalonia; CiU = Convergence and Union; PNV = Basque Nationalist Party; AIC = Canarian Independent Assembly; CC = Canarian Coalition; HB = United People; PCE = Spanish Communist Party; PSUC = Socialist United Party of Catalonia; IU-IC = United Left-Initiative for Catalonia; CDS = Democratic and Social Center; UCD = Union of the Democratic Center.

Table 9.3. The Votes-Seats Transformation for Senate Party Groups, 1977–1996

Votes and Seats	Elections Held On						
	June 15, 1977	Mar. 1, 1979	Oct. 28, 1982	June 22, 1986	Oct. 29, 1989	June 6, 1993	Mar. 3, 1996
Winning party	UCD	UCD	PSOE	PSOE	PSOE	PSOE	PP
% Votes CofD	34.6	35.0	48.3	43.4	39.5	38.6	38.8
% Seats CofD	47.4	47.7	57.5	52.5	50.0	45.4	44.5
% Seats Senate	52.6	56.7	64.9	59.6	51.4	46.1	53.3
Difference	+18.0	+21.7	+16.6	+16.2	+11.9	+7.5	+14.5
Second party	PSOE	PSOE	AP	CP	PP	PP	PSOE
% Votes CofD	29.2	30.4	26.2	26.0	25.8	34.8	37.4
% Seats CofD	33.7	34.5	30.2	30.0	30.5	40.2	40.2
% Seats Senate	21.2	34.1	25.4	29.8	37.5	44.7	38.9
Difference	−8.0	−3.7	−.8	+3.8	+11.7	+9.9	+1.5
Third party	PCE	PCE	UCD	CDS	IU-IC	IU	IU
% Votes CofD	9.3	10.8	6.9	9.2	9.0	9.5	10.5
% Seats CofD	5.7	6.5	3.4	5.4	4.8	5.1	6.0
% Seats Senate	0	0	1.9	1.4	.4	0	0
Difference	−9.3	−10.8	−5.0	−7.8	−8.6	−9.5	−10.5
Main nationalist party	PDC	CiU	CiU	CiU	CiU	CiU	CiU
% Votes CofD	2.8	2.6	3.6	5.0	5.0	4.9	4.6
% Seats CofD	3.1	2.5	3.4	5.1	5.1	4.8	4.5
% Seats Senate	.4	.4	3.3	3.8	4.8	4.8	3.8
Difference	−2.4	−2.2	−.3	−1.2	−.2	−.1	−.8

Notes: The party groups in the Senate include: UCD = Union of the Democratic Center; PSOE = Spanish Socialist Workers' Party; PP = People's Party; AP = Popular Alliance; CP = Popular Coalition; PCE = Spanish Communist Party; PDC = Democratic Pact for Catalonia; CDS = Democratic and Social Center; IU-IC = United Left-Initiative for Catalonia; CiU = Convergence and Union.

"Difference" refers to the % difference between the proportion of senate seats won by a party and the % of the national vote that party won in the election of members of the lower house.

CofD = Congress of Deputies.

legislative powers) have assumed the legal right to appoint senators and have conferred this responsibility upon their legislative assemblies. A few have passed specific laws governing the designation process, while the rest have made the appropriate provision in the rules of procedure of their assemblies. Most communities require senators to be selected from among the deputies of the autonomous assembly, and many have taken the position that a member who loses his or her seat in the territorial Parliament must resign as senator.

The constitutional requirement of "ensuring in any case an adequate proportional representation" habitually has been fulfilled through an application of the d'Hondt formula to the number of seats won by each party at the territorial assembly, carried out by the Parliament's board. With this system, parties may know in advance how many Senate seats they can fill, and accordingly they can propose candidates to be presented jointly to and voted on by the plenary. However, when there is only one senator to designate, the process is reduced to a simple vote among the nominated candidates.

Very interesting has been the question of the relationship between the autonomous assembly or, in a broader perspective, the political institutions of an autonomous community and the senators designated by it. Some scholars (like Aja and Arbós 1980, 63–66) have offered a "federalizing" interpretation of the Constitution that would create a special link between the autonomous senators and the chamber that designated them, a link that might even give way to instructions and recall mechanisms and thereby transform these senators into permanent delegates of the autonomous communities within the central institutions of the state. However, most scholars (García-Escudero Márquez and Pendás 1984, 69; Embid Irujo 1987, 192) have understood that the Constitution created two types of selection processes, but not two kinds of senators, and that the rights, duties, and privileges of provincial and autonomous senators are identical. But as Sevilla Merino (1987, 2.257) has underlined, "However reasonable that interpretation might be, practice has not been prone to corroborate it."

Organization of the Senate

Following the requirements of the Constitution (in Article 73), both houses of Parliament meet annually in two ordinary sessions, one running from September to December and the other from February to June. Extraordinary sessions may be requested by the government, the Permanent Deputation, or an absolute majority of the members of either chamber. In principle, the duration of sessions is identical for both houses, following a traditional practice in Spanish parliamentary history forbidding one chamber to meet while the other is not meeting. This does not mean that both houses have to hold their sessions simultaneously. This only means that they should be able to do so (Santaolalla 1990, 100–101).

Most important, this constitutional clause means that Parliament is virtually always in session. When it is not, special standing committees in each house, the so-called Permanent Deputations, are responsible for running the chambers' affairs. The Senate version of this committee has to be constituted as soon as the house is convened, with no fewer than twenty-one members who are elected by the plenary upon nomination by parliamentary groups in proportion to their size. The committee is chaired by the speaker of the Senate, assisted by two vice speakers and two secretaries elected from among its members. It meets at the request of the president, the government, or one-fourth of its members.

The Permanent Deputations also exercise the functions of the chambers upon the expiration of their mandate or between their being dissolved and the summoning of a new parliament, and their very existence has been strongly criticized. For a start, the institution dates back to when sessions were short and deputies and senators could not easily be summoned to attend extraordinary sessions, so it is argued this institution is no longer needed (Alonso de Antonio 1992). In addition, the extent of its freedom to make its own decisions, as well as the precise nature of its relationship to the house itself, are issues that have long been hotly debated with no entirely satisfactory conclusions having been reached.

Party Groups and Governing Bodies

The parliamentary groups are the key building blocks from which the Permanent Deputation is formed, and their important role is the norm in the Senate at large as well as in the lower house. Although the Constitution refers to them only in the specific case of the Permanent Deputations, parliamentary groups are "the real conductors of debates, the promoters of initiatives, and the almost unique subjects of the immense majority of the parliamentary procedures . . . [and] it can be said without hesitation that the upper house operates now basically thanks to the groups" (Pérez-Serrano Jáuregui 1989, 218, 213).

In table 9.4 the party group composition of the Senate is shown for the constituent legislature and the six subsequent parliaments. Following the requirements of the Senate's standing orders, parliamentary groups can only be created within five days from the date of the constitution of the house. A minimum of ten senators is required to create a group, and a minimum of six is necessary to keep it in operation afterwards; senators cannot join more than one group, and if they do not join one voluntarily,

Table 9.4. Parliamentary Parties and Groups in the Spanish Senate, 1977–1996

Legislatures	Parties and Groups	Seats Beginning	Seats End
Constituent Legislature (July 22, 1977 to Dec. 30, 1978)	Union of the Democratic Center (UCD)	115	114
	Socialist (PSOE and federated parties)	48	51
	Independent Socialists and Progressives	22	20
	Catalonians' Agreement	16	16
	Independent Group	13	12
	Independent parliamentarians	10	10
	Basque	10	9
	Mixed	14	15
1st Legislature (Mar. 27, 1979 to Aug. 31, 1982)	Union of the Democratic Center (UCD)	122	107
	Socialist (PSOE and some federated parties)	40	42
	Andalusian Socialists (PSOE-Andalusia)	19	22
	Catalonia, Democracy and Socialism (PSC-PSOE)	10	9
	Basque (PNV, CDC, UDC)	10	12
	Mixed (CD, HB, ex-UCD)	7	22
2d Legislature (Nov. 18, 1982 to Apr. 23, 1986)	Socialist (PSOE and federated parties)	163	155
	Popular (AP, PDP, and other regional parties)	69	67
	Basque Nationalist (PNV)	10	9
	Catalonia at the Senate (CiU, AIC)	14	7
	Mixed (AIC, ex-CiU, and others)	7	17
3d Legislature (July 15, 1986 to Sept. 2, 1989)	Socialist (PSOE and federated parties)	147	144
	Popular Coalition (AP, PDP, PL)	64	67
	Convergence and Union (CDC, UDC)	11	10
	Basque Nationalist (PNV)	10	6
	Democratic and Social Center (CDS)	—	11
	Mixed (AIC, CdG, PDP, PL, CDS, PAR, IU, ERC)	18	14
4th Legislature (Nov. 21, 1989 to Apr. 13, 1993)	Socialist (PSOE and federated parties)	124	128
	Popular (PP, UPN, CG)	86	92
	Democratic and Social Center (CDS)	11	—
	Catalonian at the Senate (CDC, UDC)	10	14
	Basque Nationalist (PNV)	10	6
	Mixed (AIC, HB, IU, UV, CDS, PAR, ERC)	5	15
5th Legislature (June 29, 1993 to Jan. 4, 1996)	Socialist (PSOE and federated parties)	116	111
	Popular (PP, UPN)	105	114

Table 9.4. (*Continued*)

Legislatures	Parties and Groups	Seats Beginning	Seats End
	Catalonian of Convergence and Union (CDC, UDC)	10	12
	Basque Nationalist (PNV, CDC)	10	6
	Canarian Coalition at the Senate (ATI, others)	12	5
	Mixed (IU, EA, PIL, PAR, ERC, HB, UV, CDN, PR)	7	8
6th Legislature	Popular (PP, UPN, PAR)	133	
(Mar. 27, 1996 to the present)	Socialist (PSOE and federated parties)	96	
	Catalonian of Convergence and Union (CDC, UDC)	11	
	Basque Nationalist (PNV)	6	
	Mixed (IU, CC, EA, PIL, EFS, ERC, UV, CDN)	10	

Note: The party groups are as follows:

AP/CD/CP/PP = Popular Alliance in 1977, Democratic Coalition in 1979, AP-PDP in 1982, Popular Coalition (AP, PDP, PL, CdG) in 1986, Popular Party from 1989 on.

AIC/CC = Canarian Independent Groups, comprising Independent Assembly from El Hierro (AHI), Majorera Assembly (AM), Independent Assembly from Tenerife (ATI), Canarian Initiative (IC), and Independents from Lanzarote IL; from 1993, Canarian Coalition.

CDN = Convergence of Navarran Democrats.

CDS = Democratic and Social Center.

CG = Galician Coalition.

CdG = Galician Centrists.

CiU = Convergence and Union, comprising Democratic Convergence of Catalonia (CDC) and Democratic Union of Catalonia (UDC); in 1977, only Democratic Convergence of Catalonia; in 1982, as Catalonia to the Senate.

EA = Basque Solidarity.

EFS = Ibiza and Formentera for the Senate.

ERC = Republican Left of Catalonia.

HB = United (Basque) People.

PAR = Regionalist Party of Aragon.

PCE-PSUC/IU-IC = Spanish Communist Party-Socialist Unified Party of Catalonia until 1986; integrated into the coalition United Left-Initiative for Catalonia from then on.

PDP = Popular Democratic Party.

PIL = Independent Party of Lanzarote.

PL = Liberal Party.

PNV = Basque Nationalist Party.

PR = Party of Rioja.

PSOE = Spanish Socialist Workers' Party, comprising as federated parties the Socialist Party of the Basque Country (PSE-PSOE), the Party of Catalonian Socialists (PSE-PSOE), the Spanish Socialist Workers' Party of Andalusia (PSOE-A), the Party of the Galician Socialists (PSG), and the Basque Left (EE).

UCD = Union of the Democratic Center, in coalition with Catalonian Centrists in 1979.

UPN = Union of the Navarran People.

UV = Valencian Union.

they are necessarily allocated to the "mixed group." Senators campaigning for the same party or coalition cannot create more than one group, while groups have to identify themselves with names similar to those of the parties for which their members campaigned. Senators can leave their original group at any time to join the mixed group or any other group (a choice not accorded to deputies). Although parliamentary groups are equal in rights as far as their participation in the tasks performed by the house are concerned, they receive committee assignments, subsidies, and office space in proportion to their number of members.

The most noteworthy peculiarity of the regulation of parliamentary groups in the Senate compared with the Congress is the existence of the so-called territorial groups. These can be created within a given parliamentary group by no less than three senators elected by the voters or designated by the Parliament of a specific autonomous community. But if their introduction in 1982 was aimed at strengthening the ability of the Senate to become an effective arena for the debate of territorial issues, their meager performance has led to a great deal of dissatisfaction and skepticism (García Fernández 1984, 159–60).

The speaker, the board, and the Spokesmen's Joint Committee exist both in the Congress and in the Senate and are usually referred to as "the governing bodies" of the houses (Torres Muro 1987). The Constitution explicitly provides that each house of Parliament elect a speaker, who exercises "all administrative powers and police authority" within the chamber. In addition, the Constitution provides that each chamber elect a board, but it makes no mention of the Spokesmen's Joint Committee. Just like the speaker of the Congress, the speaker of the Senate is elected by a majority vote with runoff, while the other members of the board, two vice chairmen and four secretaries, are elected by employing the "single nontransferable vote" and "limited vote," respectively. Therefore, while the chairmanship of the house is always in the hands of the majority party, the board is a rather plural body, a feature that has a decisive influence on its performance.

In principle, the Constitution provides the speaker with powers so far-reaching that the board is made to look like his useless appendage (Santaolalla 1990, 164–65). However, through the standing orders, both houses have sought to introduce some balance into this relationship, even at the cost of some contradictions. In the Senate, the speaker is empowered to represent and act in the name of the chamber, to call, chair, and moderate plenary sessions and board meetings, to call and chair the meetings of any committee, to interact with the government and other institutions, to interpret the standing orders and to complete them in case of omission, and to apply disciplinary measures and provide for the observation of parliamentary courtesy. Among the many powers of the Board of the Senate, perhaps the most important are the determination of the plenary and committees agendas, the reception, admission, and evaluation of every parliamentary document submitted to the chamber, and the distribution of bills among committees.

The Spokesmen's Joint Committee has been described as "a body for the participation of parliamentary groups in the preparation and coordination of the exercise of the functions of the Chamber" (Santaolalla 1990, 172). It is composed of the speaker of the Senate, who calls and chairs its meetings, and the spokesmen of the existing parliamentary groups. The standing orders also provide for the presence of a representative of the government, and up to two representatives of the territorial groups created within the parliamentary groups, at meetings of the Spokesmen's Joint Committee. Moreover, in perhaps the most interesting innovation regarding congressional regulations, whenever a meeting is convened to address matters affecting a specific autonomous community, the speaker may invite senators from the territorial groups concerned to attend. The Spokesmen's Joint Committee advises the speaker and the Board, in the sense that it presents them in advance with the opinions of the parliamentary groups on the way the work of the house should be organized. It has to be listened to—but not necessarily obeyed—in order to set the beginning and the end of a period of sessions, to approve the agenda of plenary sessions, to interpret and supply the standing orders, and to organize the debates of the house, among other cases.

Parliamentary Committees

Committees are the basic "working bodies" of Parliament. In former times, they were simply "restricted meetings of a certain number of deputies or senators in order to get to know more deeply the bills and other issues requiring the approval of the house, and to present it with their proposals or evaluations" (Santaolalla 1990, 174). But since the 1978 Constitution assumed that the chambers would work through committees as well as plenary sessions, that in certain fields permanent legislative committees could enjoy full legislative competencies by delegation of the plenary, and that the houses, together or separately, "may appoint investigating commissions on any subject of public interest" (Article 76.1), their role has been dramatically enhanced. Committees have additional legitimacy and effectiveness because their members are appointed by the parliamentary groups in proportion to their number of seats and members have specialized knowledge as a result of serving on a permanent rather than ad hoc basis.

There are two basic types of Senate committee, standing and investigative or special. Standing committees, created for the life of a Parliament, may be legislative or nonlegislative. Legislative standing committees are devoted to lawmaking, and they are named after the subjects with which they deal: constitutional issues, internal affairs and civil service, justice, defense, foreign affairs, economy and finance, budget, and so on. Nonlegislative standing committees are devoted to the internal affairs of the house and its members. They include committees on standing orders, conflicts of interest, applications for indictment of senators, and petitions.

Investigative or special committees are created in order to study or investigate specific issues, and they are dissolved as soon as their assignment is completed or at the end of the Parliament. Mixed committees are composed of members from both houses (not evenly distributed, however, as they comprise twenty-two deputies and seventeen senators), and created by constitutional mandate, by law, or through agreement between the two houses. Joint committees are occasionally formed by members of various standing committees from the same house to deal with interdisciplinary issues.

Committee members are nominated by parliamentary groups, following the guidelines issued at the beginning of each session by the Senate's Board regarding the number of seats awarded to each party group. Group freedom to appoint and substitute their representatives on each committee is so undisputed that it has become a decisive political tool, especially useful for reducing discontent or sending disloyal parliamentarians into political oblivion. However, committee meetings are open to senators who are not members of the committee, to members of the government, and even to deputies. Senators who are not committee members may take the floor only when they have amendments of their own to defend.

A major transformation in the Senate's committee structure took place in January 1994, when the General Committee for the Autonomous Communities was created (see Visiedo Mazón 1997). During a protracted debate on the ability of the Senate to perform as a chamber for territorial representation, the creation of this special committee was a momentary triumph for those who believed that an intelligent reform of the Senate's standing orders could be enough to allow the transformation of the upper chamber into the real forum for making decisions on territorial issues, as opposed to those who foresaw that this goal could only be achieved by constitutional reform, transforming the electoral system and enhancing the powers of the Senate.

The physiognomy and the internal dynamics of the General Committee are so peculiar that some scholars have been moved to write that they reveal an interest on the part of legislators to make it an intermediary between the plenary and the rest of the committees (Da Silva Ochoa 1994, 30) or even that "a Senate within the Senate" has been created (Sánchez Amor 1994, 114). This committee has a larger board and twice as many members as ordinary committees; every senator designated by the autonomous parliaments can be present and take the floor at its meetings, a right extended to the central and to the autonomous governments but not to provincial senators. Its meetings may be called not only upon request of the Senate's or the committee's chairs, or upon request of a third of its members, but also upon petition from the central or any of the autonomous governments.

However, the most exceptional feature of this special committee is its extensive list of powers casuistically enumerated across the twenty-three paragraphs of the Constitution's Article 56 of the Standing Orders. Critics argue that many of these paragraphs are redundant, that others refer to competencies which existing committees had already been granted, that some are virtually meaningless, and that a few even seem to conflict with powers of other bodies (Sánchez Amor 1994, 115–22). Basically, they can be classified into six groups: (1) to "inform about the autonomous content of any initiative," prior to its debate in the competent committee and the plenary; (2) to debate initiatives of an essentially autonomous content; (3) to exercise legislative initiative; (4) to receive information from the central and autonomous governments about issues of an autonomous nature lying within their respective scope of competence, and eventually to debate them; (5) to debate cooperation agreements which autonomous communities may want to sign; and (6) to make proposals to the government regarding the representation of Spain in international institutions where regions are represented.

However, the most eye-catching power of the General Committee is probably the one mandating the holding of an annual debate "in order to evaluate the situation of the State of the Autonomies," in which those taking the floor can use Spanish or any official regional language. Moreover, Article 56 of the Standing Orders, introduced within the same reform package, contained a similar mandate in reference to the plenary, obviously intended to create a replica of the "Debate on the State of the Nation" that is traditionally held in Congress every autumn with the participation of all major party leaders.

The Powers of the Senate

During the constituent debates, the lack of a coherent vision of the form the Senate should take explains to a large extent why the Constitution does not include a coherent and precise enumeration of its powers and, consequently, why the upper chamber has not been given a relevant and intelligible political role in the new democracy. If criticism of its constitutional powers has been less intense than that of its composition, it is only because discussions about the need to reform the way the house is composed have drowned out meaningful debate on other crucial matters. In fact, this same story characterized the constituent debates themselves; the attention paid to the question of Senate powers was almost completely overshadowed by debates about its institutional structure. As a result, decisions were taken after no more than a superficial debate in the Congress. Senatorial debate may have been slightly more substantial, but it was also strongly influenced by positions already taken in the lower house and the lack of time to rethink completely the Senate's role. That the major parties had no clear view about what bicameralism should mean in the new democracy had a lot to do with this definitional failure.

Thus, the Senate was not conceived as a "technical house" that would polish and improve legislative proposals hastily crafted by the Congress; nor was it conceived as a "mirror house" equal in power to the lower house; nor was it granted preferential or exclusive competence in specific policy areas, like those pertaining to the territorial structure of the country, turning it into a "territorial house." Broadly speaking, it is possible to classify the powers of the Senate into six major categories: constitutional reform, self-regulation, lawmaking, government control, territorial issues, and nominations (Martínez Sospedra 1989, 349ff.).

The Senate enjoys special powers in the area of constitutional reform. As Valencian jurist Martínez Sospedra has argued, "The position of the Senate in the processes of constitutional reform is enhanced in comparison with the role it plays in ordinary lawmaking. A fact that is not unusual, or surprising, if we take into consideration that without this strengthened position the upper house would be dependent on the goodwill of the lower house and would be unable to guarantee its own position and to fulfill its role as guarantor of other constitutionally protected institutions and interests" (1989, 349–50). The Constitution explicitly confers the initiative for constitutional reform on the Senate as well as the Congress, the government, and the autonomous communities. The proposal has to be initiated by no less than fifty senators, twice the number required to propose an ordinary or an organic law, and to be accepted by at least a plurality of senators meeting in plenary session.

However, this vote is only the starting point of the reform process, which in the Spanish case is twofold, depending on whether the reform does or does not affect basic constitutional principles, fundamental rights, the Crown, or the constitutional structure itself. In any case, the Congress is the first house to debate a reform initiative, regardless of who proposed it. Except for this "strategic" advantage, in the case of an aggravated reform, one affecting basic constitutional principles, fundamental rights, the Crown, or the constitutional structure itself, the position of both houses is identical in that a two-thirds majority in both houses has to approve the reform project. Parliament then has to be dissolved immediately, new elections have to be called, the initiative has to be readopted by the newly elected houses, and the final bill has to be passed in both houses, again by a two-thirds majority. In the final stage, the reform proposal is submitted to referendum. However, the position of the Senate is slightly weaker than that of the Congress in the so-called ordinary reform process. In no way can a reform of this kind be passed against the will of the Senate, but in the case of deadlock between the two houses, the Constitution allows the Congress, with an extraordinary majority, "to supply" the lack of enthusiasm on the Senate side.

Both houses of Parliament have the same power to determine their internal organization and operations (Santaolalla 1990, 40–43). Both adopt their own standing orders, approve their annual budget, choose their own chairs, and elect the members of their board. The Constitution sensibly limits this autonomy partly because many key matters previously addressed by parliamentary standing orders are now written into the Constitution itself and partly because the standing orders themselves are subject to scrutiny by the Constitutional Court (Revenga Sánchez and Morales Arroyo 1987, 2.021–43). But, within these limits, both houses can regulate themselves without interference from each other or the government. In addition, the Statute of Parliamentary Personnel and the Cortes's Standing Orders, regulating the joint sessions of both houses, require the approval of each house in entirely identical terms, although the superiority of the Congress is underscored by the constitutional stipulation that joint sessions be chaired by the Congress's chair.

Lawmaking is the most fundamental power of any parliament, and in bicameral legislatures the position of the upper chamber in the legislative process is the single most important factor to consider when attempting to characterize the bicameral system. In the case of Spain, the legislative power of the state is clearly conferred on the Cortes Generales, "constituted by the Congress of Deputies and the Senate" (Article 66). This amounts to saying that the Senate participates in the legislative process in its own right, not merely as an advisory body or a review chamber but as a coequal body whose participation cannot be circumvented. Moreover, the legislative competence of the Senate is general in the sense that, like the lower house, it encompasses any matter falling within the province of the central institutions of the state. Hence, there are no matters excluded from the Senate's scope of action. By the same token, there are no matters reserved for its exclusive legislative competence. This does not mean that it enjoys equality with the Congress in the lawmaking process. To the contrary, its position is far weaker than that of its counterpart, so much so that the Spanish Senate falls among the weakest of democratic upper houses.

To be sure, it can take legislative initiatives by supporting, or "taking into consideration," a legislative proposal signed by no fewer than twenty-five senators or put forward by a parliamentary group. But even here, the bill must first be debated in the Congress (with the one exception of the Interterritorial Compensation Fund). Consequently, the Senate does no more than to respond to bills already discussed and passed by the Congress, so senators' ability to introduce major changes in the structure and contents of legislation is thereby diminished. Further diminishing its influence is that every party has consistently placed its political leaders and heavyweights on the benches of the lower house.

Article 90 of the Constitution enumerates the limited range of options open to the upper house when debating bills coming from the Congress:

1. Once an ordinary or organic bill has been approved by the Congress, its Speaker shall immediately notify the Speaker of the Senate, who shall submit it for its deliberation.

2. The Senate, within two months of receiving the text, may, through a message explaining the reasons, veto it or introduce amendments to it. The veto must be approved by an absolute majority. The bill cannot be submitted to the king for approval unless the Congress ratifies the initial text in the case of a veto by an absolute majority, or by a simple majority once two months have passed since the presentation of the text, or expresses itself on the amendments, stating whether or not it accepts them by a simple majority.

3. The period of two months in which the Senate has to veto or amend the bill shall be reduced to twenty calendar days for those bills declared urgent by the government or by the Congress.

Article 90 applies to all legislation regardless of who initiated it; Senate vetoes of organic bills can be overturned only by an absolute majority vote of Congress, even after the two-month deadline. The short time allowed to the Senate to make its position known counts among the shortest known in bicameral systems, but it has been lengthened a little thanks to a generous interpretation of the Senate's standing orders. Counting begins not when the Congress's bill is received but when it is published in the Senate's *Bulletin,* and counting stops when the Senate enters any of its vacation periods. Second, to make it possible for the house to meet the constitutional deadlines, its standing orders provide a large catalog of antifilibuster mechanisms, a number of urgency procedures, and the option to delegate lawmaking to standing committees.

Above all, Article 90 has attracted the attention of scholars for its political and constitutional implications. After reviewing the legislative powers of upper houses across Europe, Martínez Sospedra (1989, 362) concluded that the powerlessness of the Spanish Senate is comparable only to that of the Austrian Bundesrat and lies not far away from that of the Council of the Republic depicted at the original 1946 French Constitution, which declared that legislative powers were vested exclusively in the National Assembly.

Hence, some scholars (see González Navarro 1987, 386) have even claimed that the Spanish Senate has no legislative powers, since it cannot impose its will on the Congress, can only delay the enactment of the bill for a short time, and can influence the content of bills only if the lower chamber accepts its amendments. This assessment of the Senate's real power may seem extreme and clearly incompatible with the wording of Article 66. Yet it has been argued that "when designing an uneven bicameralism, it seems that the constituents went too far. . . . It is not just that the upper house is placed in a weaker position, which would be logical: what happens is that on any matter, before any kind of bill, the will of the Senate is perfectly and totally dispensable" (Martínez Sospedra 1989, 362).

The Senate is in a strikingly different position when it comes to oversight of the executive. Its oversight powers are virtually identical to those of the Congress. Like the Congress, it may engage in debate, scrutinize, assess, or request information about governmental policies. Its fundamental weakness remains, though, that when it comes to demanding the ultimate political responsibility—that is, government resignation—the Senate is completely powerless, just as it is at the moment of choosing a new government (Montero Gibert and García Morillo 1984, 36–45).

The constitution allows the Senate to create committees of inquiry "on any matter of public interest" and to participate in joint committees with deputies, as well as to demand cooperation from citizens and institutions (Article 76). The Senate may receive "individual and collective petitions, always in writing" and forward them to the government, obliging it "to explain itself on the contents" whenever the Senate so requests (Article 77). It may demand full information from the government on those international treaties which do not require the consent of Parliament (Article 94.2) or on any other topic (Article 109). And it may summon members of the government and high-ranking state officials to appear before it (Article 110); it can question and interpellate the president and government ministers (Article 111) and subsequently express its position on an issue under debate by means of a motion; it receives, along with the Congress, the annual report of the ombudsman (Article 54) and the General Council of the Judiciary, and it may also request information from the authorities in the autonomous communities.

Despite this arsenal of oversight powers, the Senate has absolutely no voice in the selection and the permanence in office of the executive. When new elections are held, the presidential candidate proposed by the king is required only to present his government's political program to, and win the confidence of, the Congress. Despite the fact that his failure to obtain it may lead to the dissolution of both houses, the upper chamber has no formal role whatsoever in the process of investiture. Consequently, it plays no role when the president presents a question of confidence or when a vote of no confidence or motion of censure is proposed. Moreover, the Senate's peripheral role in government making and unmaking influences the way it exercises its oversight powers. In the end, the political relevance of devices like questions, interpellations, or motions depends on the impact they have on public opinion. Here, the political "weight" of the people putting them forward and sitting in the house becomes crucial, and recruitment patterns, in turn, hinge largely on the ability of the house to determine or influence the government's composition and tenure of office (Martínez Sospedra 1989, 370). If the Senate is irrelevant in these matters, then the likelihood of its being influential in government decision making will be close to zero as well.

Nor is it elected in such a way as to make it a good vehicle for the effective participation of the autonomous communities in the shaping of the state's policies (see Fernández Segado 1985). This explains why, despite being labeled "the chamber for territorial representation," it lacks special powers in the domain of territorial policies, and why in this field its position is largely the same as in other policy areas: one of subordination to the Congress's will. Moreover, it also explains why in recent years bilateral and multilateral agreements between the central and the autonomous governments have become the standard means for the resolution of autonomous problems, bypassing the intervention of Parliament and thereby substantially reducing the Senate's role and authority (Da Silva Ochoa 1994, 20–23, 34–35). At the same time, there is language in the constitution regarding the role of the upper house that makes it marginally more relevant regarding territorial issues than it is in ordinary lawmaking. Moreover, the Constitution also provides the single instance in which the Senate may make a political decision in which the Congress has no say: the so-called federal execution clause.

Senate approval was indispensable for the enactment of those Statutes of Autonomy drafted through the process described in Article 151 of the Constitution, the process followed by the historical nationalities who sought the largest possible level of self-government in the shortest possible time. However, the Senate did not participate in the drafting of the text itself, and its vote was scheduled after the draft bill negotiated between the Congress's Constitutional Committee and a delegation of representatives of the territories concerned had been put to referendum of the people of the community-to-be. Under these conditions, the Senate was not in a position to impose any objection. Beyond this limited arena, the Senate's legislative role has not been a powerful one.

The cornerstone of the strengthened position of the Senate in this area is the constitutional provision that significantly modifies the ordinary legislative process, postponing the moment that Congress is allowed to impose its will on the Senate's in three specific instances: the approval of the most relevant international treaties, the authorization of cooperation agreements between the autonomous communities, and the distribution of resources pertaining to the Interterritorial Compensation Fund. In these cases, the consent of both chambers is needed in the first instance. If no agreement can be reached, a joint commission composed of an equal number of deputies and senators may be established to iron out disagreements and submit an agreed proposal to both chambers. If this proposal is not approved by both, the Congress makes a final decision by majority vote. More relevantly, perhaps, the Senate becomes the first chamber to debate the bills concerning cooperation agreements and the Interterritorial Compensation Fund, an exceptional procedure aimed at reinforcing its position in the entire process which, paradoxically, has been subject in practice to a very restrictive interpretation (see Rodrigo Fernández 1987, 2.118–24).

A controversial provision of the Constitution (Article 150.3) allows Parliament to "dictate laws which establish the principles necessary to harmonize the norms of the autonomous communities even in the case of matters attributed to their competence when the general interest so demands." Although these lawmaking powers are to be carried out through the usual legislative procedures, a "state of necessity" must be determined by Parliament, by a majority vote in each chamber, and with no mediation or action allowing the Congress to impose its will on the Senate. Finally, Article 155.1 contains the only power granted solely to the Senate: the approval of coercive measures against an autonomous community acting against the general interest of Spain. This is an extreme measure which, fortunately, still remains unapplied: "If an autonomous community does not fulfill the obligations imposed upon it by the constitution or other laws, or should act in a manner seriously prejudicing the general interest of Spain, the government, after lodging a complaint with the president of the Autonomous Community and failing to receive satisfaction therefore, may, following approval granted by an absolute majority of the Senate, adopt the means necessary in order to oblige the latter forcibly to meet said obligations, or in order to protect the above-mentioned general interest."

The Senate participates in the selection of staff for many of the most important governmental institutions. In some instances, it does so because this role belongs to Parliament as a whole, and senators take part in the selection process through their participation in the joint session of the Cortes, just as deputies do. In others, the Constitution and laws divide the right to nominate between the two chambers of Parliament. In the specific case of the ombudsman, both houses have to agree on a nominee in order to comply with the selection procedure, although the houses vote separately. With the exception of the president of the government, there are no instances in which the members of a state institution are elected by one house without the participation of the other.

Parliament meets in joint sessions when matters concerning the Crown are involved: both houses vote jointly to provide for succession to the Crown in case the royal dynasty were to end, to appoint a regent or regents whenever the monarch cannot exercise his or her authority and no one can exercise the regency in his or her own right, and to appoint a tutor for a king or queen who is a minor. Also, the houses of the Cortes act jointly to prohibit the marriage of the prince or princess, to recognize the incapacity of the monarch, to witness the oath of the new royal heir, and to declare war or conclude peace. In all these cases, Senate influence depends directly on the relative size of the membership of each house. The Constitution is flexible in both cases: Congress may swing from 300 to 400 members, and the exact number of senators depends on the population of each autonomous community. The fact remains that currently the 256 senators are far outnumbered by the 350 deputies, and this places the upper house at an obvious numerical disadvantage.

Both houses of Parliament are involved in selecting governmental officials in three cases in which the houses deliberate and decide separately. These involve members of the Constitutional Court, the General Council of the Judiciary, and the Court of Accounts. In each case, both houses nominate the same number of members, and they do so through essentially identical procedures, so there is complete parity between them.

Additionally, consider the case of the ombudsman, the *Defensor del Pueblo*. Article 54 requires that this official be elected by Parliament. Candidates are proposed by a joint committee, but each house votes separately. Congress votes first on every candidate, and the Senate is asked to confirm or reject candidates approved by the Congress within twenty days. Confirmation requires a three-fifths majority in each house, but when the two houses disagree, the candidates supported by the Congress are appointed, provided they win the support of at least a majority of the votes in the upper house.

Finally, there are three major political decisions which the Constitution places under the exclusive authority of the Congress, and the Senate is given no power in making these decisions. These decisions include the validation of decree laws (see Santolaya Machetti 1988); the calling of consultative referenda (see Cruz Villalón 1980); and control over the states of alarm, emergency, and siege (see Entrena Cuesta 1985). In circumstances of national emergency, the government may issue provisional legislative decisions that take the form of decree laws. Within thirty days the decree law must be submitted for debate and a vote by the Congress, which may validate or derogate it. Unless Parliament decides to transform the decree into ordinary law—by means of an extraordinary urgency procedure—the Senate has no opportunity to express its opinion about it.

A national referendum may be called by the monarch upon a proposal of the president of the government "after previous authorization by the Congress of Deputies," and in this process the Senate plays no institutional role. Concerning the parliamentary response to "alarm, emergency, and siege," the Constitution envisaged different procedures for the declaration of each of these "states," but in none of these procedures has the Senate any official voice: the state of alarm is declared by the government, subsequently informing the Congress; the state of emergency is declared by the government following an authorization from the Congress; and the state of siege is proposed by the government and declared by a majority vote of the Congress.

Reform of the Senate?

Its ill-defined constitutional functions and powers soon precipitated criticism of the Senate's political role and, inevitably, of its performance. In the beginning, these criticisms were partly muted by the hope that the autonomous senators, added to the Senate's membership only in the early 1980s when the new autonomous communities were first constituted, would somehow transform the essentially province-based profile of the upper house (Aja and Arbós 1980, 63–66). Still later, it was anticipated that the creation of territorial groups would make senators more conscious of their territorial than of their partisan constituencies, or that the existence of the Committee for Autonomies would translate into a sharper focus on territorial issues. But time and experience led to the conclusion that such hopes for the institution were largely futile, and the belief took shape that substantial reform was needed. Reform proposals of all kinds were launched, including the revitalization of the Senate through a broad pact among Parliament, parties, government, and autonomous communities (Fontán 1991, 6); the modification of the electoral system for the upper house (Aragón Reyes 1991, 210); the renewal of the Senate's role through constitutional conventions leading to a redefined institution (Ripollés Serrano 1993, 123); and the substantial reform of the Senate's standing orders.

This last option appeared for some time to be the most promising and feasible reform. In 1987 and again in 1989 subcommittees were created within the Committee for Standing Orders to reform the Senate's standing orders so as to "reinforce its territorial functions" and "allow and reinforce the presence and the participation of the autonomous institutions in the houses's tasks" (García-Escudero Márquez 1994, 42). This reform effort led to the creation of the General Committee for the Autonomous Communities, the only significant reform of the organization of the Senate since the formalization of its standing orders in 1982 when the provisional rules adopted in 1977 had been replaced. But despite having the right to reform its own standing orders, this reform took no less than six years to complete, dragged on across three legislatures, and created more frustration than satisfaction. This episode also served to feed the belief that constitutional reform was the only possible solution to the deficiencies of the Senate.

Subsequently, parliamentary parties, autonomous institutions, legal scholars, political scientists, and even mathematicians have become involved in the debate over Senate reform. However, the seemingly endless reform proposals and schemes have fallen far short of sharing a single focus. The contradictory goals of major and minor and national and peripheral parties, the conflicting interests of the larger and smaller and the more- and less-developed autonomous communities, and the political leanings of scholars involved have produced a veritable Babel of propositions, programs, projects, and plans.

The author of the first monograph on Senate reform, Martínez Sospedra, a former senator, argued that irrespective of reformist goals, efforts to make the Senate more effective should attend to four closely related constraints (1990, 41–43). First, reform should be consensual, at least to the same extent as the original Constitution. In his view, it would be politically devastating if reform proposals were to be carried with the backing of only a bare parliamentary majority, especially if the mainstream political party groups were to succeed in carrying the day against the peripheral party groups. Second, Senate reform efforts should not touch the constitutional settlement over the territorial organization of the country because it might be interpreted as a subversion of the fundamental structure of the regime and would be unlikely to generate consensus. Third, reform should be crafted so as to be achievable through the "ordinary" reform procedures allowed for in the Constitution, since so-called aggravated reform is highly demanding procedurally and implies more sweeping constitutional change that is not only unthinkable in present political circumstances but also disproportionate to the upper house reform project. Fourth, reform should respect the basic structure of parliamentary democracy as defined by the existing constitutional provisions and practices. In particular, reformers should not seek the "Italian solution," requiring governments to win and retain the confidence of the Senate as well as of the lower house.

Within these broad constraints, many plausible options were available to reformers (Martínez Sospedra 1994, 33–35). They could seek to minimize any lack of institutional legitimacy by eliminating the striking contrast between the Senate's function of territorial representation and the provincially based election of most of its members. The electoral machinery could be reformed so as to give greater recognition to the autonomous communities without altering the fundamental powers of the body. Again, so as to optimize its performance as a lawmaking institution, the Senate could be provided with more time to debate and be given a stronger position from which to negotiate disagreements with the Congress. Alternatively, the Senate could be transformed into a full-fledged federal chamber, the unabashed locus for the representation of the autonomous communities and the carrier of a heavier workload on territorial issues. Finally, the Senate's capacity to provide adequate participation for the autonomous communities could be strengthened, giving it a role in bilateral (national/autonomous community) or multilateral (national/ several autonomous communities, or among several communities) negotiations. To do this, the presence of the autonomous communities in the Senate would have to be enlarged substantially.

But even the most cursory glance at the reform projects considered reveals that improvement of the Senate's lawmaking ability has not been high on the agendas of parties and scholars. The political history of second chambers in Spain and elsewhere shows just how troublesome a powerful second chamber can be. New technologies have clearly proved that reliable information, good organization, and skilled staff can do more than bicameralism to improve the quality of legislation. Besides, reform of the Senate's electoral system to bring it in line with the realities of autonomous communities and thereby end its widely perceived lack of legitimacy could never be a goal in its own right. A Senate elected directly by the people in districts coincidental with the existing autonomous communities would turn out to be as representative of the popular will as the Congress, if not more so, making it likely that the Senate would then challenge its secondary position in the parliamentary firmament. One way or another, the emergence of two equally powerful houses would become unavoidable.

Another position has been that the ideal formula for a reformed Senate would be its transformation into a permanent (i.e., not subject to dissolution) house composed of senators appointed either by the governments or by the parliaments of the autonomous communities and granted special powers in territorial matters. Such an institution could be constrained by instruction and recall mechanisms, devices that would provide the autonomous communities with cohesive, politically unified representation (Punset Blanco 1993, 83–86). However, such a reform—obviously patterned after the German Bundesrat—seems extremely unlikely under present circumstances inasmuch as there is an obvious lack of political will to take the reform process this far. Neither public nor elite opinion seems yet ready to accept formulas like recall, instructions, or even majority rule in senatorial elections, not to mention the unsurmountable difficulty of adequately differentiating the role of the Senate in common and territorial lawmaking, in view of the already complex lawmaking system created by the 1978 Constitution (Punset Blanco 1990, 196–97).

Reform aimed at strengthening the role of the autonomous communities in the formulation of national policies, by contrast, appears a reasonable and realistic objective. But attempting to put it into practice opens a Pandora's box of conflicting proposals, preferences, and problems. One concern is the way in which senators are to be chosen. López Garrido (1994, 10–11) argues that if the Senate is to represent citizens "as members of a region or nationality," it should be directly elected in districts falling within the boundaries of the existing autonomous communities. But most scholars reject this recommendation, arguing that it would give the Senate a degree of legitimacy that is incompatible with its subordination to the Congress (Martínez Sospedra 1994, 43). Moreover, it is held, such a change would not guarantee adequate representation of the autonomous communities, since such an upper house would very likely exhibit the partisan dynamics already seen in the Congress (Garrorena Morales 1995, 26). Hence, indirect election or designation by an existing body like the autonomous parliaments appears the most promising alternative.

A second issue concerns which territorial unit this "chamber for territorial representation" should represent. The overwhelming majority of scholars agree that the Senate should represent the people of the different autonomous communities, while other reformers have defended the need to maintain a number of senators as direct representatives of the provinces, since the Constitution clearly enumerates the provinces among the territorial units of Spain, and indeed they are entities very deeply rooted in many regions (see Martínez López-Muñiz 1997). The most radical approach along these lines has been put forward by Manuel Fraga Iribarne, former PP party leader and current Galician president. In an address before the Senate's Constitutional Committee, he argued in favor of a Senate composed of 158 popularly elected members, plus 131 members designated by the parliaments in the autonomous communities.

Yet another proposal for reform, particularly hotly contested, concerns the criteria for the distribution of senatorial seats among the constituencies. The basic question here is how many seats should each community be awarded, and why? One proposal involves making the seats awarded to each autonomous community dependent on the number of provinces it encompasses, despite the fact that these senators would not be elected in or by the provinces. This proposal has fallen on deaf ears. Garrorena Morales (1995, 23–26), by contrast, argues for the American or Swiss formula of equal representation of territorial units on the grounds that this is the only course compatible with the principle of territorial, as opposed to popular, representation. Again, this proposal has gone nowhere in the face of the markedly unequal population sizes of the existing communities and the highly probable opposition of the larger ones to any plan for equal representation of territorial units.

A cacophony of reform plans has been proposed in recent years, with most of them falling in the very wide range stretching from an entirely egalitarian, territorially based distribution of seats to a rigid application of population-size criteria (see Franch i Ferrer and Martín Cubas, 1997). Most have been closer to the latter than the former pole. Further complicating the picture has been that they have moved beyond representational specifications to embrace wider issues of appropriate powers for an upper house. Most recommend that a new Senate should not be subject to dissolution; that presidents of the autonomous communities should be designated ex officio senators or, minimally, that each autonomous government should be allowed to designate a senator to defend its point of view; that the selection of the remaining senators representing the autonomous community should be carried out by its legislature either by proportional representation or by limited vote; and that senators should not be subject to instructions or mandates from the regional assemblies, although their terms of office would depend on the duration of these assemblies.

Added to the question of how the Senate is elected is the question of what kinds of issues the Senate should deal with. The complexity of lawmaking procedures and control mechanisms in the Spanish parliamentary system means that the precise formulae possible are innumerable. To simplify the terms of the debate, we will stress three points of consensus and one major point of dissent. To begin with, there seems to be consensus that reform should not enhance senatorial control of the government and certainly not to the point of its being involved in the selection of the prime minister and cabinet or in a position to force their resignation. There also seems to be a consensus that the Senate should become "the place where the basic core of cooperation, encounter, and conciliation relations which characterize a complex State should be developed" (Garrorena Morales 1995, 37). This amounts to saying that the upper chamber should become the central, albeit not the exclusive, forum for multilateral bargaining and agreement among all the central and peripheral actors involved. Finally, there also seems to be consensus that the Senate should in some way enhance its legislative powers whenever bills have an autonomous dimension.

But herein lies the problem. Is it enough to equalize its authority with that of the lower house, forcing compromises all the way, or should it be able to impose its will on the Congress in some specific cases? Or should Spain embrace the most radical approach and provide the Senate with exclusive powers in some specified policy areas? Who should determine which bills do or do not have an autonomous relevance? And what about the Senate's legislative powers in matters lacking a territorial dimension? Should the Senate be stripped of this power? Would conflicts of power not arise between the two chambers, and possibly between their opposed partisan majorities, on a regular basis?

If the litany of reform proposals has been virtually endless, the number of questions that remain unanswered is probably even larger. And here the risk is doubled, since it would be a mistake to engage in ill-conceived reform. But, for the sake of the confidence of the Spanish people in its institutions, it would be even more harmful to reform the Senate in a way that brought to everyone's mind the classic Horace quote: "Parturiunt montes, nascetur ridiculus mus" [The mountains were in labor; a ridiculous mouse was born].

Bibliographical Note

All constitutions, draft constitutions, and basic political documents mentioned throughout the historical introduction can be found in Diego Sevilla Andrés, ed., *Constituciones y otras leyes y proyectos políticos de España*, 2 vols. (Madrid: Editora

Nacional, 1969). Most of them can also be found in Enrique Tierno Galván, ed., *Leyes políticas españolas fundamentales (1808–1978)*, 2d ed. (Madrid: Tecnos, 1984), which includes the Law for Political Reform, the 1978 Constitution (CE), and all the electoral laws in force until the March 18, 1977, decree law. The debates and the preparatory documents of the 1978 Constitution can be found in F. Sáinz Moreno, ed., *Constitución Española: Trabajos Parlamentarios*, 4 vols. (Madrid: Cortes Generales, 1980), as well as in the Congress's (DSCD) and the Senate's (DSS) *Diario de Sesiones*. The Standing Orders of the Senate (May 26, 1982) and the Electoral Law (June 19, 1985) can be found, among many other legal instruments, in Eliseo Aja and Enoch Alberti, eds., *Leyes políticas del Estado*, 14th ed. (Madrid: Civitas, 1996). The Statutes of Autonomy have been compiled by Joaquín Tornos Mas and F. Javier Machado Martín in *Estatutos de Autonomía y legislación complementaria* (Madrid: Tecnos, 1995). The major source of information about the Senate's activity is the *Memorias* edited by the house itself every legislature; so far, there are four volumes: *Memoria de la I Legislatura del Senado, 1979–1982* (Madrid: Secretaría General del Senado, 1994); *Memoria de la II Legislatura del Senado, 1982–1986* (Madrid: Secretaría General del Senado, 1987); *Memoria de la III Legislatura del Senado, 1986–1989* (Madrid: Secretaría General del Senado, 1990); *Memoria de la IV Legislatura del Senado, 1989–1993* (Madrid: Secretaría General del Senado, 1995). Sources for tables 9.1 through 9.4 are Luis Aguiar de Luque and R. Blanco Canales, *Constitución Española, 1978–1988*, vol. 3 (Madrid: Centro de Estudios Constitucionales, 1988); *Anuario Autonómico 1996* (Barcelona: Planeta-DeAgostini, 1995); Manuel Martínez Sospedra, *Introducción a los partidos políticos* (Barcelona: Ariel, 1996); *La Vanguardia*, March 5, 1996, and the above-mentioned *Memorias*.

References

Aja, Eliseo, and Xavier Arbós. 1980. "El Senado, cámara posible de las Autonomías." *Revista de Estudios Políticos* 17: 27–66.

Alonso de Antonio, Ángel Luis. 1992. *La Diputación Permanente en la Constitución Española de 1978*. Madrid: Servicio de Publicaciones de la Facultad de Derecho de la Universidad Complutense de Madrid.

Aragón Reyes, Manuel. 1991. Intervention in "Debate sobre la Reforma del Senado." *Anuario de Derecho Constitucional y Parlamentario* 3: 210ff.

Argüelles, Agustín de. 1981. *Discurso preliminar a la Constitución de 1812*. Madrid: Centro de Estudios Constitucionales.

Bertelsen, Repetto. 1974. *El Senado en España*. Madrid: Instituto de Estudios Administrativos.

Carro Martínez, Antonio. 1952. *La Constitución española de 1869*. Madrid: Ediciones de Cultura Hispánica.

Casanova Aguilar, Isabel. 1985. *Aproximación a la Constitución nonnata de 1856*. Murcia: Universidad de Murcia.

Coronas González, S. M. 1989. "Los orígenes del sistema bicameral en España." In *Materiales para el estudio de la Constitución de 1812,* ed. J. Cano. Madrid: Parlamento de Andalucía-Tecnos.

Cruz Villalón, Pedro. 1980. "El referendum consultivo como modelo de racionalización." *Revista de Estudios Políticos* 13:145–68.

Da Silva Ochoa, Juan Carlos. 1994. "El Senado en la encrucijada: La reforma reglamentaria de 11 de enero de 1994." In VV. AA.: *La reforma del Senado.* Madrid: Senado/Centro de Estudios Constitucionales.

De los Ríos. 1927. *Reflexiones sobre una posible reforma constitucional.* Madrid.

De Vega, Pedro. 1985. *La reforma constitucional y la problemática del poder constituyente.* Madrid: Tecnos.

Embid Irujo, Antonio. 1987. *Los parlamentos territoriales.* Madrid: Tecnos.

Entrena Cuesta, R. 1985. "Comentario al artículo 155." In *Comentarios a la Constitución,* ed. Fernando Garrido Falla. Madrid: Tecnos.

Fernández Segado, Francisco. 1984. "La configuración del Senado en el 'iter' constituyente." *Revista de Estudios Políticos* 38:63–125.

———. 1985. "La funcionalidad del Senado en cuanto cámara de representación territorial." *Revista Vasca de Administración Pública* 13:7–44.

———. 1986. *Las constituciones históricas españolas: Un análisis histórico jurídico.* Madrid: Civitas.

Ferrando Badía, Juan. 1973. *La Primera República Española: Historia político-parlamentaria de la República de 1873.* Madrid: Edicusa.

Flores Juberías, Carlos. 1990. "La Revolución Francesa como fuente del primer constitucionalismo español." *Aportes* 12:78–86.

Franch i Ferrer, Vicent, and Joaquín Martín Cubas. 1997. "Reflexiones en torno a una posible reforma del sistema de asignación de encaños en el Senado." *Cuadernos Constitucionales de la Cátedra Fadrique Furió* 18/19:21–42.

Fontán, Antonio. 1991. "El Senado de las Autonomías." *Nueva Revista* 19:6ff.

García Canales, Mariano. 1980. *El problema constitucional de la Dictadura de Primo de Rivera.* Madrid: Centro de Estudios Constitucionales.

García Fernández, Javier. 1984. "Los grupos territoriales del Senado." *Revista de Derecho Político* 21:141–60.

García Valdecasas, Antonio. 1983. "La elaboración del texto constitucional." *Revista de Estudios Políticos* 31/32:57–70.

García-Escudero Márquez, Piedad. 1994. "La Comisión General de las Comunidades Autónomas: Balance de seis meses de reforma de Reglamento del Senado." In VV. AA.: *La reforma del Senado.* Madrid: Senado/Centro de Estudios Constitucionales.

———. 1995. *Los senadores designados por las Comunidades Autónomas.* Madrid: Centro de Estudios Constitucionales, Cortes Generales.

García-Escudero Márquez, Piedad, and Benigno Pendás. 1984. "El Senado en el sistema constitucional español: Realidades y perspectivas." *Revista de las Cortes Generales* 2:51–112.

Garrorena Morales, Ángel. 1995. "Una propuesta para la reforma constitucional del Senado." *Revista de las Cortes Generales* 34:7–50.

González Navarro, J. 1987. *Derecho administrativo español*. Pamplona: Ediciones de la Universidad de Navarra (EUNSA).

Lijphart, Arend, Rafael López Pintor, and Yasunori Sone. 1986. "The Limited Vote and the Single Nontransferable Vote: Lessons from the Japanese and Spanish Experiences." In *Electoral Laws and Their Political Consequences*, ed. Bernard Grofman and Arend Lijphart. New York: Agathon Press.

López Garrido, Diego. 1994. "Hacia un nuevo Senado: Propuesta de reforma constitucional." *Revista de las Cortes Generales* 33:7–26.

Lucas Verdú, Pablo. 1976. *La octava Ley Fundamental: Crítica jurídico-política de la Reforma Suárez*. Madrid: Tecnos.

Martínez Cuadrado, Manuel. 1973. *La burguesía conservadora, 1874–1931*. Madrid: Alianza Editorial.

Martínez López-Muñiz, José Luis. 1997. "El Senado de la España vertebrada." *Revista Española de Derecho Constitucional* 49:119–44.

Martínez Sospedra, Manuel. 1978. *La Constitución de 1812 y el primer liberalismo español*. Valencia: Cátedra Fadrique Furió Ceriol.

———. 1989. "El Senado constitucional: Sus facultades." In *Diez años de régimen constitucional*, ed. E. Álvarez Conde. Madrid: Tecnos.

———. 1990. *La reforma del Senado*. Valencia: Fundación Universitaria San Pablo CEU.

———. 1994. "Forma de Estado y estructura del Parlamento: Notas sobre la reforma del Senado constitucional." *Revista de las Cortes Generales* 33:27–62.

Montero Gibert, José R., and Joaquín García Morillo. 1984. *El control parlamentario del Gobierno*. Madrid: Tecnos.

Oltra Pons, Joaquín. 1972. *La influencia norteamericana en la Constitución Española de 1869*. Madrid: Instituto Nacional de Administración Pública.

Pérez-Serrano Jáuregui, Nicolás. 1989. *Los grupos parlamentarios*. Madrid: Tecnos.

Punset Blanco, Ramón. 1990. "El Senado en el procedimiento legislativo: Una reforma imposible." In *El Parlamento y sus transformaciones actuales*, ed. Ángel Garrorena Morales. Madrid: Tecnos.

———. 1993. "La territorialización del Senado y la reforma de la Constitución." *Revista Española de Derecho Constitucional* 37:81–90.

Revenga Sánchez, Miguel, and José M. Morales Arroyo. 1987. "Las fuentes del Derecho parlamentario: La jurisprudencia constitucional." In *Las Cortes Generales*, vol. 3. Madrid: Instituto de Estudios Políticos.

Ripollés Serrano, María Rosa. 1993. "La funcionalidad del Senado en el Estado de las Autonomías." *Revista Española de Derecho Constitucional* 37:91–126.

Rodrigo Fernández, José Ignacio. 1987. "Las competecias financieras del Senado." In *Las Cortes Generales*, vol. 3, 2.095–2.124. Madrid: Instituto de Estudios Políticos.

Sánchez Agesta, Luis. 1964. *Historia del constitucionalismo español*. 2d ed. Madrid: Instituto de Estudios Políticos.

Sánchez Amor, Ignacio. 1994. "El Senado y las Comunidades Autónomas: Crónica de un desencuentro." In VV. AA.: *La reforma del Senado.* Madrid: Senado/Centro de Estudios Constitucionales.

Sánchez Férriz, Remedio. 1984. *La Restauración y su Constitución política.* Valencia: Departamento de Derecho Político.

Sánchez Férriz, Remedio, and Julia Sevilla Merino. 1980. "La provincia y el Senado en la Constitución Española de 1978." In *Estudios sobre la Constitución Española de 1978.* Valencia: Universidad de Valencia.

Santaolalla, Fernando. 1990. *Derecho parlamentario español.* Madrid: Espasa Calpe.

Santolaya Machetti, Pablo. 1988. *El régimen constitucional de los decretos-leyes.* Madrid: Tecnos.

Sevilla Merino, Julia. 1987. "Los senadores autonómicos." In *Las Cortes Generales,* vol. 3. Madrid: Instituto de Estudios Fiscales.

Tomás Villarroya, Joaquín. 1968. *El sistema político del Estatuto Real, 1834–1836.* Madrid: Instituto de Estudios Políticos.

―――. 1982. *Breve historia del constitucionalismo español.* 2d ed. Madrid: Centro de Estudios Constitucionales.

―――. 1985. *El Estatuto Real de 1834 y la Constitución de 1837.* Madrid: Ediciones SM.

Torres Muro, Ignacio. 1987. *Los órganos de gobierno de las Cámaras Legislativas: Presidente, Mesa y Junta de Portavoces.* Madrid: Publicaciones del Congreso de los Diputados.

Trujillo, Gumersindo. 1967. *El federalismo español.* Madrid: Edicusa.

Visiedo Mazón, Francisco J. 1997. *La reforma del Senado: Territorialización del Senado.* Comisión General de las Comunidades Autónomas. Madrid: Departamento de Publicaciones del Senado.

Zafra Valverde, José. 1973. *El régimen político de España.* Pamplona: Ediciones de la Universidad de Navarra (EUNSA).

10 From Electoral Symbol to Legislative Puzzle: The Polish Senat

DAVID M. OLSON

The rapid collapse of communism has led to the slow development of democratic institutions and practices in Eastern and Central Europe (see Hibbing and Patterson 1994). Parliaments are at the heart of the transformation process in the new postcommunist democracies as both participant and object. Not only are they the product of the democratic transformation but they are active participants in the transitional process itself. Their dual status in the democratization events of Central Europe is nowhere better illustrated than in the case of the newly created Senate of the Polish Parliament.

Parliaments, Democratization, and Bicameralism

In new democracies, everything is in flux and in early developmental stages, including the definition of executive-legislative relations, the party system, and the place of second chambers in bicameral parliaments. Upon the collapse of communism, the Communist-era legislative bodies immediately became free to act independently of single-party control. Within a few short months, new election laws had been adopted to make possible the first freely contested elections to new democratic parliaments. But nothing else about parliaments had changed. That the newly elected members met in old buildings was a metaphor for the lack of rules, procedures, internal structures, and staff developed in democratic legislatures over decades if not centuries. The new members in revitalized legislatures had simultaneously to enact new policies, create and supervise new cabinets, and develop their own internal structures and procedures. Their meager internal resources were overwhelmed by the need to act in their changed political and economic systems.

Deciding whether the chamber structure of their parliament should be unicameral or bicameral was one of the many steps facing new democracies. Those countries which had a bicameral structure in the 1920s and 1930s returned to that pattern. Poland, Romania, and the Czech Republic are bicameral, while Bulgaria, Hungary, and Slovakia are unicameral. In the Balkans, Slovenia and Croatia are bicameral, while Albania, Macedonia, and Serbia are unicameral. Of the former republics of the USSR, only Russia is bicameral. Of all the bicameral countries, only Russia is federal in structure.

Unicameral countries of Central Europe continue to express interest in a second chamber. Hungary, for example, did not return to its bicameral past, but it is often suggested that it should do so. In the Czech Republic, the surviving legislative body from communism was unicameral; a second chamber was soon adopted, at least partly in imitation of their prewar parliamentary structure. Most second chambers are directly elected, but their powers are truncated. Most have limited legislative powers and almost no role in the selection or removal of cabinets and prime ministers. Only in Romania are the two chambers equal in legislative authority.

The limited legal jurisdiction of second chambers contrasts with a direct election that conveys the legitimacy of representation. Depending on the distribution of seats among the many parties characteristic of the new democracies, it would be possible for the balance of power to be exercised by a truncated second chamber if the lower and more powerful chamber were immobilized through internal party divisions. Since Poland, like many of the new democracies, has both a president and a prime minister, a second chamber could also act decisively in the instance of deadlock between president and the lower chamber.

In this chapter the unique origins of the Senate are set forth, the events and controversies of its elections are reviewed, its committee structure and place in the legislative process of the Parliament are analyzed, and its changing status in relationship to the president and the constitution-writing process is traced.

Origins

The contemporary Polish Senate is an artifact of the postcommunist democratization process. It was created as an integral part of the negotiated settlement between the ruling Communist government and the labor union Solidarity in spring 1989. Though its immediate purpose as an electoral device for regime transformation had disappeared within the year, the institution continues. Its opportunities and actions have differed greatly since then in response to the changing political composition of the more powerful chamber, the Sejm.

The Negotiated Chamber

The Senate was created at the Roundtable negotiations between the Communists (PZPR, or United Polish Workers' Party) and Solidarity in spring 1989. Unexpectedly, those negotiations led to the first noncommunist government in the entire Soviet bloc in August of that same year. The Senate was a critical part of the negotiated agreement and the dynamics leading to the first noncommunist government. The goal of the Communist government in the Roundtable was to engage Solidarity in responsibility for the economy, while the goal of Solidarity was to regain its legal status, which had been suspended during martial law in December 1981 (Kurczewski 1993, 201; "Poland Has a New Constitution" 1992; Rapaczynski 1991, 598–601).

The Communist government offered Solidarity the opportunity to run candidates for the Sejm, but in the usual manner of using either single-list slates or specially designated districts. Solidarity rejected these efforts to implicate them in controlled elections. The idea of the Senate resolved this dilemma, for the Communist offer to Solidarity was to create a small new chamber to which elections would be "free." The reasoning of the Communist side was that the Senate with truncated powers of suspensive veto would not threaten Communist legislation, and that its small size would not deprive the Communists of their needed margin of votes in the two chambers meeting as a single body in the National Assembly. As one participant commented, the Communists used the mentality of arithmetic, unable to anticipate the entirely new dynamic that a "free" election to any office would generate in a population hostile to the Communist government.

There had been speculation in the 1980s about a second chamber, perhaps based on a corporatist model (Gebethner 1992b, 61; Orlowski 1994, 52–56). The goal, during Communist rule and martial law, was to find a means by which public policy could be debated without constraining or threatening party control. In the controversy over the structure and functions of the Senate that has continued into the current postcommunist decade, it is now the postcommunist party, the Alliance of the Democratic Left, which has argued that the Senate should be replaced by a social and economic council (Hausner and Morawski 1994; Jaskiernia 1994, 18–24). In the new postcommunist democracies, the desire to escape the narrow constraints of partisanship is a frequently expressed aspiration that a second chamber would be designed to realize, but it is also a continuation of the Communist search for a means to escape political control.

In the 1989 Polish Roundtable, the arithmetic of power combined the size of each chamber with the allocation of seats among political forces in the unique "compartmentalized" election system of the 1989 election (Olson 1993a). The 460 seats in the continuing Sejm and the 100 in the new Senate were allocated to different participants, thus allowing for, but also limiting, different types of electoral contest. Most of the seats (65%) were allocated to the Communist Party or one of its satellite parties. Within each set of allocated seats, all candidates running for a single seat would come from the party to which the seat had been allocated. In the Sejm, 35 percent of the seats were reserved for noncommunist candidates, and while the Senate itself constituted only one of the allocated sets of seats, it was the only one open to candidates from all parties. The Sejm was quickly dubbed the "contract" house because the elections of its members were only "semifree," while the Senate was selected through "free" elections. This example of electoral engineering was the culmination of two decades of experiments by which the Communist Party of Poland attempted to introduce a semblance of competition and choice without sacrificing control. The numbers of seats in each electoral compartment were calculated to preserve for the Communists the majority that was needed in the whole National Assembly to elect General Wojciech Jaruzelski, leader of the Communist Party, to the new office of president (Elster 1993). His being in that office would be the guarantee to both Polish Communists and the Soviets of continued stability in Communist rule.

The idea of the Senate as an electoral arena of free and open competition offered to the government the legitimacy of the election of its president and the inducement to Solidarity to enter the political arena (Gebethner 1992b, 57–60; Sokolewicz 1992, 78). The trade could have been summed from the Solidarity side as "Your President completely; our Senate partially."

The Communist majority, however, began to disappear during the six-week 1989 election campaign. The anticipated majority was based on the careful allocation of seats in the Sejm to each political party (hence the term *compartmentalized election system*), as well as an estimate of how many seats the Communists could win in the Senate's genuinely competitive elections. The Communist and its allied similar parties, termed a "coalition," were guaranteed 299 seats (of 460) in the Sejm, while the remainder (161 seats) were open to independent candidates, as were all of the 100 Senate seats. That a ruling Communist Party had to resort to such complicated mechanics and hopeful arithmetic is itself a measure of the extent to which Communist rule was in a state of collapse in the 1988–89 period.

The results, compared with expectations, of the 1989 election are shown in table 10.1. Solidarity won all of the 35 percent of Sejm seats for which it was eligible to run candidates, and won 99 of the 100 Senate seats. The Communists held on to their majority in the National Assembly, but it was much smaller than calculated during the negotiations. In

Table 10.1. Actual and Expected Distribution of Parliamentary Seats
in Poland by Communist-Solidarity Alignment, 1989

Political Side and Compartment	Actual		Expected	
	N	%	N	%
Communist Party Coalition				
Sejm Party Coalition	299		299	
Sejm Independent	0		50	
Senate	1		30	
Total	300	53	379	67
Solidarity				
Sejm Independent	161		111	
Senate	99		70	
Total	260	47	181	33
Total	560	100	560	100

the ensuing presidential selection, General Jaruzelski was elected president by the National Assembly only with the tacit support of Solidarity (Sokolewicz 1992, 79).

While this specific set of negotiations and events was unique to Poland, its effects were not confined to that country. Rather, as the first breach in Communist hegemony, these events set in motion the collapse of Communist rule in the whole region.

The Senate was vital in this process of regime change because of its electoral roots. As the only "fully free" electoral organ, it contrasted with the "contract" Sejm selected through the compartmentalized election system. Its importance lay not in its potential for independent action on legislation after the election, but in its being an integral part of regime transformation—a new set of offices to be filled by election. The idea of the Senate as a new electoral compartment was the solution to a bargaining objective—how to engage Solidarity in the electoral process—but became a key element in the unexpected democratic transformation stemming from the unanticipated dynamics of the spring 1989 election campaign.

The Institutional Inheritance

Although Poland's pre–World War II bicameral structure was continued immediately after the war, the Communist system beginning in the late

1940s converted the Parliament to a unicameral body. Despite the Senate's long tradition in thought and practice in Polish history (Burda 1978, 6–16; Jedruch 1992), from the moment of its election in 1989 the new Senate took its internal structural features from the unicameral Parliament that had slowly evolved under Communism. This inheritance from the lower chamber decisively shaped the organization and procedures of the newly created Senate.

The Sejm had developed a comprehensive committee system, paralleling the configuration of government ministries, toward the end of the Communist era. The committees had evolved ways of monitoring the conduct of ministry affairs and of reviewing submitted legislation (Olson and Simon 1982). The potential for independent action by committees was dramatically, though briefly, revealed during the 1980–81 eruption of Solidarity strikes immediately before martial law was imposed (Mason 1991; Zakrzewski 1982).

The leadership structure of presiding officers and a steering committee was also retained after the postcommunist transition. The presiding officer, the marshal, had several vice marshals, who, with committee chairs, decided schedules, assigned committee memberships, and referred bills to committee. The high prestige of this office, inherited from the medieval origins of the parliamentary institution, has continued through the Communist period into the present.

Although the newly created Senate and the revitalized Sejm could adapt the existing committee system and leadership structure to democracy, the party system was far more problematic. The Communist Party, though clearly in control, worked in Parliament with two satellite parties as well as a complement of independents. Each of the three parties was formally organized as a party group within Parliament, each met as a party group prior to floor sessions (several times annually), and each had formal membership on the steering committee of the Sejm. The rules and procedures formally allocated preference and authority to party groups, but they were never tested through overt party conflict.

The Communist period had seen experimentation with different ways in which voters could make a choice among several candidates for parliamentary office, though never in a way that permitted competition between parties. The party seat allocations, decided in advance, were implemented, but could never be challenged, in elections. The unique 1989 election system of compartments was an improvised adaptation of the

Communist-era election procedures. Since the end of communism, the party system has changed with each election. The one party of communism has been replaced by a constantly changing multiparty system, affecting both chambers of Parliament equally.

Elections, Districts, and Party System

In the four elections since 1989, both the Senate and the Sejm have had similar party majorities, although the specific majority and the shape of the party system have changed with each election. The parties are grouped in table 10.2 by alliance structure, to show the Solidarity-based majority in 1991 and 1997 and the postcommunist-based majority in 1993. Each election has produced dramatically different results, and in each, the number, names, and identities of parties and other electoral groupings have changed, illustrating the fragile and shifting character of party formation typical of the new postcommunist democracies (Jasiewicz 1992b; Lewis 1990, 1995; Olson 1993b, 1998a; Wightman 1995).

In this shifting kaleidoscope of parties, the survivors of the Communist era are more stable than those emerging from the Solidarity movement. The Alliance of the Democratic Left is a coalition of groups in a postcommunist leftist party, while the current Polish Peasants' Party (PSL) is a continuation of the former United Peasant Party, which was allied with the ruling Communist Party after 1949. The many parties listed in the Solidarity category in table 10.2 reflect the diversity of its groups. That polyglot electoral coalition and anticommunist reform movement was united only in its opposition to communism. Since its unifying goal has been achieved, its many participants have sought an organizational vehicle and a set of issue appeals for electoral victory. The formula of diversity for success against communism has proven a liability in the competitive electoral politics of democracy. The 1997 election showed the consequences of election systems: they tend to force small unsuccessful groups into larger groupings to win.

Election Systems

The electoral system was changed following the splintering of parties in the 1991 election to both the Sejm and Senate. Though the Sejm consistently has had varieties of multimember districts and proportional representation elections, the Senate has consistently had two- and three-member districts, with either majority or plurality election rules. In this variation of a field experiment, the party results are strikingly similar between the two chambers, even though the electoral and district systems are entirely different (Gebethner 1993; Jasiewicz 1992a; Wiatr 1992). Simultaneous election permits the parties to wage cross-chamber election campaigns, and it encourages voters to respond consistently to parties, even though the votes are counted differently.

The Senate's seat distribution does, however, exaggerate the size of the majority resulting from each election, reflecting a consistent difference in the seat allocation results of the different electoral systems. In addition, in the 1993 election, two small parties each gained entry to one chamber but not to the other.

Electoral Districts

The forty-nine voivodships, or administrative districts, inherited from the Communist system were used as electoral districts for the new Senate. This choice, consistent at the time of the 1989 Roundtable with existing Communist-era boundaries, has been increasingly questioned following the change of regime.

The whole system of local and regional organization and the desirability of self-government have been under constant discussion since democratization. At the time of dissolution of the Sejm in 1993, the Solidarity-based government had prepared a new system of regional government, whereby new, fewer, and larger regional units would replace the older voivodships. That plan was immediately abandoned by the new postcommunist government coalition when it won office in fall 1993. Local and regional reorganization threatened the existing network of local offices controlled by the postcommunist Alliance of the Democratic Left and especially by the Polish Peasants' Party. By the end of the four-year term of a government controlled by these two parties (1993–97), no agreement had been reached on this question.

However, the path for local and regional reorganization has been laid by the new constitution adopted in 1997, with the deceptively simple statement that the Senate would be elected (Art. 97, Sec. 2). Notably absent from the new formulation is a definition of district. By contrast, the

Table 10.2. Political Party Seats in the Polish Parliament, 1991, 1993

Political Parties by Origin	1991 Election Sejm Seats N	%	Senate Seats N	1993 Election Sejm Seats N	%	Senate Seats N	1997 Election Sejm Seats N	%	Senate Seats N
Solidarity									
Democratic Union (UD)	62	13.5	21	74	16.1	6	60	13.04	8
Christian National Union (ZChN)	49	10.7	9	0	0.0	0		0.00	
Center Citizen Alliance (POC)	44	9.6	9	0	0.0	0		0.00	
Liberal Democratic Congress (KLD)	37	8.0	6	0	0.0	0		0.00	
Peasant Alliance (PL)	28	6.1	7	0	0.0	0		0.00	
Solidarity Trade Union (NSZZ-S)	27	5.9	11	0	0.0	12		0.00	
Union Labor/Solidarity (UP/SP)	4	.9	0	41	8.9	0		0.00	
Nonparty Bloc (BBWR)	0	0.0	0	16	3.5	2		0.00	
Elect Action Solidarity (AWS)							210	43.70	51
Movmt Reconstruction (ROP)							6	1.30	5
Subtotal	251	54.6	63	131	28.5	20	267	58.04	64
Communist									
Alliance of the Democratic Left (SLD)	60	13.0	4	171	37.2	37	164	35.65	28
Polish Peasants' Party (PSL)	48	10.4	8	132	28.7	36	27	5.87	3
Christian Democracy (ChD)	5	1.1	1	0	0.0	0			
Subtotal	113	24.6	13	303	65.9	73	191	41.52	31

Minority								
German Minority (NM)	7	1.5	1	4	.9	0	2	0.43
Silesian Movement (RAS)	2	.4	0	0	0.0	0		
Polish Western Union (PZZ)	4	.9	0	0	0.0	0		
Subtotal	13	2.8	1	4	.9	0	2	0.43
Others								
Confederation Independent Poland (KPN)	46	10.0	4	22	4.8	0	0	0.00
Beer Lovers Party (PPPP)	16	3.5	0	0	0.0	0	0	0.00
Union of Real Politics (UPR)	3	.7	0	0	0.0	0	0	0.00
Party of Christian Democrats (PChD)	4	.9	3	0	0.0	0	0	0.00
Party X (PX)	3	.7	0	0	0.0	0	0	0.00
One-seat group & independents	11	2.4	16	0	0.0	7	5	0.00
Subtotal	83	18.0	23	22	4.8	7	5	0.00
Total	460	100.0	100	460	100.0	100	460	100.00

Sources: Jasiewicz 1991, 1993; Dirksen Electoral Archive 1997; Rose, Munro, and Mackie 1998.

Note: ZChN ran originally as Catholic Action (WAK); Democratic Union (UD) has become Union of Freedom (UW).

interim constitution of 1992 continued to state that senators were elected from voivodships (Ch. 2, Art. 3). The omission of that designation from the 1997 constitution permits consideration of regional reorganization and creates the need to rewrite the Senate election law.

Senate districts range in size from 178,000 eligible voters to almost 3 million. The disparities in population were recognized by the allocation of an additional seat to each of the two largest regions: Warsaw and Katowice (Gebethner 1995, 36). The remaining large disparities are easily explained by the model chosen by the Communists at the Roundtable—the American Senate.

Most of the plans for regional reorganization (as of 1997) would simplify the forty-nine existing voivodships into eight to twenty-five regions, to reflect both history and population size. Under most plans, the regions would be governed by directly elected regional councils (Jalowiecki 1996, 74–76). The new regions could become the basis for new senatorial districts. If the new regions were to have powers of self-government, those entities could claim a right to be represented in the Senate. The purpose for the Senate, since its anticommunist electoral function has been fulfilled, has always been a source of controversy. To connect it to reformed self-government at the local level would provide the institution with a rationale that it now lacks.

However, it would be possible to draw Senate districts on some other basis. The consistency of new senatorial electoral districts with the definition of new regions and the relationship of new Senate districts to population size have become open issues. Similar questions are also raised for the Sejm's district system, as it, too, is now based on the voivodship. Thus, districting questions, opened by the pending regional government reforms, would require the redefinition of electoral systems for both chambers.

The issue of regional reform in Poland is extremely volatile, since it raises different concerns for different political parties. Recent attempts to create new units of local government have been actively resisted by the Peasants' Party against its own government coalition partners in the 1993–97 term (Donosy, May 28, 1996). In the first parliament of the new democracy, the regional governors (Voivods), who continue to be appointed by the central government, were also eligible to be elected to either parliamentary chamber. That possibility was altered by the "Little Constitution" of 1992, which defined a wide range of offices as incompatible with parliamentary membership (Vinton 1992).

Parliament's Formal Powers

The original purpose of the Senate has been its catalytic function in the regime change process. Following the collapse of the Communist system, the institution had to be created. It had members, but it had no internal organization and no place to meet. Since the dramatic moment of its creation and first election in May–June 1989, it has turned to more mundane legislative tasks. Such tasks, however, have been a source of both constitutional confusion and continued dispute.

Legislation

The formal legislative powers of the Senate are to review Sejm bills, in response to which it may either reject the whole bill or propose amendments. The Sejm, in turn, may accept or reject the Senate's actions. The Senate may also initiate its own bills. The legislative process is complicated and lengthened by the presidential prerogative of veto, but the Senate is excluded from the Sejm's option of having the right to override a presidential veto.

One of the Senate's original functions, to select the president through its participation with the Sejm in a combined National Assembly, was soon removed. Within two years of democratization, the presidency became a directly elected office (Jasiewicz 1997). The Senate's function has been further reduced with the adoption of a constitution in 1997. That document, like the original presidential selection, was considered and voted upon in the National Assembly.

With both adoption of the Constitution and direct election of the president, the Senate has been reduced to a limited jurisdiction over ordinary legislation—with one exception. It, rather than the Sejm, has the power to agree to or block presidential requests for a referendum. Several times, President Lech Walesa proposed referenda, and each time the Senate refused permission. The main chamber, the Sejm, was not part of that approval process, though Walesa's requests were part of his long struggle with the Sejm. On this type of question, the Senate must act within fourteen days (Donosy, November 6, 1995).

The Senate can also participate with the Sejm in defense of Parliament against the president. Several times, when Walesa threatened the dissolution or even suspension of Parliament, the marshals (presiding officers) of the two chambers acted in concert against him (Karpinski 1995). The president is required to consult, at least formally, with both marshals before dissolving Parliament.

Legislative Activities

Over the first two terms (of two years each) and in the first two years of the 1993–97 term, the Senate vetoed fifteen bills from the Sejm, but proposed amendments to over two hundred of them (see table 10.3). It also adopted forty-eight bills on its own initiative, twenty-five of which were approved by the Sejm. The Sejm for its part may both override the Senate's suspensive veto and reject Senate amendments by an absolute majority. While ordinary Sejm action on legislation requires only a majority of a quorum, the majority of the full Sejm membership is needed to override the Senate. No formal action has been taken by the Senate on most Sejm bills, which gives automatic approval of, or at least acquiescence to, Sejm action. However, the Senate has amended over one-third of all Sejm legislation, and the Sejm has accepted at least some of these amendments.

The Senate works under time limits in reacting to Sejm legislation. For ordinary legislation, the Senate must act within thirty days, but on budget amendments, the Senate must act within twenty days. The budget bill cannot be rejected. The government may request expedited action from both chambers by designating a bill "urgent." Though there are many exceptions to this option, the government made extensive use of that practice in the 1991–93 term, in reaction to which the procedure has been limited. In the new Constitution of 1997, the Senate is limited to only seven days in which to act upon Sejm bills under this special procedure. There is no similar restriction on the Sejm.

Especially during the rapid democratic reforms of its first term, the Solidarity-controlled Senate approved Sejm legislation. Its task was to assist and support, not oppose or even quibble about reform legislation

Table 10.3. Legislative Activity of the Polish Senate, 1989–1995

Legislative Actions	Senate I Sejm X (1989–91)	Senate II Sejm I (1991–93)	Senate III Sejm II (1993–95)	Total
Sejm bills				
Bills passed by the Sejm	248	102	207	557
Bills amended by the Senate	84	47	80	211
Sejm agreed to all amendments	18	13	16	47
Sejm agreed to some amendments	49	24	53	126
Sejm rejected all amendments	11	6	8	25
Other	6	4	3	13
Bills vetoed by the Senate	6	7	2	15
Vetoes overridden	3	4	1	8
Vetoes sustained	3	3	1	7
Senate bills				
Bills passed by the Senate	27	9	12	48
Bills adopted by the Sejm	17	4	4	25
No action by the Sejm	9	5	4	18

Sources: Senate, *Wybrane dane o pracy,* I, II, kadencji; Sejm, *Informacja* Kadencja, 1993–95, 2:22; Sejm Research Office.

(Sokolewicz 1992, 71). Solidarity's control of the Senate was a considerable encouragement to the reformers in the more problematic Sejm. But the Senate initiated more legislation in the first than in subsequent terms. The ferment of the opportunity to reform the existing Communist system was reflected in the conflicts and uncertainties expressed in Senate debate. Though all senators were elected as anticommunists, there was little agreement among them on how the system could best be changed (Los 1994, 1995, 1996).

In the second term, the fragmented and changing party structures and alignments both reduced the sheer number of bills from the Sejm and increased the proportion (46%) of Sejm bills that the Senate amended. Not only was there interchamber disagreement and also interparty disagreement, but the post-Solidarity party groups were in flux. They were in a process of disintegration and change, and had little capacity to coordinate their own party members either within or between the chambers.

A unique form of legislative stalemate ("pat," from the game of chess) occurred in the first two terms until the Little Constitution of 1992. It had been possible for the Sejm to take two types of action on Senate amendments, each requiring a different size of majority. The Sejm could either accept a Senate amendment with a simple majority or reject a Senate amendment with a two-thirds majority. Several bills were stymied, because the Sejm could meet neither target: motions to accept and reject the same amendment were both defeated. The revised procedure is much simpler: the Sejm now acts on Senate amendments through a single motion, requiring an absolute majority for rejection ("Poland Has a New Constitution" 1992; Sarnecki 1995, 70–71; Vinton 1992; Wojtyczek 1994). In table 10.3, the stalemated bills are listed in the "other" category: that number has decreased in the third term.

In negotiations over the Little Constitution itself, interchamber relations fell to their lowest point. The Senate had offered many amendments to the Sejm bill detailing the constitutional changes. Of its own volition, the Sejm changed its standing orders to consider Senate amendments under the expedited procedure outlined above, in response to which "most" senators were "outraged." Several senators filed suit against the Sejm in the Constitutional Tribunal, which quickly found that the Sejm had not violated the constitution (Gebethner and Jasiewicz 1993, 533–34).

Party Coordination

Variations in the Senate's legislative actions lie in the character of parliamentary party organization: the party clubs are bicameral (Jackiewicz and Jackiewicz 1996, 372–74). That is, each parliamentary party is itself an instrument for coordination among its own members between the two chambers. Thus, since the different election systems have produced similar party majorities in the two chambers, party majorities, when and if they exist, are able to coordinate between the two chambers.

The 1993–97 Parliament, with a two-party majority coalition of Peasants and reformed Communists, was better able to develop bicameral coordination than was the Solidarity-based majorities of 1991–93. The inability of the Solidarity movement and of the many post-Solidarity parties to coordinate their diverse views is amply conveyed by the reference to the "unruly" Senate in a discussion of constitution writing in the first term (Rapaczynski 1991, 604).

In Term II, 1991–93, the Solidarity-based majority in both chambers fragmented into several parties, none of which was cohesive. Thus, the Senate was able to become more independent of the Sejm in that term of office than in the subsequent one. In Term III, 1993–97, Senate-Sejm differences were expressed in those bills on which the parties had not developed a common view and on which they did not impose party discipline. This term also saw, however, volatile issues on which parties either had changed positions or split. The issues of abortion law, local government reform, and censorship not only encouraged differences between the two chambers (*OMRI Daily Digest,* October 10, 1994; Donosy, July 8, 1996). They also led to divisions of opinions within each party. The sequence of chamber action—first in the Sejm and second in the Senate—has provided an interval of time during which party views can change. In these instances, the suspensive veto function of the Senate reflects disagreement not so much between the two chambers as within single political parties.

The Senate is also a platform, offering its members the opportunity to become major actors in their respective political parties, on legislation as well as in government formation. For example, former prime minister Hanna Suchocka observed that the marshal of the Senate was one of the "important negotiators" in the formation of her Solidarity-based multiparty government in Term II (Osiatynski 1996). Likewise, in the discussions surrounding the reorganization of the Peasant–Democratic Left government in the middle of Term III, the office of prime minister was taken by the Alliance of the Democratic Left, while the junior partner in the government coalition, the Polish Peasants' Party, was allocated the position of marshal in both chambers (*OMRI Daily Digest,* March 6, 1995).

Parties and Committees

Although the Senate has restricted legislative jurisdiction, it utilizes the typical forms of legislative internal organization, parties, and committees to manage its workload and to organize its members.

The Committee System

The Polish Senate has a structure of thirteen permanent committees, as opposed to the Sejm's twenty-four committees (Olson et al. 1998). The smaller number of committees in the Senate reflects both its smaller size and its limited authority (Rundquist 1994). Senate committees have a

Table 10.4. Polish Parliamentary Chamber and Committee Seats, 1993

Political Parties by Alignment	Sejm Chamber N	Sejm Chamber %	Sejm Committees N	Sejm Committees %	Senate Chamber N	Senate Committees N	Senate Committees %
Government							
Alliance of the Democratic Left (SLD)	171	37.2	277	36.1	37	73	40.1
Polish Peasants' Party (PSL)	132	28.7	211	27.5	36	61	33.5
Subtotal	303	65.9	488	63.6	73	134	73.6
Nongovernment							
Democratic/Freedom Union (UD/UW)	74	16.1	122	15.9	6	11	6.0
Union of Labor (UP)	41	8.9	74	9.7	0	0	0.0
Solidarity (NSSZ "S")	0	0.0	0	0.0	12	22	12.1
Confederation of Ind. Poland (KPN)	22	4.8	35	4.6	0	0	0.0
Nonparty Reform Bloc (BBWR)	16	3.5	25	3.3	2	4	2.2
Independent/Other	4	.9	23	3.0	7	11	6.0
Subtotal	157	34.1	279	36.4	27	48	26.4
Total	460	100.0	767	100.0	100	182	100.0

Sources: Sejm Membership Directory, 1993; Senate Membership Directory, 1993.

Note: Permanent committees in each chamber at the beginning of the term following the 1993 election.

defined policy jurisdiction corresponding to sets of ministries. Like the Sejm's committees, they can ask ministers to meet with them. However, apparently ministers often send subordinates on the grounds that their own tenure depends on the confidence of the Sejm rather than of the Senate.

However subordinate the Senate is to the Sejm, the parties do not neglect control over committees. The distribution of committee seats among the parties is closely proportional to their chamber size (see table 10.4). The two government parties held 74 percent of all committee seats in the 1993–97 term. There are sizable variations both in relative government coalition strength and in individual party strength. On all committees in the Senate in the 1993–97 term, the two governing parties held a clear majority, ranging from 62 percent (defense) up to 92 percent (agriculture) of the seats. Other committees with disproportionate government strength were those on culture (91%) and legislative work (88%). The two government parties also held the preponderance of committee chair and vice chair positions. These variations tend to parallel the variations found among Sejm committees (Olson et al. 1998) and reflect the importance of each committee to each governing party in terms of the distribution of power within the Senate, their salience to its electorate, or both.

Party Power on Committees

Individual party preference for committee assignments may be expressed in two tangible ways: through membership ratios and leadership positions. Both the opposition parties and the two governing parties prefer different committees. Party ratios on committees are defined in broad ranges of seats, while each party allocates its own members to its share of seats on any given committee.

Not only is there a consideration of the balance between government and opposition parties, but also individual parties have their own concerns and priorities. The size relationship between the two governing parties, for example, varies by committee. Though in 1993–97 the Alliance of the Democatic Left (SLD) held one seat more in the chamber than the Polish Peasants' Party (PSL), the latter outnumbered the former on five of the thirteen committees. The largest discrepancies were in the committees on Poles abroad and agriculture. The other and slightly larger coalition partner, SLD, was also oversized on some committees, especially culture, social policy, and rules.

Likewise, the distribution of committee leadership positions signals party preferences. The committees typically have one chair and two vice chair positions that are almost entirely monopolized by the two governing parties. Of these two parties, the smaller PSL held seven chair positions to SLD's five in the 1993–97 term, while the larger SLD held almost twice as many vice chair positions as did its partner. The combination in which one government party holds both the chairmanship and one of the two vice chairs is a measure of concentration of party attention and power. Committees in which one party holds two vice chair positions, while the other holds the chair position, more evenly distributes power between the two governing parties.

Both measures, membership and leadership, are combined into an estimate of party power in the committee system. Table 10.5 lists committees in three categories: committees in which power is concentrated in a single governing party, those in which power is concentrated equally

Table 10.5. Party and Government Power on Senate Committees in Poland, 1993

Concentration of Committees	Committee Size	% Government Parties' Seats
Party-concentrated		
Polish Peasants' Party (PSL)		
Agriculture	13	92
Environment	14	71
Alliance of the Democratic Left (SLD)		
Culture	11	91
Rules	11	73
Justice	12	67
Average	12.2	78.8
Government-concentrated		
Legislative work	8	88
Local government	15	80
Education/science	14	79
Average	12.3	82.3
Dispersed		
Poles abroad	17	76
Foreign affairs	18	67
National economy	20	65
Social policy/health	16	63
National defense	13	62
Average	16.8	66.6

Source: Senate Membership Directory, 1993.

Note: Within categories, committees are listed by descending size of the government party coalition.

between the two governing parties, and those in which power is more dispersed.

In the "party concentrated" committees, the designated government party holds a preponderance of seats and leadership positions. Of the five committees in this category, PSL power is concentrated in the committees on environment and agriculture, both of which are related to the policy concerns and electoral base of the PSL. If constituency is a major concern for PSL, power in the Senate would appear a similar concern for the SLD. It controls the leadership positions and is disproportionately large on three committees. The committee on rules illustrates the concern with internal power, while the committees on culture and justice reflect power over broad sectors of public policy.

The "government concentrated" committees have a high governing party membership, but either the sizes are more evenly balanced or leadership positions are more evenly shared between the two government parties than in the previous category. The committee on legislative work is the predominant coordinating committee in the Senate on legislation, while the local government committee holds jurisdiction on a question that deeply divides the two parties of government—regional reorganization.

On the "dispersed committees," the government majority is not as large as on the previous two sets of "concentrated" committees. Among these, however, PSL has a much larger membership, and holds the chair on the Poles abroad committee, while SLD has a similar position on the social policy and health committee. Both the coalition and single government party-concentrated committees tend to be smaller in size than the dispersed committees, perhaps because small committees are easier to control than are large ones.

The committee on legislative work is the key coordination committee, sharing jurisdiction on virtually all legislation with the subject matter committees. Its key placement is indicated by its small size and high proportion of government party members. Furthermore, the relationship between the two government parties is more balanced than in the single-party concentrated committees.

Minority Parties

The several small minority parties in Term III faced the classic choice of either concentrating their members on some committees or attempting to cover them all. The Solidarity Union members are concentrated in the committees on justice, Poles living abroad, national economy, social policy, and national defense, while the Freedom Union, which had members on most committees, concentrated slightly on the committees on foreign affairs and environment. Independent members opted for the committees on national economy and foreign affairs. The committee choices of the small parties reflect their constituencies, while the independent members can select committees on the basis of personal preference. Thus, these committees are mostly in the "dispersed" category in table 10.5.

Committee Coordination

Senate committees do the preparatory work on both Sejm bills and on their own. Bills initiated in the Senate go through two sets of committees. The proposal for a Senate bill is initially examined by the Committee on Legislation. Following its approval and Senate plenary debate, the draft is referred to the relevant subject matter committees. Even with relatively few committees, transition-era legislation frequency cuts across committee jurisdictions. Coordination among committees is achieved by procedures similar to those in the Sejm (Olson et al. 1998). Committees may meet jointly or form ad hoc joint subcommittees. In addition, the legislation committee shares jurisdiction on most bills and serves as the basic coordinating committee for the chamber.

The budget requires its own coordination mechanisms among Senate committees. Consideration of possible amendments to the Sejm's budget bill is coordinated through the committee on national economy. Specific portions of the budget are referred to each of the subject matter committees, which in turn report to the national economy committee. Both the budget bill and those bills designated by the government as "urgent" place severe time constraints on Senate committees.

Members

There is no clear pattern of membership mobility from one chamber to the other over the series of four elections in postcommunist Poland. The more visible phenomenon is that incumbents do not seek reelection to either their own or the other chamber. On the one hand, the greater political importance of the Sejm would suggest that party leaders and persons interested in public policy would seek election to the Sejm more than to the Senate. On the other hand, the different electoral systems give more scope to individual Senate candidates to test their campaign abilities and voter acceptance than in party list Sejm elections. There are isolated instances in which popular, though unelected, Senate candidates have been placed on Sejm party lists in a succeeding election.

The occupational structure of both chambers is broadly similar, as are the patterns of previous political and governmental experience. With economic reform, however, a new category of member is entering Parliament. While the previous members were largely in professional and artistic occupations, businessmen as owners and managers began to enter the Senate from the 1991 election onwards.

The members of both bodies are largely university educated; 87 of the 100 senators in 1991 were university graduates. The proportion of women in the Senate grew from 7 to 13 percent between 1989 and 1993 elections, roughly matching the proportion in the Sejm. The biggest demographic difference in membership between the two chambers is age: while almost 37 percent of the Sejm members elected in 1991 were below the age of forty, only 19 percent of senators were below that age. The average age of senators has ranged from forty-nine to fifty-four years over three elections.

Legislative Workload and Resources

At the time of the idea to use the Senate as a bargaining tool in negotiations to induce Solidarity's participation in a semicontrolled election system, the Senate had no members, no workload, no schedule, no facilities, and no staff. On the day following the 1989 election, the Senate had members but no other resources. Their activities and resources have been developed since that dramatic day.

The Senate, having fewer bills to consider than the Sejm and not having responsibility for government formation, meets less often and for shorter periods than does the main chamber (see table 10.6). Though the number of "sessions" of the two chambers is similar over two terms, they last twice as long in the Sejm (177 and 136 days each term) as in the Senate (90 and 69 days each). Likewise, the steering groups of the chambers differ in the frequency of their meetings. The Presidium met 87 times in the Senate's Term II, while the Sejm's Presidium met 230 times in the same period. There was an even greater difference in the frequency of meetings of the two Convents of Seniors, the coordinating body among party leaders.

The discrepancy in committee meetings, however, was not as great. The most active Sejm committee met 225 times in the 1991–93 term, while in the Senate, the most active committee met 170 times. In each chamber, the most active committee was the coordinating committee on law and legislation.

Table 10.6. Sejm and Senate Activity in Poland, 1989–1995

	Sejm			Senate		
Activity	X (1989–91)	I (1991–93)	III (1993–95)	I (1989–91)	II (1991–93)	III (1993–95)
Plenary meetings						
Sessions	79	45	68	61	40	31
Days	177	136	171	90	69	39
Steering group meetings						
Presidium	178	230	246	110	87	49
Convent of seniors	274	218	230	*	45	25
Committee meetings						
Most frequent	*	225	*	155	170	91

Sources: See Table 10.3.

Note: Sejm II and Senate III = 1993–95 (partial term).

*Not applicable.

It was easier to invent the Senate in a quick negotiation than to find a place for it to convene. The comparison with Hungary is ironic: Hungary has a unicameral parliament but two physical meeting chambers in one building, while Poland had two functioning bodies but only one physical chamber. A new chamber has been constructed in an office building within the Sejm complex of separate but attached structures. The small membership simplified the physical task of fitting a plenum hall within a relatively narrow office building. The physical arrangement is symbolic: a remodeled addition, off to the side.

The Senate has created its own staff and support offices, not only of clerks but of advisers and experts. The Senate has its own legal staff and a committee staff. Its research staff is housed separately from that of the Sejm. Each research group occupies a different office building near the main parliamentary complex of buildings. Because they are in joint party clubs, however, senators and Sejm members are served for individual and constituency purposes in the same facilities and by the same staff. Members do not have individual offices or secretaries; such support comes through the party. Likewise, their constituency offices are supplied on a party basis.

The contrast between chamber separateness and party togetherness reflects the improvisations of early 1989. The Sejm, dominated by the two-thirds Communist-era majority and staffed only and minimally by

Communist holdovers, could not be relied on by a Solidarity-dominated Senate. The new Senate attempted to duplicate for itself the pattern of Sejm staff support offices (e.g., legal staff, committee staff, clerical support) precisely because it could not use those Sejm structures.

The new Senate could also duplicate the practice of the Communist Party in that member services were organized more through the party club than through the chamber; hence the Solidarity party club began to provide for its members what the Communist group did for its—only more so. As well-educated reformers full of enthusiasm and skilled in the use of symbols, they rapidly developed both an activist party office and a Senate staff (Orlowski 1994, 137–50). As soon as the balance of political power shifted in the Sejm (i.e., the parties allied with the ruling Communist Party became independent), the Sejm, too, rapidly expanded its support facilities. As the larger and more active chamber, the Sejm soon built a much larger staff than did the Senate.

The Senate in the National Assembly

The existence of the National Assembly—the members of the two chambers together—as a functioning body with its own rules suggests a form of tricameralism in the Polish Parliament. Its original function, electing the president, was rapidly abandoned in favor of direct popular election (Sokolewicz 1992, 88–89). Although the National Assembly did elect Wojciech Jaruzelski as president, his successors, Lech Walesa of Solidarity and Aleksander Kwasniewski of the Alliance of the Democratic Left, were directly elected in 1990 and 1995, respectively. The Senate thereby lost its most important function.

The other task of the National Assembly has been much more difficult and lasting: to enact a constitution. The Roundtable "contract," though intended as a short-term and onetime agreement in 1989, became a substitute constitution, along with limited amendments enacted as the "Little Constitution" of 1992 (Kurczewski 1993, 203; Sokolewicz 1992, 78). The revisions of 1992 assigned constitution writing to the National Assembly and defined the Senate as an integral participant in that task. The Senate thus gained in importance relative to the original 1989 pact.

The long-term task of writing a completely new and democratic constitution, rather than relying on amendments to a Communist-era one, led to formation in 1992 of the Constitution Committee, which functioned as a committee of the National Assembly rather than as a joint committee of the two chambers (Gebethner 1992a, 246–47; Sokolewicz 1992, 91–93; Winczorek 1993). The committee consisted of 10 percent of the membership of the whole National Assembly: ten from the Senate, forty-six from the Sejm. The two coalition parties held thirty-six, or 64 percent, of the committee seats. The membership consisted of legal experts as well as the party leaders from both chambers. Since there was a considerable turnover in party leadership, often by assuming executive office, there has been a corresponding instability on the political side of this committee's membership.

Before forming the Assembly committee, each chamber had formed its own Constitution Committee. The early differences between the two chambers in 1989–91 led the Senate to adopt a draft constitution that was very different from versions considered in the Sejm, largely in its emphasis on religious and cultural values ("Interim Constitution," 1992; "Poland Has a New Constitution," 1992; Rapaczynski 1991; Winczorek 1993). The Roman Catholic Conference of Bishops directed its statement on the constitution in the first term to the Senate committee, not to the Sejm's (Lisicka 1994).

While a new constitution had been predicted with confidence at the beginning of each year, it was only in summer 1996 that the Constitution Committee agreed on a document to report to the National Assembly (Karpinski 1996). The final version of the new constitution was adopted on April 3, 1997, by a 451–40 vote in the National Assembly ("Constitution Watch: Poland," 1997). In the National Assembly, the whole Parliament as a single body, the 560 members (460 from the Sejm; 100 from the Senate) vote individually, with each member's vote having equal weight. The constitution was accepted in a national referendum on May 25, 1997, by a narrow vote (57%) with a rather low voter turnout of less than 40 percent (de Weydenthal 1997).

The 1997 constitution does not markedly alter either the organization or functions of the Senate, although of course the district basis of the Senate has become an unresolved question (Constitution, Art. 97). But in the Constitution Committee, a proposal to abolish the Senate had earlier been defeated by only a three-vote margin (*OMRI Daily Digest,* January 27, 1995). Many difficult issues, such as the place of the Roman

Catholic Church (Bingen 1996) and the structure of regional and local government (Michta 1997), crowded out controversy over the Senate in both the National Assembly's and the public's deliberations and in voting on the constitution in the final months prior to the referendum.

Although the 1997 constitution retains the Senate, controversy continues about its powers and dignity. For example, the National Assembly retains responsibilities concerning the president, thereby elevating the importance of the Senate. Both the impeachment and swearing in of the president belong to the National Assembly. During the conflictual presidency of Lech Walesa, impeachment was something more than an abstract concept (Jasiewicz 1997). The difficulties of working through the National Assembly are illustrated by the choices and distinctions made at the inauguration of the new president in 1995. The swearing-in ceremony was conducted by the National Assembly. After a brief recess, the president then addressed the same parliamentarians in a different form, as a joint session of the Sejm and Senate (Donosy, December 28, 1995).

The Senate in Retrospect

In postcommunist Central Europe with bicameral parliaments, the Polish Senate illustrates the typical circumstances of an upper chamber that finds itself secondary in legislative authority and function. It is subordinate and inferior to the Sejm, or main chamber, of the Polish Parliament.

The Polish Senate is an institution in search of a mission. A stable democratic Poland might not create a new Senate if one did not already exist. The Senate emerged a democratic token, offered by the Communists to Solidarity, and it became a key component of the electoral dynamic that, unexpectedly to all participants, led to the change of regime. But once having served its function as electoral symbol, it has become a legislative puzzle. What can it do constructively? Coordination between the two chambers is a political problem, while the timing and sequencing of Senate action relative to the Sejm have become difficult practical problems to resolve.

The Polish Senate has experienced several changes in its first decade of existence. Those changes have been more in its external relations than in its internal organization and procedure. As a new body, the Senate simply began with the institutional structure of the Sejm. The more important changes for the Senate in the initial decade of postcommunist democratization have been in its relationship with the Sejm. First, the Senate's Constitution Committee was absorbed into a National Assembly with its own Constitution Committee, thereby reducing the autonomy of Senate-centric decision making on that topic. Second, its lively disagreements with the Sejm were made more subject to the Sejm's final decisions through simplification of the Sejm's own internal rules. Third, its disagreements with the Sejm on policy and its resentment of the Sejm's unilateral rules changes were dismissed by the judgment of an external judicial body.

In the context set by these externally induced changes, the Senate has actively exercised its review function over Sejm-adopted legislation. A sizable proportion of Sejm bills have been amended and a few rejected. Although the statistics are imprecise on this point, it appears that the Sejm has accepted at least some Senate amendments to most of the bills on which it has proposed amendments. The Senate's initiative on new legislation, however, has been less successful in the Sejm.

Both the purposes and structure of the Senate have been in dispute. It is now continued as a legislative chamber, but it could have been supplanted by a corporatist body. Its electoral basis is likely to be greatly altered through a redefinition of its districts. Should the two chambers diverge greatly in party composition, one of them could support the president against the other. The more likely these possibilities are, however, the more we might anticipate political parties to coordinate their campaigns before the election and their party clubs afterward. Nevertheless, the most important contribution of the Senate to the new postcommunist democracy of Poland has been in the regime transformation process itself. The mark of its success as electoral symbol is that its current rationale in the legislative process in a stable democracy has been, and remains, open to question.

References

Bingen, Dieter. 1996. "Katholische Kirche un Demokratie in Polen, 1990–1995." *Berichte des Bundesinstituts für ostwissenschaftliche und internationale Studien* (Cologne), no. 1.

Burda, Andrzej. 1978. *Parliament of the Polish People's Republic.* Wrocław: Ossolineum.

"Constitution Watch: Poland." 1997. *East European Constitutional Review* 6:20–22.

de Weydenthal, Jan. 1997. "Poland/Slovakia: The Tale of Two Referenda." *RFE/RL News Feature* (May 26) (World Wide Web).

Dirksen Electoral Archive. 1997. Elections in Poland. (Www.Agora.stm.it/elections/election/poland.htm).

Donosy 1995–96. (Warsaw; via email.)

Elster, Jon. 1993. "Constitution-making in Eastern Europe: Rebuilding the Boat in the Open Sea." In *Administrative Transformation in Central and Eastern Europe*, ed. Joachim Jens Hesse. Oxford: Blackwell.

Gebethner, Stanislaw. 1992a. "Political Institutions in the Process of Transition to a Postsocialist Formation: Polish and Comparative Perspectives." In *Escape from Socialism: The Polish Route*, ed. Walter D. Connor and Piotr Ploszajski. Warsaw: IFiS.

———. 1992b. "Political Reform in the Process of Round Table Negotiations." In *Democratization in Poland, 1988–90*, ed. George Sanford. New York: St. Martin's Press.

———. 1993. "Political Parties in Poland (1989–1993)." In *Die politischen Kulturen Ostmitteleuropas im Umbruch*, ed. Gerd Meyer. Tübingen: Francke Verlag.

———. 1995. "System Wyborczy: Deformacja czy Reprezentacja?" In *Wybory Parlamentarne 1991 i 1993*, ed. Stanislaw Gebethner. Warsaw: Wydawnictwo Sejmowe.

Gebethner, Stanislaw, and Krzysztof Jasiewicz. 1993. "Poland." *European Journal of Political Research* 24:519–35.

Hausner, Jerzy, and Witold Morawski. 1994. "Tripartism in Poland." In *Tripartism in Central and Eastern Europe: Roundtable Conference National Reports*, vol. 2. Budapest.

Hibbing, John R., and Samuel C. Patterson. 1994. "The Emergence of Democratic Parliaments in Central and Eastern Europe." In *Parliaments in the Modern World*, ed. Gary W. Copeland and Samuel C. Patterson. Ann Arbor: University of Michigan Press.

"Interim Constitution Approved in Poland." 1992. *East European Constitutional Review* 1 (summer): 2 (World Wide Web).

Jackiewicz, Irena, and Zbigniew Jackiewicz. 1996. "The Polish Parliament in Transition: Search for a Model." In *Parliaments and Organized Interests: The Second Steps*, ed. Attila Ágh and Gabriella Ilonski. Budapest: Hungarian Center for Democracy Studies.

Jalowiecki, Bohdan. 1996. *Oblicza polskich regionow*. Warsaw: University of Warsaw, Europejski Instytut, Studia Regionalne i Loakalne.

Jasiewicz, Krzysztof. 1992a. "Poland." *European Journal of Political Research* 22:489–504.

———. 1992b. "Elections and Political Change in Eastern Europe." In *Developments in East European Politics*, ed. Stephen White, Judy Batt, and Paul Lewis. Durham, N.C.: Duke University Press.

———. 1997. "Poland: Walesa's Legacy to the Presidency." In *Postcommunist Presidents*, ed. Ray Taras. Cambridge: Cambridge University Press.

Jaskiernia, Jerzy. 1994. *Wizja parlamentu w nowej konstytucji Rzecspos-politej Polskiej.* Warsaw: Wyd. Sejmowe.

Jedruch, Jacek. 1992. "Revival of the Senate of Poland in the Light of Its History." In *Bicameralisme, Tweekamerstelsel vroeger en nu,* 395–408. Handelingen van de Internationale Conferentie ter gelegenheid van het 175-jarig bestaan van de Eerste Kamer der Staten Generaal in de Nederlanden.

Karpinski, Jakub. 1995. "Setting the Stage for the Presidential Election." *Transition* 1 (November 20): 40–43.

———. 1996. "Poland Has a Constitution Draft." *OMRI Analytical Brief* 1 (June 20): 187 (World Wide Web).

Kurczewski, Jacek. 1993. "Democracy and the Rule of Law: Poland after 1989." In *Constitutionalism and Politics: Proceedings Fourth International Bratislava Symposium,* ed. Irena Grudzinska Gross. Bratislava: Slovak Committee of the European Cultural Foundation and American Council of Learned Societies.

Lewis, Paul. 1990. "Non-Competitive Elections and Regime Change: Poland 1989." *Parliamentary Affairs* 43:90–107.

———. 1995. "Poland's New Parties in the Postcommunist Political System." In *Party Formation in East-Central Europe,* ed. Gordon Wightman. Aldershot, U.K.: Edward Elgar.

Lisicka, Halina. 1994. "Role Kosciola Katolickiego w Systemie Politycznym RP." In *Ewolucja Polskiego Systemu Politycznego po 1989 Roku w Swietle Komparatystycznej Teorii Polityki,* ed. Andrzej Antoszewski. Wrocław: Wyd. Universytetu Wroclawskiego.

Los, Maria. 1994. "Property Rights, Market and Historical Justice: Legislative Discourses in Poland." *International Journal of the Sociology of Law* 22:39–58.

———. 1995. "Lustration and Truth Claims: Unfinished Revolutions in Central Europe." *Law and Social Inquiry* 20:117–61.

———. 1996. "In the Shadow of Totalitarian Law." In *Totalitarian and Post-Totalitarian Law,* ed. Adam Podgorecki and Vittorio Olgiati. Aldershot, U.K.: Dartmouth.

Mason, David. 1991. "The Polish Parliament and Labour Legislation during Solidarity." In *Legislatures in the Policy Process,* ed. David M. Olson and Michael L. Mezey. Cambridge: Cambridge University Press.

Michta, Andrew A. 1997. "Poland after Communism: The Question of Democratic Consolidation." In *The Consolidation of Democracy in East Central Europe,* ed. Karen Dawisha and Bruce Parrott. Cambridge: Cambridge University Press.

Olson, David M. 1993a. "Compartmentalized Competition: The Managed Transitional Election System of Poland." *Journal of Politics* 55:415–41.

———. 1993b. "Political Parties and Party Systems in Regime Transformation: Inner Transition in the New Democracies of Central Europe." *American Review of Politics* 14:619–58.

———. 1998a. "Party Formation and Party System Consolidation in the New Democracies of Central Europe." *Political Studies* (UK) 40.3:432–64.

————. 1998b. "The Parliaments of New Democracies and the Politics of Representation." In *Developments in Central and East European Politics,* 2d ed., ed. Stephen White et al. London: Macmillan.

Olson, David M., and Maurice D. Simon. 1982. "The Institutional Development of a Minimal Parliament: The Case of the Polish Sejm." In *Communist Legislatures in Comparative Perspective,* ed. Daniel Nelson and Stephen White. London: Macmillan.

Olson, David M., Ania van der Meer-Krok-Paszkowska, Maurice D. Simon, and Irena Jackiewicz. 1998. "Committees in the Post-Communist Polish Sejm: Structure, Activity, and Members." *Journal of Legislative Studies* 4:101–23.

Open Media Research Institute (OMRI) Daily Digest. 1994–96 (World Wide Web).

Orlowski, Wojciech. 1994. "Senat Rzeczypospolitej Polskiej I kadencji 1989–1991." Lublin: Uniwersytet Marii Curie-Sklodowskiej, Wydzial Prawa i Administracji. Rozprawa doktorska napisana pod kierunk iem naukowym.

Osiatynski, Wiktor. 1996. "An Interview with Hanna Suchocka on Church-State Relations." *East European Constitutional Review* 5:48–50.

"Poland Has a New Constitution as Conflict between Two Chambers of Parliament Continues." 1992. *East European Constitutional Review* 1:3 (World Wide Web).

Poland. Sejm. 1994. Przewodnik, II Kadencja (Membership Directory, Term II). Warsaw: Sejm Publishers.

————. Sejm. 1995. Informacja o dzialalnosci Sejmu, II Kadencja, 1993–1995 (Information on Sejm Activity, Term II). Warsaw: Sejm Publishers.

————. Sejm. 1997. Private communications. Sejm Research Office.

Poland. Senate. 1991. Wybrane dane o pracy Senatu Rzeczypospolitej Polskiej, I Kadancja (Selected Data on the Activities of the Senate of the Polish Republic, Term I). Warsaw: Senate Chancellery.

————. Senate. 1993 III Kadencja (Membership Directory, Term III). Warsaw: Senate Chancellery.

————. Senate. 1993. Wybrane dane o pracy Senatu Rzeczypospolitej Polskie, II Kadencja (Selected Data on the Activities of the Senate of the Polish Republic, Term II). Warsaw Senate Chancellery.

————. Senate. 1994. Wybrane dane o pracy Senatu Rzeczypospolitej Polskiej, III Kadencya (15 X 1993 r. Do 14 X 1994 r.) (Selected Data on the Activities of the Senate of the Polish Republic, Term III, Oct. 15, 1993–Oct. 14, 1994). Warsaw: Senate Chancellery.

Rapaczynski, Andrej. 1991. "Constitutional Politics in Poland: A Report on the Constitutional Committee of the Polish Parliament." *University of Chicago Law Review* 58:595–631.

Rose, Richard, Neil Munro, and Tom Mackie. 1998. "Elections in Central and Eastern Europe since 1990." *Studies in Public Policy #300.* Glasgow: Centre for the Study of Public Policy.

Rundquist, Paul. 1994. "Institutionalizing the Polish Parliament." Paper presented at the annual meeting of the International Political Science Association, Berlin.

Sarnecki, Pawel. 1995. *Senat RP a Sejm i Zgromadzenie Narodowe.* Warsaw: Wydawnictwo Sejmowe.

Sokolewicz, Wojciech. 1992. "The Legal-Constitutional Bases of Democratisation in Poland: Systemic and Constitutional Change." In *Democratization in Poland, 1988–90,* ed. George Sanford. New York: St. Martin's Press.

Vinton, Louisa. 1992. "Poland's 'Little Constitution' Clarifies Walesa's Powers." *RFE/RL Research Report* 35 (September 4): 19–26.

Wiatr, Jerzy. 1992. "Fragmented Parties in a New Democracy: Poland." Paper presented at a conference on Political Parties in the New Democracies, Vienna.

Wightman, Gordon. 1995. "The Development of the Party System and the Breakup of Czechoslovakia." In *Party Formation in East-Central Europe,* ed. Gordon Wightman. Aldershot, U.K.: Edward Elgar.

Winczorek, Piotr. 1993. "Political Aspects of Constitutional Reforms in the Republic of Poland during Years 1989–1993." Paper presented at a conference, Indiana University.

Wojtyczek, Krzysztof. 1994. "Un nouveau régime parlementaire rationalisé: La Pologne." *Revue du Droit Public et de la Science Politique en France et à l'Etranger* 110: 379–99.

Zakrzewski, Witold. 1982. "Die gesetzgeberische Taetigkeit des Parlaments (Sejm) der Volkerepublik Polen in der VIII Legislaturperiode bis 13, December 1981." *Ost-Europa Recht* 3:210–14.

11 Senates: A Comparative Perspective

ANTHONY MUGHAN AND SAMUEL C. PATTERSON

One of the more momentous and sweeping political developments of modern times has been the tide of democratization that has engulfed the formerly authoritarian regimes of Eastern Europe, Southern Europe, and Latin America over the last two decades or so. Among the welcome consequences of this quest for democracy has been a resurgence of interest among political scientists and policy makers alike in constitutions, constitutional engineering, and institution building. Specifically, the question now widely asked is: What are the institutional arrangements making for lasting, stable, and effective democratic government?

The plethora of efforts to answer this question has produced a large literature on the relative advantages and shortcomings of parliamentary as opposed to quasi-presidential and presidential forms of government (e.g., Lijphart 1992; Linz and Valenzuela 1994; Sartori 1997; von Mettenheim 1997; and Weaver and Rockman 1993). Likewise, the merits and demerits of various types and mixes of electoral systems have been subjected to extensive analysis with a view to determining, among other things, their origins and their effects on the structure of party systems, patterns of representation, and the making and unmaking of governments (e.g., Cox 1997; Farrell 1997; Lijphart 1994). But perhaps the sharpest break with the past has come with the restoration, after decades of close to total neglect, of bicameralism to the status of an institutional arrangement worthy of investigation and discussion outside the narrow confines of the United States, with its clearly powerful and influential upper house (e.g., Levmore 1992; Mastias and Grangé 1987; Riker 1992a, 1992b; Trivelli 1975; and Tsebelis and Money 1997).

Political science interest in such topics as presidentialism vs. parliamentarism and majoritarian vs. proportional electoral systems was kept alive during the cold war era by concern about the policy immobilism and democratic instability that was, or had at some point been, characteristic of political life in a number of Western European countries. Was French democracy better served by the abandonment in the Fifth Republic of the traditional republican ethos of parliamentary supremacy and its replacement by a presidentialist regime? What has been the role of electoral systems in explaining the rapid governmental turnover and policy deadlock characteristic of Weimar Germany, postwar Italy, and the Third and Fourth French Republics? Conversely, what has been the contribution of Germany's mixed proportional, first-past-the-post electoral system to the stable and effective democratic government that has been that country's post–World War II political hallmark?

Invisible Upper Houses

Studies addressing these and similar questions inevitably and unquestioningly focused on the directly elected lower house of national parliaments. With the glaring exception of the United States where the Senate was universally accepted as being central to the policy-making process, the role of upper houses in shaping how governments perform and what they do was largely ignored. The de facto working model for the world's parliamentary democracies seems to have been a British House of Lords that the 1911 and 1949 Acts of Parliament had stripped of all its powers except the ability to delay nonfinancial legislation for up to one year. As Tsebelis and Money (1997, 1) point out, one measure of the common and longstanding disregard for upper houses is not only that Norton's (1990) "collection of the most influential articles written about legislatures fails to include a single article on bicameralism, but also . . . the articles themselves do not address the distinction between unicameral and bicameral legislatures."

This neglect of the political role and performance of upper houses in parliamentary democracies is to be regretted for at least two reasons. In the first place, it discouraged recognition of the basic fact that their relationship to lower houses is variable; not all senates are, or were in the past, as constitutionally helpless vis-à-vis the lower house as the British House of Lords. Constitutionally speaking, for example, the Italian and Romanian senates enjoy the same legislative powers as their lower houses.

In the second place, and in direct consequence, neglecting a significant actor in the legislative process encouraged a no more than partial understanding of the actions and inactions of democratic governments. A case in point is the democratic stability literature in which the party system was usually the keystone of explanations of the rapid turnover of coalition governments. Especially notable is Sartori's (1966) seminal argument that this turnover was a function not of multiple parties and coalition government per se but of "polarized pluralism." In other words, the essence of the instability problem in France, Italy, and the like was the existence of popular antisystem parties at the left and right poles of the party system that forced relatively centrist, pro-system parties into uneasy and fragile coalitions that often split apart when difficult decisions had to be made. Ignored in such party system-based explanations of patterns of governmental instability, however, were differences in constitutional and institutional structure. What, for example, was the impact on their longevity of Italian governments being, unlike their French or Weimar German counterparts, answerable to both houses and having to secure majority support for their policy initiatives in both houses and not just effectively in the lower one?

Nor is the neglect of senates restricted to this particular body of literature. Rather, it has been, and continues to be, pervasive. Take, for example, a 1997 textbook on European politics that came across our desks by chance. After distinguishing between unicameralism and bicameralism and providing information on the names of the two chambers in individual national parliaments, the number of seats in them, and the term lengths of members, it then goes on to ignore the upper houses. Discussing the "work of parliaments," it quickly narrows its focus to encompass lower houses only. "In general terms, parliaments act as a means of communication between the people and the government. They (or at least their lower chambers) are composed of elected representatives of the people. Together, these elected representatives have the authority to hold the government accountable to the people" (Roberts and Hogwood 1997, 196–97). Skirted is the question of whether senates play a significant role in making governments accountable. If they do, or indeed if they do not, what work do they do? How do they organize themselves to go about doing it? With what consequences? As in the textbooks generally, these and similar questions are assumed to be irrelevant to the study of parliamentary government and democracy.

Senates: A Reappraisal

This book essentially puts this assumption to the empirical test in a number of countries deliberately chosen for their variation in characteristics, like state structure, constitutional status of the upper house, and the method of recruitment of its members, which can be expected to influence the political role that upper houses play in democratic political systems. This test has necessarily involved two objectives. The first of them is descriptive. For want especially of relevant English-language literature, it has been incumbent on the individual chapters of this book to provide details about how upper houses in a range of countries actually work. At the moment, basic descriptive information of the kind that is plentiful about lower houses, political executives, and other institutions of government is simply lacking when it comes to second chambers. With the exception of the U.S. Senate, little is known about upper houses individually, and even less is known about them in comparison with each other.[1] How were they formed, and with what purposes? Where do their members come from, and how did they get there? What is their constitutional role in the legislative process, and how reflective is it of the role they actually play?

Our second objective has been to highlight what should have long been obvious from even the most cursory glance at the constitutions of many new and established democracies: upper houses exist for a reason, and bicameralism is important for the theory and practice of democratic government. The importance of these parliamentary institutions is manifold, potentially encompassing instrumental considerations like influence on legislation, and symbolic ones like enhancing democratic legitimacy by checking the majoritarian impulses of single-party governments. In this volume, issues of space and complexity have meant that importance has been defined narrowly to encompass senates' performance of the two functions most commonly attributed to them: representation and redundancy.

The immediate impression to emerge from these studies of upper houses in many of the more important new and established democracies today is one of a variety and complexity that might seem at first glance to stand in the way of progress toward a systematic understanding of the factors conditioning their political performance. All are unique in a number of important respects, some because, as with the House of Lords, their evolution is deeply rooted in an atypical pattern of national historical and political development, and others because, as with the Polish Senate, they represent the result of a negotiated settlement between conservatives and reformers, the product of a constellation of political forces and circumstances at a particular juncture in the nation's political development. Some have large memberships, and some have small ones. Some are elected bodies, some appointed, and still others employ mixed recruitment criteria. Some exist in federal systems of government, and some exist in unitary ones. Some have a territorial representational base, whereas others do not. Some enjoy coequal powers with the lower house, while the majority are constitutionally and self-consciously subordinated to it because they do not enjoy the same democratic legitimacy that comes with direct, popular election.

Lessons from Nine Senates

The list could go on, but no amount of detail on differences should be allowed to shortchange what senates have in common. Variety and complexity notwithstanding, a number of general conclusions emerge clearly from the case studies in this volume.

Cameral Inequality

The first, and most general, of these conclusions relates to the position of upper houses in the larger political system. The United States Senate has come to enjoy remarkable prestige and power. But senates in parliamentary systems of government generally enjoy less prestige and power than lower houses. Most often, as in the case of the House of Lords and the Canadian, French, and Spanish senates, this is the result of constitutional dictate. But even when constitutions mandate formal equality between the houses, this does not always translate into actual equality. Italy is a good example. Its two houses are directly elected and coequal in power, yet dissatisfaction with bicameralism has translated into proposals to abolish the Senate and not the Chamber of Deputies. Lodici explains lower house primacy in a formally equal bicameral system in terms of "the major influences on Italian public opinion" coming from the Chamber of Deputies, "which prefers a senate whose role is one of mediation, wisdom, and moderation, and not a senate with coequal legislative or government-making power."

Essentially Contested Institutions

This argument leads directly to the second general conclusion to emerge from the chapters in this volume, and it is that, be they fixtures of unitary or federal states and regardless of their power relative to the lower house, parliamentary upper houses are "essentially contested" institutions in the sense that their very existence is inherently a matter of dispute (Gallie 1955–56). Many countries choose not to have one, others have them but then do away with them, and still others keep them but are engaged in an apparently incessant dialogue about how they should be reformed. None of this is true, of course, of the United States where a governing philosophy of minoritarian democracy and a constitutional separation of powers legitimize opposition to the House of Representatives, even if it comes from political actors who, unlike members of the lower house, are not themselves directly elected, e.g., the president, justices of the Supreme Court, or senators before 1913. The overriding goal of democratic government is to protect the interests of minorities against the potential tyranny of the majority. By contrast, parliamentary systems of government are based on a majoritarian philosophy of democracy and a fusion of governmental powers. Their overriding goal is to allow the popular will, as expressed in periodic elections, to be put into practice for as long as the government legally holds office and can retain the support of a majority of elected representatives.

The problem with upper houses is their very existence places parliamentary democracies on the horns of a dilemma. On the one hand, senates can be politically useful in practice. They can, for example, provide representation to self-consciously distinctive territorial or functional groups, thereby assuring them that their rights are protected in national government. Examples are the states in federal systems like Australia, the localities and autonomous communities in unitary states like France and Spain, respectively, or the hereditary aristocracy in Britain. Equally, upper houses can do much useful work reviewing lower house legislative proposals, offering more or less friendly amendments and tidying up their language—busy work that overcommitted lower houses generally do not have the time or the inclination to do for themselves. But performance of these representational and redundancy functions is bought at a price, which is that upper house influence runs counter to the basic principle of majoritarian democracy that political authority derives only from election by the people. The quandary, therefore, is how to reconcile the usefulness of institutions that are not always directly elected with an influence on policy that is not their democratic right.

The simple answer might seem to be to have them directly elected, just like lower houses, but there are good theoretical and practical reasons why this recourse is not a solution to the problem. The theoretical impediment is that, in dispersing democratic authority, the principle of the fusion of powers, with its concentration of decision-making power in the lower house, is breached and the direct and focused governmental accountability that is the hallmark of parliamentary democracy is diluted. The practical disincentives are two. First, for parliamentary governments to create directly elected upper houses would be potentially to create a whip for their own backs. Direct election would endow senates with the same democratic legitimacy as lower houses and, especially when controlled by a different partisan majority, would turn them into a competitor for the political authority and decision-making power that lower houses now generally monopolize. Second, a potential casualty of coequal powers, apparent to would-be reformers of Italy's coequal senate, is legislative efficiency; it simply takes longer to pass legislation if the reconciliation of differences has to be pursued within and between lower and upper houses coequal in power and status.

The upshot of this situation is that senates in parliamentary democracies are forever under the microscope of parliamentary reform. Rarely are all significant political actors satisfied with the balance that is achieved between the criteria according to which senators are recruited and the powers of influence and veto that they enjoy. Governments in lower houses want senates that are useful to them in largely administrative and apolitical ways and that do not compete with them for influence, sometimes final decision, in the legislative process. This ideal may come close to realization when partisan majorities in the two houses coincide, but a foul is called when the senate majority is different and demands concessions in return for its legislative cooperation and agreement.

The democratic reality of alternating governments thus dooms senates to a life of uncertainty, and their general lack of democratic legitimacy leaves them in a weak position to defend themselves against political opponents demanding their reform. It is not important that demands for reform may arise less out of consideration for representative democracy and more out of the frustration of governments constituted from lower houses whose legislative proposals have met with repeated upper house resistance. The reality is that, whatever the reason, senate reform is a perennial item on the political agenda of parliamentary democracies, perhaps because the threat of reform provides valuable leverage for governments wanting to influence senate behavior. Again, the U.S. Senate stands as unusually immune from most such demands because of its exalted constitutional status in a system of separated powers.

Senates Matter: Representation

The pervasive and apparently endless debate about senate reform leads inexorably to our next conclusion: senates are influential and important parliamentary bodies. If they were not, why would lower houses strive so hard to strike a more appropriate balance—from their perspective— between themselves and upper house usefulness and influence? However, it is manifest that the extent to which senates are consequential varies according to the function performed; generally speaking, their behavior is structured less by performance of the representation function than by the redundancy one. Accordingly, we consider senate functions separately, taking representation first.

There are a number of reasons why the notion of representing a constituency, be it territorially or functionally defined, is less relevant to understanding the work and achievements of senates than is the notion of overseeing and influencing the actions of government. One is that members of upper houses do not always have clear constituencies that they represent and to which they are accountable. This is especially obvious in cases where members acquire their position through right of birth or governmental appointment and retain it for life, as, for example, in the British House of Lords and the Canadian Senate. The most that can be said in such instances is that members' responsibility is to the constitution, good government, improving the quality of legislation, or the like. This is not representation in the usual sense in which that concept is used (Pitkin 1967).

A second reason is that even where there is a clear territorial base to senate representation, the behavior of the upper house can be more sensitive to the dictates of partisan competition with a lower house controlled by a different political party or combinations of parties. In some cases, interhouse conflict may signal representative democracy at work in the sense that the elected partisan majorities in the two houses represent different constituencies, and their disagreements properly reflect the contrasting interests of these constituencies. A particularly clear example of this situation occurs when the U.S. Senate is controlled by one party and the House of Representatives by the other. In parliamentary Germany, the federal government frequently has been dominated by one major party, currently the Christian Democrats (CDU/CSU), and state governments have been controlled by its rival, the Socialists (SPD).

However, the upper house's performance of a legitimate representative function becomes far more questionable when its entrenched and unelected partisan majority is able to hinder, and even thwart, the will of the popular majority in the lower house. This situation was evident in the obstructionism of the appointed Liberal majority in the Canadian Senate during the time that Prime Minister Mulroney's Progressive Conservative government was in office. Even direct election does not always guarantee the primacy of representative over partisan motivations in upper house behavior. In Australia's version of "divided government," for example, determined Senate minorities have thwarted a succession of majority governments in pursuit of their own partisan agenda.

In sum, then, it is clear that senates do not always represent a constituency, territorial or otherwise, to which they are democratically accountable. They do sometimes, and their actions reflect it. But it is also the case that their actions are sometimes explicable only in terms of their "knee jerk" desire to influence, perhaps even foil, the ambitions of a partisan majority in the lower house with which they instinctively disagree.

Senates Matter: Redundancy

Whether senates pursue partisan goals, representative ones, or a mixture of the two, they do have in common their performance of the redundancy function; they serve to bring a "bicameral perspective" and influence to bear on the legislative process. Our fourth conclusion follows directly from this observation: senates tend to have an important impact on the shaping of legislative policy outputs. Of course, constitutional provision and political circumstance mean that senates are at different points in time influential to different degrees in their performance of the redundancy function. At the same time, the essays in this volume give no indication that any of the nine upper houses investigated can be dismissed as being unworthy of detailed study for want, to use Bagehot's apt phrase, of playing no more than a "dignified" role in government. This conclusion is hardly novel and is perhaps best taken as simply emphasizing a point too infrequently appreciated and made by scholars of national legislatures other than the U.S. Congress. After all, if upper houses are widely perceived to play no useful role in their country's legislative process, then their elimination, seen in post–World War II Denmark, New Zealand, and Sweden, would be a more common phenomenon.

Still, it remains the case that the role of upper houses in the legislative process has long been ignored. At least part of the reason seems to be conflicting perceptions of what "mattering" means in this context. The maximalist position is that it entails some kind of power equality with the lower house. In Spain, for example, some proponents of senate reform argue that if the Senate has no role in appointing or dismissing governments, then its "influence in other respects will be close to zero," as Flores points out. By this measure, of upper houses studied in this book located in parliamentary systems, only Italy can be said to have a senate that matters. To make this claim, though, is clearly untenable given, for example, that slightly more than half the bills passed in Germany require the Bundesrat's consent.

The more moderate and realistic position would seem that senate influence does not manifest itself only through victory in open clashes of will with the lower house and its governing majority. Upper houses also have real influence when their anticipated reaction is taken into account in the writing of a bill, when they amend or improve the text of government proposals, or when they oblige the government or lower house to make concessions in, for example, conference committee to prevent recourse to the suspensory veto at one extreme or, where it is constitutionally possible, outright rejection at the other. Examples of this more subtle kind of influence in its various manifestations are legion in political systems like Britain, Canada, France, Poland, and Spain, where the upper house boasts no more than the most modest constitutional powers vis-à-vis the lower house.

The Growing Importance of Senates

The fifth conclusion to be suggested by these chapters is the most interesting and exciting of all: senates take on greater institutional importance today in the shaping of legislative policy outputs than they did in the not-so-distant past. That is, they have become more legislatively assertive in relation to the lower houses despite the constitutional rules governing their interaction not having changed. In the Canadian case, Franks traces this change to the elevation to office in 1984 of a Progressive Conservative majority government after a protracted period of Liberal hegemony and the Liberal Party's continuing domination of the senate. A little less precisely, Uhr attributes the rejuvenation of the Australian Senate to "the arrival (in the late 1960s) of the second wave of minor parties which were less committed to shoring up the major parties in government." Shell, in contrast, writes in relatively unspecific terms of the House of Lords having "in the past few decades actually become of greater significance." Similar disjunctures, or cycles of assertiveness, can be identified in France, the United States, and other countries.

Whatever its timing in individual cases, this development underscores the need for students of comparative democratic politics to take senates more seriously than they have done in the past, not least because the reasons for it make it most unlikely that it is a development that will be reversed. These reasons are interactive and can be placed in three categories: (1) partisan competition, (2) respect, and (3) the crystallization of competing philosophies of government in lower and upper houses.

The most obvious reason for the increased competition for legislative influence between lower and upper houses is the more frequent incidence of ideological differences between the political parties in control of the two chambers. This is starkly obvious in the case of Canada where, after a long period of Liberal government and a long train of Liberal appointees to the Senate, a Progressive Conservative government came to power in the 1980s. The Liberal-dominated Senate decided to break with tradition and use the constitutional and political resources at its disposal systematically to frustrate the will of the popularly elected Conservative government in the House of Commons. Similar tensions have been periodically evident in France, whose centrist senate has often found itself strongly opposed to policies favored by left- and right-wing presidents with their often compliant governing majorities in the Chamber of Deputies. Patzelt notes as well that "a great deal of criticism has been leveled at the Bundesrat for functioning as a partisan 'second opposition' to the federal government. Most of it has been motivated by considerations of political expediency as partisan groups seek to discredit competitors in the public eye."

However, partisan competition alone does not explain increased upper house assertiveness. The House of Lords, for example, retained its built-in Conservative majority throughout the eighteen years of Conservative government from 1979 to 1997, but it still functioned during this period as what Shell terms "the other Opposition." Equally, Mastias shows the French Senate to have had better relations with some Socialist governments than others during the Mitterand presidencies. This is because a second factor affecting interhouse relations independently of partisan competition has been the respect shown to upper houses by their lower house counterparts. At the extreme, such respect has been notable for its total absence—witness General de Gaulle's attempt to deprive the French Senate of all political power in the 1969 referendum.

More commonly, senates have shown resentment of, and resistance to, lower houses' efforts to bypass their scrutiny by ignoring or overriding their recommendations for change to legislative proposals, setting their agendas, and overburdening them with work, especially at critical points in the legislative calendar. Among the reactions of angry governments has been public denigration. Thus, Canadian Prime Minister Mulroney described his country's senators as "has-beens and never-weres," while Paul Keating, the Australian prime minister, depicted their antipodean counterparts as the "unrepresentative swill" of Australian politics. In a similarly derogatory vein, a senior Labour politician in Britain recently justified government plans to restrict the powers of hereditary peers by dismissing them as "that cast of a Gilbert and Sullivan opera in the House of Lords" (*Guardian,* September 11, 1997).

Both the cause and consequence of such tensions is perhaps the most durable source of increased senate assertiveness, and it is the crystalliza-tion of divergent views of the nature of democracy itself in lower and upper houses. The lower house view is the conventional majoritarian one that legitimate political power and its exercise emanates, and should ema-nate, from the mandate conferred by direct, popular election and the maintenance of majority support in the lower house. Under these circum-stances, senates with no popular mandate do not have the democratic right to question and frustrate the wishes of the lower house. Franks sum-marizes this conception of democracy nicely for Canada: "Effective par-liamentary democracy demands both an opposition which can present itself as a credible alternative to the government, and parliamentary pro-cesses which enable the opposition to criticize government policies effec-tively, and hold the government accountable for its stewardship. These core activities are highly partisan in nature, and their legitimacy derives from their support through the democratic election of members to the House of Commons. The Senate is appointed, not elected." Upper house members themselves have shown that they do not always hove to this view. One counter argument they have made is that, even if not elected, upper houses still have a constitutional duty to perform and cannot stand by passively when they see governments with a safe, disciplined majority in the lower house overstep their powers, especially when, as in Britain, they are not accountable for their actions to a higher constitutional au-thority. In the words of one Conservative peer in the House of Lords jus-tifying resistance in the 1970s to highly contentious Labour government legislation proposing to hedge freedom of the press: "We have no personal interest to defend in this matter: we have a constitutional duty to perform, and a constitutional responsibility to carry out. We have sought to discharge that duty and responsibility" (quoted in Baldwin 1995, 226).

Less spectacular than constitutional confrontation is the risk that majoritarianism degenerates into tyranny and disregard for the rights of minorities. For instance, echoing America's Founders, Riker (1992a) holds that a powerful upper house is to be welcomed for the role it plays in preventing majority tyranny and protecting minority interests. For this minoritarian conception of democracy, what is important is to have effective devices, like independent upper houses, that help to prevent majoritarian government, protect minorities, and thereby discourage the passage of legislation for which there may be an inevitably transient parliamentary majority, but for which there is no underlying consensus in the society as a whole. Thus, Australian and Canadian senators have justified their obstructionism by arguing that their actions better allow for the representation and protection of minorities in the general context of disciplined, majoritarian decision taking in the lower house. French senators, for their part, have sought to achieve this same goal by another route, namely, by resorting to the Constitutional Council to protect individual rights and freedoms in particular.

Partisan competition, private and public respect, and divergent conceptions of democracy all conspire to ensure an ongoing tension and conflict of interests between lower and upper houses in bicameral systems of government. Short of sweeping reform, there is little likelihood that the resultant competition between them will disappear. It may well ebb and flow as, for example, majorities in the two houses become more or less alike, but the reality, and likely persistence in lower houses, of executive dominance, disciplined voting, and disregard for opposing viewpoints means that intercameral tension and disagreement will remain part of the grist of "normal" democratic politics and, as such, will need to figure as a matter of course in accounts of the legislative process and governmental policy outputs.

Concluding Remarks

In sum, upper houses are important for legislative politics and outcomes, even in parliamentary democracies where they are endowed with few constitutional powers. In member states of the European Union, at least, their role in the legislative process is even likely to grow as domestic parliaments have to deal with more and more legislative initiatives emanating from Brussels and Strasbourg. The German Bundesrat is a good example of an institution that has already turned the flow of European legislation to its political advantage. As Patzelt notes, "There have been few serious discussions of reform of the Bundesrat." It has "adapted to new situations by taking preemptive measures when the clear need for reform has arisen. The best example has been the creation of its EU-Chamber in response to the growing volume and importance of European legislation."

The future points to upper houses having an evident, perhaps growing, and minimally cyclical importance in the democratic legislative process. Their political role therefore needs to be better understood in at least two respects. First, the internal decision-making dynamics of senates need to be better understood. Until now, upper houses have tended to be seen from a bicameral perspective, and their interactions with lower houses and the government of the day have been the central analytical focus. Questions concerning the outcome of conference committees or the results derived from shuttling legislative proposals between legislative houses, the number of upper house amendments accepted or overturned in the lower house, and government strategies for building and maintaining support in the upper house have dominated the scholarship on senates. Relatively little research has been conducted on the dynamics by which senates arrive at the positions they take to the conference committee table or by which they choose to veto legislative proposals rather than amend them. In short, little is known about the inner workings of upper houses, about what goes on within them, before they interact with the lower house.

This point is nicely illustrated by Sinclair's analysis of the U.S. Senate. The other country chapters have a distinctly bicameral perspective, focusing mainly on the various interactions between governments and upper houses. Relatively little is said about the internal organizational characteristics and political dynamics of the upper houses themselves. By contrast, the analysis of the U.S. Senate mainly concerns the institution in its own right, with only secondary consideration given to the Senate's relations with the House of Representatives, and tertiary attention to the interactions of the Senate with the president.

The same kind of approach, yielding the same kind of information, needs to be adopted in the study of other upper houses. Do senatorial parties organize themselves in the same disciplined way they do in lower houses? How do standing committee systems operate? Are upper house members subjected to systematic and sustained lobbying by interest groups? Where appropriate, how are senatorial election campaigns funded and with what implications for their parliamentary behavior? These questions are but a small sampling of the matters that need to be investigated and clarified before we can gain comparative insights into how senates organize themselves, and why they behave as they do in their own right as well as in their interactions with their respective lower houses.

The second aspect of senates that needs inquiry is their relationship to public opinion and the implications of this relationship for the legitimacy of the larger political system. Is the territorial representation provided by senates instrumental in holding diverse regions in multiethnic states together, or does it simply exacerbate sentiments of exclusivity and heighten tensions? In his analysis of the Italian Senate, Lodici notes that national public opinion evidences a strong antiparliamentary prejudice. But just how deep is the knowledge of the senate's contribution to the country's protracted instability, and does it get the same blame for it as does the lower house? What value, if any, does the mass public see in upper houses? Is public opinion a resource for them in their disagreements with their more democratic lower house counterparts? Again, the list of specific questions, many of them already asked and answered about lower houses, could go on and on. The important point is that in the nine parliamentary settings we have examined, senates enjoy some importance and influence in the relatively narrow confines of the legislative environment, but an intriguing question is whether they have a role and an influence in the larger national political systems of which they are a part.

Note

1. This observation is especially true of the English-language political science literature, but see Tsebelis and Money (1997). Exceptions in French are Mastias and Grangé (1987) and Trivelli (1975). Even in English, there are good studies of single upper chambers, including Shell (1992) and Sinclair (1989).

References

Baldwin, Nicholas D. 1995. "The House of Lords and the Labour Government, 1974–79." *Journal of Legislative Studies* 1:218–42.

Cox, Gary W. 1997. *Making Votes Count: Strategic Coordination in the World's Electoral Systems.* New York: Cambridge University Press.

Farrell, David M. 1997. *Comparing Electoral Systems.* London: Prentice Hall / Harvester Wheatsheaf.

Gallie, W. B. 1955–56. "Essentially Contested Concepts." *Proceedings of the Aristotelian Society* 56:167–98.

Levmore, Saul. 1992. "Bicameralism: When Are Two Decisions Better than One?" *International Review of Law and Economics* 12:145–62.

Lijphart, Arend, ed. 1992. *Parliamentary versus Presidential Government.* New York: Oxford University Press.

———. 1994. *Electoral Systems and Party Systems: A Study of Twenty-seven Democracies.* New York: Oxford University Press.

Linz, Juan, and Arturo Valenzuela, eds. 1994. *The Failure of Presidential Democracy.* 2 vols. Baltimore: Johns Hopkins University Press.

Mastias, Jean, and Jean Grangé. 1987. *Les secondes chambres du Parlement en Europe occidentale.* Paris: Economica.

Norton, Philip, ed. 1990. *Legislatures.* New York: Oxford University Press.

Pitkin, Hannah. 1967. *The Concept of Representation.* Berkeley: University of California Press.

Riker, William H. 1992a. "The Justification of Bicameralism." *International Political Science Review* 13:101–16.

———. 1992b. "The Merits of Bicameralism." *International Review of Law and Economics* 12:166–68.

Roberts, Geoffrey K., and Patricia Hogwood. 1997. *European Politics Today.* Manchester: Manchester University Press.

Sartori, Giovanni. 1966. "European Political Parties: The Case of Polarized Pluralism." In *Political Parties and Political Development,* ed. Joseph La Palombara and Myron Weiner. Princeton: Princeton University Press.

———. 1997. *Comparative Constitutional Engineering: An Inquiry into Structures, Incentives, and Outcomes.* 2d ed. New York: New York University Press.

Shell, Donald. 1992. *The House of Lords.* 2d ed. New York: Harvester Wheatsheaf.

Sinclair, Barbara. 1989. *The Transformation of the U.S. Senate.* Baltimore: Johns Hopkins University Press.

Trivelli, Laurent. 1975. *Le bicameralisme—institutions comparées—études historiques, statistiques, et critiques des rapports entre le Conseil National et le Conseil des Etats.* Lausanne: Payot.

Tsebelis, George, and Jeanette Money. 1997. *Bicameralism.* New York: Cambridge University Press.

von Mettenheim, Kurt, ed. 1997. *Presidential Institutions and Democratic Politics: Comparing Regional and National Contexts.* Baltimore: Johns Hopkins University Press.

Weaver, M. Kent, and Bert Rockman, eds. 1993. *Do Institutions Matter? Government Capabilities in the United States and Abroad.* Washington, D.C.: Brookings Institution.

C. E. S. Franks is professor of political studies at Queen's University, Kingston, Ontario. His research interests include parliamentary government and public administration in Canada, public service in the Canadian North, the police power in society, northern travel, and sport and politics. Among his books are *The Canoe and White Water* (1977), *The Parliament of Canada* (1987), *Sport and Politics in Canada* (1987), *Public Administration Questions relating to Aboriginal Self-Government* (1987), *Dissent and the State* (1989), and *The Myths and Symbols of the Confederation Debates* (1993). In 1994 he was elected a Fellow of the Royal Geographical Society of Canada in recognition of his contributions to understanding Canadian development and exploration.

Carlos Flores Juberías is professor of constitutional law at the University of Valencia, Spain. From 1993 to 1995, he was a Fulbright visitor and then a visiting lecturer at the University of California, San Diego. He has written widely on electoral processes, party systems, and institution building, especially in Eastern and Central Europe and Russia. He edited *Las nuevas instituciones politicas de la Europa oriental* (1997), and he serves as editor of *Cuadernos Constitucionales*, a quarterly journal published by the Department of Constitutional Law, University of Valencia. He is a member of the executive committee of the Comparative Representation and Electoral Systems Research Committee of the International Political Science Association.

Claudio Lodici is adviser for public affairs to the Office of the Speaker of the Italian Senate. He worked in the Ministry of Budget (1982) and in the Ministry of Defense (1985–87). From 1987 to 1994 he was special assistant and top aide to the speaker of the Italian Senate. From 1985 to 1989 he was vice president of the Atlantic Association of Young Political Leaders, Washington, D.C. He has written several research articles on international affairs and security policies. He has worked on the European integration process in the Theodor Heuss Akademie, Gummersbach, Germany. He contributed a chapter on labor relations in Italy to *Storia delle relazioni* *industriali in Italia dal 1958 al 1970* (1982), and he coauthored a study of Italian industrial policies, *Storia delle politiche industriali in Italia dal dopoguerra al 1984* (1984). His latest book, on the history of the Democratic Party in the United States, is *L'America del Democratici: Da Thomas Jefferson a Bill Clinton* (1996). Also, he writes for Italy's oldest scientific review, *La Nuova Antologia*.

Jean Mastias teaches at the Sorbonne, Université Paris I, in the Department of Political Science. He specializes in political institutions, parliamentary politics, political communication, and public law. He is director of graduate programs in communication, and runs the Center for Local Communication, which is concerned with both research and policy. He has written several scholarly articles and books, including *Le Sénat de la Vème République: Réforme et renouveau* (1980) and *Les secondes chambres du Parlement en Europe occidentale* (1987). He has also written on issues concerning civic education and French local communities.

Anthony Mughan is professor of political science and director of the undergraduate international studies program at Ohio State University. His research interests lie in Western European politics, focusing on parliamentary behavior, national elections, and political leadership. He wrote *Aid and Arms to the Third World* (1985) and *Party and Participation in British Elections* (1986). In addition, he was coeditor of *Political Leadership in Democratic Societies* (1992) and *The Mass Media and Democracy* (1998). His research articles have appeared in the *American Political Science Review,* the *British Journal of Political Science, Comparative Political Studies,* the *Legislative Studies Quarterly,* and the *European Journal of Political Research.* He was senior research fellow at the Australian National University's Institute for Advanced Study from 1985 to 1988.

David M. Olson is professor of political science at the University of North Carolina, Greensboro, and director of the Parliamentary Documents Center for Central Europe. He has written or edited four books on parliaments: *The New Parliaments of Central and Eastern Europe* (1996), *Democratic Legislative Institutions* (1994), *Legislatures in the Policy Process: The Dilemmas of Economic Policy* (1991), and *Two into One: The Politics and Processes of National Legislative Cameral Change* (1991). He was Fulbright Professor of Political Science at Charles University, Prague, in 1992.

Samuel C. Patterson is professor emeritus of political science at Ohio State University. He is the coauthor of *The Legislative Process in the United States* (4th ed., 1986), *Representatives and Represented* (1975), and *Comparing Legislatures* (1979), and coeditor of *Comparative Legislative Behavior* (1972), *Handbook of Legislative Research* (1985), *Political Leadership in Democratic Societies* (1992), *Parliaments in the Modern World* (1994), and *Great Theater: The American Congress in the 1990s* (1997). He has also written many research articles on state legislatures, Congress, and other parliaments. He was editor of the *American Journal of Political Science* from 1970 to 1973, coeditor of the *Legislative Studies Quarterly* from 1982 to 1985, and managing editor of the *American Political Science Review* from 1985 to 1991. He was a Guggenheim Fellow in 1984–85 and a Fellow of the Center for Advanced Study in the Behavioral Sciences during 1993–94. In 1996 he occupied the Fulbright chair in political science at the University of Bologna.

Werner J. Patzelt is professor of political science at the Technical University of Dresden. He is the author of *Sozial-wissenschaftliche Forschungslogik* [The logic of social science research] (1985), *Grundlagen der Ethnomethodologie* [Foundations of ethnomethodology] (1987), *Abgeordnete und Repräsentation* [Legislators and representation] (1993), and *Abgeordnete und ihr Beruf* [Members of Parliament and their job] (1995). In addition, he has written numerous research articles on parliamentarism, German MPs, and German political institutions. In 1997 he was named coeditor of *Zeitschrift für Parlamentsfragen,* the leading German journal on legislative research.

Donald Shell is senior lecturer in politics at the University of Bristol. He is the author of *The House of Lords* (2d ed., 1992), and the editor of *The House of Lords at Work* (1993) and *Churchill to Major: The British Premiership since 1945* (1995). He has also written many articles, especially on developments in the British Constitution. He has served as academic secretary of the Study of Parliament Group in the United Kingdom.

Barbara Sinclair is Marvin Hoffenberg Professor of American Politics at the University of California, Los Angeles. Her publications on Congress include articles in the *American Political Science Review,* the *American Journal of Political Science,* the *Journal of Politics,* and the *Legislative Studies*

Quarterly. She wrote *Congressional Realignment* (1982); *Majority Leadership in the U.S. House* (1983); *The Transformation of the U.S. Senate* (1989), winner of the 1989 Richard F. Fenno Prize of the American Political Science Association, and the D. B. Hardeman Prize for the outstanding book on Congress published in 1989–90; *Legislators, Leaders, and Lawmaking: The U.S. House of Representatives in the Post-Reform Era* (1995); and *Unorthodox Lawmaking: New Legislative Processes in the U.S. Congress* (1997). She has served on the editorial boards of all the major political science journals in the United States, and she is an elected member of the American Academy of Arts and Sciences.

John Uhr is senior fellow in the political science program at the Australian National University. He has published widely in Australian government and public administration, and has edited three books for the Federalism Research Centre, of which he was a director: *Program Evaluation* (1991), *Ethical Practice in Government: Improving Organisational Management* (1996), and *Evaluating Policy Advice: Learning from Commonwealth Experience* (1996). Between 1982 and 1989 he was a committee secretary, then director of research, with the Australian Senate, and he was a Harkness Fellow in the United States in 1985–87. From 1987 to 1992 he edited the journal *Legislative Studies,* published by the Australasian Study of Parliament Group.